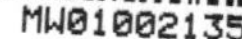

OXFORD
An Architectural Guide

Geoffrey Tyack

OXFORD
UNIVERSITY PRESS

OXFORD
UNIVERSITY PRESS

Great Clarendon Street, Oxford OX2 6DP

Oxford University Press is a department of the University of Oxford. It furthers the University's objective of excellence in research, scholarship, and education by publishing worldwide in

Oxford New York

Athens Auckland Bangkok Bogotá Buenos Aires Cape Town Chennai Dar es Salaam Delhi Florence Hong Kong Istanbul Karachi Kolkata Kuala Lumpur Madrid Melbourne Mexico City Mumbai Nairobi Paris São Paulo Shanghai Taipei Tokyo Toronto Warsaw

Published in the United States
by Oxford University Press Inc., New York

First published 1998

British Library Cataloguing in Publication Data
Data available

Library of Congress Cataloging in Publication Data
Data available

ISBN 978-0-19-817423-3

10 9 8 7

Picture research by Lisa Agate
Maps drawn by Artworks Design
Typeset by George Hammond Design
Printed in China

Frontispiece: the Bodleian Library, the Radcliffe Camera, and the spire of St Mary's church from Hertford College

Contents

Colour Plates and Maps

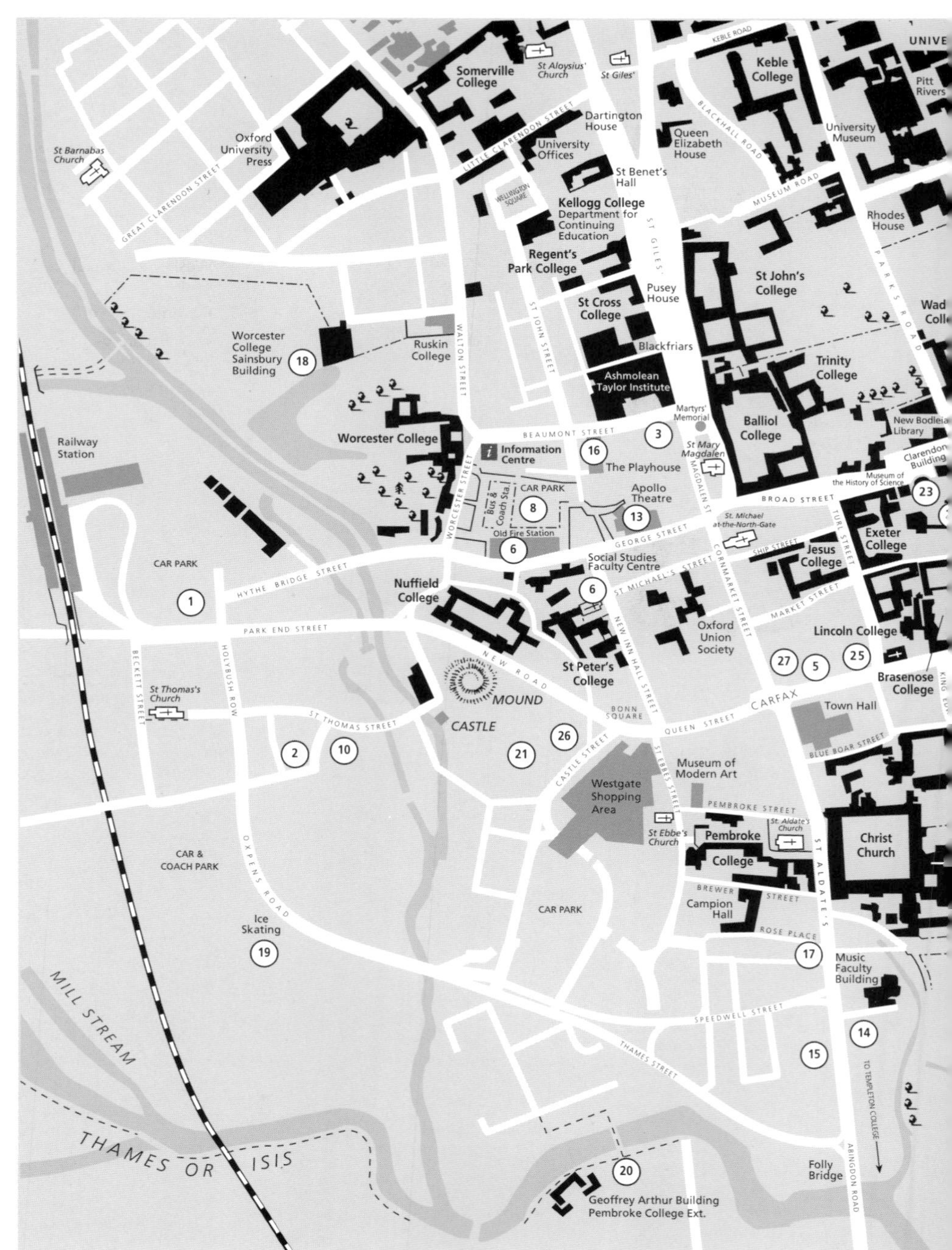
Somerville College
St Aloysius' Church
St Giles'
Keble College
Pitt Rivers
Oxford University Press
St Barnabas Church
Dartington House
University Offices
Queen Elizabeth House
University Museum
St Benet's Hall
Kellogg College
Department for Continuing Education
Rhodes House
Regent's Park College
St John's College
St Cross College
Pusey House
Worcester College Sainsbury Building
Ruskin College
Blackfriars
Trinity College
Ashmolean Taylor Institute
Martyrs' Memorial
Balliol College
New Bodleian Library
Railway Station
Worcester College
Information Centre
The Playhouse
St Mary Magdalen
Clarendon Building
Museum of the History of Science
CAR PARK
Bus & Coach Sta.
Apollo Theatre
Old Fire Station
St. Michael at-the-North-Gate
Jesus College
Exeter College
Social Studies Faculty Centre
Nuffield College
Oxford Union Society
Lincoln College
St Peter's College
Brasenose College
St Thomas's Church
MOUND
CASTLE
BONN SQUARE
Town Hall
Museum of Modern Art
Westgate Shopping Area
St Ebbe's Church
St Aldate's Church
Pembroke College
Christ Church
CAR & COACH PARK
Campion Hall
Ice Skating
Music Faculty Building
MILL STREAM
THAMES OR ISIS
Folly Bridge
Geoffrey Arthur Building Pembroke College Ext.
TO TEMPLETON COLLEGE
KEBLE ROAD
BLACKHALL ROAD
MUSEUM ROAD
PARKS ROAD
LITTLE CLARENDON STREET
GREAT CLARENDON STREET
WELLINGTON SQUARE
ST GILES'
ST JOHN STREET
WALTON STREET
BEAUMONT STREET
MAGDALEN ST
BROAD STREET
TURL STREET
WORCESTER STREET
GEORGE STREET
SHIP STREET
HYTHE BRIDGE STREET
ST MICHAEL'S STREET
CORNMARKET STREET
MARKET STREET
PARK END STREET
NEW ROAD
NEW INN HALL STREET
BECKETT STREET
HOLYBUSH ROW
ST THOMAS STREET
CARFAX
QUEEN STREET
BLUE BOAR STREET
CASTLE STREET
ST EBBE'S STREET
PEMBROKE STREET
OXPENS ROAD
BREWER STREET
ST ALDATE'S
ROSE PLACE
SPEEDWELL STREET
THAMES STREET
ABINGDON ROAD
CAR PARK
1
2
3
5
6
8
10
13
14
15
16
17
18
19
20
21
23
25
26
27

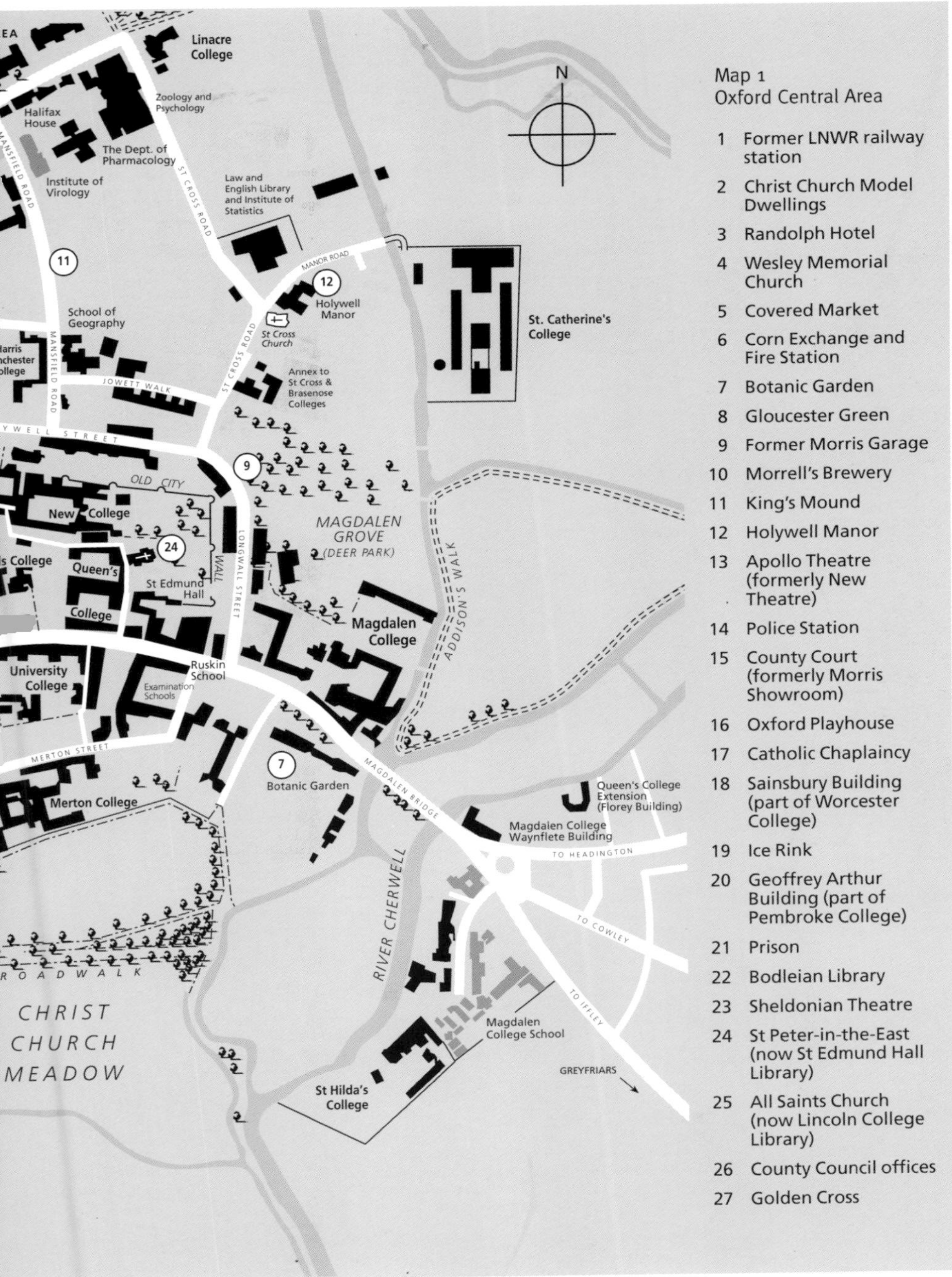
Map 1
Oxford Central Area
1 Former LNWR railway station
2 Christ Church Model Dwellings
3 Randolph Hotel
4 Wesley Memorial Church
5 Covered Market
6 Corn Exchange and Fire Station
7 Botanic Garden
8 Gloucester Green
9 Former Morris Garage
10 Morrell's Brewery
11 King's Mound
12 Holywell Manor
13 Apollo Theatre (formerly New Theatre)
14 Police Station
15 County Court (formerly Morris Showroom)
16 Oxford Playhouse
17 Catholic Chaplaincy
18 Sainsbury Building (part of Worcester College)
19 Ice Rink
20 Geoffrey Arthur Building (part of Pembroke College)
21 Prison
22 Bodleian Library
23 Sheldonian Theatre
24 St Peter-in-the-East (now St Edmund Hall Library)
25 All Saints Church (now Lincoln College Library)
26 County Council offices
27 Golden Cross
N
Linacre College
Zoology and Psychology
Halifax House
The Dept. of Pharmacology
Institute of Virology
Law and English Library and Institute of Statistics
MANSFIELD ROAD
ST CROSS ROAD
MANOR ROAD
Holywell Manor
St Cross Church
St. Catherine's College
School of Geography
Harris Manchester College
JOWETT WALK
Annex to St Cross & Brasenose Colleges
HOLYWELL STREET
OLD CITY WALL
New College
MAGDALEN GROVE (DEER PARK)
ADDISON'S WALK
Queen's College
St Edmund Hall
LONGWALL STREET
Magdalen College
University College
Ruskin School
Examination Schools
MERTON STREET
Botanic Garden
MAGDALEN BRIDGE
Queen's College Extension (Florey Building)
Merton College
Magdalen College Waynflete Building
TO HEADINGTON
RIVER CHERWELL
TO COWLEY
ROADWALK
TO IFFLEY
CHRIST CHURCH MEADOW
Magdalen College School
GREYFRIARS
St Hilda's College

Introduction

Few cities contain more magnificent buildings within a relatively small area than Oxford. More than eight centuries of lavish architectural patronage, combined with the extraordinary institutional continuity and persisting vitality of one of the oldest universities in the world, have ensured that a moderately sized English provincial town has been adorned with and, in the eyes of many, personified by buildings worthy of a capital city. Quite apart from the University's immense contributions to human knowledge, Oxford is one of the great cities of the world simply because of its architecture.

My reason for writing this book is a simple one: the want of an accessible and up-to-date account of the architectural history of Oxford in a single volume. This is not to say that Oxford has lacked architectural historians; far from it. Most of the colleges, and many of the University's other buildings, have been exhaustively chronicled. The older buildings of the city, both the extant and the lost ones, have also received devoted attention from historians and archaeologists. What has been missing is a single synoptic account of how the Oxford of today has come to be what it is, an account able to be used not only by residents but also by the growing number of visitors who seek a greater understanding of what they see. I have tried to steer a path between excessive subjectivity and a Gradgrindish concern for the accumulation of facts for their own sake. I have given greater emphasis to buildings that still exist than to those which have vanished or, for one reason or another, were never built. And I have placed the evolution of Oxford's architecture against the background of the historical development of both the University and its often ignored and neglected older sister—or Siamese twin?—the city. This means that there is a greater emphasis on the architecture of the 19th and 20th centuries than will be found in most books on Oxford. It also means, I hope, that users of the book will find signposts to lead them away from well-trodden paths into byways which, so often, reveal something of the inner life of the place.

W. H. Fox Talbot's photograph of the High Street looking east in the early 1840s, showing the spire of St Mary's church before its restoration. The houses in the foreground stood on the site of the High Street front to Brasenose College by T. G. Jackson (1881–1911). The façade of All Souls College is in the background

The chapel of Exeter College from the south

The book has been written as a chronological history and is designed to be read from cover to cover. Those who also wish to use it as a guide on their explorations are encouraged to refer to the maps at the back in which four tours are suggested, covering medieval, early modern, late 18th- and 19th-century, and 20th-century Oxford. The contents list indicates the buildings of greatest architectural significance which no visitor should ignore. Those who wish to refer to descriptions of any particular building should also use the index, where the main entries are indicated in bold type. Given the extreme variety and unreliability of college opening times, no attempt has been made to say whether or when buildings are accessible to the public. It should be emphasized, however, that the inclusion of a building in this book does not imply that visitors can gain access to it. For understandable reasons of security, some colleges are rarely or ever open nowadays, or are open only at restricted times, and some parts of most colleges that are open, especially libraries, are always closed to visitors. Oxford is not only one of the most visited cities in the world; it also houses a working university of some 14,000 members whose interests are, not surprisingly, paramount.

In writing this book I have relied mainly on published sources, and those who wish to dig deeper are urged to use the bibliographical notes at the end. Anyone writing on Oxford's architectural history soon discovers that published sources are much more copious for older than for relatively recent buildings, and some of the information in the last three chapters has been drawn from manuscript sources, for access to which I am indebted to the keepers of various collegiate and other archives. It would be invidious to mention by name all of the many people who have supplied me with information or answered enquiries, but I would like to single out those who kindly read and commented on parts of the text: Malcolm Airs, John Ashdown, John Blair, Edward Chaney, and Chris Day. I have also learnt a great deal from fellow-members of the Oxford Architectural History Seminar and from successive generations of students from both Britain and the United States. At the Oxford University Press I have been encouraged throughout by Anne Ashby, Lisa Agate, George Hammond, Paul Luna, and Sandra Raphael. And, as always, the book would never have got off the ground at all without the constant help and support of my wife and family.

GEOFFREY TYACK

Oxford,
May 1997

1 Origins: 900 to 1350

Like many important English provincial towns, Oxford owes its origins to the great expansion of urban life which occurred in the late 9th and 10th centuries. Recent archaeological research suggests that it was probably first laid out in the 890s by Aethelred, ealdorman of Mercia, or by his daughter-in-law Aethelflaed, 'Lady of the Mercians'. Her father was Alfred, King of Wessex, whose territory extended to the south or Berkshire side of the River Thames, which passes to the south and west of medieval Oxford on its course from the Cotswold hills to London and the North Sea. Oxford thus seems to have began life as a frontier town on the border of the two most powerful political units in southern England, and in many fundamental respects it has always remained a border town, fully identified neither with the Midlands nor with the south and west of England.

Oxford first appears by name in a document known as the Burghal Hidage, dating from *c.*900, and the town was mentioned in the Anglo-Saxon Chronicle for the year 912. The name commemorates a 'ford for oxen' across the Thames which existed long before the town acquired any distinct urban identity. The medieval town was built on a gravel terrace above the river's flood-plain, with hills to the east and west, and flatter land to the north and south. For many years it was assumed that the original 'ox ford' was to the west, along the present Botley Road. But the recent discovery of an 8th-century stone causeway near Folly Bridge suggests that Oxford was named after a crossing to the south of the place where the town later grew up. This was the obvious place for an important river crossing, enabling people, goods, and animals from the Midlands to pass safely to the south of England, and vice versa. Oxford's prosperity, in the Middle Ages and later, owed much to the town's situation on this north–south trade route, which ran roughly along the line of the present A34 road; the east–west route through the town, equivalent to today's A40, counted for less at first. Today's constant procession of cars and heavy lorries on Oxford's bypass roads is a reminder of the town's continuing importance as a nexus for long-distance trade.

Oxford Castle, St George's Tower

The causeway was probably made during the reign of Offa, King of Mercia from 757 to 796, and led across the swampy flood-plain to the north of the Thames crossing; even today the low-lying ground near the river floods frequently in winter, and the city has long been notorious for its damp, stagnant air and enervating climate, conducive, some would say, to academic introspection and melancholy. Overlooking the causeway from the edge of the gravel terrace was a church, which stood near the present Christ Church Cathedral. According to medieval legend, a Mercian princess, Frideswide, escaping the unwanted attentions of a royal suitor, founded a community of holy women here, and after her death in 727 a religious community of some sort grew up around her shrine; recent dating of skeletons dug up from the cloister of Christ Church suggests that the community already existed in the 9th century. So, even before it became a town, Oxford was a centre of religious observance, with a minster church (*monasterium*) and a local saint of its own .

The Anglo-Saxon town was laid out with a grid plan of metalled streets enclosed within a defensive wall of earth and timber, strengthened with stone in the 10th century. The wall was pierced by narrow gates across the main routes leading north, south, east, and west: Cornmarket Street to the north, St Aldate's to the south, High Street to the east, and Queen Street to the west, to give them their modern names. The streets intersected at a crossing place later known as Carfax, probably meaning 'four forks', from the Latin *quadrifurcus*. The market was here, later spreading out into the surrounding streets. Elsewhere were the detached houses of merchants and rural landlords, interspersed with churches, some of which seem to have started life as private chapels. And in the south-east corner, just within the walls, was St Frideswide's minster.

By the middle of the 11th century Oxford had become one of the more important provincial towns in England, ranking with places like Winchester and Lincoln, though smaller than York or Norwich. There were over 1000 houses and perhaps 4000 or 5000 people. Royal councils were held in Oxford from time to time, and one king, Edmund Ironside, was murdered there. As the population grew and prosperity increased during the first two-thirds of the 11th century the large garden plots of the 10th-century houses began to be divided up, gradually producing the characteristic pattern of narrow frontages to the main streets with long burgage plots behind. At some time in the 11th century the walled area was extended to the east, taking in more agricultural land; this led to the celebrated bend in the High Street, just east of the church of St Mary, as it curves south towards its

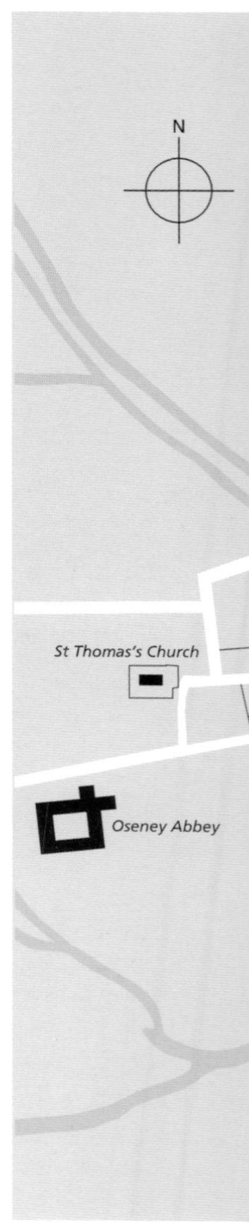

Map 2 Oxford *c.*1250

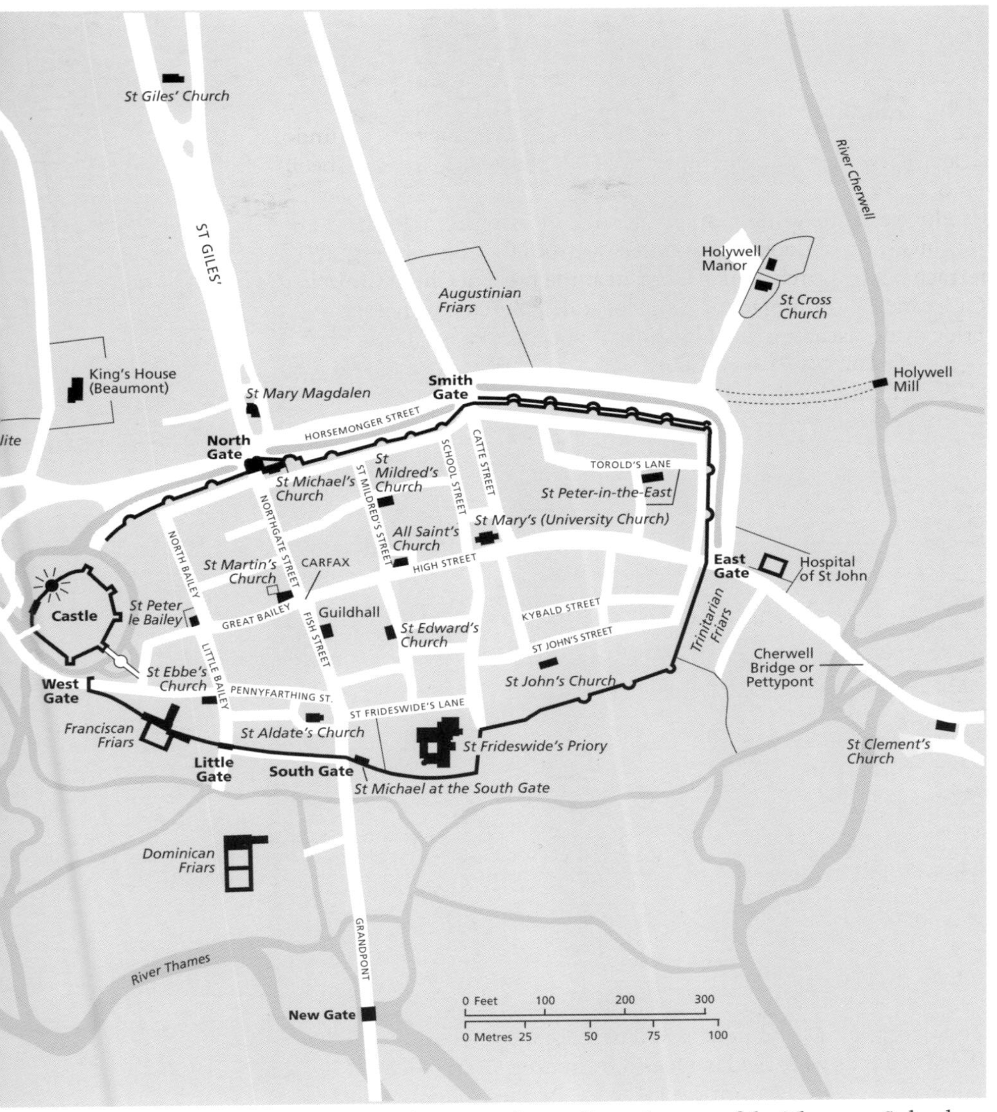

crossing over the River Cherwell, a tributary of the Thames. Suburbs also began to grow outside the walls, both to the north and towards the 'oxen ford' to the south. Thus the street plan of Oxford acquired the shape which it retained with remarkably little alteration up to the early 19th century and even today.

Oxford's oldest surviving building dates from the early to mid-11th century. Now the tower of the church of **St Michael** in Cornmarket

St Michael at the North Gate: tower

Street, it originated as a semi-defensive structure, four storeys high, at the place where the north gate pierced the town wall; the church probably stood south of the tower and not, like the present church, to the east. A doorway led from the tower onto the ramparts, and people could shelter in the upper storeys during dangerous times. The defensive function of the building is certainly suggested by its formidably plain architecture. The walls are of coral rag, a local limestone quarried in the Cumnor hills, three miles west of the town; this stone, though tough and remarkably resistant to weathering, could not be carved or cut into regular blocks, and the only external detail takes the form of the upper windows or bell openings, each of two lights divided by bulbous baluster-like columns of dressed limestone—a type found in other English churches of the period like Barton-on-Humber (Lincolnshire) and Earls Barton (Northants).

The Norman Conquest of 1066 initially had a disastrous effect on Oxford. Nearly half the houses were recorded as having been laid waste when Domesday Book was compiled in 1086, and it was not until the early 12th century that the town's economy fully recovered. Norman power was consolidated in 1071 by the building of **Oxford Castle** next to one of the branches of the River Thames on the western side of the town, its construction entailing the demolition of several houses. The builder, Robert d'Oilly, was a Norman knight who

The North Gate from the south, before its demolition in 1771, with the battlemented tower of St Michael's church in the background and the former New Inn on the right. The town gaol ('Bocardo') was over the gateway

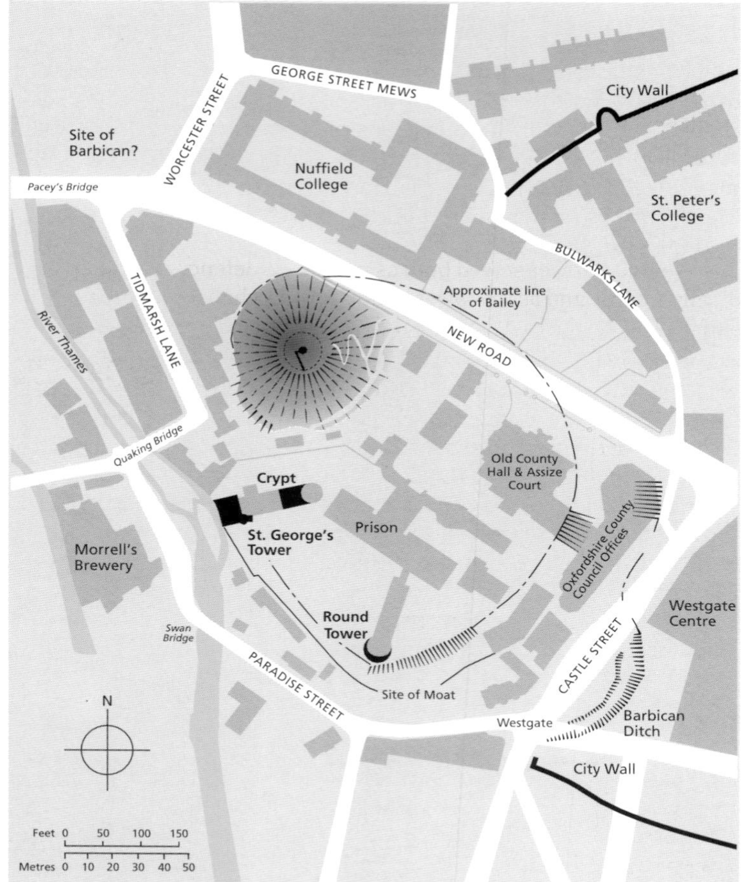

The site of Oxford Castle today

acquired large estates in the vicinity of Oxford and garrisoned the castle on behalf of the king, using it meanwhile as the centre of his own territorial authority. His overbearing presence is still visible in the sole surviving structure, a massive stone tower (St George's Tower) overlooking the river on the scruffy western fringe of the modern city centre. Norman castles were defensible enclosures, not single buildings, and it is clear from the first accurate map of Oxford, made by Ralph Agas (1578), that St George's Tower was the tallest of a number of towers which by that time punctuated the stone defensive wall of the enclosure or bailey. Its unusual height can probably be attributed to the fact that it was fairly close to the old west gate of the Anglo-Saxon town; it would have been the first part of the castle and town to be seen by anyone coming from the west. It thus fulfilled a function analogous to the tower of St Michael's church by the north gate. Like that tower, it is built of coral rag, with thick walls made up of small blocks of stone laid in horizontal courses, but it is much larger, and it lacks even the rudimentary adornments of the earlier building. Presumably for reasons of stability, the tower is much narrower at the top than the bottom, somehow contributing to the effect of brutal strength.

St George's Tower served both as part of the defences of Robert d'Oilly's castle and as the tower of St George's chapel, a church situated inside the castle bailey and served by a college of priests founded by Robert d'Oilly and Roger d'Ivry in 1074. This was a long building with a nave, a chancel, and an apsidal sanctuary which survived into the 18th century, long after the rest of the church was demolished. Even this fragment fell victim to the building of a prison within the former castle walls at the end of the 18th century, and now the only part of the chapel to survive is part of the crypt, with six sturdy columns—moved from their original places—supporting a reconstructed stone vault. The columns have capitals crudely carved with simple linear motifs, and the whole ensemble, like the tower, bears witness to the starkness of much early Norman building in England.

Apart from St George's Tower, the only part of the castle visible to the public today is the late 11th-century artificial earth mound or motte, situated on the north-western side of the bailey. The motte was

The crypt of St George's chapel in Oxford Castle

Folly Bridge and 'Friar Bacon's Study' before its destruction in 1779. The bridge was replaced in 1825–7. The drawing, like that on p. 5, was based on one made by J. B. Malchair in 1772

intended as a defensible strong point of last resort, and deep inside it there is a vaulted well-chamber dating from the 13th century, but the ten-sided stone tower or shell keep which once stood at the top of the mound has gone. So too have the residential buildings within the castle walls and also the walls themselves with their flanking towers, except for the base of a round tower of 1235, which survives within the former prison grounds. After Robert d'Oilly's death the castle was used intermittently by royalty, most notably in 1142, when the Empress Matilda was beseiged there during the civil war of King Stephen's reign (she allegedly escaped across a snow-covered landscape, clad in a white cloak). In the later Middle Ages it became a centre for county administration, like many other castles in English county towns, but most of the buildings were demolished during the Interregnum in 1649–52. A degree of continuity was maintained, however, by the presence of the county gaol, rebuilt *c.*1785 and again in the19th century, and also by the 19th-century county assize court (see p. 203). Today Oxfordshire is still administered from within the old castle precincts, the county bureaucrats currently occupying a singularly unprepossessing building (Macclesfield House, 1969) close to the site of the west gate of the medieval town.

Robert d'Oilly was responsible not only for the building of Oxford's castle, but also for its first stone bridge, the so-called Grandpont over the Thames near the 'oxen ford'; the site is now occupied by **Folly Bridge**, dating in its present form from 1825–7. At the southern end of the medieval bridge a defensive tower and gateway was later built, like the one which still survives on the bridge at Monmouth; this picturesque structure came to be known as 'Friar Bacon's Study', after the Franciscan friar Roger Bacon, one of the leading luminaries of Oxford's intellectual life in the 13th century. It was demolished in 1779, but part of the late 11th-century approach to the bridge is still visible at the southern end; it is constructed of rubble stone, and three round arches are visible from the river towpath. From this point a causeway under the present Abingdon Road led south along the marshy ground on the Berkshire side of the river, complementing that on the northern side which led into the town.

Oxford seems to have recovered from the depredations of the Norman Conquest fairly quickly, and in the 12th century the town flourished once more as a commercial and ecclesiastical centre. Further prestige came from a revival of the town's links with royalty. Henry I visited Oxford in 1133, and stayed at his house or palace called Beaumont, outside the northern wall near the present Worcester College; the site is marked by a plaque on a wall at the junction of Beaumont Street and Walton Street, and some fragments of masonry were removed to the garden of a house in Woodstock Road in about 1830. Two future kings, Richard the Lionheart and John, were born in Beaumont Palace, but it ceased to be used by royalty in the 13th century and the buildings were later taken over by a Carmelite friary.

Some important new churches were built in Oxford in the 12th century, a time of extensive ecclesiastical building throughout western Europe. The largest and most magnificent was the Augustinian priory of **Oseney**, founded in 1129 by Robert d'Oilly's nephew, another Robert, on open ground to the west of the castle and river. It soon took over the collegiate foundation of St George in the Castle, with its revenues, and was elevated to the status of an abbey in 1154. There was a major rebuilding in the first half of the 13th century, a Lady Chapel was added in the mid-14th century, and outer aisles were built onto the nave aisles a century later; by the early 16th century the church was 300 feet (92 metres) long, with a central tower and a tall western tower which commanded the western approaches to the city. Had events taken a different course in the last years of Henry VIII's reign, this magnificent church would now be Oxford's cathedral, but now it has vanished without trace, save for a small 15th-century building which lurks, inaccessible to the public, among industrial premises close to Osney Lock. For four years from 1542, after the expulsion of the Augustinian canons and the seizure of its revenues by the king, Oseney Abbey served as mother church of a new diocese carved out of the diocese of Lincoln, in which Oxford and the surrounding country had stood since the 11th century. But in 1546, shortly before the king's death, the former priory church of St Frideswide became both the mother church of the new diocese and the chapel of Christ Church, the king's new collegiate foundation. Oseney Abbey was gradually demolished, leaving only the west tower and sundry ruins which lasted into the mid-17th century. The destruction of the abbey blighted the surrounding area, now a wilderness of gravestones (a cemetery was built over part of the site in 1847) and railway sidings. All in all, it is Oxford's greatest architectural loss.

Wenceslaus Hollar's drawing of the ruins of Oseney Abbey in the mid-17th century

St Peter-in-the-East in 1809

Despite the destruction of Oseney Abbey, there are still three major examples of 12th-century ecclesiastical architecture left in Oxford. The earliest of these is the parish church of **St Peter-in-the-East**, which stands on the site of an Anglo-Saxon church in the part of the town incorporated within the walls in the 11th century. The richest living in medieval Oxford, St Peter's came under the patronage of the d'Oilly family after the Conquest, and presumably the younger Robert d'Oilly played a part in funding the present building, which may have been begun in the 1130s. In its original form it consisted of an aisleless nave and a chancel built over a vaulted crypt, which survives virtually unaltered. A crypt is an unusual feature in an English parish church, but its existence here is explained by the presence at its western end of a *confessio* or relic chamber of the kind which is sometimes found under the main altar in Continental churches. The chamber was flanked by staircases leading down from the main body of the church, and must have been the focus of the cult of an unknown saint. The rest of the crypt, to the east of the relic chamber, is similar in character to the crypt of Worcester Cathedral, begun in 1084. The aisled space is roofed by groined vaults supported on eight slender columns with capitals, three of which have carved ornament; one of the capitals features imaginary beasts of a kind like those still to be seen in the crypt of Canterbury Cathedral, consecrated in 1130, and also in the vast, and now largely demolished, Benedictine abbey at Reading (Berkshire), founded in 1123 by Henry I.

There is more sculpture in the main body of the church, which may not have been built until the 1160s. The rounded south doorway of the

St Peter-in-the-East: crypt

nave, now hidden by a 15th-century porch, is elaborately framed with zigzag (chevron) carvings enclosing a ring of beakheads: monstrous heads with staring eyes and long beaks curving over the roll moulding around the doorway. Chevron carving, a common feature of mid-12th-century English Romanesque architecture, also appears inside the church, on the ribs of the western bay of the vaulted chancel, probably Oxford's first ribbed vault; the ribs of the second or eastern bay, however, are decorated with an unusual chain-like motif, possibly representing the chains of St Peter. Later medieval alterations have transformed the nave, and also, for the most part, the exterior of the church, but much of the original ragstone rubble walling still survives on the south side, and at the east end there are two pyramid-capped staircase turrets which date from the 12th century and led originally to a room over the chancel. The church is now the library of St Edmund Hall (see p. 328), named after the 13th-century scholar Edmund of Abingdon, who is said to have built the Lady Chapel on the north side of the chancel out of the profits of his teaching.

Romanesque carving of the mid-12th century can be found around the re-set west doorway of St Ebbe's church, to the south-west of Carfax, and also around the chancel arch of the parish church at Headington, a village (now a suburb) in the hills to the east of the medieval town. But the most impressive piece of Romanesque architecture in Oxford, barring only St Frideswide's Priory, is the parish church at **Iffley**, another village perched on a bluff overlooking the River Thames to the south of the town and now, like Headington, incorporated within the city boundary. It was built, possibly in the 1170s, by Robert of St Remy, lord of the manor, or by his daughter

Iffley church from the south-west

Juliana, who gave the patronage to the newly-founded Kenilworth Priory (Warwickshire) shortly before 1190. A long, narrow building of rubble stone, almost certainly quarried nearby, it consists of an aisleless nave, a tower, and a vaulted chancel (the east end was rebuilt in the 13th century). This was a fairly common plan for a 12th-century parish church, but what lifts Iffley church above the commonplace is the quality of the stone carving, especially on the west front and around the south door; as at St Peter-in-the-East, there are resemblances to work at Reading Abbey, and it is possible that the same masons and carvers worked on both buildings. The west front is one of the most satisfying architectural compositions of its date in England, combining almost classical proportions with exuberant detail, as in some contemporary churches in western France. The façade is divided into three sections. At ground level there are blind arches flanking the west doorway, which is liberally adorned with chevron and beakhead carving and representations of the signs of the zodiac and symbols of the Evangelists under the outer moulding.

The interior of Iffley church, looking east

Above, there is a round window dating in its present form from a restoration carried out by J. C. Buckler in 1860—a 15th-century window is shown in early views of the church—and the upper level is made up of three windows, the central one slightly taller than the other two, all three deeply recessed into the wall surface and surrounded by chevron carving, with paired columns supporting the outer arches. The much-restored carving on the south door is equally elaborate, with engaged columns supporting the outer arches, intricate carvings (two knights in combat; a centaur suckling a child; Samson and the lion) on the capitals of the inner columns, and a mixture of rosettes, heads, and strange beasts around the doorway itself.

The dark, numinous interior is clearly demarcated into four main sections, with the floor level gradually rising from west to east (the church is built on a slope). As if to symbolize the Christian's initiation into the mysteries of the Faith, there is a massive stone font immediately inside the west door, designed for total immersion. At the east end of the nave an archway flanked by Tournai marble columns—one of the first architectural uses of marble in medieval England—leads into the space under the tower, and from here a similar arch leads into the rib-vaulted chancel of the 12th-century church; the easternmost bay, with its 13th-century ribbed vault and Gothic details, is a replacement of the original east end, which may have terminated in a rounded apse, like that in the equally celebrated church at Kilpeck (Herefordshire). Chevron carving is liberally employed around the arches and on the vault ribs, and the overall effect is of a solemn majesty characteristic of the best architecture of this period.

Oxford's importance in the history of 12th-century architecture derives mainly from the priory church of St Frideswide (now the **Cathedral**). This curious, fascinating building was erected, like the larger church at Oseney, for Augustinian canons, but here they took over an existing building, the Anglo-Saxon minster church, rebuilt in 1004, in which Oxford's patron saint was buried. The priory was founded *c.*1111–22 by Bishop Roger of Salisbury, King Stephen's justiciar and one of the most powerful prelates of his time, but the establishment was not a wealthy one at first, and it was not until the middle of the 12th century that new building began, under the priorship of Robert of Cricklade, one of the learned clerics who began to give Oxford a reputation for scholarship in the 12th century. The Anglo-Saxon church probably stood to the north of the present Cathedral, on the site of the north transept and the Dean's garden, and it seems that the canons began work with the construction of a new cloister in the 1140s ; this was built some distance to the south of the original church, just inside the town wall, which was moved southwards for the purpose. The main visual evidence for this phase is the doorway to the chapter house, in the east walk of the cloister. It has the chevron carving familar from St Peter-in-the-East and Iffley church but, though built of the local buff-coloured stone, it is now reddened, probably as a result of a fire which was said by the Chronicle of Oseney Abbey to have consumed 'the greater part of the town of Oxford' in 1190.

Recent research suggests that the present church was begun in the second half of the 1160s, and that the chancel and transepts were largely completed by 1180, when the relics of St Frideswide were translated to a chapel on the east side of the north transept, probably close to where they had lain in the Anglo-Saxon church. The nave was probably built in the 1180s, and there were presumably repairs after the fire of 1190 which, it has recently been argued, must have destroyed the roofs but not the vaulted interior. Building was thus going on at a time when Romanesque architecture was giving way to Gothic in England (the choir of Canterbury Cathedral, the first great Gothic building in this country, was built in 1175–84), and St Frideswide's, though still Romanesque in its essentials—round arches, massive supports, thick walls—shows signs of the transition to Gothic. It was not very large by the standards of the great Romanesque abbeys of western Europe—at 200 feet (61.5 metres) it was only two-thirds as long as Oseney Abbey—but it had all the accoutrements of a major monastic church: an aisled nave of seven bays (reduced to four in the 1520s), aisled transepts, and an aisled chancel (see pp. 74–5). The aisles to the transepts are an unusual feature in a church of this size; almost certainly an afterthought resulting from the growing popularity of the saint following the construction of the shrine, they give the church a multiplicity of cross-vistas which greatly enhances its appeal to modern eyes.

The larger monastic churches of the 11th and 12th centuries were built in three layers, with a main arcade at ground level surmounted by either a triforium—a row of arches in front of the aisle roofs—or a full-scale tribune gallery, and a clerestory at the top through which light penetrated into the central parts of the building. This system was employed at St Frideswide's, but the walls here were only about 40 feet (12 metres) high (compared with 70 feet (21.5 metres) for Durham Cathedral) and, in order to give an effect of apparent height, both the triforium and the lower arcade are enclosed within single arches resting on giant piers, circular in the chancel and transepts, alternately circular and octagonal in the nave (an idea which may have

Christ Church Cathedral (formerly St Frideswide's Priory): north transept from crossing

been inspired by Canterbury Cathedral). The internal elevations at St Frideswide's are certainly distinctive, though not unique: giant orders of Romanesque arches can also be seen at Romsey Abbey (Hampshire) and Jedburgh Abbey in Scotland. But there is something slightly disturbing about the way in which the triforium is squashed in between the arches of the lower arcade and those resting on the giant piers—a defect which is admittedly more apparent in photographs than it is when looking at the building itself. And, in order to give the giant piers an uninterrupted face, the capitals of the lower arches are cut off halfway around the circumference of each pier: an understandable compromise, but one which is visually jarring. The capitals themselves are delicately and inventively carved, with the Romanesque motifs of the chancel and transepts giving way in the nave to others inspired by Canterbury, notably the acanthus leaf which both recalls the Corinthian order in classical architecture and anticipates the 'stiff leaf' of Early English Gothic. The growing appeal of Gothic can also be seen in the use of pointed arches in the nave clerestory. For all its eccentricities, the 12th-century St Frideswide's was a highly original and adventurous building, and it still repays close and careful study.

Even allowing for the subsequent loss of the three western bays of the nave, we do not now see the church in its original form. Though the original aisle vaults survive, the high stone vault which was almost certainly built over the nave and chancel has gone, to be replaced in the chancel by the present magnificent stone vault of *c.*1500 (see p. 69) and in the transepts and nave by 16th-century timber roofs. As a result of the addition of chapels on the north side of the chancel in the 13th and 14th centuries the east end of the church has acquired a highly unusual, lopsided ground plan which adds greatly to the picturesque charm of the building. The first of these chapels was the Lady Chapel, added on to the northern side of the north chancel aisle *c.*1230 by masons who worked at, or were at least familiar with, Pershore Abbey (Worcestershire). Lady Chapels became *de rigueur* in

Christ Church Cathedral: north choir aisle and Lady Chapel. The canopied tomb on the left commemorates Prior Sutton (d.1316), and the glass in the east aisle window (1874–5) was designed by Edward Burne-Jones

Christ Church Cathedral from the north-west. The north transept is in the foreground and the Latin Chapel at the left

the 13th century as the cult of the Virgin Mary grew in popularity, but they were usually placed to the east of the high altar in major English churches. It has often been claimed that expansion in that direction at St Frideswide's was difficult because of the proximity of the town wall, though this had not prevented the canons from expanding the cloister southwards in the 12th century; a more likely explanation might be a concern to build the chapel as close as possible to the local saint's shrine. The Lady Chapel, as would be expected from its date, is a fully developed example of Early English Gothic, with clusters of vertical shafts in the piers, deep mouldings to enhance and exaggerate the linear feeling, and abundant stiff-leaf carving on the capitals: features made all the more telling by the immediate proximity of the late Romanesque chancel and north aisle.

The other major 13th-century additions to St Frideswide's were the building of a central tower and spire, and the rebuilding of the chapter house. In both, the early Gothic style is adopted in its unadulterated form. The spire probably dates from the first quarter of the century and is thus not only the first of Oxford's 'dreaming spires' but also one of the first in England to be built of stone. Short by later standards, and rather stumpy in appearance, it is an unmistakable focal point of the jumbled complex of buildings which constitutes the former monastery. It rises from the upper storey of the central tower, and there are pinnacles at the corners: a pattern found in churches in Normandy which may have served as an inspiration to the unknown masons responsible for the design. The chapter house, probably built a little later (*c.*1230–50), is a more delicate, elegant structure: a rectangular room with a ribbed vault, uninterrupted by internal supports and flooded with light entering through tall lancet windows. It has the taut, linear quality which distinguishes Early English Gothic architecture in its maturity, and it retains some of its original painted decoration. There is also some excellent sculpture, in the roof bosses, the stiff-leaf capitals, and in some of the corbels supporting the vaulting shafts. Though encumbered with counters and display cases (it now serves as the Cathedral shop and a museum of church plate), it remains the finest example of early Gothic architecture in Oxford.

There was a certain amount of work on the town's parish churches in the 13th century, notably at St Giles, which stood at the far end of the northern suburb, at the place where the roads to Banbury and Woodstock diverge; though occupying an earlier site, and much altered in later centuries, the church is still essentially an example of the Early English style, with an aisled nave lit by the lancet windows characteristic of the period and a western tower. Elsewhere outside the walls, where space was plentiful, new monastic foundations sprang up, so that by 1300 the town had acquired what has been called 'an agglomeration of varied monastic and mendicant settlements unsurpassed elsewhere in England'. The most important of these were the houses of the mendicant orders: the Dominicans or Black Friars, who arrived in 1221, the Franciscans or Grey Friars (between 1225 and 1236), Carmelites (1256), and the Augustinian or Austin Friars (1267). Their buildings all suffered grievously after the Reformation, but recent archaeology has at least established the basic layout of the Dominican friary, the largest in England outside London. It was built, starting in 1236, on low-lying ground between the southern stretch of the town wall and the river, and the church, much resorted to by townspeople and members of the growing university, was longer than St Frideswide's Priory; part of the north or outer gateway is embedded in a house in Albion Place which now serves as the Deaf and Hard of Hearing Centre. The smaller Franciscan church

The chapter house of Christ Church Cathedral

stood further to the north, beneath the present Westgate shopping centre; it had the same long, narrow plan as the Dominican church, but there was also a northward extension or 'preaching transept'. Less is known about the Carmelite house, which took over the buildings of Beaumont Palace, or that of the Austin Friars, which stood to the north of the town wall, on the site of Wadham College. Oxford's last monastic foundation took place in 1280 with the establishment of a Cistercian house, Rewley Abbey, to the north-west of the castle on the banks of one of the branches of the Thames. It served briefly as a 'house of studies' for the Cistercian order, but here too the original buildings have virtually all gone, except for a 15th-century doorway embedded in a wall on the west bank of the Oxford Canal, on the edge of a new housing development to the north of Hythe Bridge Street.

Medieval Oxford also had two establishments dedicated to the relief of the sick. Henry I founded a leper hospital dedicated to St Bartholomew ('Bartlemas') on an empty site in the parish of Cowley, to the east of the River Cherwell, in 1126, and its small 14th-century chapel still survives in an improbably rural setting amid the suburban sprawl to the north of Cowley Road; it was built by Oriel College, to which the management and revenues were transferred in 1329, and the residential buildings subsequently became an almshouse, before being turned into a private house. A more ambitious foundation, the Hospital of St John the Baptist, was established between the east gate of the town and the bridge over the Cherwell ('Pettypont', on the site of Magdalen Bridge) in the 12th century; it was enlarged in the 1190s and refounded by Henry III in 1231 for 'the care of the sick and the benefit of poor students and other miserable persons'. There was a chapel flanking the street, a two-aisled infirmary, and a hall, part of which survives as the Junior Common Room of Magdalen College, which took over the buildings and endowments in 1458 (see p. 61).

The quantity of church building in 12th- and 13th-century Oxford is a sign of the prosperity of the town at that time. The population was rising, and in about 1155 Henry II granted a charter confirming the right of the citizens to manage their own affairs, subject to the royal officers. A seal attached to a document of 1191—the oldest such seal to survive in England—shows that the nucleus of a municipal government existed by the end of the century. At first the burgesses seem to have met in a house in what is now Queen Street, to the west of Carfax, but in 1229 they bought a house on the east side of St Aldate's, formerly belonging to a wealthy Jew, and here they established a Guildhall which lasted until 1751; it occupied part of the site of the present Town Hall, and contained a large upstairs court room lit by two-light Gothic windows, with vaulted cellars below which were let out as taverns.

One of the main responsibilities of the civic authority was the maintenance of Oxford's defences. They were necessary not only to protect the citizens from marauders and to defend them in time of civil war; they also asserted the corporate prestige of a town which was still in the early 13th century one of the largest in England. Between 1226 and 1240 therefore the **walls** were thoroughly rebuilt, using large blocks of the local coral rag. Judging from the most complete surviving section, in the grounds of New College, the walls were as impressive as any in medieval England. They were crenellated, with a raised walkway on the inner side, and at intervals there were semicircular bastions, with arrow-slits to allow defenders to fire outwards. Less well-preserved sections, with some bastions, survive behind houses on the south side of Broad Street; in the grounds of the present Social Studies library to the north of the Castle; and also on the southern boundaries of Pembroke, Corpus Christi, and Merton Colleges. The gates which controlled access into the main streets and some of the smaller ones have all disappeared, the south and west

Part of the town wall, in New College garden

gates in the early 17th century, the north and east gates as a result of street improvements in 1771. So too has the outer wall—a unique feature in medieval town defences—which ran north of the main wall between Smith Gate, at the northern end of Catte Street, and the eastern end of the present Holywell Street.

None of the houses of Oxford's early medieval citizens survives complete. The oldest domestic structure to have been identified is the barrel-vaulted cellar or semi-basement of a house built, probably in the first half of the 12th century, on a block of land between Cornmarket Street and New Inn Hall Street in the western part of the town. In the latter part of the century the property belonged to Geoffrey fitz Durand, one of Oxford's most prominent citizens; having been incorporated into St Mary's College, a short-lived foundation for Augustinian canons (see p. 55), it later passed to Brasenose College, which now uses it as a graduate hostel, under the name of Frewin Hall. The basement, now used as a common-room, is a plain structure of no architectural pretension; there is no evidence for the original appearance of the house above it.

A bastion of the town wall, seen from within New College

There was a great deal of domestic building in 13th-century Oxford, much of it by the major religious houses, which invested heavily in property in the town. As a result of the subdivision of the larger Anglo-Saxon and Norman holdings, most houses, especially in the central district, had relatively narrow frontages to the street: the usual arrangement found in towns throughout northern Europe. In many cases the street frontage was given over to workshops or retail shops; in the late 13th century there were twelve shops in the first 70 feet (21.5 metres) of Cornmarket Street on the eastern side going north from Carfax. The shops were often built over stone-vaulted cellars, like that which still survives under the Mitre Hotel in the High Street, probably dating from the late 13th century. The houses were usually built of timber, though stone was often used for party walls and sometimes for outer walls too; the long-vanished Haberdasher's Hall, in the High Street, was described in 1256 as a 'great stone house'. In any house the most important room was the hall, which was at least partially open to the roof, to allow the smoke from the fire to escape (chimneys are not mentioned in contemporary documents until the 15th century); the hall could be placed behind the shop or shops, or alongside the street, or facing a passage or alleyway behind the street frontage. Chambers or bedrooms were usually upstairs, in rooms described as solars in the documents which are our main source of knowledge about the houses of this period. Kitchens were detached, because of the risk of fire. The house on the site of the Mitre Hotel had six chambers, a hall, and a courtyard with a kitchen and stabling: a miniature version of the houses of the country gentry of this period. But it is not until the 14th century that any traces of Oxford's houses survive above ground, and by then the architectural development of the town was beginning to be influenced by the presence of the University.

Oxford University, in the words of Sir Richard Southern, 'was not created; it emerged'. Learned clerics were attached to some of Oxford's religious houses in the 12th century; they included the historian Geoffrey of Monmouth, a canon of St George in the Castle, and the theologian Robert of Cricklade, the second Prior of St Frideswide's. Some higher instruction no doubt went on in 12th-century Oxford, as it did in comparable towns like Northampton and Exeter, but there is no indication of any organization worthy of the name of university until the very end of the century. By then Oxford had become well known not only as an ecclesiastical centre, the home of an archdeaconry, but also as a place for hearing cases in the Church courts. By 1190, civil and canon law was being taught in the town, to foreigners as well as Englishmen, and the curriculum was soon extended to include the liberal arts and theology. Both the Church and the secular authorities needed able administrators, and during the Anglo-French wars of 1193–1204 it was no longer possible for students to attend the University of Paris, at that time the most illustrious seat of learning in Europe. By the early 13th century there were 200–300 students and 70 masters (graduate teachers), and the appointment of a Chancellor in 1214 marked the recognition of the University as a corporate entity, self-governing, and with its own, albeit limited, income.

The University flourished, and by the early years of the 14th century there were probably about 2000 students. They were drawn from a wide area; Oxford has always been a residential university, and the idea of attending university in one's home town never caught on in England. In the earliest days the students lived in private houses, often with fellow-students from the same part of the country. But by the middle of the 13th century a new type of residence had come into being: the academic hall. These halls were houses, many of them belonging to the local monasteries, which were leased out to graduate principals who made a profit from letting out rooms and providing meals for students; in time all halls were licensed by the University, which required the principals to provide a measure of discipline. In their heyday in the early 14th century there were probably over 100 of these establishments, most of them situated in the eastern part of the town, with especially large concentrations to the north-west of St Mary's church, close to the schools where lectures were given, and to the north and north-east of St Frideswide's Priory. The number of halls dropped as the student population declined in the second half of the century, but for much of the 15th century there were seventy at any one time, housing about nine-tenths of the total student body and supplying members with both bed and board and also a measure of communal life, then as now an important aspect of student experience in England.

Tackley's Inn (number 107 High Street) from the south *c.*1750

The architectural history of the academic hall is virtually indistinguishable from that of the larger houses of late medieval Oxford. Many halls were set up in existing houses, but some were purpose-built, like **Tackley's Inn**, whose early 14th-century hall still survives behind a shop on the south side of the High Street (number 107), not far from St Mary's church. Described as newly built in 1324, its name derives from its builder and promoter Roger le Mareschal, vicar of Tackley, a few miles north of Oxford. In its original form the building consisted of an open-roofed hall, used for dining and perhaps also for lectures, behind a row of five shops, which brought in an income to supplement that supplied by the students. There was a handsome vaulted cellar under the shops, and next to the hall there was a chamber block in which the students lived five to a room; the hall was reached from the street by a passage between the shops, and there was a detached kitchen in the garden space behind. The shops have been rebuilt, but the hall, with its remodelled two-light window and its early 16th-century arch-braced roof, still survives as part of an insurance office, and the cellar remains intact.

Oxford's academic halls eventually gave way to the colleges, and very few of their medieval buildings survive today. Colleges are the most distinctive feature of the Universities of Oxford and Cambridge, both for their architecture and for their extraordinary resilience and longevity. Yet for the first 250 years of their existence they catered for only a minority of the academic community, something which is easy to forget today. The idea of a college devoted to academic study can be traced back to the University of Paris; here there were thirteen such institutions by the mid-13th century, when Oxford's first colleges came into being. But, unlike those of Paris, the colleges of Oxford survived and flourished, eventually all but taking over the University (a process which has to some extent been reversed in the 20th century). Colleges differed from academic halls chiefly in the fact that they were endowed, sometimes very generously, with land, rents, and church revenues. The endowments conferred an institutional and financial independence which the halls lacked; they also enabled the colleges to build extensively and lavishly. And, despite economic and political vicissitudes, this wealth has remained inviolate and their legal independence untouched down to modern times.

Colleges were founded for two main reasons: to further the education of particular groups of scholars, usually graduates at first, enabling them to proceed to higher degrees; and to ensure the regular performance of the *opus dei*, including the saying of Masses for the souls of founders and benefactors—an important aspect of late medieval religious culture. Unlike the early academic halls, they invariably acquired chapels in due course, even if they did not possess them at the time of their original foundation. In their combination of a communal celibate life with a strongly religious emphasis, the medieval colleges of Oxford bore a distinct resemblance to monasteries; a famous 15th-century drawing of New College underlines the point by showing the students and their teachers wearing monastic-style habits, with their heads shaved after the fashion of monks. An even closer parallel is with the colleges of secular priests which had existed since before the Norman Conquest; these foundations proliferated in late medieval England as noblemen demanded ever more elaborate provision for prayers and Masses for the dead. It is in such establishments too that some of the main influences on Oxford's collegiate architecture can be found.

The character and subsequent history of the Oxford colleges depended to a great extent on the circumstances of their foundation. Of the three oldest colleges—Merton, Balliol, and University—only

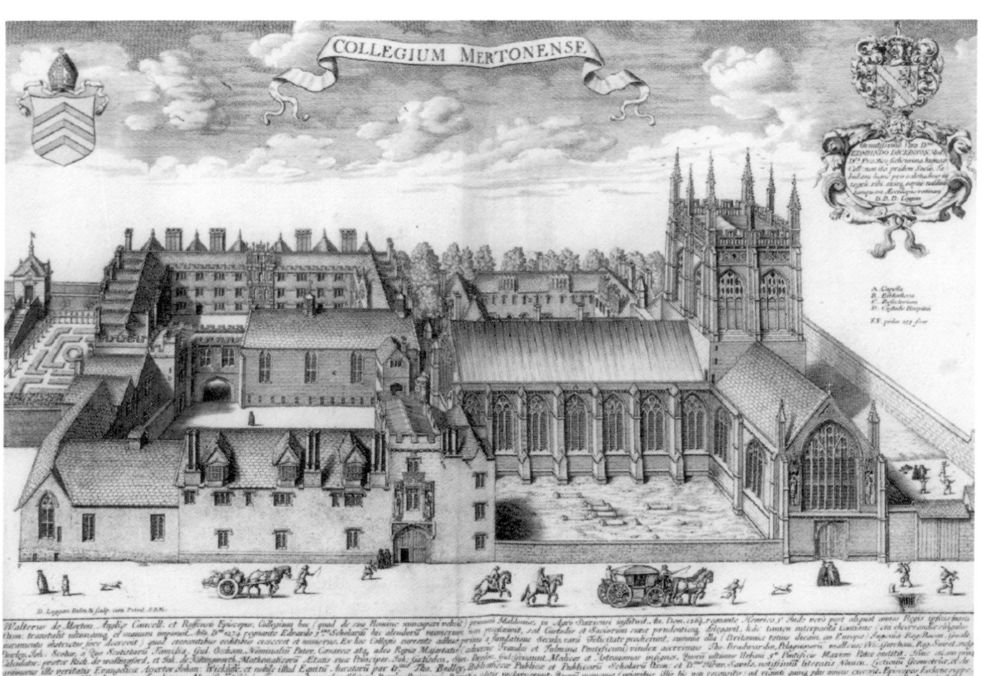

Merton College from the north in 1675. On the left is the main quadrangle, with the Warden's Lodging on the extreme left of the street front and the Hall on the far side; behind it is the 17th-century Fellows' Quadrangle. The Chapel is to the right of the gatehouse, and behind it is Mob Quad

Merton was recognizable as a college in the modern sense in its earliest days. It was founded in 1264 by a successful ecclesiastical administrator, Walter de Merton (d.1277), twice Chancellor of England and later Bishop of Rochester; his aim was to 'make some return in honour of [God's] name for the abundance of his bounty towards me in this life'. As set out in the College statutes of 1274, this involved providing housing and sustenance for between thirty and forty members (*socii*, or Fellows), including some of his own relatives (he had seven sisters). The establishment was thus to be comparable in size to a medium-sized monastery of the time. The Fellows were to be mostly graduates, teaching the liberal arts—the basis of the curriculum up to the bachelor's degree—while studying for the higher degrees of law, medicine, and, most important of all, theology. They were to be self-governing, and were supported by a generous endowment, which eventually included ten manors, in Surrey and elsewhere, and ten appropriated churches; the manors included that of Holywell, to the north-east of the town, where the University spread prodigiously in the 19th and 20th centuries. The generous scale of the foundation contrasts sharply with that of Balliol, in its early days little more than an endowed academic hall for undergraduates, and even more with University College, an impoverished establishment which

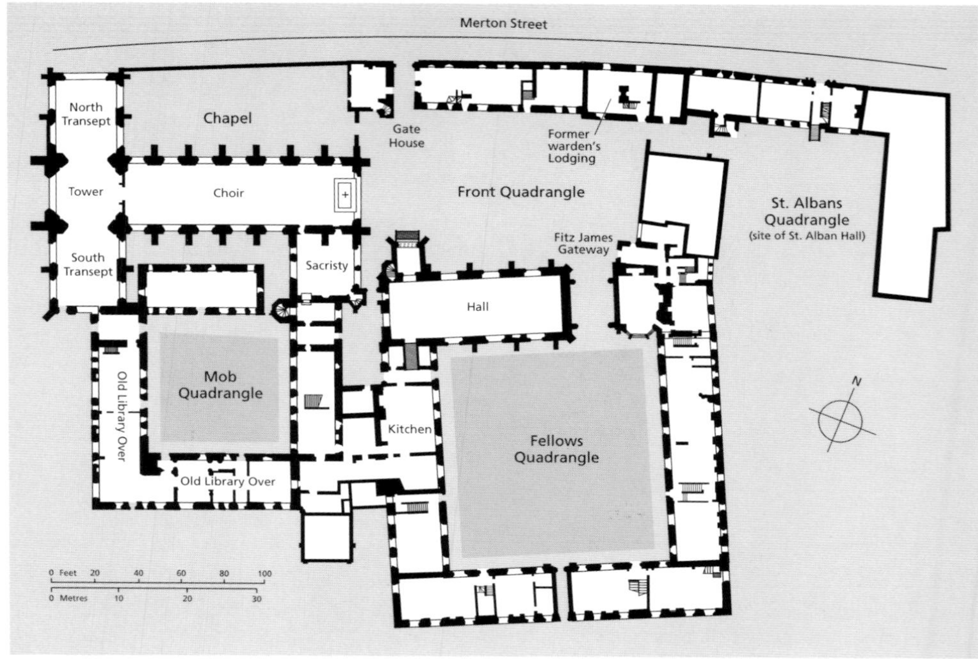

Plan of Merton College

had only four members at first, and did not acquire any buildings of its own until well into the 14th century.

When Merton College was founded there was no model of what an Oxford college should look like. The buildings developed piecemeal, starting in 1266–8, on a site within the developing academic quarter, immediately to the east of the church of St John the Baptist, and just within the southern wall of the town. It comprised a vacant plot of ground and three houses, one of which belonged to St Frideswide's Priory, one to a Jew called Jacob, and the third to Robert Flixthorpe. Here, on the gardens of the two houses east of the church, the first of the College's buildings was constructed before 1277: a Hall where lectures could be given and where all the Fellows could dine communally. It was a substantial free-standing structure of stone, raised up over a basement, and it had an open timber roof; though substantially remodelled by James Wyatt in 1790–4, and almost totally rebuilt by Gilbert Scott in 1872–4, some of the original walling survives, and so too does the main door, beautifully adorned with swirling ironwork. David Loggan's drawing of the College in 1675 (see p. 27) shows the Hall with three tall two-light windows on the north wall, a lantern near the high-table or 'upper' end, marking the site of the louvre through which the smoke from the central hearth or brazier—the only heating—could be extracted, and a two-storeyed porch at the west or 'lower' end; this must have been close to the detached kitchen.

The Hall formed the south side of a rudimentary quadrangle like those found in contemporary bishops' palaces and in some of the grander houses of the nobility and gentry. On the northern side were the houses bought in 1266–7, to the east was an academic hall belonging to St Frideswide's Priory (later known as St Alban Hall and eventually acquired by the College, like much of the property in Merton Street), and to the west was the church of St John the Baptist. This was appropriated by the College, though the parish retained its identity until 1891. But in 1290–4 the existing church, which stood on the site of the present Mob Quad, was replaced by the chancel of the present magnificent Chapel, the finest late 13th-century building in Oxford. As first envisaged, the Chapel (or, more correctly, St John's church) was to have been a full-scale monastic-style church with transepts and an aisled nave, some 200–240 feet (61.5–74 metres) long, and comparable in length to St Frideswide's Priory before the western bays of the nave were lopped off in 1525. In the event, the nave was never built, but the chancel still dwarfs the other early buildings of the College. It is a spacious, aisleless structure, wide in relation to its height like many 13th-century English churches, with a wooden roof and massive gabled buttresses on the street front, from the top of which project gargoyles or water-spouts. Like the earlier chapter house of St Frideswide's Priory, it is flooded with light, but here the light enters through large traceried windows. Geometrical bar tracery was derived from contemporary French Gothic architecture and first appeared in England at Westminster Abbey in the 1250s, from which the new fashion soon spread to the cathedrals at Lincoln, Lichfield, and elsewhere. The windows at Merton Chapel are more complex in design than these, reflecting recent developments in London, notably in the chapel of the Bishop of Ely's London house in Holborn (now the church of St Etheldreda, Ely Place), the proportions of which are very similar to those of Merton Chapel. The window tracery is varied in form, with circular and triangular shapes interspersed with three-lobed designs recalling the leaves of a horse-chestnut tree; the east window, lighting the high altar, is one of the most impressive of its date in England, with its row of seven sharply pointed lancets and a circular rose above. The beauty and interest of the building is enhanced by the fact that it still retains a good deal of its original stained glass, some of the oldest in Oxford; it was given by Henry de Mamesfield, a Fellow of the College and later Chancellor of the University, and he is represented in twelve of the side windows, kneeling in prayer on either side of the figure of a saint.

Merton College Chapel looking east. The floor, fittings, and roof decoration date from William Butterfield's restoration of 1849–56.

In the earliest days of Merton College the Fellows shared rooms in the existing houses on the site and elsewhere in Merton Street. The first purpose-built residence was an L-shaped house built for the head of the College (*custos* or Warden) on the site of Robert Flixthorpe's house and extended in 1299–1300. A substantial part of the Hall of this house survives as the College's Middle Common Room, including a two-light window and a timber roof, both of *c.*1300; here the Warden, a senior ecclesiastic, dined except on festive or formal occasions, when he took his place at the high table at the 'upper' end of the College Hall, like the abbot or prior of a monastery. The expansion of the Warden's house reduced the accommodation available for the Fellows, so a new L-shaped set of chambers was built of rubble stone to the south of the Chapel *c.*1304–11, on the site of the old church of St John. Each chamber was made up of a large room with beds for three or four Fellows and a partitioned-off study cubicle for each occupant, each with its own small window. The accommodation must have been uncomfortable by modern standards—medieval Oxford colleges were the homes of poor scholars, not privileged young aristocrats—though it was probably better than what was available elsewhere in the town. There was no heating, the windows were unglazed, and the rooms on the ground floor had earth floors. The blocks were just one room deep, with the chambers placed on either side of a lobby and staircase, approached through a pointed-arched doorway: an arrangement which was soon taken up in Cambridge, at Corpus Christi College, and which thereafter became the usual method of arranging residential accommodation in the colleges of Oxford and Cambridge down to modern times. The staircase plan can also be seen in late medieval colleges of chantry priests and in the lodgings of some late 14th-century great houses, like Dartington Hall (Devon), and its widespread and rapid acceptance in Oxford and Cambridge must be explained by the nature of medieval colleges: communal institutions, in many ways like monasteries, but also requiring a degree of privacy for the members, who did not take monastic vows.

The chambers of *c.*1304–11 now form the north and east ranges of Mob Quad, the first reasonably complete and architecturally uniform collection of residential quarters for students in Oxford. But, contrary to first appearances, the quadrangle evolved as the result of gradual accretion, not conscious design. At the junction of the north and east ranges is the former Treasury, built *c.*1288–91 to house the College's valuables: not only money but also the statutes and charters which gave it its constitution and legal independence. Architecturally, its most notable feature is the unusually steep-pitched roof, covered not

The west and north ranges of Mob Quad at Merton College. The Library is on the first floor of the west range, to the left. The Chapel tower in the background was built in 1448–52

with stone slates like the rest of the quadrangle, but with slabs of limestone. The south and west ranges were not built until 1373–8, with money provided by a former Bursar, William Rede, Bishop of Chichester. They contained chambers on the ground floor, but the upper floors were given over to a Library, the oldest in Oxford, with single-light windows illuminating the spaces between the stalls in which the chained books were kept. This system first appeared in the late 13th-century library in the College of the Sorbonne in Paris, but the immediate influence may have been the library of the Dominicans (Black Friars) in London, which the Warden and the master mason, William Humberville, visited before work began. Thus Oxford acquired its oldest surviving library, and one of the finest surviving medieval libraries anywhere.

The building accounts for the south and west ranges of Mob Quad show that the walls are of a rough, durable stone from Wheatley, a few miles to the east of Oxford; this was formed on the Corallian beds but, unlike the coral rag used for Oxford's oldest buildings, it could be cut into smallish blocks and laid in regular courses. It was not suitable for the door and window frames, any more than it had been for the elaborate carved detail of the Chapel windows, and for these purposes freestone had to be brought by road and river from the oolitic limestone quarries at Taynton, near Burford, some twenty miles to the west; similar stone must have been used for the carvings of Oxford's 12th- and 13th-century buildings, and for the spire of St Frideswide's Priory. The other materials were the roofing slates, which came from near Stow on the Wold in the Cotswolds, and timber brought from the College's estates in Surrey.

The number of students in Oxford increased during the early 14th century, and the academic halls flourished. Meanwhile three new colleges were founded, all of them in the eastern part of the town: Exeter in 1314, Oriel in 1326, and Queen's in 1341. These new foundations were smaller and poorer than Merton. None had more than about a dozen members at first, making them comparable in size to the smaller colleges of chantry priests. Their 14th-century buildings have all disappeared, but early illustrations indicate that, as at Merton, they were arranged piecemeal around open spaces which gradually coalesced into quadrangles. Loggan's drawing of Queen's shows a gateway to Queen's Lane with chambers on either side, a

Loggan's view of Queen's College in 1675. The entrance was from Queen's Lane, and the Hall was on the far side of the quadrangle. To the right is the Williamson Building of 1671–2, which still survives, though externally remodelled

Chapel with elaborate Decorated tracery in the east window on the south side, and a Hall lit by three two-light windows on the west; work on these buildings began in 1352, and the quadrangle was finished by the end of the century, only to be swept away in the 18th century.

The University of Oxford did not acquire its first purpose-built structures until the early 14th century. By then it already possessed a handful of houses in the town, but it had no strictly architectural identity of its own. Unlike the colleges, it was poorly endowed, and it could not erect buildings without help from private benefactors: something which has remained generally true down to modern times. Teaching took place in schools (lecture-rooms), holding an average of thirty to fifty students apiece, most of them rented from the local monasteries like Oseney Abbey, which had invested heavily in urban property in the 12th and 13th centuries. They were clustered in the area between St Mary's church in the High Street and the northern town wall, bounded on the west by School Street and on the east by Catte Street. This area has remained the physical heart of Oxford's academic quarter, just as the heart of the town is, and always was, at Carfax and the streets leading into it.

St Mary's church, at the junction of School Street and the High Street, was the University's main meeting-place. Though the parish was small, the living was an important one, in the gift of the Crown since the early 12th century. And, from at least the middle of the 13th century, the church was used for meetings of Convocation, the supreme governing body of the University, and of its disciplinary body, the Chancellor's Court. These took place in the chancel, and academic exercises or disputations sometimes took place in the porch. The oldest visible part of the building is the steeple, with its magnificent spire, externally the most striking example of Decorated Gothic in Oxford. Dating from some time in the early 14th century (the precise date is unknown), it stands on the north side of the building: an unusual position explained by the lack of space to the west. There are pinnacles at the four corners of the tower, as in the earlier spire of St Frideswide's, but here they are in pairs, and each of them incorporates statues of saints under gables encrusted with ball-flower ornament, with another pinnacle creeping up the face of the spire behind each of the lower pairs of pinnacles: an extraordinarily lavish conceit. The pinnacles have been repaired on several occasions, most recently by T. G. Jackson in 1894, when new statues by George Frampton were installed; the original statues were then removed to the cloister of New College, where they can still be seen.

The body of St Mary's church was totally rebuilt in the 15th century, but a chantry chapel of *c.*1328 still survives on the north side, built by

St Mary's church (the University Church) from the north in 1754. To the left of the steeple is the University's Convocation House, externally remodelled in the 15th century

the Rector, Adam de Brome, founder of Oriel College. And to the east is the oldest of the University's buildings: the Convocation House (now a coffee shop), erected in the 1320s out of funds contributed by Thomas Cobham, Bishop of Worcester. It is two storeys high, with a dark, vaulted ground floor used originally as both a muniment room and a treasury, and as a meeting-place for Congregation—the body comprising all resident Masters of Arts. The room upstairs was intended as the University's own library, housing manuscripts donated from Cobham's own collection. With the completion of this unpretentious structure, the University had a tangible nucleus.

The unpretentious tower of St Martin, Carfax (see p. 262)—one of the main landmarks of modern Oxford—also dates from the early 14th century, but the church itself has gone and its tower now stands in an isolation which was never intended. The only other parish church to show important work of the period is **St Mary Magdalen's**, beyond the town's northern gate, to the north of the street now known as Broad Street, which ran alongside the town ditch outside the wall. Here the work took the form of adding an outer south aisle lit by Decorated Gothic traceried windows onto the existing late 12th-century church, making it wider than it is long. The new aisle was endowed by a wealthy parishioner and served as a chantry chapel, dedicated to the Virgin Mary; the north aisle, replaced by Gilbert Scott in 1841, was used for many years by the adjacent Balliol College. The church's interior, rich in candles and images dimly visible through Victorian stained-glass windows, still has something of an air of

St Mary Magdalen from the south in 1840

medieval devotion, albeit overlaid with the fashionable Baroque trappings of 20th-century Anglo-Catholicism.

St Frideswide's Priory church remained the most impressive ecclesiastical building within the walls of medieval Oxford down to the end of the 14th century. Its continuing prestige is confirmed by the building of a sumptuous new shrine to the patron saint in 1289, and in about 1338 a new chapel—now known as the Latin Chapel—was built to the north of the Lady Chapel, serving, it seems, both as a new and more worthy setting for the relics of the saint and as a chantry chapel for the souls of the important persons whose bodies were interred nearby. The saint's shrine was destroyed at the Reformation, but parts of the elaborately carved superstructure were reconstructed on a new base, and in a new setting at the east end of the Lady Chapel, in 1889. Less damaged are the tombs of Prior Sutton (d.1316?), whose effigy rests under a gabled canopy enriched with ball-flower ornament, and Lady Elizabeth Montague, who founded a chantry in the church in 1346; their monuments still occupy their original positions in the south arcade of the new chapel. Similar in its proportions to Merton College Chapel, the Latin Chapel is vaulted in stone and is lit from the north by four large windows with flowing tracery and excellent contemporary stained glass in the lower lights, featuring sinuous figures of mostly female saints under elaborate

The north side of the Latin Chapel in Christ Church Cathedral. The early 15th-century effigy in the foreground may be of Sir George Nowers, lord of the manor of Tackley, and the bust on the pier above commemorates Robert Burton (d.1640), author of *The Anatomy of Melancholy*

canopies; one of the saints is Frideswide herself, gazing down onto what may have been the site of her shrine close to the second bay from the east end. There is more flowing tracery, and more good early 14th-century glass, in the east window of St Lucy's chapel in the south transept. These were the last examples of Decorated Gothic architecture in Oxford. By the middle of the 14th century the Black Death had struck, decimating the town's population and clearing the way for the adoption of a different style in whose development Oxford played a central part.

2 The Later Middle Ages

When the University first came into being Oxford was one of the most flourishing provincial towns in England, but in the early 14th century it fell into an economic decline from which it did not really recover for 200 years. The initial cause is probably connected with the migration of the wool and cloth trades—source of much of the town's earlier wealth—westwards into the Cotswolds. Economic problems were probably worsened by changes in the pattern of long-distance trade: a decline in the importance of the road route from the Midlands to the south coast; the realignment of the increasingly important east–west route from London into South Wales through Abingdon, where a new stone bridge was built in 1416; and finally obstructions in the navigation along the River Thames. By the 15th century Oxford's economy had came to rely to a large extent on marketing and services, and on the food and drink trades, all of which were heavily influenced by the presence of large numbers of students and scholars, which were subject to seasonal fluctuations. The coming of the Black Death in the 1340s made matters much worse. The population fell and large numbers of houses, especially in the suburbs, fell into dereliction. This change in fortunes affected the social and economic life of Oxford down to modern times.

The decline of the Town was seized as an opportunity by the Gown. The eastern part of Oxford, away from the castle and the market, was especially hard hit by demographic and economic decline, enabling vacant plots in and around the academic quarter to be bought up by academic halls and, especially, the colleges. The fall in population after the Black Death seems to have been especially marked in the north-eastern corner of the town, and it was here that William of Wykeham, Bishop of Winchester and Chancellor of England, started buying up property in 1369 with a view to founding a new college dedicated to the Virgin Mary. **New College** was founded in 1379, the year in which Merton's Mob Quad was finally completed, and work on the new buildings began in the following year. Like Walter de Merton, Wykeham was an ecclesiastical grandee of the first order, and he

The Divinity School, looking west

endowed the new foundation lavishly with manors and appropriated churches acquired especially for the purpose. With a Warden and seventy Fellows, many of whom were undergraduates (a relative novelty), it was larger than all the other 14th-century colleges combined, and twice the size of Merton. It was also the first college to be conceived as part of a dual foundation, with a 'feeder' school at Winchester, from which the Fellows were exclusively recruited down to the 19th century: an idea which was imitated by Henry VI in his foundation of Eton College and King's College, Cambridge, in 1446. The site, made up largely of fifty-one deserted tenements just inside the walls, was unprecedentedly spacious. For the first time in Oxford, all the buildings were conceived as a coherent architectural whole, with the disparate elements of earlier colleges—Hall, Chapel, Library, chambers for Fellows, lodgings for the head of the College, kitchen—all grouped together in a single magnificent set of buildings, larger than anything built within the walls since the construction of St Frideswide's Priory 200 years before.

Wykeham was the first of a series of wealthy and ambitious clerics who transformed the architectural face of Oxford in the later Middle Ages. He first became familiar with the management of large-scale building projects through his work as surveyor to Edward III at Windsor Castle and elsewhere between 1356 and 1361. Among the craftsmen he met in the course of his duties was the master mason William Wynford, who was entertained several times at New College while building was in progress and eventually sent his son there; Wynford later went on to rebuild the nave of Winchester Cathedral—one of the masterpieces of English late Gothic—and his portrait was included in the east window of the chapel of Wykeham's school at Winchester. So, in so far as the two establishments had an architect in the sense that we understand the word today, it is virtually certain that Wynford was that man. Though trained as a building craftsman and not as an artist or theoretician, he was responsible for the main elements of the design, taking advice from Wykeham himself and also, it seems, from other craftsmen, including Henry Yevele, the leading master mason in the Royal Works in the late 14th century. Among the other building craftsmen employed by Wykeham was the master carpenter Hugh Herland, best known for his superb hammer-beam roof at Westminster Hall in the Palace of Westminster.

New College served as a model for collegiate architecture, in Oxford and elsewhere, down to recent times, and its buildings still vividly convey the founder's determination to provide a dignified and self-contained setting for the life of an academic community dedicated to study and to the worship of God, and organized down to the smallest

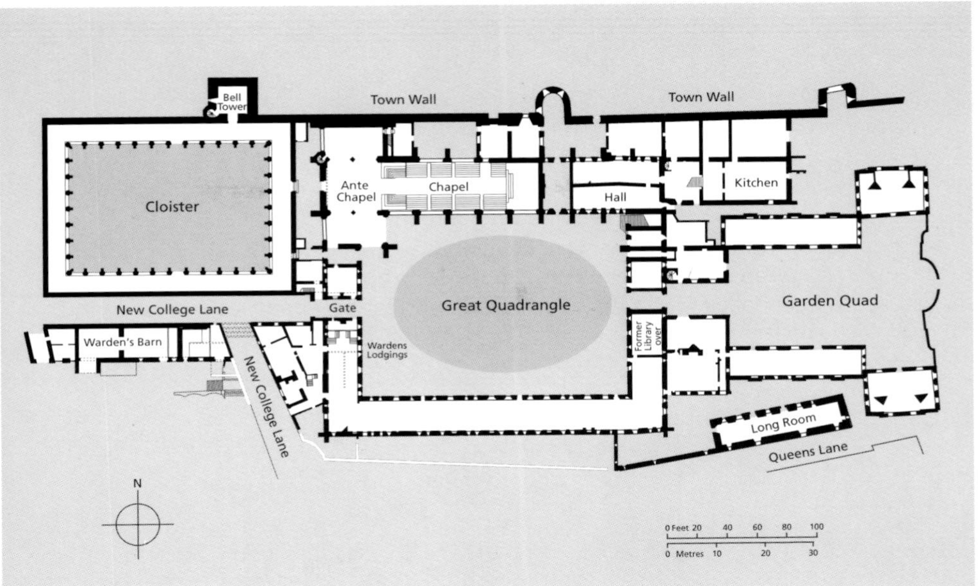

New College: plan

detail. They are grouped around a single quadrangle with the residential quarters disposed around three sides and the Hall and Chapel on the fourth: an idea which clearly owed something to monastic precedents and something to the planning of contemporary colleges of secular priests, like that at Cobham in Kent, begun to Henry Yevele's designs in 1370. The new buildings were larger and more ambitious than anything previously attempted in the colleges of either Oxford or Cambridge. The quadrangle is nearly four times the size of Merton's Mob Quad, and twice that of Corpus Christi, Cambridge, the most complete surviving early collegiate quadrangle there. Here, for the first time, the collegiate idea is convincingly expressed in three-dimensional architectural form.

New College is approached from a street (New College Lane) which has not changed in its essentials since the end of the 14th century. To the left is the south wall of the cloister (see p. 44), to the right a barn constructed to hold produce from the College's extensive rural estates, and at the end is a tall gatehouse adorned on the outside with niches containing figures of the founder, the angel of the Annunciation, and the Virgin Mary. This was the first of many Oxford collegiate gate towers; it proclaims the exclusiveness and confidence of the establishment to the outside world, and also its determination to keep riotous townspeople at bay, something which may have weighed on the founder's mind in an era of social dislocation which was most spectacularly manifested in the Peasants' Revolt of 1381.

The gate tower of New College from New College Lane. The outer wall of the cloister is on the left

The room over the gateway was, and still is, part of the Warden's house or Lodgings (a term also used in contemporary aristocratic houses), and its strategic placing enabled him to keep an eye on visitors and on the activities of the Fellows. The rest of the collegiate community was housed in the west, south, and east ranges of the quadrangle, in rooms which were disposed on two floors, with shared rooms and private studies, as in Mob Quad at Merton; a third floor was added in 1674, unfortunately spoiling the original proportions. The Library was on the upper floor of the east range, its layout no doubt influenced by that of Merton College. To the east of the quadrangle was a large open space bounded on two sides by the town wall, and it was here that the College's garden was eventually laid out. A block of latrines, the Long Room, was built to the south, alongside Queen's Lane, and is still used in part for its original purpose.

The quadrangle of New College looking east. The Chapel, Hall, and Muniment Tower are on the left. The top floor of the east and south ranges dates from 1674, and the sash windows were inserted in the 18th century

The buildings were all constructed of durable local rubble stone, with stone dressings from the quarries at Taynton, near Burford.

The north range of the quadrangle is given over to the Chapel and Hall: the core of the religious and communal life of the College. Taller and more richly detailed than the other buildings in the quadrangle, their traceried windows are separated by boldly projecting buttresses surmounted by miniature spires or pinnacles embellished with crockets: a favourite motif in late medieval Oxford. The Chapel tracery, with its repetitive lines of tall stone mullions interrupted by cross bars (transoms) and the emphasis on verticality, are both characteristic of the late or 'Perpendicular' Gothic which supplanted the Decorated style in late 14th-century England. Though Perpendicular Gothic did not originate in Oxford, it was the decisive influence on the architectural character of the city in the later Middle Ages, and in the north range of New College William Wynford created one of its definitive monuments.

The Hall and Chapel were placed next to one another: a novel decision in a collegiate context, though anticipated by Edward III in his remodelling of the Upper Ward at Windsor Castle. The Hall, like that of Merton and the slightly later one built by John of Gaunt at Kenilworth Castle (Warwickshire), is raised over a vaulted ground floor, in which the boy choristers who formed part of the foundation were later taught. At the east or service end is a pinnacled tower containing the staircase, covered by a net-like lierne vault of great ingenuity and, on the upper floor, the College's Treasury, which is also vaulted. The Hall has much in common with the halls of the great aristocratic country houses of the time, which the College in some respects resembled. In the centre there was a hearth or brazier for heating, and at the 'upper' end a raised dais, from which the Warden and a handful of eminent guests could gaze down over the other tables, where the members of the College were seated according to rank. Elements of this ceremonial arrangement have remained in regular use in almost all Oxford colleges down to the present day: a vivid instance of the institutional continuity which lies behind Oxford's architectural development. The flattish timber roof was by Hugh Herland—the present roof is a reasonably accurate 19th-century replacement—and at the east or 'lower' end a staircase descends to the kitchen, flanked originally by the Buttery and Pantry for the serving of food and drink (a wooden carving over the Buttery doorway shows a man holding a jug).

The Chapel reflects the founder's determination to leave behind him a magnificent chantry in which prayers and Masses for his soul could be offered in perpetuity. The main body of the building is a tall aisleless chancel similar in proportions to the lost chapel of St Stephen in the Palace of Westminster, begun in 1292—a building which Wykeham must have known well—and lit by windows which are substantially larger than those of the Hall. Here the members of the College met together for worship, facing each other across the central aisle; the fancifully carved wooden misericords—among the most inventive and humorous examples of medieval craftsmanship in Oxford—still survive under the hinged seats. Because the Hall is behind the east wall there was no possibility of introducing an east window; instead, there is a richly carved screen, full of figures of saints and prophets, now dating entirely from the later 19th century (see p. 226). The founder may have intended at first to build a long, aisled nave to the west of the chancel, with the aisles as high as the nave: in other words a 'hall church', of a type highly unusual in England at that time. But a nave would have been an expensive luxury, since New College Chapel was never a parish church like that of Merton, nor was it a popular preaching house like the churches of the mendicant friars. So, although the land was purchased in 1389, the plan was abandoned and a cloister was built instead, leaving the truncated nave as an antechapel, used for College meetings and for Masses at the east-facing altars. In this way the Chapel achieved, more by accident than design, a T-shaped plan: an arrangement virtually unique to Oxford (save for the 15th-century chapel of Eton College). The antechapel has largely avoided the meddling of later generations,

The antechapel of New College Chapel, looking north. The standing figure is Jacob Epstein's *Lazarus* (1951)

and is now the least altered of the main buildings of New College. The lofty proportions are accentuated by tall, thin columns with deeply undercut mouldings, and the effect is enhanced by the survival of the original stained glass in all but the west window (the medieval glass in the chancel was replaced in the 18th century, except in the upper lights).

Immediately to the north of the Chapel and Hall is the town wall, the maintenance of which has always been one of the College's responsibilities. Here in 1396–7 a bell tower was built, to the west of the Chapel, gaunt and a little forbidding, with a crenellated roof-line and no spire. Constructed of 'hardstone' from Headington, only two miles away—the first documented instance of Headington stone being employed in Oxford—it emphasized the formidable face which the College clearly wanted to present to the outside world. And the building of the cloister to the south of the tower, also in the 1390s, deepened the sense of academic exclusiveness which was so marked a feature of William of Wykeham's foundation. A cloister was not strictly speaking an essential part of a college, since the members did not live around its covered walkways, as monks did in monasteries. But it provided space for burials of junior members—a tenth of all Fellows died within four years of matriculation in the 15th century—and it may have been used on occasion for teaching. Quiet, and usually deserted, it is now a vivid reminder of the medieval origins of

New College from the north in 1844. The mason's yard in front of the 13th-century town belonged to the Knowles family, who were responsible for remodelling many of Oxford's older buildings in the early 19th century

The cloister of New College, with the tower and the west front of the Chapel

the University, and with its completion the College remained virtually unaltered for over 250 years.

With the building of New College, the ecclesiastical and academic influence on Oxford was reinforced. Only the Norman Castle asserted the claims of the secular power on a comparable scale, and the town's demoralized citizens had neither the resources nor the motivation to compete with William of Wykeham as patrons of architecture. Their contribution was largely confined to domestic building, and here the most important innovations were the addition of extra storeys to houses and the growing importance of timber as a building material: something which sharply differentiated the town from the University down to the early 19th century. Houses of more than two storeys are first recorded in Oxford in the mid-14th century, and it is fortunate that a three-storeyed late 14th-century timber building still survives on Cornmarket Street, the busiest shopping street in the city. It has recently been shown that this structure—now largely occupied by the Laura Ashley shop—started life as the New Inn, built *c.*1386–96 on a site just inside the North Gate at the corner of Ship Street, which ran parallel to the city wall. Begun by a vintner, John Gibbes, Mayor of Oxford and three times Member of Parliament, it was completed by his son who descibed it as the 'Neweyn within the Northgate' in 1396.

The former New Inn, Cornmarket Street

In its original form the complex of buildings consisted of a three-gabled frontage to Cornmarket Street, with two long parallel two-storeyed ranges of stone and timber extending backwards to enclose an open courtyard. The street front is three storeys high, and originally incorporated a row of five shops at ground level with chambers and attic rooms above. It was built entirely of timber framing, with the upper stories projecting—'jettied'—out over the lower: a method of building found all over northern Europe. After many changes—the building is all but unrecognizable in early 20th-century photographs—the northern part of the street front was restored in 1950–2, the rest following in 1985–7.

The houses of Oxford's leading late medieval citizens clustered near Carfax, each with a narrow gabled frontage of two, three, or even four storeys to the street: a pattern which lasted into the 17th century and even later. A much rebuilt example of this type of house survives at number 126 High Street. Built as one of a pair of houses in the late 15th or early 16th century, it stands on ground originally belonging to St Frideswide's Priory; the builder may have been Henry Mychegood (d.1501), Squire Bedel to the University. The house is four storeys high, originally jettied, with a single gable to the street; new windows were inserted in the late 17th century, but much of the original structure still survives, including the carved bargeboards under the wooden gables. Away from the centre of the town, houses were usually only two storeys high, and where space was not at a premium, as it was in the streets around Carfax, the main rooms extended along the whole of the street frontage, with an open-roofed hall flanked by one or more chambers and service rooms. This was the arrangement at Beam Hall, a small 15th-century stone-built academic hall which still survives, albeit somewhat rebuilt, on the north side of Merton Street, opposite Merton College Chapel, and also at the much-remodelled Littlemore Hall—now occupied in part by the Elizabeth Restaurant—in the southern suburb of the city, outside the south gate. The meticulous drawings of the early 19th-century artist John Buckler and his son J. C. Buckler show other late medieval houses, now lost, including one at the corner of St Thomas Street and Hollybush Row in the western suburb between the Castle and Oseney Abbey, its central hall recessed behind two jettied wings like many 'Wealden' farmhouses in the south and east of England. But in general it is striking how little secular architecture of note there is, or probably ever was, in late medieval Oxford, especially when compared with other important provincial towns like Coventry or York, not to mention Continental European cities like Bruges and Florence. There is no clearer indication of the growing importance of the University *vis-à-vis* the town.

It was in the 15th century that the colleges made their decisive architectural impact on the urban fabric of Oxford. The first new collegiate foundation was **Lincoln**, established in 1427 by Richard Fleming, Bishop of Lincoln (and Oxford's diocesan bishop). It was a much smaller establishment than New College, housing only a Rector and seven graduate Fellows at first, and was dedicated to promoting religious orthodoxy at a time when many members of the Oxford academic community had been influenced by the reforming views of John Wycliffe. The site, formerly occupied by the church of St Mildred and some academic halls, was on the eastern side of Turl Street, just south of Exeter College, and the present west or entrance range was probably begun before Fleming's death in 1431. Loggan's engraving shows a somewhat forbidding stone block fronting the street, two storeys high, with tiny windows and a low tower rising up above the gateway; though much remodelled externally in the 19th century (see p. 194), this range still survives. By 1437 two more ranges had been built, comprising the north and east sides of the present Front Quadrangle. There was a Chapel and a small Library on the first floor of the north range, and much of the east range was occupied by a Hall, not raised up over a basement like those of Merton and New College, but entered directly from the quadrangle through a passage at the north-east corner. This led to the detached Kitchen, which still exists,

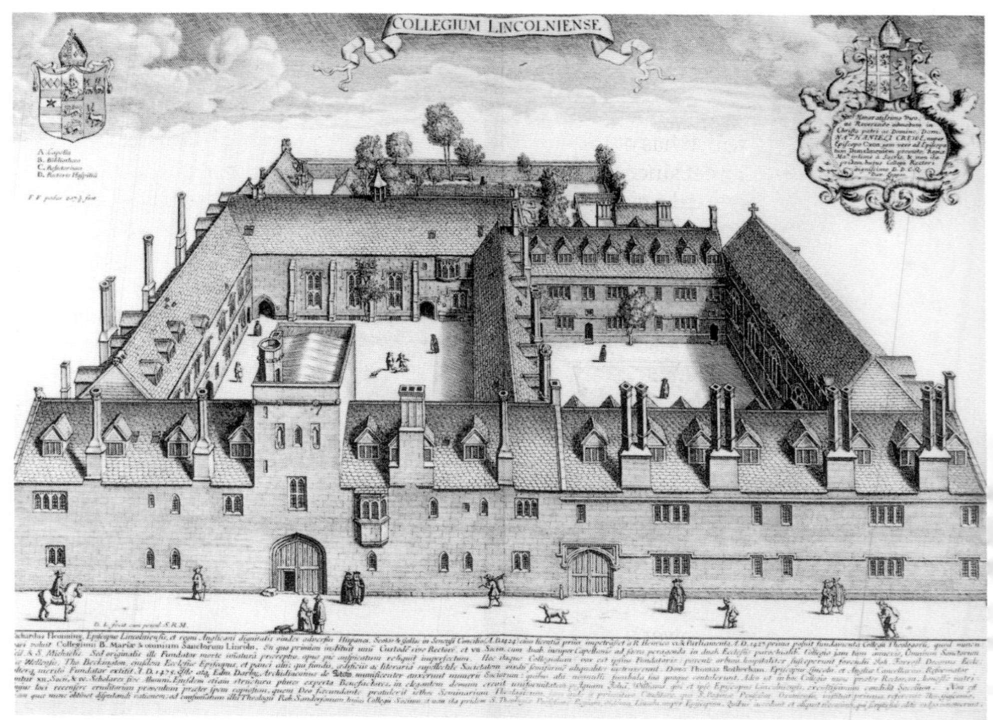

Loggan's view of Lincoln College from the west in 1675. The 15th-century buildings are to the left, and to the right is the second quadrangle, started in 1608

with the Buttery placed opposite the Hall on the north side of the passage; access to the Hall was through a wooden screen. More than any other surviving Oxford college, Lincoln retains the comfortable sense of corporate security which characterized all the smaller late medieval colleges, echoing the inward-looking protective character of contemporary gentlemen's country houses, like Cotehele (Cornwall). The Hall still retains its original arch-braced roof of timber, much steeper pitched than that of New College, and is surmounted by a replica of the louvre through which the smoke from the open hearth passed until the building of a wall fireplace at the end of the 17th century. New lodgings for the Rector were built at the southern end of the Hall in 1465–70, and the quadrangle was completed with the building of the south range, containing chambers for extra Fellows, in 1475–9.

Collegiate building in the 15th century was not confined to new foundations. The smaller and less well endowed of the older colleges had started life in houses which hardly differed in appearance from the academic halls, but in the 15th century they succeeded in erecting buildings which, though domestic in scale like those of Lincoln College, were none the less more extensive than any of the unendowed halls to which most of the undergraduates still belonged. The process was usually slow and piecemeal. University College, which has occupied its present site on the south side of the High Street since 1332, built a new Chapel *c.*1396–8 and subsequently created a quadrangle with a Hall, buttery, and kitchen of 1448–9 in the east range, all of which were totally swept away in the mid-17th century. A similar process occurred at **Balliol**, which had owned property on the north side of Broad Street, just outside the town walls, since 1284. Here more property was acquired in the early 15th century and a quadrangle (the present Front Quadrangle) gradually took shape, starting with the Hall (completed by 1430) on the west side and the first-floor Library in the north range, begun in 1431 but extended *c.*1475–83 to house books donated by William Gray, Bishop of Ely. The Hall (turned into the main library in the 19th century) is at ground level, like that at Lincoln, and is lit by four two-light windows; the Library is more distinctive, with a long succession of windows under flattened arches, characteristic of the period. Next to the Library was the Chapel, rebuilt in the 1520s and replaced in the 19th century, and on the south side of the quadrangle a range of chambers with a gate tower was erected *c.*1495 (also replaced), thus completing the quadrangle.

The front quadrangle of Balliol College, with the 15th-century Hall in the west range to the left and the Library on the right. The battlements were added by James Wyatt in 1791–4

At Exeter, the smallest and least well endowed of the medieval colleges, the only medieval survival is the former gate tower of 1432 (now known as Palmer's Tower), which stands rather incongruously in the north-eastern corner of the college's Front Quadrangle, dwarfed by the vast Victorian Chapel; it originally gave access to the college's rather inchoate collection of buildings from a now-vanished street just inside the northern town wall, but it lost its original function when a new entrance from Turl Street was created in the 17th century. Nothing at all survives of medieval Oriel College, rebuilt in an agglomerative fashion in the 15th century, but, like University College, rebuilt again in the 17th century. To the north, however, a range of 15th-century buildings survives from St Mary Hall, one of the larger academic halls which swallowed up some adjacent halls, only to be incorporated into Oriel in the 19th century.

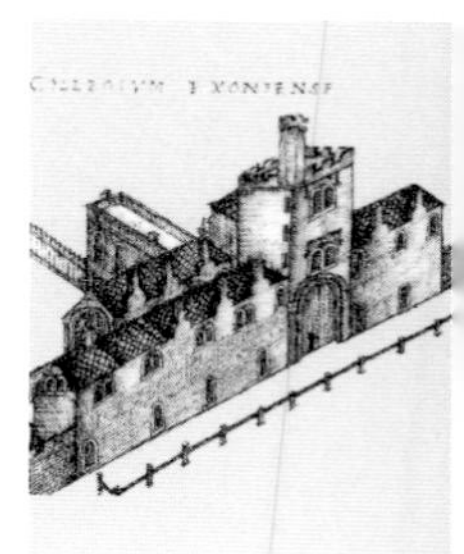

Exeter College in 1566. The gate tower (Palmer's Tower) and the adjoining buildings faced north to the town wall; the tower still survives, but the rest of the buildings depicted have been demolished

The largest and wealthiest of the older colleges was **Merton**, and here too there was a certain amount of building in the 15th century. Attention was focused at first on the completion of the Chapel: something which, in the event, never occurred. The Chapel was originally intended as a large cruciform structure with transepts and an aisled nave, as well as the chancel built in the 1290s. But the initial momentum was not maintained, and the impressive crossing arches with their clustered shafts were not built until the 1330s, followed by the south transept, possibly begun *c.*1368, and then by the north transept, probably built *c.*1419–25 and lit by large windows with Perpendicular tracery like that of New College Chapel; the doorway to Merton Street is flanked by statues of the Virgin Mary and St John the Baptist, the patron saint of the church. With the nave still unbuilt, the Chapel was now, like that of New College, shaped like the letter T, and so it has remained, the site of the intended nave being occupied now by Corpus Christi College (see p. 71). Finally, in 1448–52, a massive tower was built over the crossing, standing guard over the southern wall of the town in the same way as the bell-tower of New College looks out to the north. Low and wide in comparison with some 15th-century church towers, the surfaces are broken up by large traceried windows, and the skyline is punctuated by tall crocketed pinnacles separated by an openwork parapet—something also seen in the central tower of Gloucester Cathedral. The contrast to the tower of New College is striking, the austerity of Wykeham's building giving way to a new delicacy which was to be characteristic of Oxford architecture in the late 15th century.

The man responsible for Merton tower was Robert Janyns, founder of what was to become one of the most important dynasties of master masons in late medieval England. He had already been second-in-command to the master mason at All Souls College (see pp. 57–60)—a building much influenced by New College—and he went on to build the gatehouse at Merton. First conceived in 1418, it was not built until 1465, but with its completion the College acquired a street façade comparable to those of other, later foundations; its most notable feature is a carving, now immediately above the gateway but originally higher up, depicting the founder, Walter de Merton, kneeling in prayer, with John the Baptist to the right, and mythical animals including a unicorn emerging from a background of trees. The last major 15th-century addition to the College was an enlargement of the Warden's Lodgings on the east side of the quadrangle. This took the form of a room over a vaulted archway to the east of the Hall, known as the Fitzjames Arch from the Warden who commissioned the work in 1497; the room formed part of an 'apartment' or suite of rooms given over to queens of England when they visited Oxford, as Henry VIII's first wife, Catherine of Aragon, did in 1518.

There was also extensive building in the 15th century by the monastic colleges which were founded, mostly on sites outside the city walls, in order to give a higher education to monks from certain specified monasteries and religious orders. If the abortive 'house of

Merton Street looking west, with the entrance range and gate tower of Merton College in the foreground and Corpus Christi College in the distance

Loggan's view of Trinity (formerly Durham) College from the south in 1675. The detached building beyond the quadrangle was built to the designs of Christopher Wren in 1665–8

studies' for Cistercians at Rewley Abbey (see p. 21) is discounted, the first of these establishments was Durham College, established *c.*1290 for Benedictine monks from Durham on land next to Balliol, and refounded in 1381 with a secure source of income from appropriated churches. Here a quadrangle of buildings took shape in the late 14th and 15th centuries, with a gatehouse of 1397 and a Chapel (1406–9) on the south side, set well back from Broad Street and the town ditch. A Hall was later built on the western side of the quadrangle, with a north range of 1409–14 containing chambers, and an east range with a first-floor Library followed in 1417–21; it still contains some well-preserved 15th-century stained glass, some of it probably always in its present position and the remainder brought from the Chapel after the Reformation. Some of these buildings, notably the east range, still survive as part of Trinity College.

Durham College was architecturally all but indistinguishable from the smaller secular colleges, as was the now totally vanished Canterbury College, established in 1363 for a handful of monks from Canterbury Cathedral Priory, and occupying the site of the present

Canterbury Quadrangle of Christ Church. But a different system of planning was adopted at Gloucester College, begun in 1423 on open ground to the north-west of the city, near the former Beaumont Palace. Here the monks were accommodated not around a quadrangle but in houses built separately by each of the larger Benedictine monasteries which sent students to the college; they were placed next to one another in rows, resembling the houses of the secular canons in the Vicars' Close to the north of Wells Cathedral, and the Hall and Chapel were placed at the east end of the site along what later became Worcester Street. The Hall and Chapel disappeared at the beginning of the 18th century, when Worcester College took over the site (see p. 157), but some of the houses with their chambers or *camerae* still survive, notably in the southern range, where the coats of arms of the monasteries which built them in the 15th century—Pershore, Glastonbury, Malmesbury, and St Augustine's, Canterbury—can still be seen over the doorways.

The last monastic colleges in Oxford were founded by the Cistercians and the Augustinians. The Augustinian college of St Mary, founded in 1435, occupied the house now known as Frewin Hall to the east of New Inn Hall Street, and a chapel was built there in 1443. But funds were lacking and nothing more was done until the college was taken over by Cardinal Wolsey in 1518. He built a new chapel, but the refounded establishment fell victim to the

Former monastic *camerae* on the south side of the quadrangle at Worcester (formerly Gloucester) College

Reformation, after which its property was transferred to the recently founded Brasenose College; today only a gateway on the eastern side of New Inn Hall Street survives *in situ*, but the timber roof of the early Tudor chapel was moved to the Chapel of Brasenose College in 1656 (see p. 115). The Cistercian college, St Bernard's, was more fortunate. The site, to the north of the town wall and alongside the road leading to Banbury and Woodstock, was supplied by Henry Chichele, Archbishop of Canterbury, and building began soon after the foundation in 1437. The reluctance of individual Cistercian monasteries to contribute funds meant that the buildings were still less than half complete by 1479, but the project was rescued by Marmaduke Huby, Abbot of Fountains (Yorkshire), who entered into an agreement for the supply of stone with the local master mason William Orchard in 1502, and by 1517 Orchard had 'built the hall and chapel very splendidly with glass in the windows, and raised the windows of the fourth and last part of the college up to roof level'. By this time the College consisted of a spacious quadrangle around which were disposed a Hall, squeezed into the north-west corner, a much larger Kitchen and the Chapel in the north range, an incomplete east range intended for the Library, a south range made up of chambers, and a long western façade to the street with a central gate tower of *c.*1490, like that recently built by Balliol College

The front quadrangle of St John's (formerly St Bernard's) College looking north-west. The sash windows date from the 18th century

All Souls College from the south in 1598

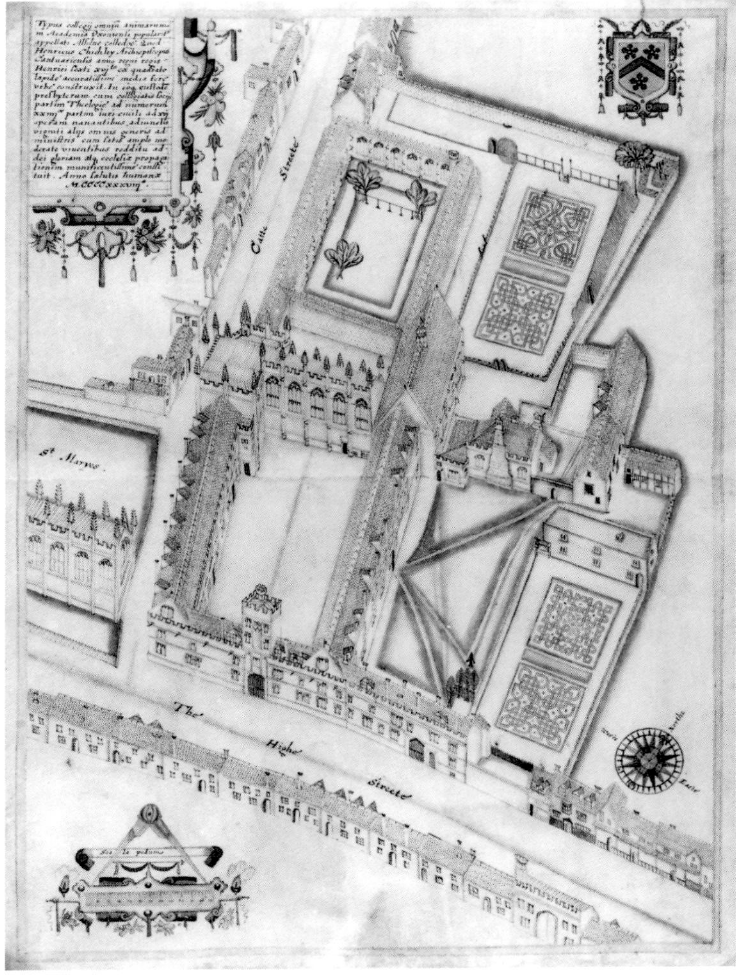

(itself influenced by the earlier façade of All Souls). From an architectural point of view, this must have been the most impressive of all the monastic colleges, and after the Reformation its buildings were taken over by the newly founded St John's College.

The largest and most magnificent of the 15th-century colleges, All Souls and Magdalen, were secular foundations, but both were built by ecclesiastical grandees who commanded vast resources. The founder of **All Souls** was Henry Chichele, who was educated at Winchester and New College before rising up the ecclesiastical hierarchy to become Archbishop of Canterbury in 1414. The College was founded in 1438 and was designed, like New College, to train secular clergy and ecclesiastical lawyers, although it did not (and still does not) admit undergraduates. All Souls was also like New College, but unlike the smaller colleges, in being a chantry foundation, and like New College it has a large and magnificent Chapel; here the members were required to pray for the souls of all the faithful departed, and especially those killed in Henry V's wars in France. But there were only forty Fellows, just over half the number at New College, and the buildings covered a smaller area. Completed in 1443, they stand on the site of six academic halls immediately to the east of St Mary's, the University Church, and the position gave the master mason, Richard Chevynton, the opportunity of building an impressive façade to the High Street. It takes the form of a range of two-storeyed stone buildings with a battlemented gate tower rising up from the centre, and a single-stair turret on the courtyard side; on the tower were statues of Henry V and Archbishop Chichele by the sculptor John Massyngham, proclaiming the close identification of Church and State which has always been a major theme in the history of Oxford University (the present statues are copies; the originals are housed in the former Buttery underneath the east end of the Chapel). With the

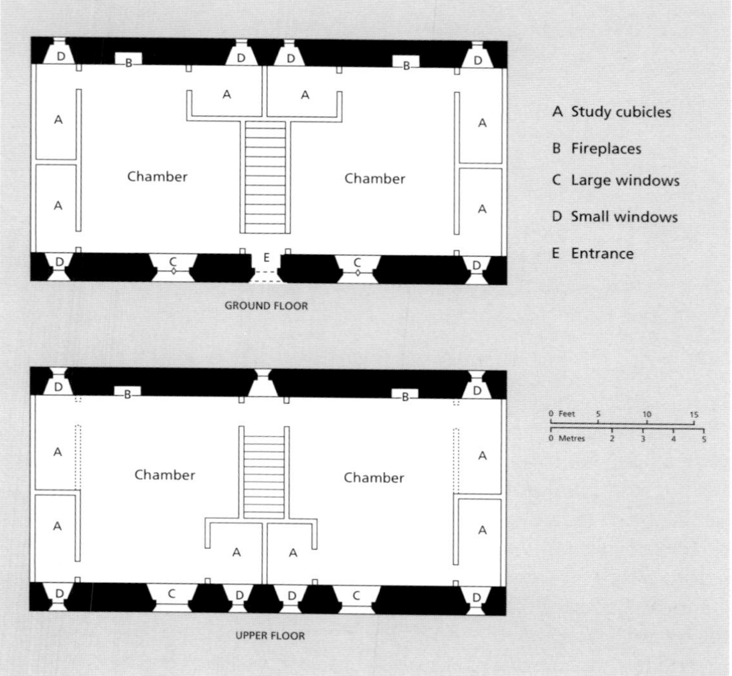

Plan of a staircase at All Souls College

The front quadrangle of All Souls College, looking towards the Chapel

completion of this impressive frontage the Oxford collegiate façade achieved its classic form, imitated again and again down to modern times.

The inner walls of the Front Quadrangle at All Souls have remained almost unaltered. The two-storeyed residential ranges still retain their steep stone staircases and their alternating pattern of two-light windows illuminating the chambers in which the Fellows slept, with smaller windows for their private studies. The Library was on the first floor of the east range, and on the north side is the Chapel, facing the gate tower and dominating the quadrangle as unmistakably as the Chapel at New College. It too is T-shaped, and the projecting buttresses and pinnacles make an impressive show. But the window arches are flatter than those of New College, and the mullions are carried up to the tops of the arches—features found in many 15th-century English churches. Inside, the most notable original features are the original (though restored) stained glass in the antechapel and the timber hammer-beam roof of the chancel—the first of its kind in Oxford—by the carpenter John Branche. The confined nature of the site meant that the Hall was placed behind the Chapel, projecting northwards, and was thus invisible from the front quadrangle. Beyond it a cloister was later built, its site now occupied by the North

The Chapel of All Souls College, looking west. The screen was completed by Sir James Thornhill in 1713–16

Quadrangle (see p. 159), and to the east of the Hall and Chapel were the kitchens and domestic offices. In 1472 the College acquired the ground flanking the High Street to the east of the Front Quadrangle, and here a new and more private residence for the Warden was eventually built.

The second of the major 15th-century collegiate foundations was **Magdalen**. Here too the founder, William Waynflete, was a high-ranking churchman who, like William of Wykeham, rose to become Bishop of Winchester and Chancellor of England. In its final manifestation Wayneflete's college was as large and ambitious as

Wykeham's, with seventy members, both graduate and undergraduate; there was also a grammar school which in its early years taught the boy choristers who sang services in the Chapel, together with sons of townspeople and undergraduates who needed grammatical teaching. The endowment was lavish: no fewer than 55 manors compared to Merton's 31, All Souls's 24, and Exeter's meagre complement of 3. And, as at All Souls, New College had a decisive influence on the final architectural form.

The College was founded in 1458, but building did not start until 1467, when the charter was confirmed by King Edward IV. The spacious site, to the east of the walled town on the banks of the River Cherwell, was already occupied by the Hospital of St John, granted to Waynflete with the intention of providing an untrammelled space for building. He accordingly suppressed the hospital and demolished its buildings, with the exception of the chapel and part of the hall, alongside the river, which eventually became the College kitchen and is now used as the Junior Common Room. The master mason (*principalis lathomus*) most closely associated with the new buildings

Magdalen College from the west in 1675 (Loggan)

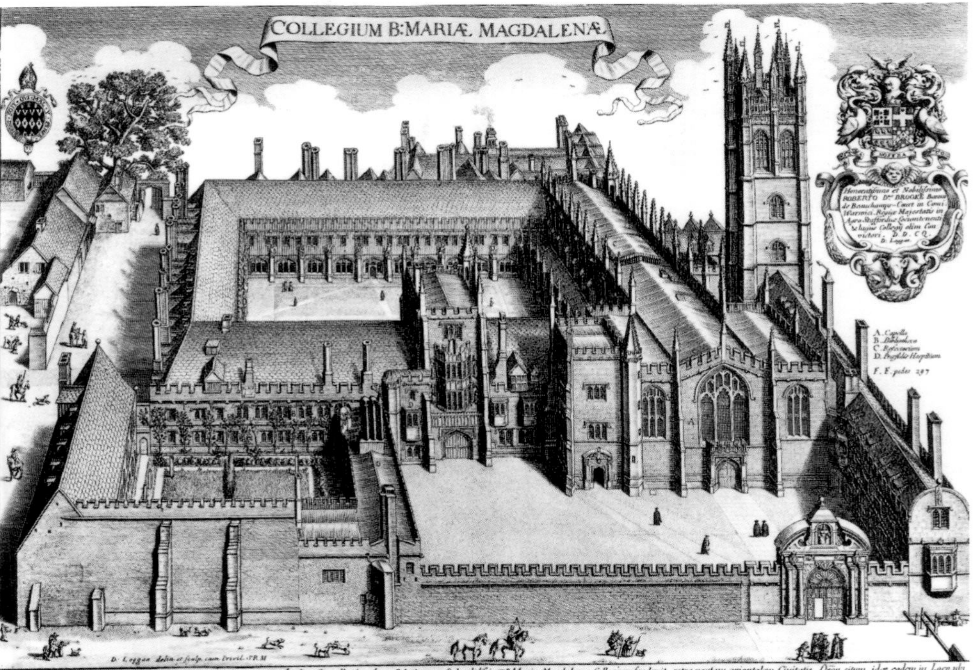

was William Orchard, and his role at Magdalen was comparable to that of William Wynford at New College. He seems to have been responsible for the overall design, and he certainly received payments for the outer boundary wall, for the Hall, Chapel, and cloister windows, and for the main gateway. He also supplied much of the stone, including a smooth ashlar for facing the walls, from quarries which he leased from the college at Barton in the parish of Headington (now a housing estate), thus allowing the college a considerable saving on the cost of carriage; this stone was supplemented, as was usual in late medieval Oxford, by Taynton stone for the carved detail. Orchard was thus the forerunner of a series of local mason contractors who over the next three centuries constructed some of the best-known buildings in Oxford, and like them he became a respected local worthy, owning and leasing property in the town and sending his son to Magdalen College (the son became a brewer, another much respected Oxford occupation).

As an architectural ensemble, Magdalen College vies with anything in late 15th-century England. The buildings stand away from the walled medieval town in extensive grounds, protected from the outside world by a battlemented wall and tower which still marks the eastern boundary along Longwall Street: a startling assertion of autonomy, even defiance. The wall went up in 1467, but seven years elapsed before work started on the College itself; most of the buildings were constructed between 1474 and 1480. The College was originally approached by a pathway (the Gravel Walk) to the north of the High Street, with the grammar school to the left and a gateway leading into an open forecourt (now St John's Quadrangle) in front; the schoolroom survived until the 19th century, latterly as part of a jumbled complex of buildings which also housed Magdalen Hall, one of the largest and longest-lasting of the academic halls (the site is now occupied by the 19th-century St Swithin's Quadrangle: see p. 247). The main buildings are arranged around a quadrangle nearly as large as that of New College, entered originally through a gatehouse (the Founder's Tower) in the west range. Buttressed, pinnacled, and decorated, especially on the west face, with elaborate carvings and mouldings, this magnificent structure proclaims the luxurious architectural tastes of Edward IV's reign (1461–83). The outer order of arches around the main doorway, and around the west doorway of the Chapel, contain 'flying ribs'—an unusual feature more commonly found in German than English late Gothic—and there is intricate panelling around and between the oriel windows on the first and second floors, lighting rooms which formed part of the President's Lodgings. Inside the gateway there are lavishly embellished vaulting

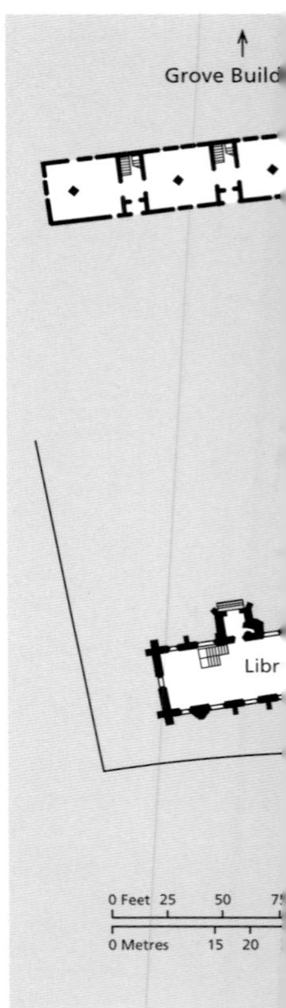

Plan of Magdalen College

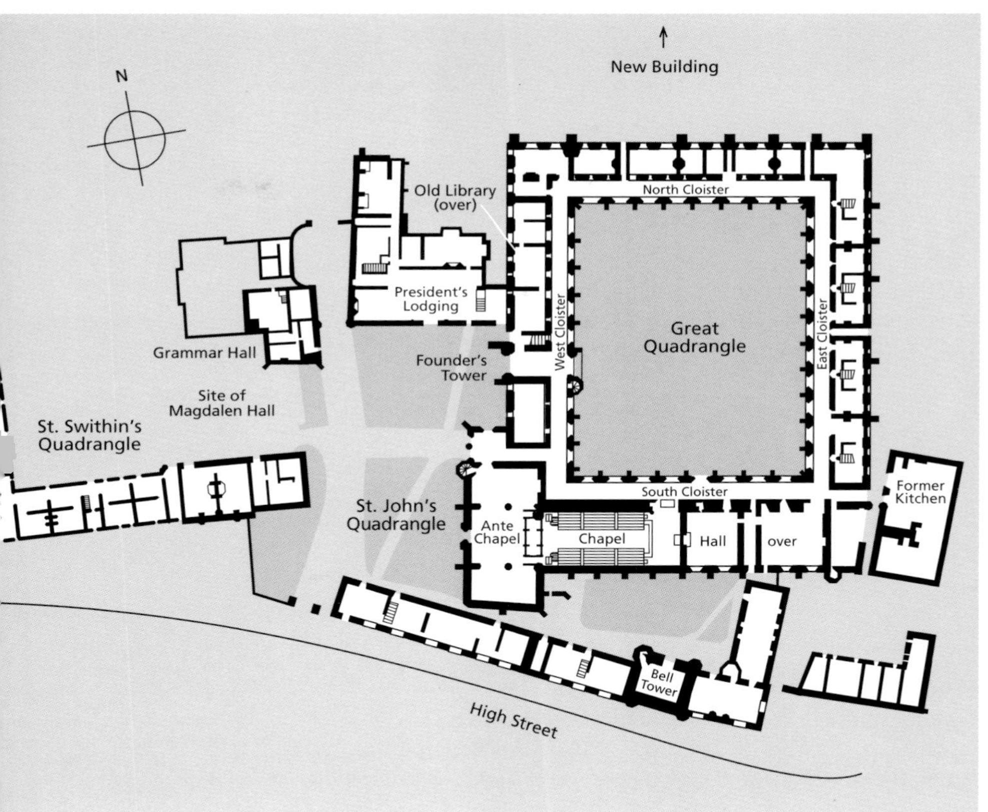

ribs and carved bosses. And, both inside and outside, the quadrangle was, in the words of a 16th-century writer, 'crowned with battlements entire in the manner worthy of gentlemen': an unmistakable assertion of seigneurial power.

The gateway at Magdalen soon ceased to serve its original purpose, except on ceremonial occasions, and from an early stage the usual entrance into the quadrangle has been through an unpretentious doorway in the lower Muniment Tower, next to the Chapel. It leads, uniquely in Oxford, into a covered walkway or cloister which runs all the way around the inner walls of the quadrangle (the south walk was an afterthought, not built until 1490, and the north range was rebuilt in the 19th century: see p. 198). The cloister windows are of the low, four-centred variety which was so popular in late 15th-century England, and above them are rows of flat-topped windows lighting the Library, in the west range, and the chambers which take up most of the north and east ranges; according to the contract of 1475, these windows were to be as good as, if not better than, those at All Souls

The quadrangle of Magdalen College looking west, with the Founder's Tower. The Chapel is on the left

College. The south side of the quadrangle is occupied by the Hall, raised up over an undercroft, and the Chapel, which has the T plan of New College and All Souls; both have been extensively altered inside, and are now as much a monument to the medievalizing tastes of later generations as to the authentic spirit of the 15th century. But in the walkways of the cloister it is still possible to experience in almost unalloyed form the quasi-monastic atmosphere with which Magdalen College has been imbued ever since its late medieval origins.

As at New College, the completion of the quadrangle was followed by the building of a bell tower. The tallest of Oxford's medieval towers (144 feet (44 metres) high), this beautifully proportioned structure was not begun until 1492, six years after Waynflete's death, but its designer remains tantalizingly unknown (a mason called William Rainold was mentioned in the accounts). It stands on the street front of the college, unmistakably announcing the presence of the University to those who approach Oxford across Magdalen Bridge from the London direction (see p. 175). Similar in some respects to the superb 15th-century church towers of Somerset, a more immediate source of inspiration may have been the unbuilt tower at King's College, Cambridge, of which a drawing of *c.*1448 survives. Both towers have polygonal corner turrets, but at Magdalen the lower stages are plain, throwing into greater relief the profuse decoration of the top stage, with its two traceried openings and its crown of crocketed pinnacles separated by an openwork parapet, like that of the earlier tower of Merton College Chapel. Here Gothic architecture in Oxford reached a degree of perfection which it was rarely, if ever, to attain in later years.

The University of Oxford, as distinct from the colleges, did not begin to be a significant patron of architecture until the 1420s, when a decision was taken to build a large and impressive lecture-room for theology—the **Divinity School**—on a site bought from Balliol College at the northern end of School Street, just inside the town wall. The University's lecture-rooms were already concentrated in this area, including Oseney Abbey's schools for lectures in the arts, rebuilt as a two-storeyed row in 1440 and since demolished. But the new building was intended to be on a grander scale, befitting the status of theology as 'the queen of the sciences'—a striking expression of faith in religious orthodoxy at a time when Oxford had been shaken by Wycliffite heresy. The foundations of the new building had been laid by 1430, when the mason Robert Winchcombe, builder of the chancel at Adderbury church near Banbury—a New College living—was appointed to 'survey the work of the new schools of theology'. It was conceived by Winchcombe as a single-storeyed structure, with most of the wall space taken up by large traceried windows under flattened arches of an unusual, almost triangular, profile (also seen in the cloisters at Magdalen). The carved stone mouldings on the present west doorway, and also on the piers of the north wall, were of great intricacy and delicacy, and the size of the buttresses indicates that a stone vault was intended from the beginning. But by 1440 work had ground to a halt for lack of funds—a perpetual problem with the chronically under-endowed University—and a new mason, Thomas Elkin, was instructed in his contract to 'hold back in future . . . such superfluous curiosity of the said work, namely in the housings of images . . . casements and fillets and other frivolous curiosities, which are not to the point and involve the university in costly expenses and the delaying of the work.' The results of this edict can be seen on the south wall piers, where Winchcombe's elaborate mouldings give way to a much plainer treatment, corresponding in character to the relatively austere contemporary work at All Souls.

A radical rethinking of the design took place in 1444, when Henry V's younger son Humfrey, Duke of Gloucester, a notable patron of humanist (classical) learning, gave a valuable collection of manuscripts to the University. These could clearly not be accommodated in the dingy room over the Convocation House

A modern drawing showing the probable appearance of Duke Humfrey's Library in the late 15th century

which then served as the University Library, and instead it was decided to house them in a new library to be built above the Divinity School: an idea which may have been taken from Winchester College, where a library had been built over the Fromond chantry chapel in the cloister in 1420. Robert Janyns, the master mason responsible for Merton tower, gave advice about the design in 1453, but further financial troubles ensued, and the building was not finally completed until after the University had resorted to a large-scale fund-raising campaign in the 1470s. The main donor, in 1478, was Thomas Kemp, Bishop of London, who gave 1000 marks (£666 13s 4d). He was assured by the University that by associating his name with the building, it would be remembered by posterity in the same way as Solomon was remembered for his Temple. This has not proved to be the case, but Kemp's initials can nevertheless still be seen, along with those of other donors, on the present stone vault of the Divinity School, which boasts no fewer than 455 carved stone bosses. The vault was erected in 1480–3, thus bringing to completion a building first conceived sixty years before, and the library above (now known as Duke Humfrey's Library) was finally opened to readers in 1488.

The vault of the Divinity School (see p. 38) is one of the *tours de force* of late medieval architecture in Europe. The decision to build a library over the School meant that the vault had to be of a lower pitch than had originally been intended in the 1420s. But what it loses in height it gains in decorative richness. By the second half of the 15th century, vaulting in England had reached a degree of inventiveness and virtuosity unmatched outside central Europe, and by the 1480s

A pendant in the Divinity School

English taste favoured prodigal display, as it had in the era of early 14th-century Decorated Gothic. Technically the Divinity School vault is a flattish stone ceiling resting on transverse arches supported from the outside by buttresses. Fan-like clusters of stone ribs sprout from pendants which hang from the transverse arches like stalactites, creating an effect of extraordinary delicacy and complexity, rich in the taut linear patterning which is so typical of late Gothic. In a return to the elaborate detailing eschewed in 1440, the pendants are carved with figures of saints in niches, and, to add even more complexity, shorter liernes link the main ribs to form lozenge-shaped patterns on the ceiling, with carved bosses at the intersections. Among the carved initials are the letters WO, possibly referring to the master mason William Orchard, who was mentioned in the accounts of the University's Proctors in 1478–9 and was paid for travelling to see Bishop Kemp of London in 1482–3. It seems likely therefore that Orchard was the designer of the vault, and also perhaps of the distinctive roof-line of the two-storeyed building, the tall crocketed pinnacles acting as counterweights to the outward thrust of the wooden roof of Duke Humfrey's Library.

The late medieval University of Oxford was governed from **St Mary's church** in the High Street. The existing building fell into disrepair in the 15th century, and in about 1462 Walter Lyhert, Bishop of Norwich and former Provost of Oriel College—the patrons of the living—paid for the rebuilding of the chancel. It is a long, narrow structure, with the large Perpendicular traceried windows found in the chapels of New College, All Souls, and Magdalen; the collegiate atmosphere is reinforced by the inward-facing stalls, which still survive, though somewhat mutilated. The rebuilding of the chancel threw the dilapidated state of the rest of the church into sharp relief, and by *c.*1490 the Chancellor of the University was lamenting that the nave had 'been reduced by age and weakness to such a state that we find no-one of good judgment who does not think it in danger of ruin'. The nave of a parish church was legally the responsibility of the parishioners, but the parish of St Mary's was tiny, and an appeal for funds to finance rebuilding was therefore launched among the old and current members of the University; there was also a gift from King Henry VII of forty oak trees from the royal forest at Shotover, a little to the east of Oxford. The building of the new nave, which took place in the 1490s, entailed the destruction of the whole of the existing church apart from the steeple, the Convocation House, and the Brome Chapel, the last two of which were later given new windows on the north side to correspond with those of the rest of the building (see p. 35). The rebuilt nave is a spacious, well-proportioned

The chancel of St Mary's church, looking east

example of late Perpendicular parish church architecture, though somewhat mechanical in its detailing and lacking the imaginative flair which makes the Divinity School such a memorable building. The usual parade of buttresses and pinnacles enlivens the frontage to the High Street (the present pinnacles are restorations, the originals having been blown down in a gale in the early 16th century, according to the Tudor traveller John Leland); the interior is roofed in timber, with flat tie-beam trusses over the nave, and there is plentiful light from the large clerestory windows, denuded of their original stained glass after the Reformation, when the screens and statuary also perished (the present woodwork dates mostly from 1826–8, and the stained glass, some of it very good, was inserted later in the 19th century).

St Mary's was the one parish church of architectural note in 15th-century Oxford, and it is significant that its rebuilding was financed by members of the University and not the townspeople. While they worshipped in surroundings of growing richness and beauty, the townspeople remained content with their existing churches, to which they made piecemeal alterations of no great architectural interest. Some work was carried out at St Thomas's, the parish church of the western suburb—though only the embattled western tower still survives reasonably intact—and also at St Cross, the parish church of Holywell. The nave of St Michael's at the North Gate was also rebuilt, and there were some relatively minor alterations at St Peter in the East. But Oxford never acquired a grand 15th-century church through which it could express whatever civic pride it had. Here again architecture—or, rather, the lack of it—confirms the historical record of a city dominated by the University which had been planted in its midst.

The rebuilding of the University Church coincided in its later stages with a major programme of alterations at St Frideswide's Priory (the Cathedral). By 1499 the cloister had been rebuilt with the proceeds of a gift from the Dean of St Paul's Cathedral, Robert Sherman, and a new Refectory constructed, which still survives in a much-altered state overlooking the southern walk. At about the same time, or slightly later, the chancel was given a new clerestory and a new stone vault, even more rich and elaborate than that of the Divinity School, which it resembles in many respects. This was clearly intended as the first stage of a re-roofing of the whole church, for in 1504 money was given for a new vault over the north transept, where the beginnings of a new clerestory can still be seen. But for some reason the project was not carried out, and only twenty years later the canons were expelled by Cardinal Wolsey (see p. 71), leaving only the spectacular chancel vault complete. As at the Divinity School, the most striking feature is the array of gravity-defying pendants, from which clusters of ribs spread over the surface. But here the pendants are pierced, and the liernes between the ribs are formed into extraordinary star-shaped patterns, reminiscent in some respects of Spanish late Gothic. The effect is matched only in the royal chapels of Windsor, Westminster Abbey, and King's College, Cambridge, all of which recieved new stone vaults in the first quarter of the 16th century. Yet while these were new buildings, the vault at St Frideswide's was created within a church more than 300 years old: a remarkable achievement. The overall similarity to the Divinity School vault suggests the hand of the same designer, William Orchard, and the attribution is supported by the fact that he was buried in the precincts of the Priory after his death

The chancel of Christ Church Cathedral, looking east, showing the vault of *c.*1500. The east wall, together with the ornamental floor and the stalls, dates from Gilbert Scott's restoration of the 1870s

in 1504. If the vaults of St Frideswide's and the Divinity School are indeed his, along with Magdalen and St Bernard's (later St John's) Colleges, he ranks among the most creative of the architects who have shaped the Oxford we see today.

The academic colonization of Oxford continued into the first quarter of the 16th century, when three new colleges were founded inside the town walls: Brasenose, Corpus Christi, and Cardinal College. Following the precedent of earlier Oxford colleges (though not those of Cambridge, where royal patronage was more important), high-ranking ecclesiastics played an important part in all three foundations, and each followed the lead of New College and Magdalen in making extensive provision for undergraduates. Brasenose was founded in 1509 by William Smith, Bishop of Lincoln, and Sir Richard Sutton, steward of the fashionable nunnery at Syon in Middlesex. The founder of Corpus Christi was Richard Fox, Bishop of Winchester and an important diplomat who had negotiated the marriage of Catherine of Aragon to Henry VII's eldest son Prince Arthur, and then, when he died, to his younger brother, the future Henry VIII; the College was originally intended for monks from St Swithin's priory in Winchester, but by the date of its inception (1517) it had become a secular foundation. Cardinal College, the largest of the three, was founded in 1525 by Henry VIII's chief minister, Thomas Wolsey, last and most magnificent of the powerful prelates in royal service who did so much to shape the institutional and architectural character of Oxford in the later Middle Ages. Wolsey suppressed the Priory of St Frideswide, then housing a mere handful of canons, and planned on the site a college intended to outstrip any other in Oxford and Cambridge in size, architectural grandeur, and academic achievement. Though never completed in the form he envisaged, much of the College was built in his lifetime, and it now forms the nucleus of the largest of Oxford's older colleges, Christ Church.

The foundation of the three new colleges coincided with a steep decline in the number of academic halls; of the fifty-two halls which existed at the beginning of the 16th century, only eighteen remained in 1513, and of these all but eight had disappeared by 1537: a sudden decline whose cause is not entirely clear. Brasenose and Corpus Christi both took over the sites of halls in the eastern part of the town: Brasenose on the western side of School Street, and Corpus to the south of Merton Street, on the site formerly set aside for the nave of Merton College Chapel. At Corpus Christi a clean sweep was made of the existing buildings, but at **Brasenose**—which drew its curious name from one of the halls on the site—the kitchen of one of the halls continued to serve the new foundation. Both colleges were built in the usual quadrangular fashion, with gate towers on the street frontage containing the lodgings of the head of the house. And both still retain their intimate, almost domestic character, typical of the smaller late medieval colleges (see colour plate facing p. 82).

Brasenose was built between 1509 and 1518, but with an eventual complement of eighty members it soon outgrew its original buildings, which were modified and extended in the 17th century. The early buildings of **Corpus Christi**, probably completed by 1517, have been less changed. The master masons were both connected with Henry VIII's Office of Works: William Vertue, who had been involved in building Bath Abbey and the vault of St George's Chapel, Windsor,

The Hall of Corpus Christi College looking south. The screen and panelling date from 1700–1

and William East. Their appointment was not welcomed by the local men, judging by an incident in 1512 when they were attacked by masons working at Brasenose. The gate tower, overlooking Merton Street, is embellished with niches on either side of the first-floor oriel window, which lit the principal chamber of the President's Lodgings, and over the entrance passageway is a fan vault, one of the first appearances of this characteristic English late Gothic feature in Oxford. The most impressive of the interiors is the Hall, with its splendid hammer-beam roof designed by Humphrey Coke, Warden of the Carpenters' Company in London and subsequently Henry VIII's chief carpenter; here, as in the roof of the almost contemporary chapel of St Mary's College (see p. 115), wooden pendants hang down from the horizontal beams, like the stone pendants on the choir vault of St Frideswide's Priory. The residential blocks are two storeys high, and, in contrast to the older colleges, the rooms were originally shared by just two occupants, a Fellow and an undergraduate or 'disciple', an arrangement which was soon to become normal in Oxford.

Unlike Brasenose and Corpus Christi, Cardinal College (the present **Christ Church**) was intended to rival and surpass the largest and most ambitious educational establishments in either Oxford or Cambridge. Wolsey's original foundation was designed to house no fewer than 176 people, including undergraduates, and it was financed by the revenues of several suppressed monasteries, including St Frideswide's, whose buildings were completely demolished, along with the church of St Michael by the South Gate and many houses. Streets were also obliterated, the present Blue Boar Street re-routed

The main façade of Christ Church to St Aldate's in 1794. The part of the building at the left was not erected until the 1660s, when the classical balustrade was extended along the whole façade. The gate tower (Tom Tower) dates from 1681–2. The houses on the right fell victim to a later street improvement

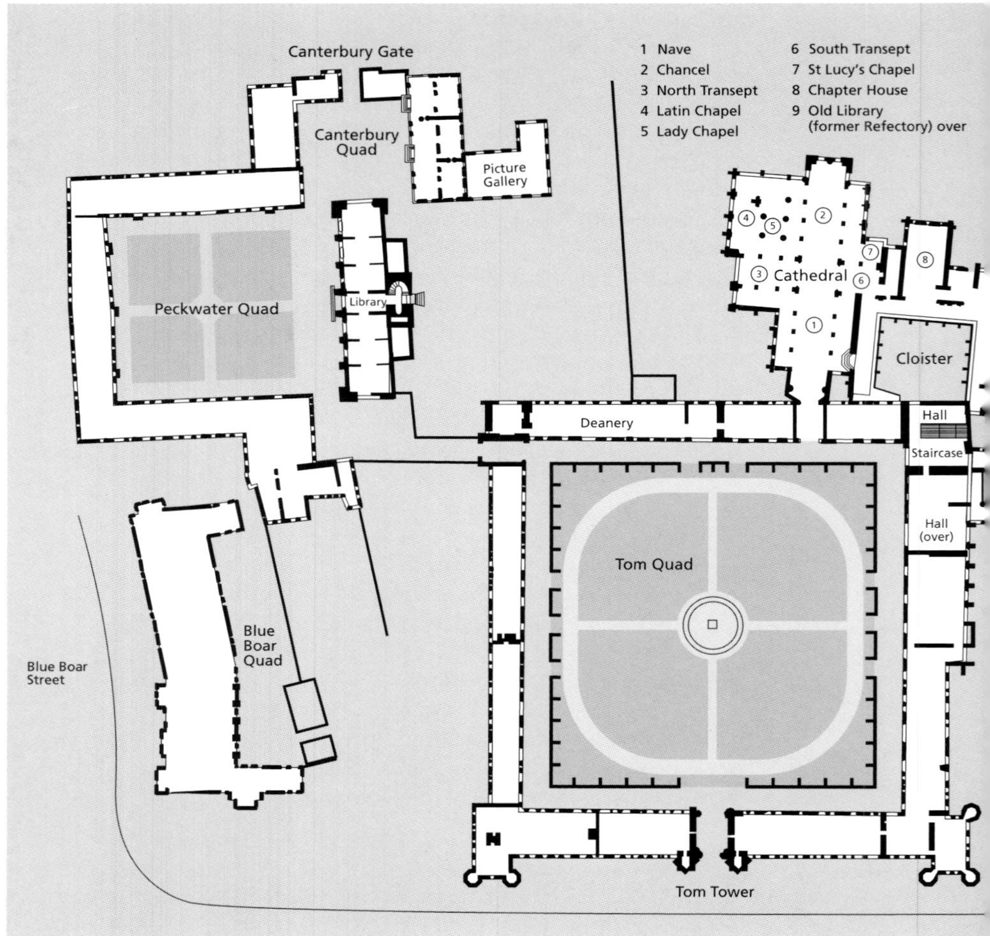

along the northern boundary, and a set of almshouses (now, after much remodelling, the Master's Lodgings of Pembroke College) built opposite the west front. Like Bishop Fox at Corpus, Wolsey eschewed Oxford's building craftsmen and entrusted the design to two experienced master masons from the Office of Works, Henry Redman and John Lubyns, who were paid for 'devising the building' and 'seeing the plat [plan] on the ground' in January 1525. Redman had already worked with William Vertue on the building of Lupton's Tower at Eton College, completed in the early 16th century, and Lubyns was involved with the building of Henry VII's Chapel at Westminster Abbey; both men had worked for Wolsey at his sumptuous country house, Hampton Court in Middlesex, begun in

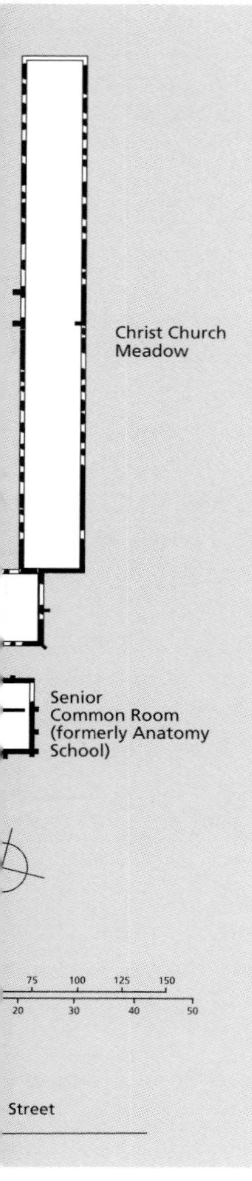

Christ Church: ground plan

1515. The master carpenter was Humphry Coke, who had worked with Redman at Eton. Thus the leading craftsmen were all intimately acquainted with the most ambitious building projects of early Tudor England, among which Wolsey's College was intended to occupy a leading place.

The main quadrangle (the present Tom Quad of Christ Church) was laid out on the site of the three western bays of the nave and the forecourt of St Frideswide's Priory. Wolsey had been a Fellow, and also Bursar, of Magdalen College in the 1490s, and, as at Magdalen, the original intention was for a cloister to be incorporated into the plan of the main quadrangle. But here the Chapel—of a size matched only by that of King's College, Cambridge—was to take up most of the north range, and the Hall, placed on the first floor like those at New College and Magdalen, was to face it on the opposite (southern) side of the quadrangle. A symmetrical street façade was planned, 300 feet (92 metres) long, with a tall gate tower in the centre and massive towers like defensive bastions at each end. Work began in 1525, and by July of that year there were 32 masons, 16 'rough layers', and 64 labourers at work on the site, as well as 20 carters bringing stone from Sherborne and Barrington in the Cotswolds to supplement the local stone from the Headington quarries. Construction proceeded quickly, and by 1526 the west range was completed, the foundations of the Hall and Chapel laid, and the Kitchen, in the words of a contemporary, Dr John London, 'finished save only the louer [louvre]; and all this Christmas the Dean and Canons had all their victuals prepared there. Behind the kitchen southward be goodly larder houses, pastry houses, lodgings for common servants, slaughter and fish houses, stables, with other such necessary buildings, substantially and goodly done in such manner as no two of the best colleges in Oxford have rooms so goodly and convenient'—an establishment more reminiscent of one of the royal palaces than a college for poor scholars. In 1529 Wolsey was informed by Thomas Cromwell, later to supplant him in the king's favour, that 'every man thinks the like was never seen for largeness, beauty [and] sumptuous curious and substantial building.'

Even in their unfinished state, Wolsey's buildings impress by their sheer magnitude. The main survivals from the original project are the bulk of the west and south ranges, including the Hall, the Kitchen, and the lower parts of the gatehouse. The rooms are higher than those in the earlier colleges, and are lit by square-headed windows with transoms, much larger than the normal collegiate two-light windows, and heated from the beginning by wall fireplaces: a novel luxury. Externally, there is profuse carving, especially around the gateway, covered with blind tracery and flanked by polygonal turrets of a kind

Christ Church: the Kitchen

also seen in Henry VII's Chapel at Westminster Abbey (see pp. 141–2); had this been completed as intended it would have thrown all earlier collegiate gate towers into the shade. And under the oriel window on the southern tower there is Oxford's first example of Renaissance carving, with putti and 'grotesques' of the kind which were currently appearing in the palaces of Henry VIII.

But the most impressive of Wolsey's works is the Hall, the largest and most splendid in either of the ancient universities. It rests on an undercroft, like the halls of New College and Magdalen, and is lit by large Perpendicular traceried windows, separated by pinnacled buttresses (the pinnacles themselves were not constructed until the 19th century), with taller bay windows lighting the 'upper' or high-table end. The wooden roof, like that of Corpus Christi, is of the hammer-beam type, but the span is wider and the pitch lower

Christ Church: Tom Quad looking south to the Hall. To the left of the Hall is G. F. Bodley's tower over the Hall staircase (1876–9)

(see colour plate facing p. 83); it was partially remodelled after a fire in 1720, when the lantern or louvre for the central hearth was removed. Vast and magnificent, Christ Church Hall marks the culmination of the tradition of lavish architectural patronage begun by William of Wykeham at New College 150 years before.

In 1529, soon after the completion of the Hall, Wolsey fell from power and work on the buildings came to an end. The following decade saw the beginning of the Reformation, which permanently altered the character of both Oxford and England. The Chapel and gate tower of Cardinal College were never built, and the intended cloister never got beyond the drawing-board, though the inner arches and the springing of the vault can still be seen along the walls of Tom Quad. By a strange turn of fortune the truncated priory church of St Frideswide survived, minus the western bays of the nave, as the Chapel of a new college, originally to be named after Henry VIII but later, in the year before the king's death (1546), refounded as Christ Church. In its final form the new foundation incorporated the Dean and Chapter of the newly founded diocese of Oxford, and, with the unfortunate abandonment of Oseney Abbey, what remained of the old Priory church became Oxford's Cathedral, while at the same time remaining the Chapel of the college. Meanwhile, despite the lavish endowment of the new College, the patronage of architecture in Oxford languished for two generations, and the completion of Tom Quad was postponed for more than a century.

REGNANTE CAROLO

3 From Reformation to Restoration

The Reformation constituted the greatest single upheaval in the history of Oxford University. For so clerical an institution, the break with Rome and the seizure of the assets of the monasteries by Henry VIII could not fail to have a devastating effect. The religious houses outside the city walls were all suppressed, their possessions dispersed and their buildings demolished. The disappearance of Oseney Abbey, Rewley Abbey, and of the Franciscan and Dominican friaries permanently scarred the southern and western suburbs, and the memory of these once magnificent institutions—grander than all but the largest of the colleges—is now perpetuated only by street names like Rewley Road and Preachers Lane, and a few forlorn fragments of masonry. The only monastic buildings to survive reasonably intact were those of St Frideswide's Priory, reprieved by the fall of Cardinal Wolsey in 1529 and recycled in 1546 to serve the king's new foundation of Christ Church.

The dissolution of the monasteries led directly to the suppression of Oxford's monastic colleges. Their buildings fared better than those of the monasteries themselves, no doubt because they were smaller and more easily adapted to academic purposes. The buildings of St Mary's College, the Augustinian foundation in New Inn Hall Street, were taken over by Brasenose College, but were largely demolished in 1580. Canterbury College, for Benedictine monks, became part of Christ Church and survived with some alterations up to the 1770s, when it was replaced by the present Canterbury Quadrangle. The former Benedictine foundation of Gloucester College was refounded in 1560 as a new academic hall, Gloucester Hall, and enjoyed a precarious existence until 1714, when it was refounded for a second time as Worcester College. Meanwhile, during the reign of the Catholic Queen Mary, the Cistercian college, St Bernard's, passed into the hands of a wealthy London merchant tailor, Sir Thomas White, who established a new college, St John's, there in 1555. And in the same year the lawyer Sir Thomas Pope, who had prospered in the service of the Crown as Treasurer of the Court of Augmentations, established

The east range of Oriel College

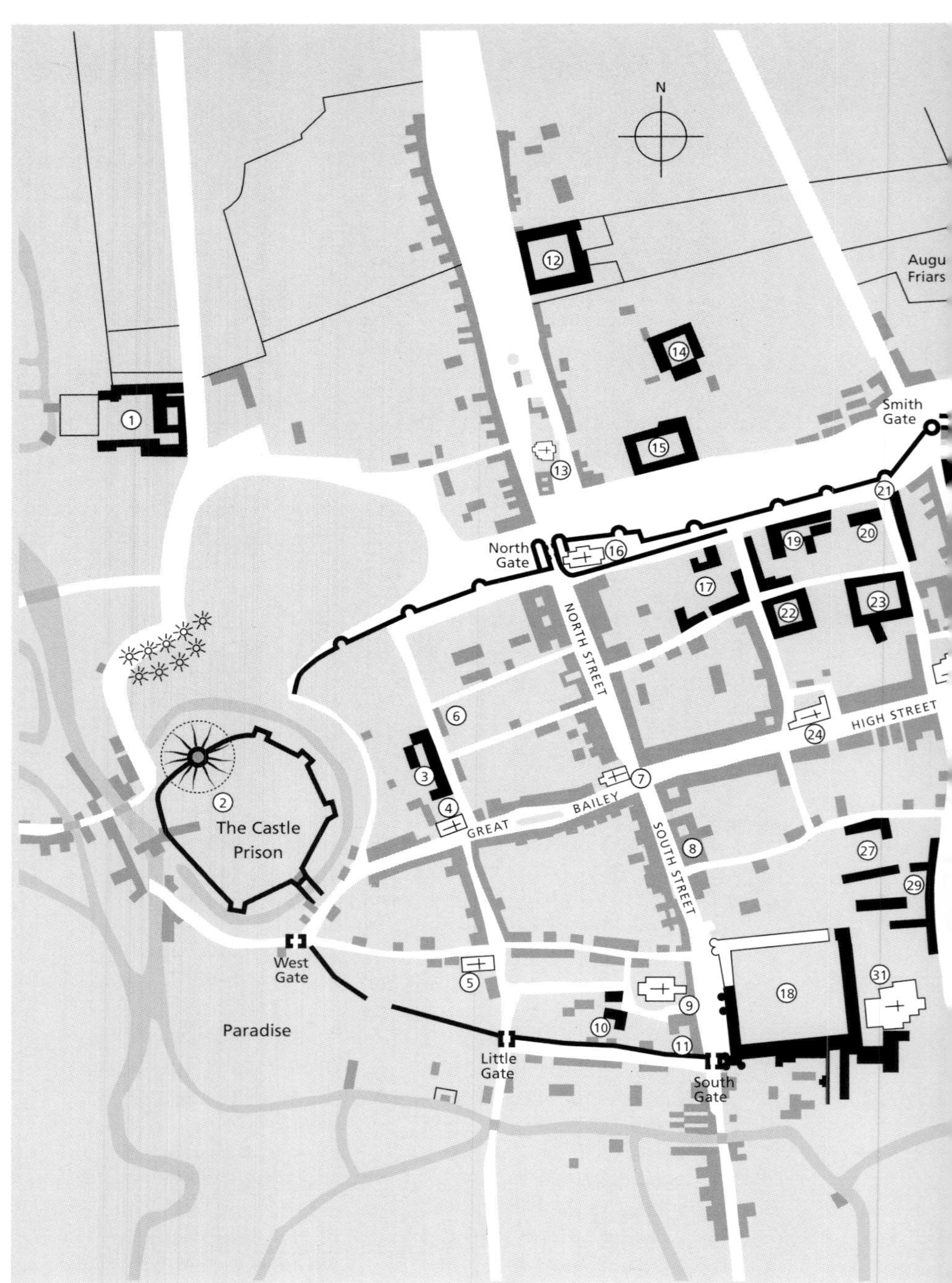
N
Augu
Friars
Smith
Gate
North
Gate
NORTH STREET
HIGH STREET
GREAT
BAILEY
SOUTH STREET
The Castle
Prison
West
Gate
Paradise
Little
Gate
South
Gate
1
2
3
4
5
6
7
8
9
10
11
12
13
14
15
16
17
18
19
20
21
22
23
24
27
29
31

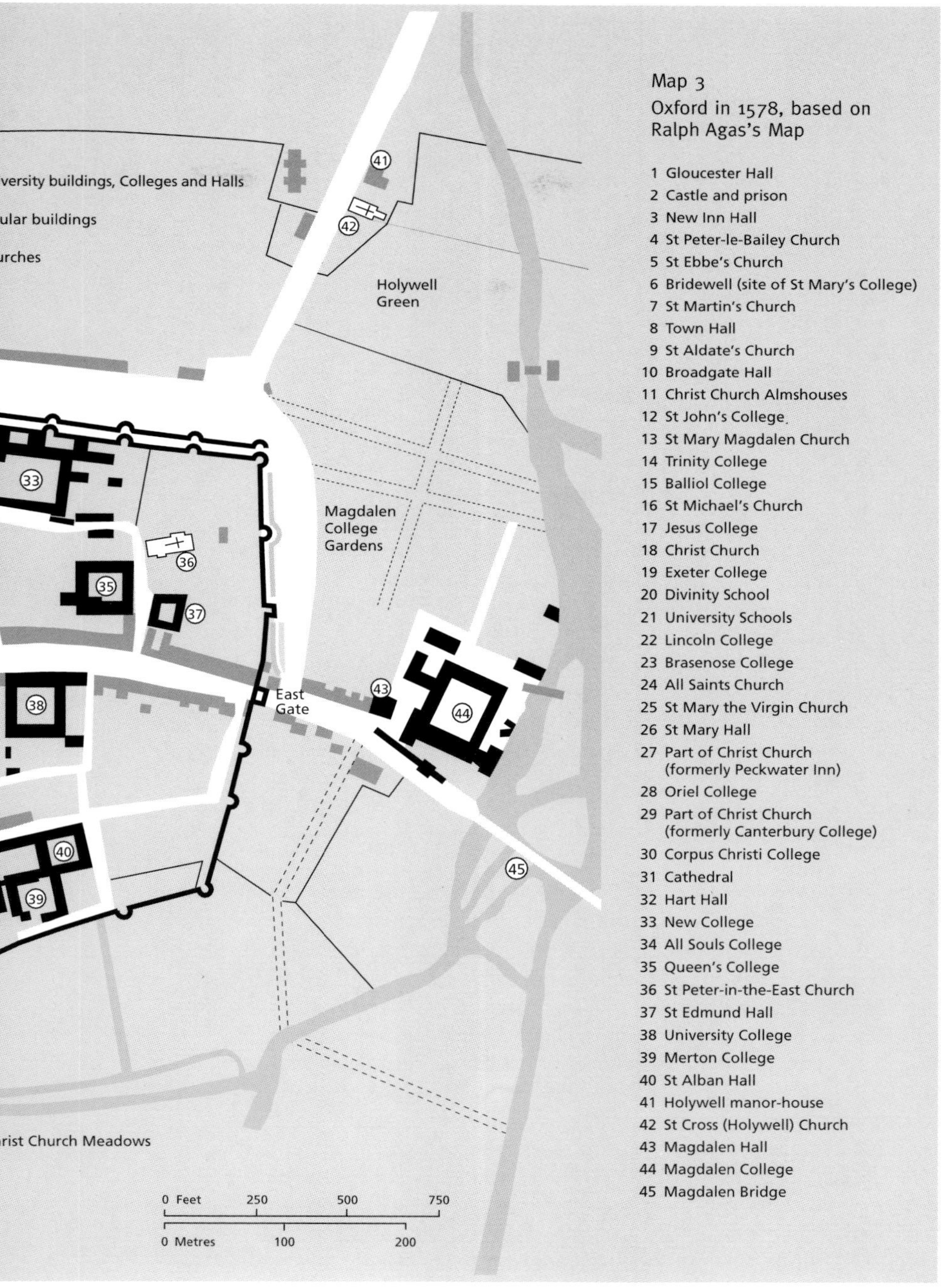
niversity buildings, Colleges and Halls
cular buildings
hurches
Holywell Green
Magdalen College Gardens
East Gate
hrist Church Meadows
0 Feet 250 500 750
0 Metres 100 200
Map 3
Oxford in 1578, based on Ralph Agas's Map
1 Gloucester Hall
2 Castle and prison
3 New Inn Hall
4 St Peter-le-Bailey Church
5 St Ebbe's Church
6 Bridewell (site of St Mary's College)
7 St Martin's Church
8 Town Hall
9 St Aldate's Church
10 Broadgate Hall
11 Christ Church Almshouses
12 St John's College
13 St Mary Magdalen Church
14 Trinity College
15 Balliol College
16 St Michael's Church
17 Jesus College
18 Christ Church
19 Exeter College
20 Divinity School
21 University Schools
22 Lincoln College
23 Brasenose College
24 All Saints Church
25 St Mary the Virgin Church
26 St Mary Hall
27 Part of Christ Church (formerly Peckwater Inn)
28 Oriel College
29 Part of Christ Church (formerly Canterbury College)
30 Corpus Christi College
31 Cathedral
32 Hart Hall
33 New College
34 All Souls College
35 Queen's College
36 St Peter-in-the-East Church
37 St Edmund Hall
38 University College
39 Merton College
40 St Alban Hall
41 Holywell manor-house
42 St Cross (Holywell) Church
43 Magdalen Hall
44 Magdalen College
45 Magdalen Bridge

another new college, Trinity, in the premises of the former Durham College. St John's and Trinity marked a new departure in being founded by laymen without royal connections. But while there was some modification of the existing premises, notably the creation of a new and larger Hall within the walls of the old kitchen at St John's, no substantial new buildings were erected for a long time.

Oxford University was allowed to survive, despite its strong association with the old faith, because in the eyes of the Crown it still had a useful function to perform in training administrators and Anglican clergy. But the political and religious uncertainty of the middle years of the century ensured that the number of students fell, reaching an all-time low in the 1550s. And the buildings suffered many depredations. Iconoclasm wreaked havoc on the college chapels, leading to the loss of 'idolatrous' stained glass and quantities of wood and stone carving. At New College 'the servants of Master Plummer' were paid in 1547 for 'taking down and breaking images in the high altar and remaining parts of the church', and in 1559, after the respite of Mary's reign, two labourers were employed for four days to destroy altars and images. Similar destruction occurred in the Chapels of All Souls and Magdalen, and in the former Priory church of St Frideswide. Libraries of religious manuscripts were also plundered, notably the University's own library over the Divinity School, which lost all of its books in 1549; according to Anthony Wood, 'some of these books . . . were burnt, some sold away for Robin Hoods pennyworths, either to Booksellers, or to Glovers to press their gloves, or Taylors to make measures, or to Bookbinders to cover books bound by them, and some also kept by the Reformers for their own use.' Six years later the library was denuded of even its desks and seating.

One of the indirect effects of the Reformation was that the University and colleges refrained from large-scale building for the rest of the 16th century. Henry VIII's new foundation, Christ Church, and the new colleges founded in Queen Mary's reign, St John's and Trinity, all took over existing buildings, and new work was kept to a minimum. The student population began to grow again in Queen Elizabeth's reign, and one new college, **Jesus**, was founded in 1571. But it lacked the generous endowments bestowed by the pre-Reformation ecclesiastical grandees, and only two ranges of buildings, on the south and eastern sides of the present Front Quadrangle, were constructed in the early years, the society otherwise making do with the premises of two former academic halls on the site; both of the 16th-century ranges have been substantially rebuilt. Otherwise, while the building of country houses by the gentry and

The front quadrangle of Corpus Christi College, looking north to the gate tower. The sundial in the foreground is dated 1581, but was altered in the 17th century and subsequently

Christ Church Hall looking west towards the high table

nobility flourished, the University of Oxford became an architectural backwater, and remained one until the beginning of the next century.

When new work was carried out, it usually took the form of modifying existing buildings. A wooden screen and wood panelling were introduced into the Hall of New College in 1533–5, and Magdalen followed suit in 1541; at New College a plaster ceiling was introduced too, doubtless to mitigate the damp chill which must have afflicted the diners for much of the year, but the ceiling has since been removed. The panelling survives, adorned with 'linenfold' of the kind found in Henry VIII's palaces and also at contemporary country houses like The Vyne (Hampshire), and there are decorative motifs deriving from the Italian Renaissance; the work was probably paid for by William Warham, Archbishop of Canterbury, whose portrait survives in the Hall, and it was carried out in London. Renaissance motifs can also be found in a remarkable series of wall paintings in an upstairs room at the former Golden Cross inn in Cornmarket Street (now the Pizza Express restaurant); they date from the middle of the century, and consist of a pattern of 'grotesques' and arabesques—possibly inspired by the title-pages of printed books—painted in white against a black background. An equally impressive, though very different, decorative scheme can be seen in the so-called Painted Room at number 3 Cornmarket Street (formerly the Crown Inn, where, according to John Aubrey, Shakespeare 'did commonly in his journey [from London to Stratford] lye'); it is made up of a trellis pattern on a red ground, and bears the initials of John Tattleton, tenant from *c.*1560 to 1591. It was through such decorative schemes that the language of classical art first achieved widespread currency in Oxford.

One important result of the Reformation was that the heads of colleges were allowed to marry. So, while the celibate Fellows continued to live in quasi-monastic discomfort in their cramped medieval quarters, more spacious and more comfortable lodgings began to be supplied for the heads of houses. Here they could install their families and entertain guests: something which has always been an important part of their public role. The Warden's Lodgings at New College had always contained extensive provision for entertaining, and in the early 1540s, even before the election of the first married Warden, an extra storey was added, together with a Gallery; some of the panelling and carved wooden chimneypieces still survive. At Corpus Christi there is an elaborate mid-16th-century plaster frieze and ceiling in what was then the principal chamber of the President's Lodgings in the gate tower; the ceiling is richly decorated with heraldic emblems and pendants like those of the late medieval stone vaults at the Divinity School and the former St Frideswide's Priory,

J. C. Buckler's view of the courtyard of the Golden Cross, looking towards Cornmarket Street in 1824. The range on the right dates from the mid-16th century and that on the left from *c.*1670

and the frieze is adorned with the coats of arms of the colleges set into Renaissance-inspired plasterwork. At the newly-founded St John's the President took over much of the east range of the quadrangle which had been left unfinished when St Bernard's College was suppressed, and at Trinity he was installed in the east range of the former Durham College, underneath the library; some late 16th-century wall paintings have been uncovered there, hidden behind later wood panelling. Elsewhere, as at All Souls and University College, new lodgings were built on property adjoining the main college buildings; those at University College were large and elaborately furnished, with six chambers, an upper and a lower hall, and a gallery.

As the numbers of undergraduates increased in Queen Elizabeth's reign, the colleges and academic halls found it more and more difficult to house all their members. By 1600 there were more students in residence than at any time since the beginning of the 14th century, and the numbers continued to grow until the 1630s. About half of the student body was made up of young men of relatively humble background who embarked on a university education as the only means of gaining employment as Anglican clergymen or schoolmasters. But the rest came from a higher social stratum and had more worldly aims. For them the University was an essential part of a gentlemanly education, and their parents were prepared to pay handsomely for them to attend. More and more colleges began to augment their revenues by taking in fee-paying commoners in addition to the scholars on the foundation: something pioneered by Magdalen in the late 15th century. Their presence was to transform the architectural face of Oxford in the 17th and 18th centuries.

Wall paintings of the mid-16th century on the upper floor of the Golden Cross inn

Many of the extra students were housed in former academic halls belonging to the colleges, or in the eight halls which still maintained an independent identity. The halls still accounted for about a third of all undergraduates in the mid-16th century, but most were now attached to one or other of the sixteen colleges, all but one of which (All Souls) contained both graduate Fellows and undergraduates. Extra space inside both the halls and the colleges could be found by creating rooms in the attics, known locally as cocklofts. This practice is first recorded at New College in 1539, but it remained uncommon until the last quarter of the century, when the pressure of numbers began to become intense. The Fellows of St John's told the Merchant Taylors' Company of London in 1573 that 'partly through coldness, partly for want of room', it had been 'constrained to overloft all the chambers in the whole college, which ariseth to no small sum of money'. The result of the alteration can still be clearly seen in the façade of the college to St Giles, with its range of dormer windows

The façade of St John's College to St Giles

surmounted by gables above the 15th-century parapet. A similar change took place at Brasenose between 1605 and 1636, but here the parapet was raised to the top of the second floor on the street front, thus dwarfing the gate tower; the attic rooms, lit on the courtyard side by dormer windows, were more comfortable than the damper rooms below, and were therefore allotted to the Fellows. At Trinity new rooms were built over the Hall and Library of the former Durham College, and the old open wooden roofs replaced by new plaster ceilings; the work was carried out in 1602 and 1618 respectively. The new top-floor rooms in these colleges were usually heated by wall fireplaces—a rarity in medieval Oxford, necessitating the provision of rows of tall chimneystacks which now vied with medieval steeples and pinnacles as incidents on the skyline.

Growing numbers of people were matched by growing numbers of books. Oxford's medieval libraries remained largely unchanged until the 1580s, when an increase in the quantity of printed books brought about important changes in the design of library furnishings. The new ideas were first implemented at Merton College in 1589–90, under the aegis of the Warden, Henry Savile, one of Queen Elizabeth's former tutors. He had travelled abroad and was a major influence on Oxford's academic life in the late 16th century, lecturing

The Library at Merton College

on Copernicus and founding two University professorships. Wooden cases made up of stacks of shelves now replaced the medieval desks on which the chained books had formerly been stored and read, and wooden screens adorned with classical architectural motifs were erected at the entrances to the main reading areas. The introduction of the new bookcases reduced the amount of light penetrating the Library through the single-light medieval windows, and dormer windows were therefore introduced into the roof space on the sides facing into Mob Quad. A similar transformation took place at All Souls in 1596–7, the College taking the opportunity meanwhile to introduce a splendid barrel-vaulted plaster ceiling embellished with armorial devices and pendants of late Gothic inspiration; the room ceased to be a library in the 1750s and is now a seminar room, but the ceiling decoration survives intact. At Christ Church the Library was housed from *c.*1563 in the former refectory of St Frideswide's Priory on the south side of the cloister, and in 1610–11 the lawyer Otho Nicholson, one of James I's Examiners in Chancery, paid for a refitting in which the ceiling was adorned with painted coats of arms; the ceiling still survives, although the Library itself was divided into undergraduate rooms in 1763 after the completion of the present Library. By 1610 new bookcases had also been installed in the existing libraries at Queen's, New College, Magdalen, and Corpus Christi. The first completely new Library to be constructed according to the new principles was at St John's. Here the President's Lodging had usurped the space originally set aside for a library in the defunct St Bernard's College, and in 1595 a new block was begun to the east of the main quadrangle, with the Library, as always, upstairs and chambers below.

Thomas Bodley's monument in Merton College Chapel

The most important new library in Oxford was that founded in 1598 by Sir Thomas Bodley. A scholar and diplomat, who held a fellowship at Merton College and was a friend of Henry Savile, he applied his fortune—acquired in part through marriage to a rich widow—towards the reinstatement of the derelict University Library over the Divinity School, making generous gifts of books himself and encouraging gifts by others. New cases were installed, of the type recently introduced at Merton, and the ceiling was repaired and painted with the coats of arms of the University. The Bodleian Library, as it became known, opened in 1602, and, as gifts and purchases accumulated, it soon became one of the most illustrious university libraries in Europe.

In the first decade of the 17th century, with the numbers of undergraduate students continuing to grow rapidly, generous benefactors resumed the pre-Reformation practice of contributing to building schemes in the colleges. The first college to expand substantially was **Merton**, and the instigator once more was Henry Savile. The foundations of a new quadrangle on the open ground between the medieval Hall and the city wall were laid in 1608, and in the following year the antiquary Brian Twyne wrote: 'Merton College men are now erecting a goodly quadrangle of building . . . for which they have all their workmen out of the North Country, not one out of the town, and they must have for that building for their work only £900.' The workmen in question included the master masons John Akroyd and John Bentley, and a master carpenter, Thomas Holt, all of whom were summoned by Savile from Halifax in his native West Riding of Yorkshire. The seemingly perverse decision to import builders from a place 170 miles away can be explained in part by the recalcitrance of the Oxford masons, who tried to dictate the price of their work through the newly-founded Company of Freemasons, Carpenters, Joiners, and Slaters. But it also reflects the dearth of obvious local talent, no major buildings having been erected in the city for eighty years. It was not until the second half of the 17th century that local men remotely approaching the calibre of William Orchard once more appeared on the scene.

The Fellows' Quadrangle at Merton—so called to distinguish it from the medieval Bachelors' Quadrangle, now Mob Quad—was the first large-scale extension to a medieval Oxford college, and it heralded a period of intensive building activity which lasted until the Civil War, as the colleges vied with each other to provied more accommodation for the growing numbers of students, and especially for the lucrative fee-paying commoners. Like all of the new residential buildings in early 17th-century Oxford colleges, the quadrangle was essentially medieval in its layout: shared bedrooms with cell-like studies, separated from each other by staircases opening into the quadrangle. The detailing—battlements on the courtyard side, mullioned windows under hood-moulds—was also deeply traditional. But in some respects the Fellows' Quadrangle marked an important new departure in collegiate architecture. It was the first set of buildings in Oxford designed with three storeys of full height throughout (see p. 27); rooms were also provided in the attics, lit by windows under gables on the outer sides. And the 'frontispiece' or Tower of the Orders at the centre of the south range, which immediately catches the eye on entering through the 15th-century Fitzjames Gateway, represents the most impressive attempt hitherto to introduce classical motifs into an Oxford college building.

Classical or 'humanist' studies had been an important part of the Oxford curriculum since the early 16th century and some colleges, like Magdalen and Corpus Christi, had always had a distinctly

The upper part of the classical 'frontispiece' to the Fellows' Quadrangle at Merton College

humanist intellectual agenda. But Oxford's dons have usually been more interested in words than images, and the best part of a century passed before they showed any obvious interest in classical architecture. In contrast to Cambridge, which can boast the classical Gates of Virtue and Honour at Gonville and Caius College (1567), examples of classicism in 16th-century Oxford were meagre indeed. Loggan's engraving of Jesus College shows a pair of Tuscan columns of indeterminate date flanking the gateway (subsequently remodelled), and a similar arrangement can still be seen around the doorway of the former St Alban Hall in Merton Street, built in 1599 with the proceeds of a bequest by Benedict Barnam, an alderman of London, having been incorporated into the street front of the present St Alban's Quadrangle of Merton College (see p. 277). But these tentative essays in the classical idiom are quite overshadowed by the 'frontispiece' in the Fellows' Quadrangle. Here pairs of classical columns, of the Doric, Ionic, Corinthian, and Composite orders, rise one above the other, correctly detailed and proportioned, albeit with Gothic as well as Renaissance motifs jostling for attention in the intervening spaces; at the top is the coat of arms of King James I with the date 1610. The idea of a 'tower of the orders' can be traced back to the château of Diane de Poitiers at Anet in France, built to the designs of Philibert de l'Orme *c.*1550 and re-erected in the 19th century at the Ecole des Beaux Arts in Paris; other precedents closer at hand included the Gate of Virtue at Gonville and Caius College, Cambridge, and the 'frontispieces' of country houses like Burghley,

Northamptonshire (1585), and Stonyhurst, Lancashire (c.1592–5). It was presumably Warden Savile—the owner of a copy of Daniele Barbaro's edition of Vitruvius (1567)—who took the initiative in commissioning the 'tower of the orders' and, if this was indeed the case, he set a precedent which was profoundly to influence Oxford's early 17th-century architecture.

Bodleian Library: Arts End looking north

Having completed the new quadrangle at Merton, the Halifax masons went on to carry out important work for the University. The **Bodleian Library** became overcrowded almost as soon as it was founded, and expansion of the 15th-century building was made imperative by the famous agreement with the Stationers' Company in London in 1610, under which a copy of every book printed by its members was deposited there. Bodley took control of the project himself, calling the Library 'one of my greatest worldly cares' and telling the Librarian, Thomas James, in 1611 that he should 'continue your care about my building, and call upon Acroide and Bentley, for the choice of their stone, and the close laying of it . . . I make no doubt but that they will be so diligent and provident, as there shall be no cause for their enemies the townsmen to insult them as they did.' The extension, which was begun to the designs of the Halifax masons in 1610, is two storeys high, and was built in front of the medieval building at its eastern end. The ground floor takes the form of a lierne-vaulted Proscholium or vestibule in front of the Divinity School (now the main entrance to the Library), and in the new room upstairs (known as Arts End) the cases, following recent Continental precedent, were arranged floor to ceiling against the walls, with the upper shelves reached from galleries: the first known instance of this arrangement in England. The ceiling beams in Arts End are painted with Renaissance-inspired 'grotesques' and arabesques, but the windows have Perpendicular Gothic tracery and the exterior is covered with a net-like pattern of blind arcading like that on the 15th-century façade of the Divinity School, still visible inside the Proscholium. The skyline, like that of the existing Library (Duke Humfrey's) is lavishly pinnacled and crenellated, as in the old library, but the pinnacles are not carried down into buttresses as would have been the case in medieval architecture: an indication that the Gothic style was chosen primarily for its visual and associational effect. That decision was surely Bodley's own, and his aim was no doubt to emphasize continuity: both between the new Library and the old, and between the Jacobean University and the illustrious University of the Middle Ages. In this respect the new buildings at the Bodleian Library deserve recognition as major examples of the survival—or should it be the revival?—of Gothic architecture in early 17th-century England,

Bodleian Library: east façade from the Schools Quadrangle

comparable with near-contemporary buildings like Sir Charles Cavendish's extraordinary 'Little Castle' at Bolsover (Derbyshire) and the third Lord Bindon's Lulworth Castle (Dorset).

Bodley was also involved in the bold decision to erect a new quadrangle to the east of the extended Library so as to provide 'better built scholes . . . than those ruinous little rooms' which had since the 15th century served as Oxford's main University lecture and examination rooms. This involved taking down the houses which stood between the Library and Catte Street and closing off part of the street which ran eastwards along the inside of the city wall from Exeter College. A public appeal was launched, which brought in £4500, and Bodley himself promised to contribute a tenth of the total cost. The new buildings were built in front of the enlarged Library, which forms the west side of the quadrangle, and the quadrangle is entered through a gate tower in Catte Street to the east. As first envisaged, the buildings were to be two storeys high, with each school occupying a single rectangular room lit by mullioned windows. The ground-floor schools (Moral Philosophy, Grammar and History, Metaphysics, Logic, Music, and Natural Philosophy) were entered through pointed-arched doorways with the name of the subject in Latin painted above; staircases built out at each corner of the quadrangle led to the schools on the first floor (Law, Greek, Arithmetic and Geometry, Astronomy, Rhetoric, and Anatomy and Medicine). Work began in 1613, and was entrusted once more to Warden Savile's team, but with Akroyd's death in the same year the chief responsibility passed to Bentley, who died in 1615 and was described on his monument as 'the most skilful architect of the library and schools'.

Bodley also died soon after the work started, and was buried in the chapel of Merton College, where he is commemorated by a splendid wall monument (see p. 87) with representations of the liberal arts and a bust flanked by classical columns in the form of piles of books: an appropriate conceit. But in his will he left money to the University to add a third storey (now the Upper Reading Room of the Bodleian Library) running around three sides of the Schools Quadrangle. This was originally intended to serve in part as a 'very large supplement for stowage of books'. But for many years it was mainly used as as a gallery housing the University's collection of portraits, similar in character to the long galleries of contemporary country houses; it was open to the public, and thus, for all the mediocre quality of the pictures on display, has claims to be the first public art gallery in Britain. A painted frieze by an unknown artist depicts the most notable of the authors represented in the library's collections, from the Church Fathers to the more recent Puritan divines admired by Bodley and his Librarian. The whole ensemble was brought to completion by Thomas Holt in 1624, the other members of the Halifax team having died in the interim.

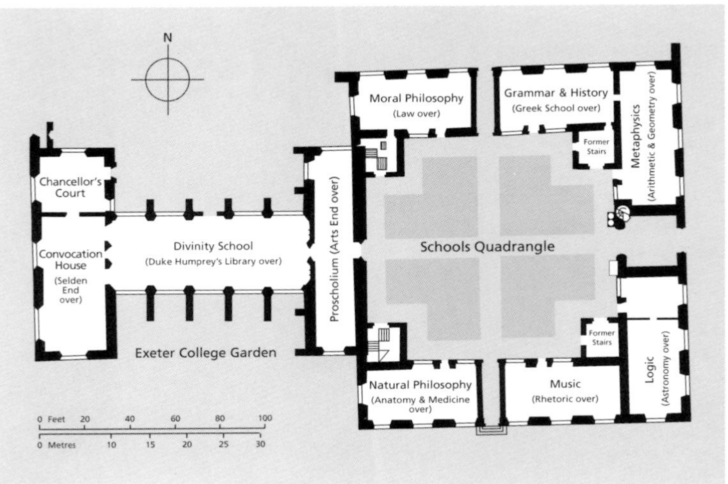

Plan of the Bodleian Library and the Schools Quadrangle, showing the original uses of the Schools

The east range of the Schools Quadrangle with the Tower of the Five Orders

The Schools Quadrangle was by far the largest architectural work yet undertaken by the University, and for all its bulky, slightly ungainly appearance—largely the result of the last-minute decision to add a third storey—it remained for many years the most impressive collection of buildings for university teaching in England. The general air of heaviness is mitigated by the battlemented and pinnacled skyline, amplifying the note of late Gothic fantasy sounded in Bodley's Library extension, and also by the gate tower, the uppermost floors of which were used to house the University's muniments and financial deposits. This too is essentially Gothic in conception, but its inner face is treated as a classical 'frontispiece', with five superimposed orders of columns (Tuscan, Doric, Ionic, Corinthian, and Composite). Warden Savile, who lived until 1621, probably played a part in the decision, taken after Bodley's death, to introduce this gigantic piece of architectural pedantry; according to Bodley, he had 'the judgement of a mason', and he was certainly influential in working out the uses of the rooms in the new quadrangle, though the juxtaposition of classical and Gothic elements in the tower is crude and amateurish in the extreme. A further modification of the design took place in 1620 in commemoration of a visit three years earlier by James I. A sculptural group (originally coloured) was now carved on the fourth storey of the tower by John Clark, a Yorkshireman who was probably the son-in-law of John Akroyd. It shows the King—the 'wisest fool in Christendom'—seated under a canopy, presenting a copy of his collected writings to a sedate female figure representing the University, attended by a beefy figure of Fame blowing a trumpet; the royal coat of arms also appears on the roof-line, framed in intricate strapwork but squeezed between the top of the stair turret and a Gothic pinnacle. Palladio and Inigo Jones would not have been amused.

The Schools Quadrangle was faced throughout in Headington ashlar stone. The advantage of Headington freestone, according to Robert Plot in his *Natural History of Oxfordshire* (1676), was that it 'cuts very soft and easie . . . but hardening continually as it lies to the weather'. Headington ashlar had been used in Oxford since the late 15th century, and without some such stone the Schools Quadrangle could never have had the smooth external finish that was much admired in the 17th century. With abundant supplies available only two miles away, it was used again and again over the next 150 years, sometimes together with stone from Burford and elsewhere in the Cotswolds. But, unlike the Headington 'hardstone' used for plinths and foundations, it had the great disadvantage of being less resistant to the atmosphere than the tougher rubble stone used in medieval

Oxford, and by the end of the 18th century it had already begun to 'blister' and crumble, with dire consequences for the future.

The final stage in the building of what is now the Bodleian Library complex took place in 1632–7, when an extension was built on to the western end of Duke Humfrey's Library, giving the whole building its present H plan. Known as Selden End in recognition of a gift of books from the lawyer John Selden, it is virtually a replica of Arts End, apart from the omission of the Gothic panelling on the outside. Here too the books are arranged along the walls, reached this time by balustraded wooden galleries resting on arches supported by Tuscan columns: visually a rather more satisfactory arrangement than the rather flimsy-looking galleries in Arts End. The room underneath is also filled with excellent woodwork and was originally covered with an elaborate plaster ceiling, replaced in 1758–9 by the present stone vault. It served as a Convocation House for the University's 'Parliament', and on at least two occasions (1665 and 1681) it was pressed into service for the national Parliament when it could not meet in London: a reminder of the important place occupied by Oxford in the affections of the Stuart monarchs. On the occasion of royal visits and other festive occasions the Library was used for serving meals, as in 1687, when James II dined in solitary state in Selden End, Anthony Wood remarking that 'none did eat but he, for he spake to nobody to eat.'

The building of the new Library and Schools provoked a riposte from the city fathers in 1615–17, when a spectacular new fountain or conduit-house was put up at Carfax, then as now the heart of mercantile Oxford. The promoter was the lawyer Otho Nicholson, who had already paid for the refitting of the Library at Christ Church; the occasion for his generosity was the visit to Oxford by James I commemorated by the University in the tower of the Schools Quadrangle. Carfax Conduit was part of an an ambitious project to bring fresh water to the city from springs at North Hinksey, a couple of miles to the west (a stone-built well-house still survives there, in a field near the western bypass). The new conduit-house consisted of a square stone-built base containing two tanks with—inevitably—separate outlets for the city and the colleges; buttresses rose from the corners to support an octagonal crown-like superstructure adorned with statues of eight kings, originally painted and gilded. The conception recalls the towers of the medieval St Mary-le-Bow in London and St Giles Cathedral in Edinburgh, but the complex detailing drew heavily on classical pattern-books, and the symbolism recalls the temporary structures erected for ceremonial entries of monarchs, immortalized in Stephen Harrison's *Arches of Triumph*

Convocation House

(1604); Anthony Wood later said that 'for its images of ancient kings . . . [its] gilding and exquisite carving, the like except in London [is] not to be seen.' The mason responsible for this singular building may have been John Clark, who also worked on the gate tower of the Bodleian. It was demolished as part of a street improvement in 1787, but was fortunately re-erected as an ornamental object in the landscaped grounds of Nuneham Courtenay, about six miles south of Oxford, where it still survives; repeated proposals to return it to Oxford have all foundered.

The upper part of Carfax Conduit

The part-classical detailing of the Schools Quadrangle and Carfax Conduit did little to mask the fact that these were still essentially Gothic buildings. Seen in a European context, early 17th-century Oxford stands out for its persistence in repeatedly choosing the Gothic style at a time when classicism had already become an international architectural *lingua franca*. Even in backward England, the Court of James I had already fallen under the spell of the sophisticated classicism of Inigo Jones by the time the Schools Quadrangle was completed. The continuing popularity of Gothic in early Stuart Oxford can be explained in part by the conservatism of the Oxford dons. But the deliberate decision to use Gothic mouldings and, in some cases, correct Gothic tracery, also implied a strong sense of architectural propriety. Gothic was still associated by most Englishmen with ecclesiastical building, and Oxford University, for all its growing interest in the classics and other branches of learning, was a bastion of religious orthodoxy, as indeed it had been for much of the Middle Ages. Anglican divines in the early 17th century were increasingly laying emphasis on the Church of England's roots in the medieval past, and from then until at least the 19th century Oxford remained the moral and intellectual heart of High Church Anglicanism. Oxford's early 17th-century Gothic buildings proclaim that message very clearly.

Oxford's continuing attachment to the architectural forms of the Middle Ages is clearly demonstrated in the design of **Wadham College**. Founded in 1610 on the site of the suppressed Augustinian Friary to the north of the city wall, and completed in 1612, Wadham was named after its founders, Sir Nicholas Wadham, a Somerset gentleman who died in 1609, and his formidable 75-year-old widow, who came from a Roman Catholic family, the Petres, and was herself accused of recusancy in 1615. Whatever her own religious proclivities, Lady Wadham saw the new College as a staunchly Anglican institution, where the members were expected to attend chapel twice daily, at 5 a.m and 8 p.m, as they did in other colleges. It is not surprising therefore that the Gothic style was employed in the Chapel,

Wadham College: the east range of the front quadrangle

the first to be built in Oxford under the Anglican dispensation, and in deference to local tradition the T-shaped plan of antechapel and chancel—most recently employed at Magdalen in the 1470s—was also adopted. Since the customs and corporate life of Wadham were consciously modelled on those of the older colleges, it also made sense to revive the medieval arrangement of an open-roofed Hall entered through a screens passage, already obsolescent in domestic architecture, and heated from a central hearth. The bedrooms and studies are arranged around a square quadrangle in front of the Hall and Chapel, and the windows, like those of the Fellows' Quadrangle at Merton, are of the two-light mullioned variety which had been used in Oxford ever since the 14th century.

Lady Wadham not only played a crucial part in framing the new college's statutes; she was also deeply involved in the design of the buildings and the choice of craftsmen. The master mason, William Arnold, was brought from Somerset on the recommendation of Sir Edward Phelips of Montacute, near Yeovil, whose impressive Elizabethan house he had recently built, and in February 1610 Lady Wadham told her half-brother Lord Petre that Arnold was 'an honest man, a perfect workman, and my near neighbour, so that he can yield me continual contentment'. Arnold not only provided the 'plot' (plan), which was approved by James I and the Archbishop of Canterbury; he also directed the building operations, supplied the stone and timber, imported workmen from the West Country (twelve of them from a single village, Stoke-sub-Hamdon), and was probably responsible for some at least of the detailing, including the peculiar window tracery of the Hall and antechapel (the more conventional windows of the Chapel proper were by another mason, John Spicer). The Headington ashlar facing of the outer walls has had to be replaced, as it has almost everywhere in Oxford, but in general the excellent state of preservation of the original buildings of the College is a tribute to the quality of the workmanship of Arnold and his team.

For all the stylistic similarities, Wadham differs from the medieval colleges in several respects. The plan is almost—though not quite—symmetrical and so too are the main elevations. The buildings are three storeys high, and the skyline is made up not of pinnacles but of gables and tall chimneystacks. There is some decorative use of Renaissance architectural motifs. The Hall and the antechapel are placed alongside each other in the east range, furthest from the street and directly opposite the gate tower, and behind them—but invisible from the quadrangle—are projections containing the main body of the Chapel and the Kitchen, with the Library above it. At the centre of

Wadham College Chapel from the antechapel, from Ackermann's *Oxford* (1814)

the east range is a classical 'frontispiece', clearly based on that at Merton; it stands over the entrance to the Hall and encloses rather gauche statues (by John Blackshaw) of the king and of the founders, Sir Nicholas Wadham and his wife, the former clad in armour. The high, spacious Hall has a splendid hammer-beam roof, by the carpenter Thomas Holt, and there is exuberant wood-carving on the screen, with pairs of Corinthian columns on either side of the two entrance doorways and fanciful strapwork devices fronting the gallery above; these motifs were taken directly from the Flemish pattern-books which had been circulating in England since the 1570s.

The Chapel is an attempt to realize the 'beauty of holiness' emphasized by the High Church divines of the period as an alternative to the iconoclasm which had wrought such havoc in the previous century. The chancel windows, with their impeccably correct Perpendicular tracery, are filled, most unusually in a place of Protestant worship, with painted glass: prophets and apostles in the side windows and the Passion, Resurrection, and Ascension of Christ in the east window, which is dated 1622. The art of stained glass-making died out in England after the Reformation, and the glass in the east window (and possibly the other windows too) was fashioned by Bernard van Linge, a craftsman from Emden in north Germany who, with his brother Abraham, carried out several important glazing schemes in early 17th-century Oxford; taken together, these windows constitute the finest collection of painted glass of the period in England (see colour plate facing p. 114). As in so much of the decorative art of early 17th-century Oxford, Flemish influence was strong, the designs having been taken from plates published in Antwerp in 1595. And the influence of Flanders also lies behind the design of the screen separating the antechapel from the chancel, carved in 1612 by John Bolton, who had worked in the Bodleian Library, and profusely embellished with strapwork and obelisks.

Inspired by the architectural example of Merton and Wadham, and fortified by the fruits of energetic fund-raising from old members and assorted well-wishers, Oxford's colleges now launched into a spree of competitive rebuilding, from which only four of the sixteen colleges (Balliol, New College, Magdalen, and All Souls) stood aside. Two of the oldest colleges, Oriel and University, made a clean sweep of their cramped medieval premises, replacing them with new quadrangles in a style plainly influenced by the new work at Merton and Wadham. At **Oriel** the work was carried out in two stages, *c.*1620–2 (west and south ranges) and *c.*1637–42 (north and east). The residential quarters consisted of thirty sets of rooms, of which over half were occupied by the Fellows and the remainder by undergraduates who shared two to a room, and, as at Wadham, the rooms were arranged on three floors. But here both the inner and the outer faces of the quadrangle are surmounted by rows of small curved gables: another Flemish motif, of which there are many examples in contemporary English country houses. The unknown designer of Oriel College was clearly influenced by the example of Wadham in placing the Hall and the antechapel next to each other in the east range, opposite the gate tower, and the peculiar window tracery, especially in the austerely decorated Chapel, is also like that at Wadham. But in place of a 'tower of the orders' there is a rather more elegant arrangement of a projecting porch reached by a flight of steps and bearing the words REGNANTE CAROLO ('in the reign of Charles I'); above it are two figures of kings under canopies (probably Edward II and James I or Charles I), and over them is a canopied representation of the Virgin and Child, alluding to the dedication of the medieval College and recalling the High Anglicanism which so enraged the Puritans in Charles I's reign (it was prudently removed during the Interregnum and not replaced until 1673–4). Enfolding the Virgin and Child is a classical niche or aedicule with a rounded (segmental) pediment, but the interior of the Hall, with its magnificent hammer-beam roof—one of the last to be built in England—is wholly medieval in character.

The rebuilding of **University College** was first mooted in 1610. Here the original intention was to employ the Halifax masons who built the Schools Quadrangle, and they were asked by the Master and Bursar to make the windows of the proposed west range 'faire [and] proportionable like Maudlein or All Soules College'. But rebuilding did not begin until 1634, by which time the Halifax masons were long dead. For a time the College toyed with the idea of erecting a classical set of buildings, with temple-like porticoes in front of the Hall (facing the entrance), the Chapel (on the east side of the quadrangle), and at the centre of the west range opposite. But nothing came of this adventurous scheme, and when work began, under the direction of the master mason Richard Maude, it was to a much more conservative design. The buildings, unlike those they replaced, are raised up above the level of the High Street; their most distinctive feature is the array of small and rather finicky gables on the roof-line. Work was interrupted by the Civil War, and the Hall and Chapel, opposite the gate tower, were not finished until 1656; the Chapel—which was much altered in 1862—contains a splendid set of painted glass windows by Abraham van Linge, dated 1641 but presumably stored until the building was completed. The project came to an end with the completion of the east range, along with a wing for the Kitchen and Library, in 1668–77.

The front quadrangle of University College: north and east ranges

Oriel and University Colleges were unusual in getting rid of their medieval buildings in their entirety. It was more common to provide extra accommodation by making piecemeal additions to the existing premises. This occurred at **Exeter College**, the smallest and poorest of the medieval foundations. The college was put on a stronger financial footing by William Petre, Lady Wadham's father, and in 1618, following a gift by Sir John Acland, a member of a well-known West Country family, a magnificent new Hall—one of the most impressive in Oxford—was built well to the south of the medieval buildings. Raised up over a basement, it is entered through a richly carved screen with classical motifs like those on the screen at Wadham, but most of the features, like the open timber roof and the Perpendicular traceried windows, would not have looked out of place two centuries earlier. A new two-aisled Chapel followed in 1623–4 on the north side of what now became the main quadrangle, but the rest of the quadrangle, like many in Oxford, grew by gradual accretion, as funds permitted; it was entered through a new gate tower on Turl Street, replacing the old entrance facing the city wall (see p. 167), and was finally completed in 1703.

At **Lincoln College**, another of the smaller medieval foundations, the 15th-century quadrangle remained largely intact, but growing

Exeter College Hall, looking west to the screen

numbers of students made it necessary to build a new set of chambers to the south, along Turl Street, starting in 1608 (see p. 50). This was followed in 1629–31 by another set of chambers and a new Chapel, funded largely by John Williams, Bishop of Lincoln, thus creating a second quadrangle. The Chapel is lit by Gothic windows with tracery very similar to that found in the Hall and antechapel windows at Oriel, but the excellent carved woodwork of the screen and stalls, with the diminutive figures of saints and prophets, owes its inspiration to the Renaissance. The ensemble is completed by another set of painted glass windows, most of them probably from the van Linge studio.

A similar process of growth by accretion took place at **Jesus College**, one of the newer and less well-endowed foundations. Here a

Lincoln College Chapel

successful appeal by the Principal, Griffith Powell, yielded sufficient funds to build a Hall in about 1617, with a richly carved screen by an unknown craftsman, surmounted by a classical balustrade; the donors came from London, Oxford, and Wales; the College's Welsh connections are underlined by the carvings of dragons on the screen. Powell also began to build a new Chapel, which was completed in 1621 by his successor, Eubule Thelwall, and Thelwall made a further successful appeal for 'the perfecting of the Quadrangle and the furnishing of the Library'; this involved clearing away the last vestiges of White Hall, which stood on the site. New Lodgings for the Principal were also built on the north side of the quadrangle, between the Hall and the Chapel, the carved wood panelling of the main rooms setting a new standard of luxury for the heads of colleges. Finally, in 1639, a second quadrangle was begun to the west, with a roof-line of curved gables clearly influenced by University College; work was interrupted by the Civil War, and the quadrangle was completed at a leisurely pace between 1676 and 1713.

The last completely new college to be founded in the 17th century was **Pembroke**, established in 1624 on the site of the medieval Broadgates Hall, within the mighty shadow of Christ Church. The new society was poorly endowed, and at first it made use of the existing buildings, together with a new set of chambers on the south side of what is now the main quadrangle; the Chapel and Library were in the south aisle of the adjoining St Aldate's church, and the present front quadrangle was not completed until 1670–99.

Meanwhile, most of the surviving halls were extended and rebuilt. Since they did not possess endowments, the funds had to come entirely from donations, often from the Principals. At St Edmund Hall a new block of chambers—part of the present north range of the main quadrangle—was built *c.*1596 and extended before the end of the century. It stands at right angles to the medieval entrance range on Queen's Lane which was pulled down by the Principal, Dr Airay, and rebuilt *c.*1635, having become 'very ruinous'; the Hall which formed part of this range was replaced in 1659. Hart Hall, to the east of Catte Street adjoining New College Lane, also consisted of an architecturally unremarkable L-shaped complex of rubble-stone buildings, with a Hall of *c.*1572 and another range dating from the early 17th century; the buildings now form part of Hertford College . A more ambitious building project took place at St Mary Hall, south of the High Street. Here too a new Hall was constructed in 1639–40, with a Chapel above, lit by round-arched windows with tracery similar to that found in the adjacent Oriel College, and quite possibly by the same masons. This attractive and rather unusual structure formed

The main gate to the Botanic Garden from the north

part of a quadrangle mostly made up of lower, mainly 15th-century buildings, and it still survives as part of Oriel, the Hall having become the college's Junior Common Room and the Chapel part of the library.

For all the tenacity of Gothic, an interest in Renaissance architecture gradually made itself felt in Oxford in the years before the Civil War. The classical orders had now become relatively common currency in a purely decorative sense, especially in the 'frontispieces' of quadrangles, the screens of college halls, the panelling of chapels, and in chimneypieces in domestic interiors. The influence of the Renaissance is also strongly felt in certain church monuments of the period, notably those to Sir Thomas Bodley and Sir Henry Savile (d.1622) in Merton College Chapel, and to the Lyttleton brothers (d.1635) in the Chapel at Magdalen, the latter featuring figures of two lightly clad youths leaning languorously on either side of the inscription. And it was in the 1630s that the first serious attempt was made systematically to integrate the language of classical architecture into the design of an Oxford building.

Oxford's first consistently classical structures were the gateways to the University's new Physic Garden (now the **Botanic Garden**). By this time elaborate gardens for recreation had already been laid out adjoining several of the colleges, including New College and Wadham. But the University's garden was a product of the growth of scientific research which was now becoming an important part of Oxford's academic life. The founder was Henry Danvers, Earl of

Danby, and the site was on low-lying ground outside the East Gate of the town, by the banks of the River Cherwell. Here a square space was set aside in 1621 for the plants, and in 1632–3 the master mason and sculptor Nicholas Stone built, presumably to his own design, three monumental gateways leading through the high stone wall. Stone had been master mason at Inigo Jones's Banqueting House at Whitehall Palace, one of the most influential buildings of the age; he also carried out work at Danby's country house, Cornbury Park, a few miles north-west of Oxford, and some of the more ambitious monuments in Oxford college chapels, like that to Sir Thomas Bodley at Merton, were produced in his workshop. The gateways represent variations on the theme of the Roman triumphal arch, but they are treated in a richly sculptural, almost Mannerist, fashion which has its counterpart in contemporary London buildings like the water gate to Buckingham (later York) House, which Stone may have designed. The main entrance to the Botanic Garden, facing Magdalen College, is especially richly carved, with the columns on the north side broken by bands of rustication, and the inner face treated quite differently—a solecism which would not have been tolerated by purists like Inigo Jones—with the keystones and voussoirs of the arch grotesquely exaggerated, and the surfaces on either side broken by niches.

The classical theme is proclaimed with great splendour in the Canterbury Quadrangle at **St John's** (1631–6). Here Oxford returned to the kind of lavish patronage by leading ecclesiastics which had been so marked a feature of the later Middle Ages. The buildings were conceived and financed by William Laud, Archbishop of Canterbury and one of the most powerful men in England during the reign of Charles I. He had been President of St John's from 1611 to 1621, and, as Chancellor of the University, used his very considerable energy and organizational skills to introduce a new set of statutes which lasted until the 19th century. The new quadrangle was built between the east range of the existing 15th-century quadrangle and the extensive garden and, as first conceived in 1630, it was to consist of two ranges with a covered walkway or loggia linking them on the east or garden side: a novel idea for Oxford, but one anticipated in Caius Court at Gonville and Caius College, Cambridge (1565–9). The south range, with its first-floor Library of 1595–1601, already existed; the north range, containing rooms for commoners, was a virtual replica. This arrangement was modified in 1632, after work had begun. A long gallery was now built over a matching loggia on the western side, flanking the President's Lodgings, and an extension to the Library constructed over the loggia on the east or garden side, blocking the view of the garden from the quadrangle. This change of plans

St. John's College: Canterbury Quadrangle

was accompanied by a change of designer. The master masons responsible for the earlier stages of the work—Hugh Davis, formerly a mason at the Palace of Whitehall, and Richard Maude, the master mason at University College—were dismissed and replaced by a new team under the direction of a Londoner, John Jackson, although it appears that he worked to designs supplied, possibly second-hand, by a London joiner, Adam Browne: a reminder that the design of many important buildings of this period was the result of collaborative effort and not the creative genius of a single individual.

In its completed form the Canterbury Quadrangle is a successful synthesis of traditional motifs with newer ideas derived ultimately from Renaissance Italy and early 17th-century Flanders and France. The north and south ranges are conventional enough, with their pointed-arched doorways and two-light mullioned windows, and similar windows light the President's long gallery in the west range and the Laudian Library in the east range, used initially to house precious books and 'rarities'; these ranges are conventionally battlemented, and gables and battlements also appear on the garden front, together with projecting oriel windows to add picturesque variety. But Laud was determined that the east and west courtyard elevations should have an emblematic, ceremonial character, and for this purpose he resorted to the forms of classical architecture. The round-arched loggias derive ultimately from Brunelleschi's Foundling Hospital in Florence (1419–24), and more immediately

The centre of the east range of the Canterbury Quadrangle at St John's College

from Nevile's Court at Trinity College, Cambridge (completed in 1612). The arches are supported by monolithic Tuscan columns of local Bletchingdon marble—the first structural use of classical columns in an Oxford building—and the spandrels filled with busts, probably by John Jackson, of the Seven Virtues and the Seven Liberal Arts, proclaiming Laud's reverence for the medieval curriculum of the University; in order to maintain symmetry an extra virtue—Religion—and an extra liberal art—Learning—had to be inserted to fill the eighth space on each side. But the eye is primarily captured by the richly carved classical 'frontispieces' at the centre of each range, made up of Doric and Ionic columns, surmounted by segmental pediments resembling that on the façade of Salomon de Brosse's church of St Gervais and St Proteus in Paris (begun in 1616). Adorned with lavish and sometimes bizarre Mannerist carving, taken from French and Flemish pattern-books, the frontispieces act as frames for

The south porch of St Mary's church

the coats of arms of the King and Archbishop, and for pedimented aedicules containing bronze statues of Charles I and his Queen, Henrietta Maria; the man responsible for the statues was, appropriately enough, a Frenchman, Hubert le Sueur. Nowhere in England is there a more vivid reminder of the union of Church and Crown, for the defence of which both Charles and Laud soon paid with their lives. Laud reiterated Oxford's close ties to the Stuart regime in 1636 by inviting the royal couple to a lavish and vastly expensive banquet in the New Library, where, in Anthony Wood's words, 'the King, Queen and Prince Elector dined at one Table . . . and Prince Rupert with all the Lords and Ladies at a long table, reaching almost from one end to the other, at which all the gallantry and beauties of the kingdom seemed to meet.'

The dramatic, almost Baroque, character of the Canterbury Quadrangle frontispieces is echoed in the new south porch at

St Mary's, the University Church, built in 1637. Here too the influence of Archbishop Laud was paramount. Determined to restore dignified worship to the Church of England, he applied pressure to remove secular activities from inside the building—something which did not finally take place until after the Civil War—and took steps to refit the interior. The porch was paid for by his former chaplain, Morgan Owen, but it was presumably Laud who proposed John Jackson as master mason (not, as used to be thought, Nicholas Stone, despite the fact that the building appears in a list of works compiled by his nephew). There is a Gothic fan vault inside, but the arched entrance is flanked by twisted Corinthian columns of the kind which Bernini had recently used in the *baldacchino* at St Peter's basilica in Rome; such columns were believed at the time to have derived from the Temple of Solomon, and they appear in one of the Raphael cartoons, acquired by Charles I for the royal art collection. The richly sculptured composition is crowned by a niche breaking through the curved pediment and enclosing a sculpture of the Virgin and Child; the image was cited as evidence of popery in Laud's trial in 1644. Nothing in Oxford, or indeed in England, represents more vividly the High Churchmanship and ultramontane artistic sympathies of the Laudian era.

Despite this flowering of classicism, the last major building undertaken in Oxford before the Civil War was carried out in the purest late Gothic style. This was the vault of the Hall staircase at **Christ Church**. An influx of students had already resulted in the rebuilding by Christ Church of the medieval Peckwater Inn—a former academic hall—and the former Canterbury College, both of them standing to the north-east of Cardinal Wolsey's incomplete buildings in Tom Quad. But no serious attempt was made to finish off Wolsey's buildings until the time of Brian Duppa, who became Dean in 1629 and carried out a thorough internal refitting of the Cathedral. Possibly inspired by rivalry with Laud's magnificent buildings at St John's, he launched an appeal for funds to complete the interior of the tower at the south-east corner of Tom Quad, clearly intended by Wolsey and his architects to serve as a magnificent formal approach to the Hall. The tower had been left an empty shell when Wolsey fell from power, with, according to Anthony Wood, 'scarce any steps, and open at the top'. Now, in 1638, the vast space was roofed with a stone fan vault made up of concave cones meeting at, and appearing to spring from, a single slender pier in the centre. The work was carried out, possibly to a lost design from Wolsey's period, by William Smith, Warden of the Mason's Company in London, a fellow parishioner of the main benefactor, Paul Bayning, son of a London shipowner.

Christ Church: the Hall staircase by James Wyatt (1801–4), with the vault of 1638

Despite its late date, this is one of the most beautiful vaults of its type in England, and with its completion Oxford acquired one of its finest Gothic interiors.

The completion of Tom Quad was held up by the onset of the Civil War. With London barred to the King after 1642, Oxford became the royalist capital of England. Following long-established conventions for royal visits, Charles I took up residence in Christ Church and Henrietta Maria at Merton. Meanwhile earth fortifications—works of engineering rather than architecture—were run up around the town, traces of which can still be seen today. Considering its strategic importance, Oxford suffered remarkably little from the conflict or, even more surprisingly, from the vindictiveness of the Parliamentary forces who captured the city in 1646. The only buildings to suffer as a direct result of the war were in the Castle, which was refortified by Parliament in 1649 and 'slighted' three years later in 1652, at the time of Charles II's abortive attempt to return as King; according to Anthony Wood, the buildings, including those of 1649, were 'in four daye's space in a whimsey quite pulled down and mutilated'. Thus Oxford lost the greatest part of its most formidable and impressive secular building. More widespread destruction was caused by a 'Great Fire' in 1644 which devastated much of the area between the present George Street, north of the city wall, and St Ebbe's church. But Oxford was fortunate to be spared the attentions of Puritan iconoclasts like the appalling William Dowsing, who wreaked havoc in Cambridge and throughout East Anglia, and a surprising quantity of its church furnishings remained intact, including even the superficially 'popish' fittings and stained-glass windows introduced into many of the chapels during the years of Laud's supremacy.

One indirect result of the prolonged political crisis of the Civil War and Interregnum was a decline in the number of students attending the University. As the pressure of numbers eased, new collegiate building came to an end, and only one major project was carried out in the years between the fall of Charles I and the return of his son as King in 1660. This was the building of a new Library and Chapel at **Brasenose College**, on a site to the south of the existing early 16th-century quadrangle. The new buildings were financed by a bequest from a former Principal, and the work was carried out between 1656 and 1663 to the designs of John Jackson. As in the Canterbury Quadrangle at St John's, where Jackson had already worked, and indeed in most early 17th-century Oxford buildings, Gothic and classical motifs coexist, but here they are combined in a novel manner hard to parallel in English architecture of the time. The Library is raised up over a partially open loggia (later filled in) and is lit by

Painted glass by Abraham van Linge (1641) in the Chapel of University College

ABRAHAM VAN
LINGE FECIT

Part of the east façade of Brasenose College to Radcliffe Square, showing the east window of the Chapel (left) and the southern bay of the Library

traceried windows, but the crenellated roof-line is interrupted at intervals by classical pediments, creating a restless Mannerist rhythm to both the courtyard and street fronts. To the south is the Chapel, the last in Oxford to be built on the medieval T plan. Here too there are traceried Gothic-arched windows, but the buttresses between them take the form of Corinthian pilasters, and above them there is an entablature supporting an urn-topped parapet. Even more bizarre are the gable-ends, sweeping up in concave curves, and the entrance loggia with its porthole-like oval windows. Inside, the most striking feature is the plaster ceiling in the form of a fan vault, which all but obscures the 15th-century hammer-beam roof brought from the former St Mary's College in New Inn Hall Street, acquired by Brasenose more than eighty years before. This strange exercise in deceit provides one more reminder of the seductive charms of late medieval architecture which have repeatedly mesmerized Oxford University through the generations.

The early 17th-century rebuilding of academic Oxford was matched by a comparable process in the city. Ralph Agas's map of 1578 (see pp. 80–1) shows a city which had still not fully recovered from the ravages

The interior of the Sheldonian Theatre, looking north

of the Black Death and the economic stagnation of the early 16th century. There are vacant plots along some of the streets, especially in the north-western and south-eastern areas; behind the street fronts there are large areas of garden ground, and open land stretches up to the walls. Many changes took place in the century between Agas's map and Loggan's (1675). The area within the walls was intensely developed, with continuous building along all the street frontages and extensive development on the garden plots behind. The walls themselves fell into disrepair, houses were built up against them in Ship Street and St Michael's Street, and there was extensive building on the site of the old town ditch to the north, leading to the emergence of Holywell Street, Broad Street, and George Street in their modern form. Growth also took place in the extra-mural suburbs of St Thomas, St Aldate's, St Clements, and St Giles. This upsurge of building was caused in part by an increase in population; the number of inhabitants is believed to have tripled in a century, from about 3000 in the mid-16th century to over 10,000 in the 1660s, largely through

J. C. Buckler's view of St Ebbe's Street in 1821, looking north to the church of St Peter-le-Bailey (1728–40), demolished in 1874. The jettied houses are characteristic of those built all over Oxford in the late 16th and early 17th centuries

A chimneypiece in number 90 High Street

migration. By the 1660s Oxford was once more one of the richest provincial towns in England, its size and prosperity a direct result of the growth in the University on which it chiefly depended.

As in the colleges, most of the new building took place in the first forty years of the 17th century. Many of the leading citizens now took the opportunity to introduce comforts which had already begun to appear in the country houses of the gentry and in the town houses of the better-off citizens of London. Draughty open-roofed medieval halls were roofed over, wood panelling introduced in place of paintings or painted cloth, and fireplaces with carved wooden overmantels constructed, along with framed wooden staircases. As in the colleges, extra rooms were created in the attics, and new and much larger glazed windows inserted. Some domestic interiors of this period survive relatively intact, often behind façades which have been subsequently rebuilt, like number 90 High Street, where a bland, largely 19th-century frontage gives no indication of the richly carved chimneypieces in the rooms behind; the house belonged to Christ Church, and was rebuilt by the tenant, John Wilkins, an apothecary, in *c.*1612–13. And some streets, like Ship Street, Holywell Street, Pembroke Street, and much of Broad Street and Turl Street, remain much as they were at the time of Loggan's map, despite inevitable alterations to the façades.

Holywell Street, looking west

The rebuilding of the city was carried out piecemeal, usually by builders employed by the leaseholders and not the ground landlords; there were no building regulations in the modern sense. Sometimes houses were built in pairs; there are examples on the south side of Pembroke Street and also in Holywell Street, where new houses were constructed in 1613 to rehouse those made homeless by the building of the Schools. More often the houses were built singly, one at a time, with one or two gables on the roof-line, and the street frontages were, and often still are, picturesquely varied. Surprisingly perhaps, in view of the predominance of stone in the University and colleges, timber framing was still widely employed for the front (though not always the side) walls of the houses, especially in the central districts near Carfax and the High Street. This persistence of timber-framing (much of it since covered over in stucco), and the general lack of monumentality enhanced the architectural distinction between Town and Gown.

Most of the new houses were built on old sites. In the main streets, where space was at a premium, they usually have narrow frontages of the medieval type, and extend a long way back on their garden plots: a pattern already familiar from inns like the Golden Cross. A good example of a narrow-fronted house is the three-storeyed building now known as the Old Palace (part of the University's Catholic Chaplaincy), erected some distance outside the south gate, next to the medieval Littlemore Hall, which was rebuilt at about the same time and contains some well-preserved panelled interiors and plaster ceilings. The Old Palace was built in about 1622–8 by a merchant, Thomas Smith, and the contemporary taste for decorative display—found in many English towns at the time—is apparent in its gabled roof-line, its profuse external plasterwork, its wooden oriel windows, and its ornate plaster ceilings; an even more lavish plastered façade was constructed at the former Three Tuns Inn in the High Street in 1642, demolished in the 19th century to make way for new buildings for University College. The narrow-fronted plan was also employed at Kettell Hall in Broad Street (next to Blackwell's travel bookshop), built by the President of Trinity College *c*.1620, and also at Black Hall at the northern end of St Giles (now part of Queen Elizabeth House); these houses were both built of stone.

Some important houses had no façade to the street, but were built on former garden plots approached by alleyways or 'yards', like the present number 1, Magpie Lane, a timber house to the south of the High Street which bears the date 1588. The most impressive house of

The 'Old Palace' in 1821, by J. C. Buckler

Kemp Hall (number 130A High Street) in 1868

this type is the one known as Kemp Hall, also to the south of the High Street, built for an alderman of the city, William Boswell, in 1637 (the date is carved over the main doorway). Here the timber frame is plastered over, as usual in Oxford, and the house (now a restaurant) is one room deep, with two main rooms on each floor, separated by a largely intact framed staircase; according to an inventory of 1678, the rooms were a kitchen, two parlours, a garden chamber, a dining-room, a bedchamber, a study, and two rooms in the attics. Sheds, outbuildings and, in at least two surviving instances, even tennis courts were also built on the old garden plots in the centre of the city; a former court behind numbers 104–105 High Street has recently been turned into lecture-rooms by Oriel College, but another to the north of Merton Street, described as 'late built' in 1595 and standing behind the stone-built house known as Postmasters' Hall—once the home of the antiquary Anthony Wood—is still used for 'real' tennis. As buildings of this kind filled the remaining open space, the centre of Oxford acquired the densely packed appearance which it still maintains today.

For a city whose main *raison d'être* was by now education, 17th-century Oxford was surprisingly deficient in elementary schools for the sons (let alone the daughters) of the citizens. An attempt to remedy the situation was made with the foundation of Nixon's charity school for boys in 1658–9. This occupied a timber-framed building to the south of the High Street, on the site of the present Town Hall. The schoolroom rested on a colonnaded ground floor, and was lit by large windows with arches over the central lights; windows of this

J. C. Buckler's view of Nixon's School in 1825 (demolished in 1896)

type first appeared in London at about the middle of the 17th century, but they soon spread to provincial towns and there is a particularly spectacular example in the house known as Sparrowes House in Ipswich (Suffolk), hence the term 'Ipswich windows' coined by recent architectural historians. Windows of the 'Ipswich' type became quite a fad in mid to late 17th-century Oxford; they can still be seen in the south range of the courtyard of the Golden Cross inn and in the front of number 126 High Street, an earlier house (see p. 48) remodelled in the second half of the 17th century, possibly by a mercer, Robert Pawling, Mayor of Oxford in 1679–80. Buildings of this kind formed the backdrop against which academic Oxford strove to immortalize itself in yet more monumental form in the next generations.

4 The Age of Classicism

The Restoration of Charles II to the throne in 1660 was one of the most important turning-points in the architectural history of Oxford. With its strong royalist sympathies and its close identification with the Church of England, the University welcomed the return of the king and enthusiastically resumed its role as a patron of architecture. But now it took the lead in promoting the classical style, acquiring in the process a collection of monumental buildings second to none in England. This revolution in taste resulted from a growth in architectural knowledge and expertise within the academic community, and also among the private patrons who contributed generously to the new buildings. Foreign travel and the dissemination of architectural literature created a dissatisfaction with the deeply conservative architecture of the previous fifty years. And as academic culture became more secular, even in Anglican Oxford, the supposedly rational, enlightened architectural idiom of the Renaissance was increasingly favoured over the Gothic of the not so distant past.

Oxford's architectural revolution of the late 17th century was heralded by the building of the **Sheldonian Theatre** in 1664–7. This singular building was designed as the ceremonial centre of a University which has always been addicted to academic pomp, and after more than three centuries it still fulfils the purpose for which it was first constructed. Academic ceremonies had formerly been conducted in St Mary's church in the High Street, but they were apt to become rowdy, especially at the time of the annual orgy of self-congratulation known as the Act or Encaenia, held each June to mark the end of the academic year. The idea of building a new ceremonial hall originated with John Fell, Dean of Christ Church and an energetic supporter of new building projects, and it was probably Fell who persuaded Gilbert Sheldon, Archbishop of Canterbury and Chancellor of the University, to provide £1000 towards the cost, in the hope that more donations could be attracted from elsewhere. In 1663 a site was acquired immediately to the north of the Divinity School, on

The Radcliffe Camera from the north. To the left is the screen wall to the north quadrangle of All Souls College

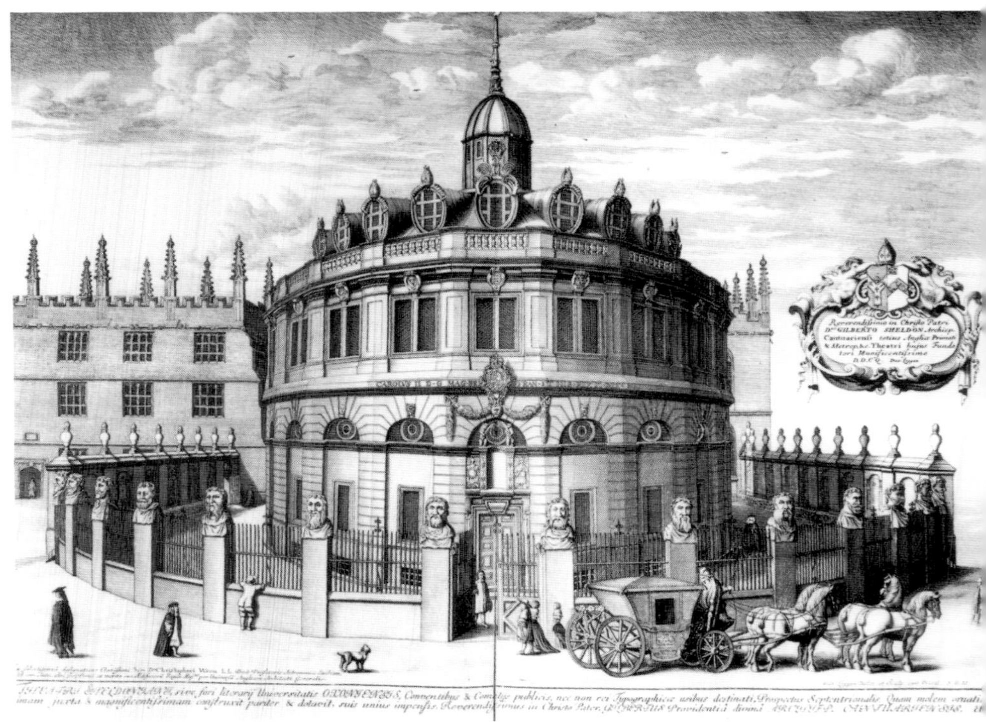

The Sheldonian Theatre from the north in 1675

land belonging to the city corporation next to the mouldering city wall. In the same year a model was prepared by the 33-year-old mathematician and scientist Christopher Wren. Work started in the following year, and the building was finally opened in 1669.

Wren's appointment marked an epoch both in his own career and in the history of architecture in Oxford. Educated at Wadham College, and subsequently a Fellow of All Souls, he was one of the most talented of a group of young men of scientific interests which coalesced around John Wilkins, Warden of Wadham in the 1650s; his friend and fellow-scientist Robert Hooke later wrote that 'there scarce ever met in one man, in so great a perfection, such a Mechanical Head, and so Philosophical a Mind.' Wren became Professor of Astronomy at Gresham College in London in 1657, but he returned to Oxford as Savilian Professor of Astronomy in 1661, the year of the formation of the Royal Society, of which he was a founder member. In the same year he was asked by the king to supervise the building of a new fortress at Tangier, but nothing came of this proposal, and his first architectural work was the building of a chapel at Pembroke College, Cambridge, for which the funds were supplied by his uncle Matthew Wren, former Bishop of Ely and a devoted royalist. But the

Sheldonian was his first large building, and it enabled him to demonstrate his talent for solving architectural problems which were deemed beyond the capabilities of any of the available master masons. It thus inaugurated a period in which the architectural initiative passed decisively into the hands of the gifted amateur.

The Sheldonian was the first building in Oxford, and one of the first in England, to be modelled directly on a structure dating from classical antiquity. The model was the U-shaped Theatre of Marcellus in Rome, which had been illustrated in the third volume of Sebastiano Serlio's *Architettura* (1540), the most popular of all Renaissance architectural books. Roman theatres were arranged with banked seating facing the stage, behind which there was usually a permanent backdrop or *scenae frons*; there was no permanent roof, but when the sun was too intense a canvas or *velarium* could be hauled across the open space, supported on cords. Several modifications had to be made before this model could be adapted to the needs of the University and the vagaries of the English climate. Most important, a roof needed to be constructed with a 70-foot (21.5 metre) span uninterrupted by internal supports—much broader than any existing roof in Oxford—thus allowing the members of the University and their guests to see and hear the ceremonies clearly. Wren's design drew on one devised in 1644 by John Wallis, the Savilian Professor of Geometry, for a wooden structure resting on long horizontal beams jointed together, supporting uprights linked by diagonal struts. Unlike the arch-braced and hammer-beam roofs which had been constructed in Oxford as recently as the 1630s, the structure of the roof was not intended to be seen. Instead, the timber-work was concealed by a huge painting carried out in London by the King's sergeant-painter Robert Streater. This takes the form of an elaborate allegory, celebrating the triumph of Religion (meaning the Anglican Church) and Learning (the University of Oxford) after the turmoils of the Civil War and its aftermath. In the centre the clouds open to reveal Truth surrounded by personifications of Theology, Law, and Medicine in their various guises, together with the arts and sciences, while at the southern end envy, rapine, and 'brutish scoffing ignorance' are being expelled; the canvas covering of a Roman theatre is shown around the edges, as if it has been drawn back to reveal the allegory, and wooden battens painted to look like gilded cords hold the different sections of the painting in place. Echoing Rubens's magnificent ceiling in the Banqueting House at Whitehall Palace, though with only a fraction of the Flemish master's creative insight and painterly skills, this elaborate absurdity heralded the arrival of a new, cosmopolitan, artistic sensibility in Oxford.

Wren had to make some important changes to the internal layout of a Roman theatre in order to adapt it to the needs of the University (see colour plate facing p. 115). The original intention was to use the building for dramatic performances and anatomical lectures as well as for degree ceremonies, but in the end this idea was dropped and the *scenae frons* was omitted from the flat (southern) end, which became the formal entrance. The focal point of the building thus became the curved northern end, where an elaborately carved chair for the Chancellor or his representative was placed. Carved wooden pulpits or rostra for the Proctors (the University's disciplinary officers) were placed on either side of the building, with represention of the *fasces* (rods and an axe, symbolizing authority to the Romans) projecting from their inner faces; the varnished and gilded carving was by a Londoner, Richard Cleer. At first-floor level there is a wooden gallery, resting on Corinthian columns of wood, but painted to look like marble, and supporting extra rows of banked seating; above this is a row of attic windows, and a Corinthian cornice runs around the whole building at roof level. In its unity of conception and richness of decoration, and above all in its emblematic intention and unswerving classicism, nothing comparable had been seen in England since the 1630s.

The exterior of the Sheldonian Theatre is aesthetically less satisfying than the interior. This may not have been entirely Wren's fault. It was presumably the University which made the decision to squash the main entrance front up opposite the Divinity School—used as a robing room on ceremonial occasions—rather than putting it in its logical place on the north side, overlooking Broad Street. Thus it is the back of the building which faces the outside world. The south front, though impressive in conception, with a huge pediment on the upper floor embracing an engaged temple front—an idea which may owe something to Palladio's conjectural reconstruction of the exterior of the Basilica of Maxentius in the Roman forum in his *Quattro Libri dell' Architettura*—is a fussy and disjointed composition, with an excess of visually indigestible carved detail. It is the curved end of the building—strangely reminiscent of the stern of a ship—which catches the eye and remains in the memory, with its 'fence' of herms (human heads on plinths, taken from ancient Roman boundary posts, but popularly known as 'Emperors' heads'), looking out onto the street. This part of the building would have looked better had Wren been allowed to introduce the tall arched upstairs windows and engaged classical columns which he presumably intended, and which were implied by the existence of the heavily rusticated ground floor. But the expected donations failed to materialize, and he was 'obliged

The south front of the Sheldonian Theatre

to put a stop to the bolder Strokes of his Pencil, and confine the Expence within the limits of a private Purse [Sheldon's]'. So the ground floor supports what looks like an attic storey, lacking the columns and arches which would have given it beauty and meaning. Further awkwardness resulted from a decision to use the roof-space as a book-store for the University's printing press, which was housed in the basement; this made it necessary to provide a row of incongruous oval windows (since removed) above the balustrade, with a meagre cupola at the apex of the roof, replaced in 1838 by the present larger cupola designed by Edward Blore.

The University's next foray into architectural patronage occurred in 1679–83 with the construction of a new building immediately to the west of the Sheldonian, now known as the **Old Ashmolean**. This was designed as a dual-purpose structure, with rooms for scientific teaching and research on the lower two floors and a museum above.

The Old Ashmolean (now the Museum of the History of Science) from the north-east

The museum, which was open to the public from the beginning, consisted of a collection of scientific and other curiosities bequeathed to the University by the antiquary, astrologer, and herald Elias Ashmole; a selection of the 'rarities', many of them first collected by the gardener and traveller John Tradescant and his son, can now be seen in the Ashmolean Museum in Beaumont Street. On the main floor, reached by a flight of steps from Broad Street, was the University's School of Natural Science, in which the first Keeper of the Museum, Robert Plot, author of the *Natural History of Oxfordshire,* gave his lectures. In the basement there was a chemistry laboratory, 'furnished,' according to Anthony Wood, 'with all sorts of furnaces and all other necessary materials'. The dignified, domestic-looking front faces north onto Broad Street, with a balustrade hiding the roof and two rows of large windows to let in the maximum amount of light; they are surmounted alternately by triangular and rounded pediments, as in Inigo Jones's Banqueting House at Whitehall Palace, and the windows are each divided by a single mullion and transom, after the normal post-Restoration fashion, sashes not yet having made their appearance (the first documented examples in Oxford are in front of the monument to Sir Thomas Pope in Trinity College Chapel, built in 1691–4). The most lavish part of the building is the east side, facing the Sheldonian. Here the dominant feature is the magnificent porch, used on rare occasions as a ceremonial entrance, with paired Corinthian columns supporting a curved pediment: a large-scale version of the dominant motif in the Canterbury Quadrangle at St John's College. The building (now the Museum of the History of Science) was designed, perhaps with the help of one of the Oxford academic *cognoscenti*, by the master mason Thomas Wood, a former assistant of William Byrd, who was responsible for the stone carving at the Sheldonian. The accomplished nature of the carving of the porch is a tribute to the speed and facility with which local craftsmen mastered the classical idiom in the post-Restoration years.

The colleges soon followed the University's lead in commissioning new buildings. This was not because of pressure of numbers; admissions even began to fall after the 1670s, and by the beginning of the 18th century there were fewer undergraduates than there had been before the Civil War. But while the overall numbers fell, the average wealth of the students increased. By 1700 only about a quarter of the undergraduates were being recruited from outside the gentry and aristocracy, and some colleges went out of their way to recruit fee-paying gentleman commoners, as they were now called, many of whom led idle, dissipated lives and left Oxford without taking a degree. Fellowships increasingly became sinecures, held by aspiring clergymen awaiting lucrative college livings. Anthony Wood was already deploring what he saw as a 'decay of learning' in 1661:

> Before the warr wee had scholars that made a thorough search in scholasticall and polemicall divinity, in humane authors, and naturall philosophy, But now scholars studie these things not more than what is just necessary to carry them through the exercises of their respective colleges and the Universitie. Their aime is not to live as students ought to do . . . but to live like gent., to keep dogs and horses, to turne their studies and coleholes into places to recieve bottles, to swash it in apparell, to weare long periwigs, etc.

Gradually the larger and wealthier colleges took on the characteristics of the country houses from whose sons their membership was increasingly drawn. An early 18th-century Frenchman thought they were 'palaces compared with the Tuileries, occupied by rich idlers [the Fellows] who sleep and get drunk one part of the day, and the rest they spend in training, clumsily enough, a parcel of uncouth youths to be clergymen', and a late 18th-century Principal of Brasenose expressed what many must have felt when he said that he 'hated a college of Paupers'. Yet whatever the implications for the University's

The Senior Common Room of Wadham College. The panelling dates from between 1690 and 1724

reputation as a seat of learning, the influx of aristocratic patronage helped create a climate in which classical architecture became not only desirable but also affordable.

The need for new buildings derived in large part from a change in social habits. Gentlemen commoners baulked at the idea of sharing rooms, as students had always done in Oxford (and as they still do in the USA). Instead, they demanded a set of at least two rooms (a bedroom, and a sitting-room in which guests could be entertained), and this became the norm for collegiate accommodation down to the middle of the 20th century. The Fellows of the colleges also expected to be housed at least as well as their wealthier students. When the traveller Celia Fiennes visited New College in 1694 she was entertained by a Fellow who had 'a very pretty appartment of dineing rooms bed chamber and studdy and a room for a Servant'. Similar considerations of comfort and conviviality led to the custom of setting aside a panelled room as a common-room 'to the end,' as Anthony

Wood remarked, 'that the Fellows might meet together (chiefly in the evening after refection) partly about business, but mostly for society's sake, which before was at each chamber by turns'. In most cases common-rooms for the Fellows were contrived within the existing buildings, as at Trinity, where one was created at the high-table end of the Hall in 1665 and panelled in 1681, or at Lincoln, where 'the chamber under the library westward [was] set apart and appropriated to the use of the fellows for their common fires and any other public meetings' in 1662. At St John's, by contrast, the common-room was housed in a detached building to the north of the old quadrangle, erected by the local mason Bartholomew Peisley in 1673–6; its panelled interior still survives largely intact.

The changing social composition of the colleges brought about fundamental changes in architecture and layout. These changes were first evident at **Trinity**, where the number of wealthy and well-connected commoners rose dramatically under the presidency of Ralph Bathurst, 'reputedly the politest Person of his Time in the whole university', according to John Ayliffe. Some of these privileged youths were housed in a new block built in 1665–8 to the designs of Christopher Wren, who had known Bathurst since the 1650s, when they had both formed part of Wilkins's scientific circle at Wadham. Financed, like many 17th-century Oxford buildings, by subscriptions (solicited in this case by Bathurst himself), the new

The garden of Trinity College from W. Williams, *Oxonia Depicta* (1733), soon after the completion of the Garden Quadrangle which incorporates Wren's building of 1665–8 (extreme right). To the left is the remodelled quadrangle of the former Durham College

building (see p. 54) was externally rather gawky, with its irregularly spaced windows and its disproportionate French-inspired mansard roof (later replaced by the present top floor). But the accommodation was unprecedentedly spacious, with sets of panelled, high-ceilinged rooms (a large room and two smaller rooms) opening off from the two staircases, and it was this spaciousness which other colleges increasingly sought to emulate. Wren originally wanted the building to stand on its own to the north of the existing quadrangle, like the earlier Fellows' Building at Christ's College, Cambridge (1640–5). But this was too radical for the donors, as Wren made clear in a letter to Bathurst:

> I perceive the name of Quadrangle will carrie it with those whom you say may possibly be your benefactors, though it be much the worse for the Chambers, and the Beauty of the College . . . [but] to be sober, if any body, as you say, will pay for a quadrangle, there is no dispute to be made; let them have a quadrangle, though a lame one, somewhat like a three-legged table.

So eventually the new building came to form part of an open-ended courtyard incorporating a west range, built in 1682, and a south range, abutting onto the existing quadrangle, which followed in 1728. The new buildings faced out onto an extensive garden, laid out as an elaborate French-inspired formal parterre, but subsequently a victim to the 19th-century craze for dull manicured lawns. Thus a new model for the layout of Oxford collegiate buildings was established.

The first open-ended courtyard to be completed in Oxford was at **New College** in 1682–1707. New College had one of the largest gardens of any of the medieval colleges, and its beauties were enhanced by the construction of a viewing mound in 1594, 'perfected with stepps of stone and setts for the Hedges about the walke' in 1648–9; Celia Fiennes remarked that the garden was 'new-makeing' when she visited Oxford in 1694, with 'a large bason of water in the middle' and 'little walkes and mazes and round mounts for the schollars to divert themselves in'. The Fellows of the College had long chafed at the cramped conditions of the 14th-century quadrangle, little changed since William of Wykeham's time, and in 1670–5 an extra storey was added, allowing them more space but irreparably spoiling the original proportions. A decision to admit gentleman commoners in 1679 made the need for yet more accommodation imperative, and the design of the new buildings was placed in the hands of William Byrd. His first proposal was for a massive three-storeyed block obstructing the view east from the medieval quadrangle to the garden, but this was fortunately shelved in favour of the present, rather subtler, scheme in which the new buildings were

The Garden Quadrangle of New College, looking west

erected in 1682–4 on either side of an open courtyard immediately to the east of the medieval quadrangle, thus creating a vista to and from the garden. The proportions and much of the detailing were classical, but visual continuity with the older buildings was maintained by the addition of battlements on the roof-line. Extra ranges set slightly back from the central axis were added to the east in 1700 and 1707, creating a sense of Baroque drama which calls to mind the entrance courtyard at Versailles or, closer to home, Wren's never-completed palace for Charles II at Winchester, where Byrd was one of the masons. Finally, in 1711, the blacksmith Thomas Robinson erected the splendid iron screen and gateway (replaced by a replica in 1894) which closes off the 'quadrangle' from the garden.

Byrd was also responsible in 1680–6 for building, and probably designing, a new Library and Chapel at **St Edmund Hall**, one of the few academic halls to have survived into the 17th century. The buildings here were smaller and more intimate in character than those of the colleges; according to Salmon, students in halls lived 'like Gentlemen in a private Family. There is not so much of that abject Submission and Ceremony observ'd, as in the Houses that are incorporated.' Space was at a premium, so the Library and Chapel were ingeniously placed together in a two-storeyed block on the eastern side of the existing quadrangle, with the Library (still largely

The front quadrangle of St Edmund Hall, with the largely late 16th-century north range and the Chapel and Library block of 1680–6.

unaltered) over the antechapel and the diminutive main body of the Chapel projecting eastwards, filled with dark woodwork by the carpenter Arthur Frogley, who was widely employed in late 17th-century Oxford. The building is only five bays wide and two storeys high, but a degree of monumentality is supplied by the giant Corinthian columns and pediment which enclose the central bay, with its doorway whimsically surmounted by a smaller pediment resting on carvings of piles of books.

The return of the Church of England after the Restoration led many of the colleges to remodel or even replace their chapels. Worship again revolved, as it had in the days of Archbishop Laud, around the regular recitation of Morning and Evening Prayer and the celebration of Holy Communion according to the Book of Common Prayer on Sundays and festivals: a pattern which necessitated the retention of inward-facing seating—something which had characterized Oxford and Cambridge college chapels, along with cathedral choirs, since the Middle Ages—and the fencing off of the altar or communion table behind rails. The renewed emphasis on the Sacrament led some colleges to construct (or reconstruct) a wooden reredos behind the altar and a screen between the antechapel and the chancel; this gave an opportunity to introduce a fashionable display of classical columns and pediments into a Gothic setting, as at University College, where the work was carried out in about 1694. Advice on refitting the chapels at Merton, All Souls, and St John's was given by Christopher Wren, a man of impeccably High Anglican credentials; most of the fittings fell victim to the medievalizing zeal of the 19th century, but the splendid wooden screen at Merton, dating from 1673, still survives, having been reinstated in 1960 after languishing in an attic for more than a century. At All Souls the painter Isaac Fuller was commissioned in the 1660s to fill the whole of the east wall behind the altar with massive compositions made up of writhing Michelangelesque figures, completely obscuring the 15th-century stone reredos which had been denuded of its 'superstitious' statuary after the Reformation; the wooden screen between the antechapel and the chancel was finally completed by Sir James Thornhill in 1713–16. Fuller was also employed at Magdalen, where a refitting along 'Laudian' lines had already taken place in 1629–35; both here and at All Souls the paintings, together with most of the other 17th-century decorations, fell foul of later antiquarianism and anti-Baroque prejudice, though part of Fuller's rather crudely executed ceiling painting at All Souls is currently displayed on the walls of the antechapel.

The finest example of late 17th-century church architecture in Oxford is the Chapel of **Trinity College**. The medieval Chapel inherited from the former Durham College suffered badly during the Interregnum, and in 1691 the President, Ralph Bathurst—who attended daily morning prayers there at 5 a.m. until his 82nd year—supplied the funds to replace it with a new one on the same site, next to a new entrance lodge and tower, which satisfyingly closes the northward vista from Turl Street. The Chapel, completed in 1694, is slightly longer than its predecessor, and is lit by large round-headed windows, separated by Corinthian pilasters, with an urn-topped balustrade on the roof-line, and statues of Theology, Medicine, Geometry, and Astronomy on the low tower, which contained a set of

All Souls College Chapel, looking east, from Ackermann's *Oxford* (1814)

panelled rooms. The exterior recalls the churches built to the designs of Christopher Wren after the Great Fire of London (1666), and in the past the building was often attributed to Wren. Wren was certainly among the 'able judges in architecture' consulted by Bathurst, but he intervened only after the preliminary design had been made and work had started. Wren suggested one or two minor changes, including the substitution of urns for pinnacles over the external balustrade, but the authorship of the original design remains a mystery.

The interior is architecturally simple but rich in decorative woodwork and plasterwork: a 'total work of art' of a kind to which all Europe aspired in the era of the Baroque. The screen and the reredos

The Chapel of Trinity College from the south

are both veneered in juniper wood, and both are surmounted by segmental pediments—a favourite motif in late 17th-century Oxford—on which are perched reclining figures, as in Michelangelo's famous Medici tombs in Florence. Over the altar there is a marquetry representation of a sunburst, symbolizing the Deity, and it is framed by extraordinarily delicate limewood carvings of fruit and flowers, possibly carried out by Grinling Gibbons, the greatest wood-carver of the age in England; Celia Fiennes said that it was 'just like that at Windsor, it being the same hand'. The remainder of the woodwork was carried out by Arthur Frogley, with the more delicate carving assigned to the carver Jonathan Maine, who also worked on some of Wren's London churches. The beauty and virtuosity of the woodwork is complemented by that of the plasterwork on the coved ceiling, with rectangular panels featuring compositions of fruit and flowers in high relief and, over the altar, representations of the Instruments of the Passion: an explicit use of religious symbolism which, together with the painting of the Ascension (by Pierre Berchet) in the central panel of the ceiling, underlines Oxford's continuing High Church sympathies.

The other major building project of the 1690s was the new Library at **Queen's College**. Like Trinity, Queen's entered the post-Restoration

Trinity College Chapel, looking east

era with a legacy of ramshackle medieval buildings, and it too became one of the most fashionable colleges in the late 17th century. As at Trinity, work started with the erection of a new building for gentleman commoners, also to the designs of Christopher Wren, and this went up in 1671–2 on a site immediately to the north of the medieval quadrangle, flanking Queen's Lane, from which the College was originally entered (see p. 33). Financed by Joseph Williamson, a former diplomat and scholar of the College, it was a plain enough structure, more elegant than Wren's building at Trinity and similar in character to many of the country houses of the time, with an eleven-bay frontage, a central pedimented feature, and a hipped roof; the exterior has since been remodelled. The Library, of 1693–6, is an

The east façade of the Library of Queen's College

altogether more ambitious edifice, facing the Williamson building across what became the Back Quadrangle after the completion of the north range in 1707. It was built to house a bequest of books by a former Provost, Thomas Barlow, who died in 1691; it was financed in large part by the current Provost, Timothy Halton, who had travelled abroad as one of the King's Ambassadors Extraordinary, and must thus have seen examples of Renaissance architecture on the Continent. The design emerged in the same way as that of the Chapel at Trinity. A preliminary version was supplied by an unknown person—perhaps Halton himself—and was subsequently engraved and passed around to the local experts, including Henry Aldrich, Dean of Christ Church, one of the 'able judges' consulted by Ralph Bathurst at Trinity. They suggested modifications which removed some of the more obvious solecisms, and building went ahead on the basis of the revised design.

The Library is a large rectangular room lit by tall round-headed windows and resting on a round-arched loggia (filled in by C. R. Cockerell in 1843–5). The idea of placing a library over a loggia was not a new one; the Laudian Library in the Canterbury Quadrangle at St John's was planned in this way, and, more recently, Christopher Wren had raised his superb library at Trinity College, Cambridge, over a Doric colonnade. Here, though, the arches spring from piers not

The interior of Queen's College Library, looking south

columns, and the ground floor is rusticated, with deep grooves cut into the stonework, after the fashion of 17th-century French architecture. The three central bays on the first floor on each side are flanked by Corinthian pilasters and surmounted by pediments containing allegorical carvings, after the manner of temple fronts; though logically absurd, since a temple front implies an entrance to a building, these features add a note of festivity characteristic of most Oxford libraries of this period. Inside, the scholarly gloom which had permeated Oxford's older libraries is banished in favour of a new feeling of space and light, indicative perhaps of the clear rationalist thinking associated with the generation of Newton and Locke.
The bookcases, placed in the traditional position at right angles to the walls, are richly carved in wood, possibly by local craftsmen, Thomas Minn, father and son, and the flat ceiling is divided into panels sumptuously framed with decorative plasterwork by James Hands, who came from London; the Rococo plasterwork within the panels was carried out by Thomas Roberts in 1756. There is equally fine plasterwork over the doorway at the south end of the room, which now gives access to the Senior Common Room. Like the Chapel at Trinity, the Library survives as a largely unaltered example of the

superbly accomplished craftsmanship of the time, and a rarely surpassed model for future library design.

The spread of classicism in late 17th-century Oxford did not completely obliterate the older manner of building. Some colleges—University, Jesus, Pembroke, and Exeter—completed projects started before the Civil War with very few concessions to modern taste, save for the carving of classical detailing on the new gate towers at Pembroke and Exeter. By far the largest scheme of this kind occurred at **Christ Church**. The guiding spirit here was the Dean, John Fell, who took over a College which still at the time of the Restoration bore the marks of Henry VIII's abrupt dismissal of Cardinal Wolsey and the consequent halting of his ambitious building schemes. The northern part of the street frontage of Tom Quad was still unbuilt, as was the tower over the gatehouse, the cloister inside the quadrangle, and most of the north range, where Wolsey had planned to put his chapel. The quadrangle was completed by 1670, and the new north range given over to houses for the canons of the Cathedral; architecturally, apart from the addition of a classical balustrade to the roof-line of Tom Quad and the street front, the work was all but indistinguishable from the earlier buildings, down even to the springings of the vault of the cloister, which was never constructed. Fell also built a new set of rooms on the site of the present Meadow Building (see p. 227), facing the newly laid out Broad Walk to the south of the college, a favourite venue for fashionable parading.

In 1681 Fell turned to the construction of a tower over Wolsey's unfinished gateway, designed to house Great Tom, the huge bell

Loggan's view of Christ Church in 1675, showing the recently completed Tom Quad before the building of Tom Tower. The larger of the two quadrangles at the top left is Peckwater Inn, the smaller the former Canterbury College

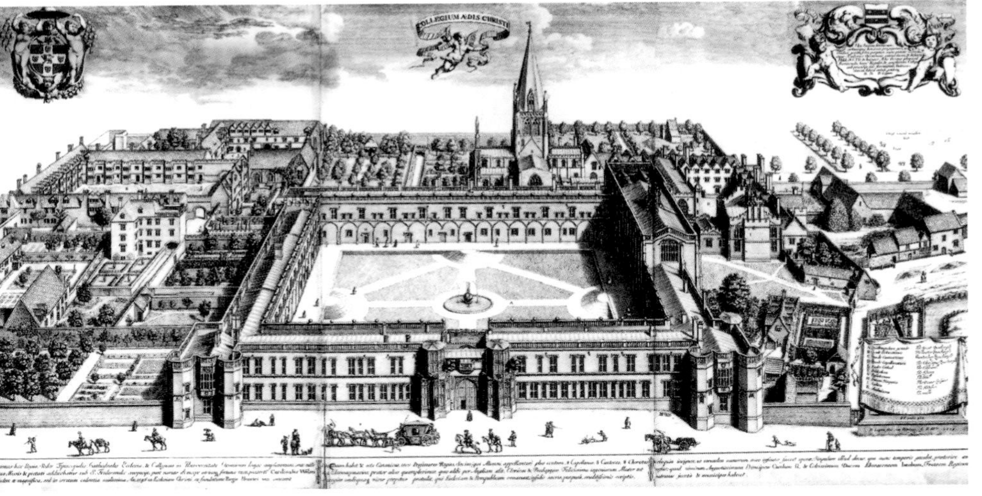

brought from Oseney Abbey after the Reformation. For this sensitive and difficult project he abandoned the local masons who had worked on his earlier enterprises and turned to Christopher Wren, now Surveyor of the King's Works and architect of the new St Paul's Cathedral in London. Wren designed Tom Tower as a personal favour to Fell, and in his letter enclosing his design he recommended the Burford mason and quarry-owner Christopher Kempster as contractor, remarking that he could not 'boast of Oxford artists, though they have a good opinion of themselves'; Kempster had worked with Wren on some of the London city churches, and later played an important part in the building of St Paul's Cathedral. Wren told Fell that he had 'resolved [the tower] ought to be Gothick to agree with the Founder's work, yet I have not continued as busy as he began,' and he later regretted that the existence of the lower portions of Wolsey's intended gate tower 'diverted us from the beginning after the better form of architecture'. These comments give a clue to the workings of his mind. Wolsey's architects seem to have intended an unusually elaborate version of the gate towers found in all late medieval colleges (e.g. the Founder's Tower at Magdalen), flanked by corner turrets, of which only the lower stages were built during his lifetime. Wren could easily have designed something along these lines, but he chose not to do so, substituting for the turreted upper portions originally intended a square tower with a tall octagonal lantern, topped by a dome whose ogee shape echoes the lush elaboration of early Tudor Court architecture. The result is masterly. Whereas Wren's first Oxford building, the Sheldonian Theatre, has a somewhat pedantic air, Tom Tower, his last, is as creative a solution to the problem of making an addition to an old building as can be found anywhere in Oxford.

Tom Tower from the west

Fell died in 1686 and was succeeded as Dean by Henry Aldrich, described by Thomas Hearne as a man 'vers'd both in Ecclesiastical and humane learning almost beyond Compare'. His pursuit of humane learning had taken him to the Continent, and there he associated with 'the eminent in architecture', returning to write a treatise on the classical orders which was not published until long after his death. In his early years as Dean he acquired a reputation in Oxford as a man whose architectural judgement could be trusted, but, despite persistent attempts to credit him with the design of the Chapel at Trinity and the Library at Queen's, the only collegiate building he is known for certain to have designed is Peckwater Quadrangle at Christ Church (1707–14). Built with the help of a bequest from one of the canons, Anthony Radcliffe, whose name is commemorated in the frieze, the quadrangle was intended to house

The north and east sides of Peckwater Quadrangle

commoners, some of whom were titled and most both rich and well-connected. It occupies the site of the medieval Peckwater Inn, north-east of Tom Quad, from which it is reached by a passageway enclosed by high walls. The sets of rooms, some of them very spacious, are grouped around staircases in the usual Oxford way, but, appropriately perhaps in view of the succession of aristocratic occupants who spent some of the formative years of their lives there, the internal elevations of the west, north, and east ranges were treated like the fronts of Italian Renaissance *palazzi*: the first time this had been done in an Oxford college (the south range was not built until after Aldrich's death: see p. 155). Each range has a rusticated ground floor, with Ionic pilasters enclosing the two upper floors and alternating triangular and segmental pediments over the windows of the first floor or *piano nobile*; the roof is hidden by a balustrade. On each side the central bays are brought slightly forward and are crowned by a pediment: an impressive gesture, though the decision to repeat it three times in the same set of buildings suggests a certain lack of imagination. The buildings are impeccably detailed and proportioned, but the overall effect is a little frigid and academic. In many ways Peckwater Quadrangle anticipates the fashionable Palladianism of the 1720s; there is a particularly close resemblance to the north side of Queen Square, Bath, built to the designs of John Wood in 1729. But the Palladian cause was not taken up in Oxford, and it was a different and more idiosyncratic style which dominated the University in the first half of the 18th century.

There was nothing in the city of Oxford in the late 17th century which could match the grandeur of Trinity Chapel, Queen's Library, or Peckwater Quadrangle. Many of England's provincial towns were being rebuilt in brick or stone at this time, but most of Oxford's citizens still continued to live in timber-framed houses, and new timber houses continued to be built well into the 18th century, like the hipped-roofed pair on the north side of Broad Street (numbers 50–51) now occupied by Blackwell's bookshop (see p. 152). According to Thomas Salmon, writing in 1744, the reason lay in the prevalence of short leases from the colleges who owned most of the city-centre property:

> As to the generality of the Inhabitants, they don't think it worth their while to build either with Brick or Stone on College leases, and this is the true Reason the private Buildings are for the most part so mean . . . The Lessees patch up their Clay Tenements as long as they can, and sometimes chuse to let their Leases run out, rather than be at the Charge of renewing them and repairing their Houses.

Many old timber houses were, however, coated in plaster and given classically proportioned windows and cornices as the taste for classical architecture spread among those with pretensions to 'politeness'; this process lasted through the 18th and early 19th centuries, transforming large stretches of the main streets in the process.

J. C. Buckler's pencil drawing of the southern side of Queen Street (formerly Butcher Row) looking east in 1822, with the spire of All Saints church in the distance. Some of the houses retain their traditional gabled façades (note especially the one on the extreme right with its 'Ipswich' windows characteristic of the mid to late 17th century), but others are classically proportioned and detailed. None of the houses survives in its original form

The eastern side of St Giles, with St Giles House in the foreground. The houses on the right were rebuilt or refronted in the 18th or early 19th centuries

The finest town house of the period was built of stone in 1702 at the northern end of St Giles, the northern suburb which Salmon thought was the pleasantest part of the city, 'especially for those that love retirement'. Now known as St Giles House, it has a well-proportioned façade to the street, with a pedimented central feature such as is found in many houses of the professsional classes in the provinces at the time. The owner was Thomas Rowney, a lawyer and one of the city's Members of Parliament, and the builder and designer was probably Bartholomew Peisley, son of the man who completed the Hall and Library at St Edmund Hall. One of the leading Oxford masons of his time, Peisley also built the equally well-proportioned Stone's Almshouses in the St Clements suburb, to the east of Magdalen Bridge, in 1697, and his son, another Bartholomew Peisley, added an impressive stone façade to his own house on the north side of St Michael's Street in about 1721, with giant Doric pilasters framing the doorway; the current name of this house (Vanbrugh House) recalls the fact that the Peisleys were among the main contractors at Blenheim Palace, only a few miles north of Oxford, begun to the designs of Sir John Vanbrugh in 1705.

The most impressive classically inspired building to be erected for the citizens of Oxford was the church of **All Saints** (now the Library of Lincoln College), built to the designs of Henry Aldrich in 1701–10 after the tower of the existing medieval church had collapsed. The new church—the first to be built in the city since the 15th century—was a surprisingly lavish building for a small parish which already

'Vanbrugh House', St Michael Street

contained several college chapels. It stands at the western end of the High Street, still flanked by old timber houses, and its tall south façade (see p. 177) makes a striking impact with its massive pedimented porch flanked by Corinthian columns and its bold display of paired Corinthian pilasters between the round-arched windows; there is a second extra layer of attic windows above the cornice. Corinthian pilasters also give scale to the light, auditorium-like interior, which is uncluttered by columns, and from each pair of pilasters an extra one projects forward to convey an effect of Baroque richness and sculptural movement: an effect far closer to the late work of Wren and the early buildings of Vanbrugh and Nicholas Hawksmoor than to the restraint of Peckwater Quadrangle. Aldrich died before the building of the steeple which so effectively terminates

All Saints church from the north-east

The interior of All Saints church before its conversion into Lincoln College Library

the view looking south along Turl Street (see p. 196), and the upper stages were added to a modified design in 1718–20. Heavier in character than the steeple shown in Aldrich's original drawing, and heavier too than Wren's London church steeples which it otherwise resembles, the source of this design lies in the Italian High Renaissance. Both the circular temple-like feature above the tower and the spire above it appear to derive from Antonio da Sangallo's scheme for the western towers at St Peter's basilica in Rome, of which Aldrich owned engravings. By choosing this bold, masculine design, whose authorship is unknown, the promoters of the church made one of the most imaginative additions to the Oxford skyline.

The first forty years of the 18th century saw the culmination of Oxford University's bid to refashion itself in a manner worthy of the ideals of Roman and Renaissance classicism. This was a period when the numbers of undergraduates continued to fall, when scholarship stagnated, and when the University as an institution fell out of political favour as the last of the Stuarts gave way in 1714 to the Hanoverians, ushering in decades of Whig hegemony. But the colleges retained their wealth and the University its share in the duopoly (with Cambridge) which monopolized the training of Anglican clergy. Most important of all, generous donors were quick to respond to appeals for funds for building. Like Venice in its decadence, Oxford turned in on itself and compensated for the loss of intellectual eminence with the pleasures of magnificent building.

After Dean Aldrich's death in 1710, architecture in Oxford was dominated by three men: William Townesend, George Clarke, and Nicholas Hawksmoor. Townesend was the son of a master mason, John Townesend, who had been an apprentice of Bartholomew Peisley and had served twice as Mayor of Oxford. The family owned quarries at Headington, and in the early 18th century William Townesend built up a reputation not only as a master mason and contractor but also as a competent designer of buildings; Thomas Hearne called him a 'proud conceited fellow who . . . hath a hand in all the Buildings in Oxford, and gets a vast deal of Money that way'. Dean Aldrich employed him as master mason at Peckwater Quadrangle at Christ Church, and he was also brought in by the 'rich and liberal' President of **Corpus Christi**, Edward Turner, to complete a programme of improvements which began with the installation of new panelling and woodwork in the Hall in 1700–1, by Arthur Frogley and Jonathan Maine (see p. 72). The new work was carried out in 1706–12 and consisted of the building of a loggia or cloister along the south side of the early 16th-century Chapel and a block of spacious, panelled rooms known as the Fellows' Building on a site to the south, overlooking Christ Church Meadow. This elegant structure, with its pilastered and pedimented façade, echoes the dignified classical architecture of Peckwater Quadrangle and many early 18th-century English country houses. There is no convincing evidence that it was designed by Aldrich or any of the other local connoisseurs, and it is quite possible that Townesend designed it himself, together with the Gentlemen Commoners' Building which followed in 1737 and the Chapel at Pembroke College (1728–32).

From 1710 onwards Townesend often collaborated with George Clarke, a Fellow of All Souls who took over Aldrich's role as unofficial architectural advisor to Oxford. Clarke was one of the Members of Parliament for the University and served as joint secretary of the Admiralty from 1701 to 1705 and again from 1710 to 1714. But his Tory politics meant that he lost office, first in 1705 and again, permanently, with the coming of the Hanoverians. In his retirement he spent a great deal of time in Oxford, where both his politics and his self-

The south façade of the Fellows Building at Corpus Christi College

taught architectural expertise found ready acceptance. He amassed a major collection of architectural books and drawings, including many by Inigo Jones, and was closely involved in most of the important architectural projects undertaken in Oxford until his death in 1736.

Through his work in the Admiralty, Clarke came into contact with Nicholas Hawksmoor, pupil of the now aged Christopher Wren and one of the most original architects of 18th-century Europe. In the first decade of the 18th century Hawksmoor emerged from the shadow of his master, collaborating with Sir John Vanbrugh at Castle Howard (Yorkshire) and at Blenheim Palace, and designing a handful of highly original buildings on his own. Clarke introduced him to Oxford in about 1708, and he responded by giving the University and colleges some of their most original and memorable buildings of that or any other era, along with plans for unexecuted buildings of a yet more grandiose nature.

Hawksmoor's first executed building in Oxford was a new University printing-house (now known as the **Clarendon Building**), erected in 1712–13 on a prominent site newly cleared of houses to the north of the old city wall and close to the Sheldonian Theatre and the Schools Quadrangle; the builder was William Townesend, who had supplied unexecuted designs. The project was funded out of the profits of one of the Press's most successful books, Lord Clarendon's

The Clarendon Building from the north-west

History of the Great Rebellion (1702–4), and it is clear that Hawksmoor saw the building not only as a utilitarian printing-house but also as a formal entrance into the heart of the University. It thus serves a rhetorical function, dominating an open space bounded to the west by the Sheldonian (now cleared of its printing presses and unsold books), to the east by Catte Street; and to the south by the Schools Quadrangle. The rectangular, two-storeyed structure is divided into two halves, corresponding to the 'learned' and 'Bible' presses, separated by a public passageway aligned on the northern entrance to the Schools Quadrangle. The approach from Broad Street leads up a flight of steps and through a giant portico—the first in Oxford—of the Doric order, enabling the building to be understood as a gateway or Propylaeum to the Acropolis of learning; on the southern side the portico is expressed as an engaged temple front, and a Doric frieze is carried around the whole building at eaves level. The east and west gable-ends are treated as pediments, in counterpoint to those on the longer north and south sides, reinforcing the identification with a classical temple and enhancing the view looking east from Broad Street; the statuary on the pediments was by James Thornhill. Hawksmoor was obsessed with the architecure of classical antiquity, which, like Wren, he knew only through drawings and engravings. But he did not simply copy the architecture of ancient Rome. He was

The eastern end of Broad Street in *c.*1800. The early 18th-century buildings now housing Blackwell's bookshop are on the left and the Sheldonian Theatre and the Clarendon Building are on the right, the former with its cupola of 1837–8 by Edward Blore. The houses in the distance stand on the site of the Indian Institute

fully aware of the expressive potential of the Doric order—the least ornamented of the classical orders of architecture, but also the most difficult to handle—and in the Clarendon Building he reinforced its solemn, dignified message by emphasizing the sculptural quality of the wall surfaces, recessing some of the bays within the surface and emphasizing the keystones and window architraves. Following soon after All Saints church, this noble building inaugurated an era of monumental Roman-inspired classicism which changed the face of Oxford.

Before the Clarendon Building was erected Hawksmoor supplied several impressive proposals for a new front quadrangle at **Queen's College**. This was an ambitious project, conceived at the end of the 17th century and continued by William Lancaster, who became Provost in 1704. He had spent some time in Paris, and shared the taste for classical architecture of his equally worldly predecessor Timothy Halton, commissioning a number of schemes in 1708 and 1709, all of which entailed the complete demolition of the College's existing 14th-century buildings and the building of a new façade to the High Street, on the site of houses which the College had started buying up twenty years before. Hawksmoor's own 'propositions', six in number, were on a grandiose scale which would have done credit to a monarch, but they were too elaborate even for Lancaster's profuse tastes. So he turned instead to George Clarke, who produced designs of his own, and these became the basis of the final scheme, work on which began in 1710. Operations were placed in the hands of William Townesend, whose father had been the mason responsible for building the new Library; the younger Townesend was described as 'architectus' in the College accounts, suggesting that the the final appearance of the College, and especially the interiors of the Hall and Chapel, owes at least as much to him as it does to Clarke.

The Front Quadrangle was, in the words of Ayliffe, 'erected upon the plan of Luxemburgh House [the Palais de Luxembourg in Paris]'. The layout is certainly French in character. As in a typical 17th-century Parisian *hôtel*, there is an open-ended courtyard screened off from the street by a wall with a porter's lodge in the centre: the first classical façade to an Oxford college. The far side of the courtyard is taken up not by living quarters, as in Paris, but by the Hall and Chapel, placed end to end as in early 17th-century colleges like Wadham, Oriel, and University, and the flanking sides are occupied by long residential wings, the western one—the first part of the quadrangle to be erected—containing a common-room and new Lodgings for the Provost. Their elevations are very French in character, with rusticated arcades on the ground floor—a feature of Hawksmoor's discarded 'Proposition A'—and two rows of windows above, recessed into the wall surfaces; at the centre of the attic level, facing the courtyard, there

The front quadrangle of Queen's College, with the west range on the left and the north range, comprising the Hall and Chapel, on the right

are segmental pediments, and there are triangular pediments on the gable-ends towards the street.

The north range, built in 1714–19, is articulated by a giant Doric pilaster order, imparting an appropriately solemn air, with an engaged temple front at the centre, as on the south side of the Clarendon Building, and a cupola above. There is a strong resemblance to Christopher Wren's Chelsea Hospital in London (1682–92), but by using stone rather than brick Clarke and Townesend achieved a grander effect. The Hall—the first in Oxford to be designed throughout in the classical style—has a barrel-vaulted ceiling of plaster hiding the roof timbers, with Doric pilasters along the walls and the tall round-arched windows breaking into the frieze; the

Queen's College Hall, looking east

The entrance to Queen's College

entrance is through a screen at the west end, above which there is a gallery with an ornamental iron balcony, used on occasion, according to Salmon, as a viewing platform from which visitors could observe the members of the College at their meals. The apsidal Chapel, by contrast, is lined with Corinthian pilasters and is entered from the tiny antechapel—no more than a lobby—through a splendid wooden screen, by an unknown craftsman, with an archway in the middle. The decoration, though rich in ornamental plasterwork, is more restrained than in the earlier Chapel at Trinity College, and the effect of solemn gravity is enhanced by the early 16th- and 17th-century stained and painted glass rescued from the former Chapel and preserved in the side windows; the east window, by Joshua Price, was made for the setting, and James Thornhill contributed the circular painting of the Ascension over the sanctuary. Virtually unaltered by later meddling, this is one of the most impressive ecclesiastical interiors of its date in England.

The front quadrangle at Queen's took a long time to complete, and because of a lack of funds the screen wall and gateway to the High Street were not built until 1733–6. In their final form they owe a great deal to Hawksmoor, who was brought in to modify and improve the original design after George II's consort, Queen Caroline, had made a contribution towards the completion of the project. The screen wall, heavily rusticated and broken up by semicircular-headed niches, is an object lesson in how to make a blank masonry surface visually interesting, and the gateway in the centre, reached by a flight of steps, supplies the necessary note of ceremonial drama. It is flanked by pairs of Doric columns interrupted by bands of rustication, and surmounted by a temple-like cupola with a dome shaped like a solar topee resting on arches supported by pairs of Doric columns radiating out from the centre: a bold and dynamic device inspired by the quasi-Baroque architecture of late Roman antiquity. The 'temple' has a commemorative and emblematic function, since it shelters a statue of Queen Caroline (by Henry Cheere) standing on a stepped pyramid. Raised up above the level of the curving High Street at the point of maximum visual impact, the front of Queen's with its domed centre-piece and tall pedimented wings is one of the most dramatic elements of the Oxford townscape. And with the final, belated completion of the east range of the quadrangle in 1756, Queen's had acquired the most consistently classical set of buildings of any Oxford college.

The note of Baroque grandeur sounded at Queen's College was echoed in the new **Library at Christ Church** (see colour plate facing p. 211), which stands on the southern side of Peckwater Quadrangle. Dean Aldrich had intended to place a free-standing block of rooms

The High Street, looking west, with the façade of Queen's to the right and the spire of St Mary's church in the distance

here, with a giant order of Corinthian columns extending the whole height of the building and a balustrade hiding the roof. But the site remained empty until 1717, when a legacy made it possible to start work, and by this time Aldrich had died. The new building was now to be, in the words of one of the canons, 'the finest library that belongs to any society in Europe', replacing the existing Library made out of the former refectory of St Frideswide's Priory and designed to hold the growing number of books and manuscripts which the College was acquiring, largely by bequest. Clarke was brought in to make the necessary modifications to Aldrich's design, and in his hands and those of the builder, William Townesend, the building took on a more massive character, contrasting with Aldrich's well-mannered elevations to the rest of the quadrangle. There were now seven bays in place of the nine originally proposed by Aldrich, and the three storeys envisaged by Aldrich were reduced to two. The Library, like that of Queen's College, is on the upper floor, with an open loggia below (enclosed in 1769), and it is lit by large rectangular windows, with richly detailed Venetian windows—the first in Oxford—on the shorter sides. A majestic line of giant Corinthian columns dominates the main façade, but Clarke also introduced a Doric pilaster order on the ground floor: an idea which derives from Michelangelo's Palazzo dei

Conservatori on the Capitol in Rome. The two orders of columns were made visually distinct by the choice of contrasting types of stone, Headington for the main body of the building and a yellower Burford stone for the lower order and capitals, replaced by Portland and Clipsham stone when the building was refaced in the 1960s. The completion of the exterior gave Oxford its grandest library façade, but a failure to raise the necessary subscriptions ensured that the building remained roofless until 1739–42, and the decoration of the interior had to wait until the 1750s, when more money became available (see pp. 179–81). By this time both Clarke and Townesend were long dead.

Clarke, Townesend, and Hawksmoor were all involved to varying degrees in the design of **Worcester College**, the first new college to be established in Oxford since Pembroke, nearly a century earlier. It was the brainchild of Benjamin Woodroffe, Principal of Gloucester Hall, which occupied the premises of the Benedictine Gloucester College, to the north-west of the city centre. He succeeded in attracting a relatively small endowment of £10,000 from a Worcestershire baronet, Sir Thomas Cookes, and the college was formally founded in 1714. Clarke took an interest in the new foundation from the beginning, and among his drawings in the library there are several schemes for new buildings to replace those inherited from Gloucester Hall and Gloucester College. The original intention was to sweep away all the old buildings and to construct on their site an open-ended courtyard facing away from the straggling outskirts of the city to the open country beyond. Work began in 1720, but shortage of money meant that it proceeded at a pace which was slow even by Oxford standards. The core of the College, consisting of Hall, Chapel, and Library, was not completed until the end of the century, and of the two long residential ranges only the northern one was ever built, leaving the southern range of 15th-century *camerae*—'like so many little colonies', as Ingram later put it—to delight future antiquarians and lovers of the picturesque.

A plan and engraving in Williams's *Oxonia Depicta* (1733) show the College as Clarke intended it to look. Two three-storeyed residential ranges stretch westwards towards the open country from a central block containing the Hall, Chapel, and Library, and, uniquely in Oxford, the Hall and Chapel extend forward to the street, enclosing a small open-ended entrance courtyard. As originally projected by Clarke and Hawksmoor, the entrance front would have been an impressive though austere composition, with Venetian windows lighting the Hall and Chapel and semicircular lunette or 'Diocletian' windows above: motifs which were currently gaining wide currency in England through the advocacy of Colen Campbell and Lord

The west façade of the Library at Worcester College

Burlington. But the design was later modified, and the only part of the central block to be completed in Clarke's lifetime was the plain but beautifully proportioned west or garden front, containing the Library in which Clarke, incensed by the acrimonious squabbles which poisoned the atmosphere of All Souls College, deposited his superb collection of architectural drawings. It is placed over a loggia and, in designing the central pedimented feature with its three linked windows, Clarke took the advice of Hawksmoor, who suggested an arrangement inspired by the Roman Arch of Germanicus at Saintes in France, which he knew through a drawing by the French architect Blondel. For many years the students lived in the old buildings of Gloucester Hall, and the first of Clarke's proposed new residential ranges, on the north side of the open courtyard, was not even begun until 1753. The builders followed Clarke's (or Townesend's) original designs, which were clearly influenced by the residential blocks at Queen's, with blind arches on the ground floor and the windows of the two upper storeys inset into the wall surface. But by then this style of architecture was looking distinctly old-fashioned, and for the Provost's Lodgings and the completion of the Hall and Chapel—projects which dragged on until the 1780s—the college commissioned new architects to make designs of a more up-to-date character (see pp. 182–3, 188).

Classical architecture never succeeded in eradicating all traces of Gothic in early 18th-century Oxford. When a benefaction from Queen Anne's physician Dr John Radcliffe enabled new buildings to be erected around an open-ended quadrangle at University College in 1717-19, the donor stipulated that the new work should be 'answerable to the [17th-century] front already built', and the masons—Bartholomew Peisley and William Townesend—were happy to oblige, even to the extent of creating a completely convincing stone fan vault under the gate tower. But the most striking and original example of early 18th-century Gothic in Oxford is at **All Souls**. This wealthy society was made up entirely of Fellows who, according to Hearne, were 'persons of great fortunes and high birth and of little morals and less learning'. They had long resented the cramped conditions imposed by their 15th-century buildings, and in about 1705 George Clarke, in his first recorded attempt at architectural design, mooted the idea of building a new set of spacious chambers and a common-room on the site of the cloister to the north of the old quadrangle.

All Souls College: plan

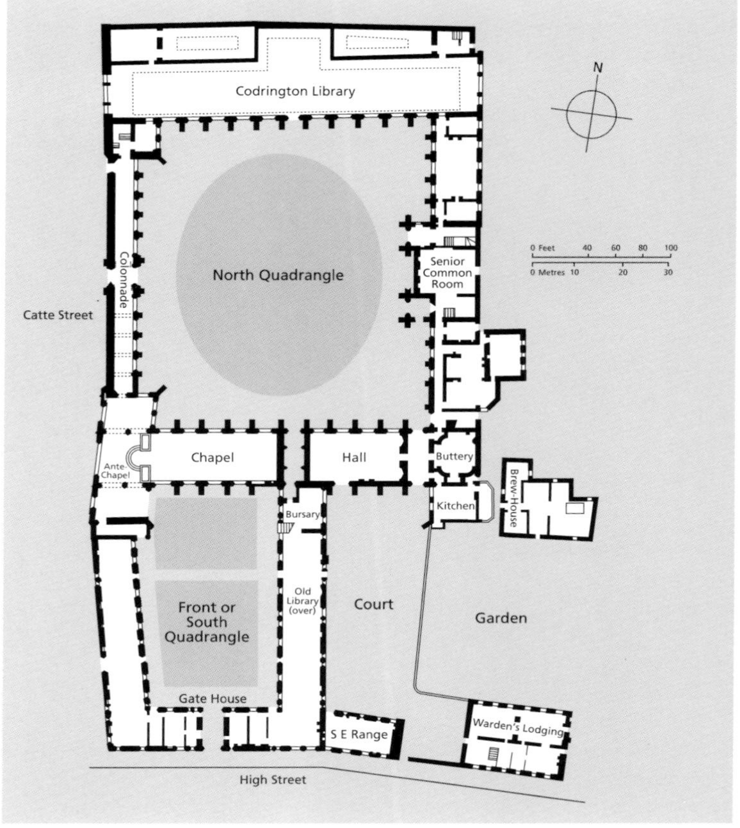

They would be contained in a dignified free-standing structure with a façade not unlike that of Peckwater Quadrangle at Christ Church; it would be linked by covered walkways to the existing quadrangle, which would at the same time be widened and rebuilt. Clarke subsequently solicited designs from other architects, both amateur and professional, including Hawksmoor, who supplied a typically inventive set of proposals, in both the classical and the Gothic idioms, in about 1708. But these plans were all discarded in 1710, when a former fellow, Christopher Codrington, a wealthy West Indies sugar planter, left the college £6000 to build a new Library and another £4000 for books. Clarke's layout was now revised so that the Library would stand on the north side of the new quadrangle, facing the existing Hall and Chapel. The residential block was to occupy the eastern side, leaving just one covered walkway or cloister to the west, flanking what was soon to become Radcliffe Square (see colour plate facing p. 210). Hawksmoor provided alternative sets of designs in 1715, in both the classical and the Gothic styles, but the Fellows opted for Gothic to match the architecture of the 15th-century Chapel, and it was in that style that work began in the following year.

The north and east ranges of the north quadrangle at All Souls College. The Codrington Library occupies the north range, to the left

Like Wren when he designed Tom Tower, Hawksmoor was obliged to use Gothic at All Souls because of the perceived need to blend a new building in with an older structure. In the printed 'Explanation' with which he accompanied the engraved version of his designs of 1715 he proclaimed that 'what ever is good in its kinde ought to be preserv'd in respect to antiquity, as well as our present advantage, for destruction can be profitable to none but Such as Live by it.' But for all his admiration for the existing buildings of the College, his own buildings at All Souls are Gothic in only a superficial sense. Their layout and fenestration is completely symmetrical, their proportions still in most essential respects classical, and their detailing inconsistent and, to any serious medievalist, unconvincing. Hawksmoor's Gothic is not part of a living tradition, nor is it a style with its own rules and principles; it is essentially stage scenery, conceived as part of a wider project to create a new and impressive public open space, and evoking an idealized medieval past in the heart of a University which viewed the recent arrival of the Hanoverian regime with deep suspicion. It was Hawksmoor's understanding of the need for a dramatic gesture which explains his decision to attach a pair of pinnacled towers with lanterns to the centre of the east range, facing towards the new square. Magnificently useless, they do not contain bells, nor do they flank an entrance, like the western towers of great medieval churches which they loosely resemble, or those of Westminster Abbey, which he later went on to build. And in the gate tower on the western side of the quadrangle the air of parody is taken even further, with an ogee-shaped dome capped by a Corinthian capital and a stone pineapple: something at which even late 20th-century post-modernists might baulk. Yet none of this really matters. At All Souls Hawksmoor gave Oxford one of its most romantic pieces of urban landscape, and for this he deserves the gratitude of all who value the capacity of architecture to lift the spirits and fire the imagination.

Hawksmoor first wanted the interior of the Codrington Library to be fitted up in the Gothic style, but this idea was vetoed by Clarke. Most of the Perpendicular tracery indicated in his earliest drawings was left out, presumably in the interests of economy and lighting, and a new design for the interior was prepared with classical fittings and large Venetian windows at the east and west ends, like those at the ends of the new Library at Christ Church (they are invisible from the outside, where a modified form of Gothic tracery was adopted). The idea of designing a building with a Gothic exterior and a classical interior infuriated later generations, but such inconsistencies are unlikely to trouble the sensibility of the late 20th century, and any

The Codrington Library, All Souls College, looking east

doubts are soon put at rest by the nobility of the internal architecture. This was the first Library in Oxford to be placed on the ground floor, and the greater height thus available, together with exceptional length (200 feet (61.5 metres), longer than any other Oxford library) creates a sense of unparalleled spaciousness, enhanced by the decision to place the bookcases along the walls, as at Arts End in the Bodleian; the furnishings and the plaster ceiling were not introduced until 1750–1, long after Hawksmoor's death.

Since the rebuilding of the College was first mooted, it had always been assumed that the building of a new north quadrangle would be accompanied by an expansion of the medieval front quadrangle to the east, making it the same width as the new buildings. At the same time a new Hall would be erected in alignment with the medieval Chapel; Hall and Chapel would then form the south range of the new quadrangle and the northern side of the extended old one. Despite advocating the retention of the masonry of the 15th-century buildings, Hawksmoor's designs of 1715 show that he was happy to contemplate the demolition of the eastern side of the front quadrangle and the refashioning of much of what was left. In the end, lack of money prevented this from happening, and the 15th-century quadrangle fortunately still survives largely intact. But the new Hall was built, and Hawksmoor was responsible for its internal design, which was carried out in 1730–3. In its somewhat severe architectural character it resembles the recently built Hall at Queen's, but there is subtler detailing in the plaster barrel ceiling and the noble stone screen of paired Ionic columns supporting a round arch. There is a contrast of mood in the Buttery, on the opposite side of the screens passage to the east. This small yet impressive room is, quite unexpectedly, oval-shaped, with a shallow coffered dome imparting a note of Borrominesque dynamism. Here Hawksmoor abandoned his habitual reserve and came as close as he ever did to the spirit of the Roman Baroque. At the end of the 'Explanation' of his designs for the

The Buttery at All Souls College

college he had said that he was 'always extreamly Satisfyed when I can be any ways Usful to ye University & when ye Gent. of that Learned Body express themselves pleasd with any of my Endeavours, it is ye highest obligation to me'. So it is fitting that it is his scowling face (in a bust by Henry Cheere) which contemplates the Fellows of the College from a niche at the northern end of the Buttery as they eat their daily lunch.

Even in the expansive mood which gripped Oxford in the early 18th century, few colleges were either willing or able seriously to contemplate rebuilding on the scale undertaken at Queen's and All Souls. Yet at the same time few remained entirely inactive. The most pressing need was for more spacious and comfortable suites of rooms, and this was a need usually met by the simple expedient of turning what had been shared bedrooms into reception rooms for single students, with the former study cubicles turned into bedrooms. At the same time the plaster walls were often masked with wood panelling, and mullioned windows replaced by sash windows which could let in more light. The latter process occurred at New College in 1718–21, and later at Lincoln, St John's, Brasenose (1724), and elsewhere, though at Brasenose it was reversed in the 19th century, when mullions were reintroduced in a fit of antiquarian enthusiasm. The results of minor alterations of this sort can still be seen all over Oxford.

Some colleges found the funds to erect new blocks of well-lit and well-proportioned rooms on sites detached from the older buildings. At **Balliol** a block of rooms to the west of the existing 15th-century quadrangle was built by William Townesend in 1716–20 out of the proceeds of a gift from the Corporation of Bristol, which also funded a number of scholarships to the College, and in 1742 the *Oxford Almanack* depicted a scheme, possibly by Townesend, for incorporating this modest block into an open-ended north-facing courtyard adjoining the older buildings, which would be refaced and otherwise remodelled in a style clearly influenced by that of Clarke and Hawksmoor; these plans were shelved, save for the rebuilding of the east and part of the south ranges of the older quadrangle in 1738–43, and they in turn fell victim to the rebuilding carried out by Alfred Waterhouse in the 1860s. More ambitious schemes were concocted at **Magdalen**, an altogether larger and wealthier foundation. They included a proposal by a Fellow of the College, Edward Holdsworth, prepared with the help of Clarke and Townesend, for a vast new quadrangle to the north of the 15th-century buildings, with a library to the west in the purest Burlingtonian neo-Palladian manner, a style hithero unrepresented in Tory Oxford; this

The New Building at Magdalen College from the tower, with the north range of the medieval quadrangle in the foreground

was shown in the *Oxford Almanack* for 1731. In the end only the northern range—the New Building—was built, in 1733–4, to a slightly modified design. Standing alone in its parkland setting, it has the air of an unusually elongated early Georgian country house, three storeys high and no fewer than twenty-seven bays long, with a plain arched ground-floor loggia and a pediment over the central bays. Yet despite its plainness, it provides an effective and unexpected foil to the profuse late Gothic architecture of the College in which the young Edward Gibbon, who matriculated in 1752, spent what he later said were some of the most unprofitable months of his life.

Another architectural endeavour of the early 18th century was the remodelling of the older college halls. This usually took the form of inserting new wood panelling over bare plastered walls, introducing wall fireplaces to replace the archaic open braziers which had sufficed since medieval times, and constructing new screens with classical architectural detailing. Several colleges also introduced new plaster ceilings beneath, or in place of, the existing exposed roof-beams, as at Lincoln in 1701 and also at Oriel in 1710, though both ceilings were removed in the 19th century, when tastes changed. But at St John's the plaster ceiling of 1730 still survives, as does the marble chimneypiece of 1731, by William Townesend, and the stone screen introduced to the design of James Gibbs in 1742, clearly echoing that built by Hawksmoor at All Souls a few years earlier; the transformation was completed by the introduction of wood panelling in 1744. At Jesus the flat ceiling with its lively Rococo plasterwork dates from 1741–2, and a

The Hall at Jesus College, looking north

few years later, in 1756, the frontage of the College to Turl Street was remodelled in the classical manner. At Brasenose a new plaster ceiling of the usual rounded shape was inserted in 1751, panelling having been introduced in 1684 and a new fireplace in 1748.

The early 18th-century rebuilding of Oxford came to a magnificent conclusion with the creation of Radcliffe Square and the construction of the Radcliffe Library (now called the **Radcliffe Camera**) in 1737–48. Among Hawksmoor's surviving drawings there are three dating from *c.*1713 for the rebuilding of the central core of the academic area of Oxford as a *Forum Universitatis*. They envisage the creation of a public

J. M. W. Turner's view of Turl Street, looking south in 1802, with the front of Exeter College on the left, Jesus College on the right, and Lincoln College and the steeple of All Saints church in the distance

open space between St Mary's church and the Schools, entailing the demolition of houses in School Street and Catte Street, the building of a new University Church, surrounded by a colonnade in the manner of a Greek or Roman temple, and, in at least one of the plans, the rebuilding of Brasenose College; this would have taken up the western side of the new square, facing the north quadrangle of All Souls on the eastern side. Hawksmoor's proposed rebuilding of Brasenose never took place, though his design of *c.*1720, with its heavily rusticated walls and massive Corinthian portico to the High Street, was included in Williams's *Oxonia Depicta*. The new University Church (which would have stood on the site of the present Hertford College) did not get beyond the drawing-board either, nor did a proposed *Forum Civitatis* at Carfax, adorned with a commemorative column. But the square north of St Mary's church was eventually laid out, and, together with that created to the north of the Schools Quadrangle after the construction of the Clarendon Building, it formed an essential part of the sequence of spaces which have defined the architectural core of the University ever since.

Hawksmoor's initial plans show the new square to the north of St Mary's devoid of buildings, save for an isolated column or statue. This was changed as the result of a bequest by the physician Dr John

A cross-section of the Radcliffe Camera

Radcliffe, in which he left £40,000 towards the building and endowment of a new library which would be, in the words of the architect, James Gibbs, 'a publick Building seen by all sorts of people who come to Oxford from different parts of the World'. Building did not begin until twenty-three years after Radclffe's death in 1714, and then only after a several changes of site and plan. The first proposal, mooted even before Radcliffe's death, was to build the library against the western side of Selden End, the westward expansion of Duke Humfrey's Library. This was abandoned because of the reluctance of the Fellows of Exeter College to part with their garden, and it was then proposed to attach the building to the southern side of the Schools. In the end the trustees of Radcliffe's bequest settled on a site in the middle of the proposed new square shown in Hawksmoor's plans.

This meant that the project had to wait until the acquisition of the existing houses on the site, a process which was not completed until 1737.

Meanwhile, in 1734, the trustees decided to solicit new designs from Hawksmoor, together with others from James Gibbs. Gibbs had been trained in Rome, and had designed several important buildings in both London and Cambridge; though a Roman Catholic, his Toryism made him acceptable in a University still notorious for its Jacobite sympathies. His design was for a rectangular library which would have taken up most of the available space. Hawksmoor, by contrast, proposed a domed circular library on a square rusticated base. Christopher Wren had prepared plans for a circular library at Trinity College, Cambridge, which was never built, and as early as *c*.1712, when the Radcliffe bequest was first publicized, Hawksmoor did a number of drawings of a domed circular library, alluding in its form and decoration to the mausolea of classical antiquity (he subsequently designed a mausoleum, one of his noblest buildings, for Lord Carlisle at Castle Howard, Yorkshire). Indeed, according to Salmon, 'whatever the Doctor designed or expected from his laying out £40,000 in building one Room, I find a great many People of Opinion that he intended to perpetuate his memory by it, and therefore give it the name of *Ratcliff's Mausoleum*.' But Hawksmoor died in 1736 before the site had been fully purchased, and it was left to Gibbs to design what has since 1862 been known as the Radcliffe Camera.

There is little doubt that a rectangular library like the one proposed by Gibbs in 1735 would have satisfied the practical needs of Oxford University more effectively than the building which was eventually erected. But practicality was not uppermost in the minds of Radcliffe's trustees—and in its early days the library had very few readers—so Gibbs was persuaded to conform to Hawksmoor's circular scheme, which he proceeded to transform. In his hands the building became lighter in effect, more richly decorated, and more imbued with that elusive architectural quality, movement: in a word, more Baroque. The ground floor, originally open, is surmounted by a shallow dome, and the architectural forms are suitably plain and massive. Upstairs is the library itself, made up of a single circular domed reading-room surrounded by an arcade with massive piers articulated by Ionic pilasters; the bookcases are all placed in the outer ambulatory, behind the arcade, with an upper row reached from a gallery, leaving the central space empty of furniture. As in the centrally planned churches of the Italian Renaissance and Baroque which Gibbs had seen and studied, light enters both through the

The interior of the main reading-room in the Radcliffe Camera from the gallery. J. M. Rysbrack's statue of John Radcliffe (1744–7) stands over the doorway

outer windows and through the drum on which the dome satisfyingly rests. And, as so often in Gibbs's buildings, the resulting effect of light and space is enhanced by the decorative plasterwork, carried out under the supervision of Gibbs's collaborator Giuseppe Artari, with the help of the Danish plasterer Charles Stanley and the local craftsman Thomas Roberts. There is no finer classical interior in Oxford, and few in England.

For the exterior, Gibbs drew on precedents stretching back through Wren's unbuilt mausoleum for Charles I at Windsor to the buildings of Renaissance Rome and ultimately to the mausolea and circular temples of classical antiquity. In essence the building consists of a masonry shell wrapped round the central domed core, but Gibbs's skill in handling the forms of classical architecture ensured that the wall surfaces take on an expressive life of their own. The reading-room is raised up on a heavily rusticated base; huge arches surmounted by pediments occupy alternate bays, with giant empty niches in the intermediate bays; the arches were enclosed when the library became part of the Bodleian in 1862. As in some of the *palazzi* of the High Renaissance, the plainness and heaviness of the ground floor makes a marked and deliberate contrast to the sculptural richness above, and the contrast is enhanced by the choice of stone: the durable Headington hardstone for the base and Burford stone for the superstructure. Here pairs of giant Corinthian three-quarter columns circle the building, irregularly spaced and interrupted alternately by niches concealing buttresses and by the windows lighting the reading areas. Thus a syncopated rhythm is introduced, alleviating the massiveness of the huge stone cylinder. The buttresses emerge into view above the cornice and balustrade; they were designed to support a stone-built dome, but in the event the dome was built of wood, covered in lead, and more rounded in form than Gibbs had originally envisaged.

In commissioning the Radcliffe Camera the trustees of John Radcliffe's will showed a complete disregard for architectural fashion. While elsewhere in England patrons were opting for the prim correctness of Palladianism, Oxford chose for its most prominent public building a full-blooded Baroque which would not have looked out of place in any of the cities of Continental Europe. In form and in style this superb building makes a startlingly cosmopolitan contrast both to the rectangular mass of the Schools Quad and the Gothic spikiness of St Mary's church and All Souls College. Rarely are the Gothic and the classic juxtaposed to such happy effect. With the completion of the Radcliffe Camera the central area of Oxford University achieved its definitive form.

5

A Century of Growth 1750 to 1850

With the completion of the Radcliffe Camera grandiose architecture fell out of fashion in Oxford. Sir Nathaniel Lloyd, one of the main sponsors of the North Quadrangle at All Souls, had already remarked in 1736 that 'Hawksmooring, and Townsending, is all Out for this Century.' With the numbers of undergraduates continuing to fall—by 1800 there were only half a dozen resident Fellows and twenty-five undergraduates at Balliol, to take one example—there was little practical incentive for the colleges to build on a large scale. Oxford had to wait until the Victorian era for an explosion of building comparable to that which had transformed the University in the early 18th century.

Many of the most ambitious architectural initiatives of the late 18th century were designed to benefit the citizens of Oxford. The improvement of the city's dilapidated stock of buildings began in 1751 with the construction of a handsome new Town Hall on the site of the much-remodelled medieval Guildhall south of Carfax. Its restrained design, by the London-based architect Isaac Ware, marked a

Carfax, looking south in 1755, with the Conduit on the left, the Town Hall of 1751 and the façade of Christ Church beyond, and the Butter Bench with its Doric colonnade of 1709–13 to the right

The portico of the Ashmolean Museum as seen from the entrance to the Taylor Institution

The Radcliffe Infirmary in 1885

significant shift away from the monumental Baroque of the Radcliffe Camera and other early 18th-century University buildings; it was replaced by the present Town Hall in the 1890s. Then in 1759–67 Oxford's first hospital, the **Radcliffe Infirmary**, was built on an open site to the north of the city, alongside the Woodstock Road. The sponsors were the Radcliffe trustees and the land was donated by Thomas Rowney, one of the city's Members of Parliament; the architect, Stiff Leadbetter, was a carpenter and surveyor from Eton who was no doubt selected on the strength of his hospital at Gloucester, built two years earlier. Like Ware's Town Hall, the Radcliffe Infirmary is a competent though unoriginal reworking of a common English Palladian model, with a pedimented centre and the main rooms arranged on a *piano nobile*, originally reached by an external staircase which was unfortunately removed in 1933; the wings were given over to large wards, and the operating theatre was on the top floor, together with rooms for patients needing 'stillness and repose'. A new workhouse followed in 1772–5, on the site of the present Wellington Square, to the west of St Giles, and in 1789 a new city gaol went up on Gloucester Green, designed by William Blackburn, and supplanting the ramshackle old gaol called Bocardo at the North Gate (see p. 5), which was demolished in 1771; the workhouse lasted until 1865 and the gaol until 1878. So Oxford, like other English county towns, began to establish the basis of the administrative and physical infrastructure without which modern urban life is inconceivable.

Further changes came about in the 1770s through a series of street improvements, celebrated by Edward Tatham, later Rector of Lincoln College, in his *Oxonia Explicata et Ornata* (1777). Financed by local rates, and carried out by a Paving Commission in which the

Magdalen Bridge, with the tower of Magdalen College before its refacing in the 1970s

University played a crucial role, they reflected Oxford's growing importance as a transport centre on the important turnpike road (the present A40) which led north-west from the capital into the west Midlands and Wales. The requirements of the lucrative coaching traffic led to the demolition of the old north and east gates of the city in 1771, allowing striking new vistas to be opened up at the eastern end of the High Street and along Cornmarket Street. Soon afterwards, in 1772–90, the decrepit **Magdalen Bridge**, which carried the London traffic over the River Cherwell, was replaced by a handsome stone-built structure designed by John Gwynn, an experienced bridge-builder and author of *London and Westminster Improved* (1766). The new bridge—Oxford's finest work of civil engineering—draws on the classical tradition, with Doric columns interrupted by heavy blocks of masonry articulating the piers which support the six arches, though Gwynn's proposed adornments on the balustrade were omitted. The construction of the bridge involved the clearance of some old houses at the eastern end of the High Street, facing Magdalen College, and by way of replacement Thomas Roberson, later Town Clerk, erected an impressive pedimented stone house (number 61 High Street), possibly to Gwynn's designs; this handsome building still announces the eastern entrance to the city centre from the London direction.

An important part of the Paving Commissioners' work involved the removal of the open market from Carfax and the surrounding streets, into which it had spilled from time immemorial. The butchers' stalls or shambles in what is now Queen Street (formerly Butcher Row) were swept away, and in 1773–4 Gwynn was employed to build a new market for the city tradesmen on the site of the present Covered Market. It was rebuilt in 1839 and again at the end of the 19th century (see p. 243), but the frontage to the High Street still exists above the row of modern shops; in its original form it consisted of a row of four houses with a central pediment, built by the fourth Duke of Marlborough 'in conformity with the architect's suggestion'. Finally, in 1787, the 17th-century Carfax Conduit was removed to Nuneham Courtenay, seat of the second Lord Harcourt, and re-erected as an ornament in his newly landscaped grounds, where it still commands a prospect encompassing the house, the River Thames, and the distant city of Oxford. Thus the old idea of the street as meeting-place began to give way to the modern concept of the street as thoroughfare.

The main streets of Oxford flourished as the coaching trade increased. The largest coaching inn, the Angel, was at the eastern end of the High Street; it was later demolished to make way for the Examination Schools (see pp. 249–51), but its imposingly columned early 19th-century coffee room still survives as part of the stuccoed 84 High Street, having been the home for many years of Frank Cooper's marmalade business. Other evidence of late 18th- and early 19th-century prosperity can be seen at 86–87 High Street, a typical 17th-century three-storeyed timber house whose ground floor was remodelled in stone with Greek Doric columns framing the new shop front, and at 92–93 High Street (now the Old Bank), completely rebuilt in stone in 1775 and 1798 for the banking partnership of William Fletcher and John Parsons. Other stone houses survive in St Giles, the tree-lined northern approach to the city. More commonly, as in Cornmarket Street, existing timber-framed houses were refronted with new stuccoed façades embellished with fashionably classical details.

The western end of the High Street looking east, with the frontage of the Covered Market, the Mitre Hotel, and All Saints church in the foreground and the façade of Brasenose College beyond

TO LET
700 SQ FT GROSS
ATHENA

Cornmarket Street looking south, by William Turner of Oxford *c.*1840, with Tom Tower in the distance.

The main street improvement west of Carfax occurred as the result of an Act of Parliament of 1766, designed to improve the western approaches to the city along the present Botley Road. The impediment here was the old castle bailey, and this was ruthlessly bisected in 1769–70 by the building of New Road; even greater changes followed in 1790 with the opening of the Oxford Canal basin to the north of New Road, on the site of the present Nuffield College. The coming of the canal reinforced the industrial character of the western part of the city, still largely made up of picturesque though decaying timber houses, several of which were recorded by the zealous topographical artist John Buckler and his son J. C. Buckler in the 1820s (most have since vanished). Some of the industries of this area expanded modestly in the 18th century, like the brewery of the Tawney (later Morrell) family, whose premises were and are situated in the shadow of the castle walls, to the west of Castle Mill Stream. Here Edward Tawney, brewer and Mayor of Oxford (and ancestor of the historian R. H. Tawney) built himself a handsome red-brick house in the 1790s, alongside almshouses of 1797 for four poor men and four poor women, all of which have fortunately survived the all but total redevelopment of the area.

As in most towns of comparable size, the second half of the 18th century saw the building of a small number of detached houses or

St Thomas Street, looking west from Quaking Bridge, with Morrell's Brewery and the late 18th-century house of Edward Tawney

villas outside the city boundaries for wealthy tradesmen or professional people. One of the first of these was Cowley House, a square and somewhat clumsily detailed three-storeyed brick building on the east bank of the River Cherwell which now forms part of St Hilda's College (see p. 280); it was built *c.*1780 for Humphrey Sibthorp, Professor of Botany, whose predecessors had resided in an official house on the edge of the Botanic Garden. Another riverside house of similar character and date is Grandpont House, built over a stream to the south of Folly Bridge by William Elias Taunton, the Town Clerk. Villas were also built in and near the villages of Headington and Iffley, on the higher ground to the east and south-east of the city. These developments faintly foreshadow the suburban growth which transformed the surroundings of Oxford in the 19th and 20th centuries.

Much of the collegiate building in the second half of the 18th century took the form of completing and embellishing existing structures. Of these the most important was **Christ Church Library**, begun in 1717. Under the guidance of David Gregory, Treasurer of Christ Church and later Dean, enough donations were secured to ensure the completion and embellishment of the Upper Library, and the work was carried out between 1752 and 1762. Like some of the great 18th-century monastic libraries of central Europe, this spacious, festive room seems at first sight more like a ballroom or an assembly room than a place for scholars and learned books. Contemporaries attributed its beauty to the 'taste and direction' of Dr Gregory, but, as in virtually all major 18th-century building enterprises, the final effect owed much to the skills of the craftsmen. The woodwork, including the galleries from which the upper bookshelves are reached, was by two London carpenters, George Shakespear and John Phillips, both of whom had worked on the Radcliffe Camera, and the plasterwork was by Thomas Roberts, a local man who had also worked at the Radcliffe Camera and at the Codrington Library, All Souls; other examples of his craftsmanship can be seen in the ceilings of the Senior Common Room at St John's (1742) and the Library at Queen's (1756). At Christ Church Library Roberts was responsible for the the swirly plasterwork on the ceiling, paid for by the sale of some of the college plate, and he also carried out the inventive high-relief cartouches on the north wall, representing Dean Aldrich's interests in music and mathematics. This is as close as Oxford ever came to capturing the exuberant and evanescent spirit of the Rococo. The Library was finally completed in

Christ Church Library, looking west

A plaster cartouche by Thomas Roberts in the Library of Christ Church

1769–72, when the ground floor—originally designed by George Clarke as an open loggia—was enclosed in order to provide a gallery for the splendid collection of Old Master paintings left to the college by General John Guise (now housed in a purpose-built picture gallery: see p. 314). Here, by contrast, the architectural embellishment was limited to pairs of Ionic columns supporting the transverse arches which divide up the space: an early indication of the austere neoclassicism which was soon to pervade Oxford.

The man responsible for the Lower Library at Christ Church was Henry Keene, the first of many London-based professional architects to be closely associated with the University. His first Oxford commission was the remodelling of the Hall at **University College**, which took place in 1766, but here the style was Gothic. Gothic architecture never entirely disappeared within the University, and in 1750 Sanderson Miller, a graduate of the Jacobite-inclined St Mary Hall and one of the leading 18th-century Gothic revivalists, employed Gothic in the remodelling of the interior of the Old Library in the Front Quadrangle at All Souls as rooms for one of the Fellows, Robert Vansittart. This was followed in 1758-9 by the rebuilding in stone of the plaster fan vault of the 17th-century Convocation House (see p. 97) by John Townesend, who had taken over as head of the family masonry firm: a clear proof of the survival of medieval traditions in the proverbial 'home of lost causes'. At University College the impetus for rebuilding came from Sir Roger Newdigate,

niversity College Hall
1814

a Warwickshire gentleman who had employed Keene at his country house, Arbury Hall, perhaps the finest of all 18th-century Gothic houses in England. Keene's Hall, with its false fan vaults hiding the 17th-century roof beams and its chimneypiece based, like some of those at Arbury, on one of the late 13th-century tombs at Westminster Abbey (where Keene was Surveyor), was no doubt intended to evoke the ancient origins of the society, believed at the time to have been founded by King Alfred. Unfortunately his work fell victim to the more solemn taste of a later generation, and all was swept away in 1904. But Newdigate's other gifts to Oxford have fared better. The Oxford Canal, of which he was one of the leading promoters, still flows, the Newdigate Prize for poetry is still competed for annually, and the two huge candelabra made up by Piranesi from fragments found at Hadrian's Villa at Tivoli, which Newdigate gave to the University, can now be seen in the Ashmolean Museum (see p. 207), alongside the celebrated Arundel Marbles, donated by his great-aunt Lady Pomfret.

Apart from the Hall at University College, all of Keene's work in Oxford was classical in character. In 1766–7 he designed a neat, domestic-looking Anatomy School—now the Senior Common Room—to the south of Tom Quad at Christ Church, financed out of a bequest by Matthew Lee, physician to Frederick, Prince of Wales, and thereafter for many years the centre of anatomy teaching in the University. Not long afterwards, in 1769–70, Balliol College employed him to design a block of rooms known as the Fisher Building on a prominent site at the western end of Broad Street (see p. 227); it was refaced and remodelled by Alfred Waterhouse in 1870, when its most distinctive feature, the Venetian windows in the end bays, were removed. But his finest surviving building in Oxford is the Provost's Lodgings at **Worcester College**. When George Clarke died in 1736 the only part of his grand design for the College (see pp. 157–8) to have been put into effect was the Hall, Chapel, and Library block, and the only room in this block to have been completed internally by the 1770s was the Library, which housed his books and architectural drawings. Chronic shortages of money meant that further progress was slow in the extreme, but a block of rooms for Fellows and undergraduates was finally erected on the north side of the proposed open courtyard in 1753, following Clarke's design, and it was extended to the west by Keene in 1773–6. The Provost's Lodgings stand at the extreme western end of this block, with a monumental west or garden front treated after the fashion of a compact Palladian villa, with a double staircase leading to the first-floor entrance and a lunette or 'Diocletian' window at the centre of the attic storey, under a pediment.

'he garden front of the 'rovost's Lodgings at Vorcester College

Such windows—derived from the baths of ancient Rome—were included by Hawksmoor in his design for the east front of the Hall and Chapel fifty years before, and in his handling of the garden front of the Provost's Lodgings, Keene showed himself to be a worthy successor to Hawksmoor.

A year before he began work at Worcester, Keene was asked by the Radcliffe trustees to provide designs for a new observatory, to be built on an open site along the Woodstock Road to the north of the Radcliffe Infirmary. The **Radcliffe Observatory** was the brainchild of Thomas Hornsby, Savilian Professor of Astronomy, and it was he who first proposed constructing a tower with a large room for 'experimental philosophy', along with lower buildings for fixed instruments and an official house for the salaried Observer. In Keene's plans a central building, surmounted by a tower, was to be flanked by lower wings, one of which would be linked by a curved corridor to the Observer's house. Work began to this design in 1773, but soon afterwards Keene was asked to modify his elevations according to a new scheme proposed by a younger architect, James Wyatt, who had recently

A late 18th-century view of the south front of the Radcliffe Observatory

achieved national celebrity with the building of the magnificent assembly room known as the Pantheon in Oxford Street, London. Wyatt's roots lay in Staffordshire, and his appointment may well have come about through the patronage of one of the Radcliffe trustees, Sir William Bagot of Blithfield (Staffordshire). When Keene died in 1776 Wyatt took over as architect, and in most important respects the building as it exists today is his; it was structurally complete by 1779, but internal and external decoration dragged on until 1794.

Wyatt was one of the most creative English architects of his generation, and in his hands the Radcliffe Observatory (now part of Green College) was transformed into one of the major monuments of English neoclassicism. It is to Wyatt that we owe the strangely jerky exterior of the central block, with the south side—originally the entrance—canted forward, the north side bulging out in a huge semicircle, and an octagonal tower perched on top, capped by a statue of Atlas and Hercules supporting the globe. The tower is clearly inspired by the Hellenistic Tower of the Winds in Athens, recently illustrated in Stuart and Revett's *Antiquities of Athens* (1762), one of the most important landmarks in the rediscovery of the architecture of ancient Greece. But it is by no means a copy of the Tower of the Winds. The sides are of unequal length, and there are large windows through which telescopes pointed towards the heavens. The neoclassical mood is enhanced by the frieze, with its relief carvings of

The top floor of the Radcliffe Observatory

The interior of the upper room at the Radcliffe Observatory in 1814

the Winds by the sculptor John Bacon (who also carved the impressive statue of the lawyer, Sir William Blackstone, in the Codrington Library at All Souls), and by the panels of the zodiac at first-floor level, made out of the newly patented conglomerate known as Coade stone by Bacon's assistant, John Charles Rossi. The former lecture-room on the first floor and the observatory in the tower, with their unusual rib-like ceilings and chaste, attenuated embellishments, represent the finest surviving examples in Oxford of the neoclassical taste in interior decoration.

Wyatt soon established himself as the most successful architect in late 18th-century Oxford. His success, due in large part to his partnership with a local builder, James Pears, marks the final triumph of the professional architect over the donnish amateur. His first completed project was the Canterbury Quadrangle at **Christ Church** (1775–8), on the site of the much-rebuilt medieval Canterbury College, to the south-east of Peckwater Quadrangle. Financed by

Canterbury Gate at Christ Church from Merton Street

Richard Robinson, Archbishop of Armagh, and designed for the exclusive use of gentleman commoners and noblemen, this rather plain, austere set of buildings is notable mainly for its eastern entrance from Merton Street, which takes the form of a triumphal arch, but with baseless Doric columns in deference to the new fashion for architectural simplicity and primitivism. Carefully placed so as to terminate the view eastwards from Merton Street, this monumental archway ranks as one of the most impressive architectural set-pieces in Oxford.

Wyatt's other major new classical building, the Library at **Oriel College**, was hidden away between the College's 17th-century quadrangle and the picturesque assemblage of buildings of different dates belonging to St Mary Hall, then still an independent entity. The Library was built by subscription after a bequest of books by the scholarly and childless fifth Lord Leigh of Stoneleigh Abbey (Warwickshire), High Steward of the University, and work began in 1788, two years after his death. Wyatt's sober and reticent façade draws on the architectural legacy of the Italian Renaissance, with its arcaded, rusticated ground floor—containing the Senior Common Room—and the first floor or *piano nobile* articulated by an uninterrupted line of engaged Ionic columns. As in most earlier

Oxford libraries, the lofty reading-room is upstairs, and the bookcases are placed along the walls in the usual 18th-century fashion, the upper shelves reached by a gallery with an iron balustrade. The decoration is plain in the extreme, but Wyatt introduced an element of drama by screening off the apsidal east end, facing the original entrance, behind paired Corinthian columns of scagliola (imitation marble): a device derived from the architecture of Imperial Rome, and much used by his rival, Robert Adam.

Wyatt was also involved in the internal decoration of several existing buildings. He played some part in 1780 in the creation of the present sparsely elegant interior of the **Holywell Music Room**, built in 1748 to the designs of Dr Thomas Camplin, Vice-Principal of St Edmund Hall; this unpretentious apsidal structure, which could easily be mistaken externally for a nonconformist chapel, is famous in

Oriel College Library from the south

The east front of Worcester College in 1832, showing Beaumont Street under construction

musical history as one of the first purpose-built places for the public performance of music in Europe. Wyatt also remodelled the Upper Library at New College (1778), and in 1780 he transformed the mid-17th-century Library at Brasenose after a gift of books from a former Principal, introducing a barrel-vaulted ceiling enriched with delicate plaster designs, and creating an apse at the southern end; the present protruding bookcases were introduced in 1894. And at **Worcester**, where he took over as architect after the death of Henry Keene, he designed the interiors of both Hall and Chapel, left as shells after the death of George Clarke. The Hall (1783–4) was embellished with delicate, attenuated plaster ornamentation of Roman inspiration, but in the Chapel (completed *c.*1790) he introduced a more elaborate decorative scheme, with an Ionic pilaster order and a coved ceiling of a kind found in some of his country houses, like Heveningham Hall (Suffolk); this was not ornate enough for the mid-Victorians, who employed William Burges to smother Wyatt's decorations with embellishments of extraordinary and exotic richness (see colour plate facing p. 242). Wyatt was also presumably responsible for the decision to omit the 'Diocletian' windows and pediments which Clarke and Hawksmoor had originally proposed for the east or street front of the Hall and Chapel block, thus creating the present somewhat austere face which the College presents to the outside world.

Towards the end of his life Wyatt's Oxford practice was dominated by the remodelling of medieval buildings. Many of these venerable structures were showing signs of age, delighting the ever-increasing number of artists who visited Oxford in search of the Picturesque, but causing anxiety to those responsible for looking after them. At the same time a burgeoning spirit of romantic medievalism and antiquarian enquiry was beginning to transform architectural taste, leading to new demands for stylistic consistency in interior decoration. These factors all came into play at **New College**, restored by Wyatt in 1788–94. Like the cathedrals at Lichfield, Salisbury, and Hereford, where he was employed at exactly the same time, New College Chapel had undergone many internal alterations in the years following the Reformation and again in the 17th century; there was a refitting along Laudian lines in the 1630s, and a new organ, screen, and marble floor were introduced in 1663. Further changes took place as the result of a fifty-year programme of replacing the medieval stained glass in the chancel, starting in 1736. Some of the new painted glass (by William Price, William Peckitt, and Thomas Jervais) is competent enough, but much of it is of embarrassing mediocrity, and even the greatest enthusiast for 18th-century English painted glass would be hard put to it to justify the removal of the original glass of William of Wykeham's time (the tracery lights were saved, as was most of the original glass in the antechapel). The *pièce de résistance* of the new glass was the west window, painted by Jervais in 1778–85 from designs supplied by Sir Joshua Reynolds, the centre-piece taking the form of a representation of the Nativity inspired by Correggio's famous *La Notte* in Dresden; when he visited the chapel in 1782, that sensitive if hypercritical traveller the Hon. John Byng preferred 'the Old high-coloured Paintings, and their strong, steady Shade, to these new and elegant-esteemed Compositions; and, to speak my mind, These twisting emblematical Figures [of the Virtues] appear to me half-dressed languishing Harlots'. In Wyatt's scheme the westward view of the new west window was 'framed' by a pointed arch placed between the two halves of the organ case on the screen separating the antechapel from the chancel. He also introduced new stalls and a plaster ribbed vault hiding the wooden roof, all in the Gothic style, and he uncovered the stone reredos behind the altar, replacing the decayed carving of the niches with imitation plasterwork by Bernato Bernasconi (though without the figures of saints which had filled the niches in the Middle Ages). The effect was highly dramatic, and had Wyatt's work been allowed to survive it would no doubt be recognized today as an impressive example of the late 18th-century Gothic Revival. But, like most of Wyatt's restorations, it fell foul of a later

New College Chapel, looking west in 1814, with the painted west window framed by the two halves of James Wyatt's organ-case. The stalls and plaster roof (imitating a stone-ribbed vault) were also by Wyatt

generation and in the 1870s the Chapel was purged of virtually all traces of his work.

Wyatt went on to carry out restoration work at Magdalen in 1790–5, installing plaster vaults in the Hall and Chapel; at the same time the damaged west window of the Chapel, an impressive Michelangelesque representation of the Last Judgement dating from the 1630s, was restored by the Birmingham glass-painter Francis Eginton. But grandiose plans concocted by Wyatt and the President, Dr Martin Routh, to expand the 15th-century quadrangle so as to incorporate the New Building of the 1730s fortunately came to nothing. At Balliol in 1791–4 Wyatt carried out minor alterations to the 15th-century Hall and Library, adding battlements (see p. 51), plaster ceilings, and bookcases projecting inwards from the walls in the medieval manner. At Christ Church he designed a stone staircase (see p. 113) under the fan-vaulted tower at the east end to act as a suitably stately approach to Cardinal Wolsey's Hall, which was embellished with neo-Tudor wood panelling; the work was carried out in 1801–4. Alterations of this sort were to form a major component of architectural activity in 19th-century Oxford, enhancing the medieval character of the University's buildings and thereby reversing the overwhelming trend towards classicism of the previous 150 years.

The growing interest in Oxford's medieval buildings was paralleled by a new concern for the aesthetic values of the Picturesque: variety, texture, and irregularity. The new taste can be seen in the drawings for the annual *Oxford Almanack*, where allegorical scenes and bird's-eye views gave way in the mid-1760s to atmospheric renderings of Oxford's older buildings, culminating in 1799 in a series of views by the young J. M. W. Turner. Garden design was also transformed. The classical buildings of late 17th- and early 18th-century Oxford were designed to look out onto formal gardens, which by then had become favourite resorts for the townspeople as well as the dons. But with the growing taste for a more 'natural'—though in reality highly artificial—treatment of the landscape, walls and formal plantations were removed, to be replaced by lawns and carefully placed clumps of trees and shrubs. Though there is nothing in Oxford on the scale of the landscaping of the Backs in Cambridge—one of the greatest achievements of English landscape gardening—those colleges which possessed large gardens, notably those to the north and west of the city centre, wrought great changes behind their jealously guarded outer walls. At St John's the wall between the Master's and Fellows' gardens was pulled down in 1778, enabling the area to the east of the College to be opened up, with a lawn overlooked by the Laudian Library and an 'inner grove' to the north, planted with the help of the local market gardener Robert Penson. A similar process occurred at Wadham, starting in 1795 under the supervision of Mr Shipley, gardener at Blenheim Palace (and allegedly a pupil of 'Capability' Brown). Nothing came of plans by Humphry Repton for the landscaping of the beautiful water meadows beside the Cherwell ('Addison's Walk') next to Magdalen. But at Worcester a new landscaped garden was created in 1817 out of a neglected orchard close to the Oxford Canal. Here the man responsible seems to have been a Fellow of the College, Richard Gresswell, and the curving tree-fringed lake and the view of the barge-boarded south range of the medieval *camerae* of Gloucester College from the lawn are among the most attractive achievements of the Picturesque aesthetic in Oxford. Some formal gardens lingered on into the 19th century, like those of

The south or garden side of the 15th-century monastic *camerae* at Worcester College shown on p. 55. The pretty bargeboards and cusped Gothic window-heads date from the early 19th century, when the garden was created

New College and Trinity, but even these finally fell victim to the Victorian love of croquet and the English taste for bare, manicured lawns.

After more than a century of falling enrolments, the number of students in the University began to rise again in the early 19th century. This increase coincided with the passing of a statute in 1809 'prohibiting more strictly than ever residence out of college'—clearly an attempt to reimpose a degree of paternalist control after the laxity of the 18th century—and with the beginning of a movement for the reform of teaching and examinations, as a result of which some colleges—notably Christ Church, Oriel, and later Balliol—shed their reputation for intellectual sloth. The increase in numbers was not sustained, and some colleges were still half empty by the middle of the century; there were only twenty undergraduates at New College in 1854, and most of the graduate Fellows there were still non-resident. But there was a resumption of building in several colleges after the end of the Napoleonic Wars in 1815, and it gathered momentum as the century progressed.

At first the results were architecturally mediocre, especially in comparison with Cambridge, where several buildings of great distinction went up in the early 19th century. Oxford University had no William Wilkins within its ranks, nor, after the death of James Wyatt in 1813, were the colleges prepared to entrust their architectural destinies to another leading architect with a nationwide practice. Sir John Soane, it is true, prepared schemes for the southward expansion of Brasenose to the High Street, but nothing came of them. John Nash, the Prince Regent's favoured architect, produced designs in conjunction with Humphry Repton for a Tudor-Gothic remodelling and expansion of the New Building at Magdalen, but, as was so often the case in that home of chronic indecision, they were set aside. Nash's contributions to Oxford were limited in the end to the design of a new porch and two fireplaces in the Hall at Exeter in 1818–20 and some minor alterations to the Principal's Lodgings at Jesus College in 1815–18; he refused payment for the latter, insisting instead that his portrait, by Sir Thomas Lawrence, should be purchased by the College and hung in the Hall, where it can still be seen. And Robert Smirke, the third of the triumvirate which dominated English public architecture after 1815, is represented only by small alterations to the Bodleian Library and Clarendon Building carried out in 1831–2.

With the leaders of the profession ignored, and the tradition of the home-bred scholar-architect all but dead, Oxford turned to local builders and lesser-known architects who could be relied upon to carry out the work cheaply. They included William Garbett, the surveyor of Winchester Cathedral, who designed the plain though well-proportioned blocks of 1820–2 on either side of the entrance to **Hertford College**, opposite the Bodleian Library in the recently widened Catte Street. Hertford had been founded on the site of the former Hart Hall in 1740, but the new society languished for want of an adequate endowment, and the site—made up of Hart Hall and

A 19th-century photograph of the west front of Hertford College (formerly Magdalen Hall), looking south along Catte Street to All Souls. The two classical blocks survive, but the low wall and the lodge between them were demolished in 1887–8 to make way for the present Hall

some newer buildings, including an 18th-century chapel (now the Library)—was sold in 1820 to the principal and students of Magdalen Hall, whose buildings next to Magdalen College had been badly damaged by fire; Magdalen Hall ceased to exist in 1874, when Hertford College was revived. The only other College to commission a classical building was Balliol, where the introduction of competitive entrance examinations led to an increase in both the numbers and the academic quality of the undergraduates. The new rooms, designed by Soane's pupil George Basevi, went up in 1826–7 on the western side of the garden, which was gradually transformed over the next decades into one of Oxford's largest and most heterogeneous quadrangles (see p. 227).

Most of the new collegiate extensions were designed in the Tudor-Gothic manner, feebly evoking the architecture of late medieval Oxford. An important incentive to the advance of Gothic architecture in 19th-century Oxford came from the decay of old stonework, hastened by the effects of sulphur from coal fires and from the gasworks, sited at the south-western edge of the city in 1819. Photographs taken in the middle of the 19th century show even quite recent buildings, like the 18th-century front of Balliol, ravaged by decay, their detailing crumbling and their walls blackened. Nathaniel Hawthorne found the effect picturesque when he visited Oxford in 1856, but noted that 'the Oxford people . . . are tired of this crumbly stone, and when repairs are necessary, they use a more durable material.' Thus the texture of Oxford's older buildings (although not the very oldest) was gradually sacrificed, a process which has continued down to recent times.

In many of the older colleges the replacement of worn stone was accompanied by the installation of new mullioned windows in place of 18th-century sashes, especially along the street façades, and the addition of battlements to enhance the medieval character. The chief effect of these alterations was to impart a spurious air of stylistic consistency which belied the cumulative effects of centuries of change. Much of the work was done in Bath stone, made easily available after the opening of the Kennet and Avon Canal which linked Bath to Reading on the River Thames (a branch to Abingdon was opened in 1810). Bath stone was used in remodelling the frontage of Lincoln College (1815–19), a task entrusted to Thomas Knowles, who had taken over the Townesends' masonry business in 1797; he also worked at Corpus Christi, Jesus, Oriel, and Exeter. Another local man involved in restoration work was Daniel Evans, who remodelled the front quadrangle and entrance range at Pembroke College in 1829–30; the work involved the removal of the deeply unfashionable

Part of the west range of St Mary Hall (now part of Oriel College)

late 17th-century classical decoration of the gate tower, but by way of compensation Evans introduced a pretty Gothic oriel window over the entrance lodge.

At All Souls the restoration of the High Street front—including the Warden's Lodgings designed in 1706 by George Clarke—took place in 1826–8 under the direction of a London architect, Daniel Robertson, probably a pupil of Robert Adam; he was widely employed in Oxford in the late 1820s but disappeared in mysterious circumstances in 1829, having rebuilt the west range of St Mary Hall (now part of Oriel College) in the Tudor-Gothic manner, and having designed the new Oxford University Press in Walton Street (see p. 199). When he left Oxford, H. J. Underwood, a pupil of Sir Robert Smirke, stepped into his shoes. Underwood first came to Oxford in 1830 and was responsible for the refacing of the Turl Street front of Exeter College in Bath stone in 1833–5, as a result of which repetitive neo-Tudor detailing was substituted for genuine work of the 17th and early 18th centuries (see p. 167), robbing the building of all its texture and most of its visual and historical interest. But, like Robertson, Underwood

was happier working in the classical than the Gothic idiom, and it is to him that we owe the elegant Grecian-detailed library and lecture-room at the Botanic Garden (now the Bursary of Magdalen College), built in 1835 on a prominent site facing Magdalen tower.

The largest and most contentious restoration programme of this period took place at **Magdalen**. Several schemes were considered, including one from John Buckler, bailiff of the College's London property and one of the most noted topographical draughtsmen of his day. But in the end the work was entrusted to a London architect and surveyor, Joseph Parkinson, who reported in 1822 that the north side

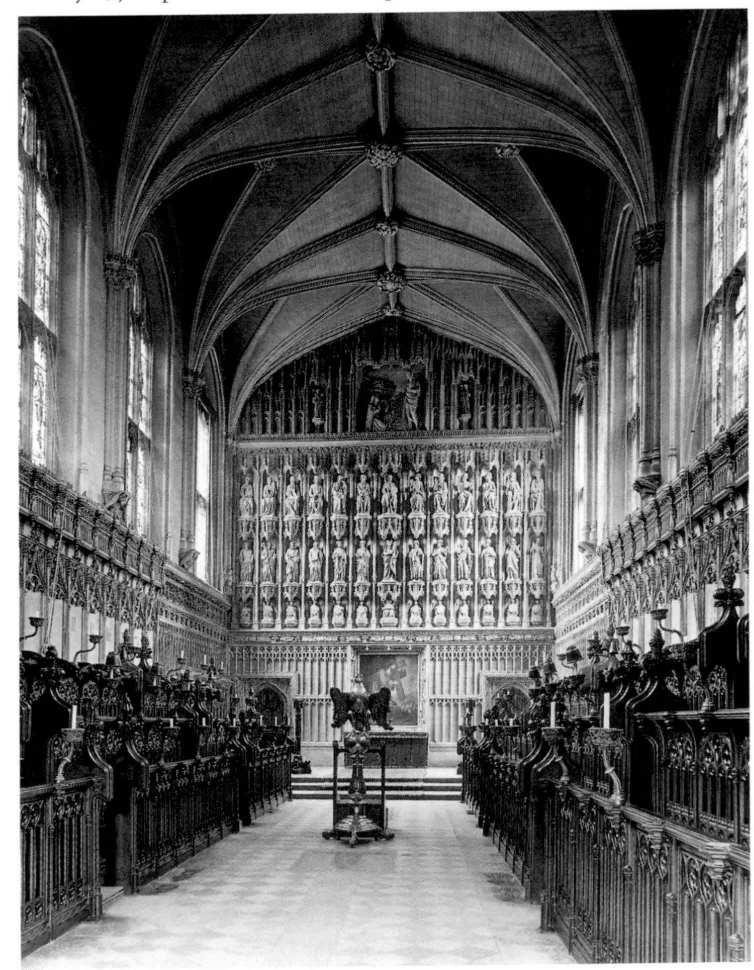

Magdalen College Chapel, looking east. The plaster vault is by James Wyatt, but the stalls and most of the craftsmanship date from Cottingham's restoration of 1829–34. The statues in the reredos were carved by Thomas Earp in the 1860s

Turl Street, looking south, with Exeter College on the left, Lincoln College in the distance, and Jesus College to the right. The steeple of All Saints church closes the view

of the old quadrangle—scheduled for demolition in Wyatt's plan for a 'Great Quadrangle'—was unsafe, whereupon Daniel Evans removed the upper storey. But after the publication in 1823 of an angry pamphlet by Buckler's son, J. C. Buckler, it was decided to reinstate the missing storey, albeit without its picturesque array of post-medieval gables (see p. 165). This alteration was carried out by Parkinson in 1824, and he went on to restore the east ranges of the cloisters, using Bath stone in place of the existing decayed Headington stone, and to remodel the Library on the upper floor of the west range. A competion was then held for the restoration of the Chapel, a process begun by Wyatt but never completed. The winner was Lewis Nockalls Cottingham, restorer of Rochester and later of Hereford Cathedrals and founder of a museum of specimens of medieval woodwork and stone carvings in London. He carried out the work in 1829–34, and his close study of medieval craftsmanship is evident in the carved wooden stalls, the stone organ screen separating the antechapel from the chancel, and the restored stonework of the reredos, revealed after the removal of Isaac Fuller's Baroque paintings. Few church restorations of the period are more convincing, and few are more sympathetic to the architecture and decoration of the later Middle Ages.

Oxford University Press, looking south along Walton Street in 1832

After a long hiatus, Oxford University resumed its role as a patron of architecture in 1826 with the construction of new premises for the **University Press** on a site in Walton Street, well to the north-west of the city. The growing worldwide demand for Bibles and prayer-books, fuelled by the Evangelical movement and the spread of British influence to the colonies, proved a lucrative source of income for the Press, but it also imposed strains on the Clarendon Building, which now became the University's registry. The first part of the new University Press was built in 1826–7 to the designs of Daniel Robertson, and the east front of the new building, facing Walton Street, is his masterpiece: a noble Roman-inspired structure, with a central entrance in the form of a triumphal arch flanked by low single-storeyed ranges ending in higher pavilions articulated, like the central archway, by Corinthian columns. The north range of the building, housing the Learned Press (as distinct from the Bible Press, which was in the south range) went up in 1829–30 under the supervision of Edward Blore, who later went on to add the present somewhat oversized lantern to the Sheldonian Theatre in 1837–8 (see p. 152).

The building of the new University Press occurred at a time when the population of the city of Oxford was expanding fast. With only some 12,000 people in 1801—about the same as Henley-on-Thames today—a tenth of whom were members of the University, Oxford, for all its wealth and intellectual prestige, now lagged well behind England's flourishing manufacturing and resort towns. But the population went up by some 50 per cent in the second and third decades of the 19th century, mostly due to the influx of poor immigrants from the surrounding rural areas. The growth in population inevitably put great strains on the city's existing housing stock, and the problem was exacerbated by the demolition of houses in the city centre for college extensions; one observer wrote in 1831 that houses had been 'pulled down to make way for college buildings, and wider streets and to improve the views. This has made building a very profitable speculation in the outskirts of the place and poor families once unpacked have not been induced to dwell so thickly as before.' The most favoured areas for new working-class housing were in the parish of St Clements to the east side of Magdalen Bridge, in the area in and around Jericho to the north of the new Oxford University Press, and above all in the low-lying district in the parish of St Ebbe's to the south and south-west of the city centre. This district had once contained the monasteries of the mendicant orders; their memory was preserved in the names of the some of the new streets, like Blackfriars Road, which were lined with small, ill-drained, and often insanitary terraced houses run up cheaply over former market

Canal House, with the 20th-century neo-Georgian buildings of St Peter's College beyond and the spire of the Wesley Memorial Church (1877–8) to the left

gardens by speculative builders in the ten or so years after the building of the new gasworks alongside the Thames in 1819.

The economy of the riverside areas of Oxford was boosted by the opening of the Oxford and Coventry Canal, linking the city with the industrial Midlands, in 1790. The canal company fixed its headquarters in a plain stone-faced house in New Inn Hall Street, built in 1797 and known as Wyaston House (later Linton House). It was superseded in 1827 by the Greek-porticoed Canal House, built to the designs of Richard Tawney, the company's surveyor, and overlooking the canal basin which occupied part of the former castle bailey to the west; the house in New Inn Hall Street now serves as the entrance lodge to St Peter's College, while Canal House is the residence of the Master of the College. Traffic along the River Thames also grew, and in 1825–7 a new **Folly Bridge** was built to the designs of Ebenezer Perry, the picturesque gateway on the old bridge known as 'Friar Bacon's Study' having been demolished in 1779. Two years later a new stone-faced warehouse (now the Head of the River pub) was built on the river bank, close to the bridge, and in about 1830 the elegant stone Wharf House (now another pub) was erected a short distance upstream. Much odder than these is the strange crenellated flint-built house immediately south of the main span of Folly Bridge, built in 1849 and known originally as 'Caudwell's Castle' after its eccentric builder, the accountant Joseph Caudwell.

As Oxford's population rose, new churches were built in the poorer areas of the city. The initiative was taken first by the non-Anglican churches. A small and very plain Roman Catholic chapel was opened up in St Clements in 1792, a year after the passing of the Catholic Relief Act, and in 1817 a large new Wesleyan Chapel went up in New Inn Hall Street, close to a building in which John Wesley, the founder of Methodism and a Fellow of Lincoln College, had held some of the earliest Methodist meetings. A year later the New Road Baptist Chapel was built to the designs of John Hudson, the Oxfordshire surveyor of bridges. The Anglicans followed suit in 1820 with a replacement for the dilapidated church of St Martin at Carfax; it was designed by John Plowman, a local architect and builder, in a rather starved version of the Gothic style, deliberately chosen no doubt as a contrast to the plain classicism employed by the Baptists and Methodists, but it lasted for less than a century (see p. 262). Plowman's son Thomas went on to install Tudor-Gothic fittings in the nave of St Mary's, the University Church, in 1826; they included the pulpit from which John Keble preached the famous Assize Sermon, generally taken to herald the beginning of the Oxford or Tractarian Movement in 1833. And in 1826–30 Daniel Robertson designed the aisled neo-Norman church of St Clement in a sylvan setting some way to the north of its medieval predecessor, which was demolished to create the open space now known as the Plain on the eastern side of Magdalen Bridge. The internal arcades of the new church were clearly influenced by the 12th-century work in Christ Church Cathedral, and they impart an air of real nobility to the building.

A very different effect was achieved at the church of St Paul, Walton Street (now Freud's Café), designed in 1836 by H. J. Underwood, and one of the few examples of Greek Revival architecture in Oxford; the Ionic portico, now sadly weatherbeaten, aptly complements the Roman grandeur of the Oxford University Press buildings opposite, to the spiritual needs of whose workers the church was intended to minister. Underwood's other surviving church in Oxford was built in 1835–6 for the inhabitants of Littlemore, a hamlet within walking distance of Oxford to the south-east (and now within the city boundary). It was designed in a plain Early English Gothic style, with lancet windows and a steep-pitched roof, and was later hailed in the

Great Clarendon Street, Jericho, with G. E. Street's St Barnabas school (1855–6) to the left and the portico of St Paul, Walton Street, in the distance

Ecclesiologist, organ of the staunchly pro-Gothic Cambridge Camden Society, as 'the first unqualified step to better things that England had long witnessed'; the tower is a later addition, of 1848. It was from this modest building that John Henry Newman, vicar of the University Church and the most charismatic figure of the Oxford Movement, exercised a large part of his ministry before being received into the Church of Rome in 1845.

The early 19th century was a period in which the social fabric of England came under serious strain, leading to growing concern about crime and public order. This presumably lay behind the building of a new **county gaol** in the castle precincts, begun to the designs of William Blackburn in 1785 and finished twenty years later under the supervision of Daniel Harris, who practised as an architect when not involved in his duties as keeper of the gaol. Though originally an impressive example of the architectural 'sublime', subsequent changes have obscured the original effect of the gaol, and now the most notable feature is a grim stone tower on which public executions took place until 1863; much of the building work was carried out by the convicts. The prison was enlarged by H. J. Underwood in 1850–2, and its ultimate fate is still under discussion at the time of writing, the prisoners having been removed elsewhere. Daniel Harris's

The entrance to Oxford Prison. The outer wall, with its crenellated gateway surmounted by the execution platform, dates from 1785–c.1805, and the cell building visible over the wall was built in 1850–2

The façade of the County Hall and Assize Court to New Road

architectural partner was John Plowman, the architect of St Martin, Carfax, and it was his younger son, another John, who designed a new **County Hall** on an adjacent site in 1839–41 to house the Oxfordshire assize courts, formerly held in the Town Hall. Plowman chose the neo-Norman style to allude to the historical origins of the castle—some gullible visitors to Oxford have been known to mistake it for a genuine medieval fortress—but the symmetrical planning is completely classical and the building has something of the air of a child's toy fort, approached from New Road through pairs of pedestals surmounted by iron *fasces*: the Roman symbol of the civil power.

A certain amount of middle-class housing went up in the 1820s and 1830s along the London Road at the foot of Headington Hill, and also in St Giles, flanking the entrance into the city from the north. But the most impressive housing development of the period took place to the west of St Giles, on land bought by St John's College in 1573, after selling the London property of the founder, Sir Thomas White. The decision to develop the southern fringe of the estate for building represents the first large planned development of middle-class housing in Oxford, and the only one dating from the first half of the 19th century. Most members of Oxford's professional and commercial classes, unlike their counterparts in larger cities, still continued to live in the city centre well into the middle of the century. But the expansion of the professions created a demand for elegant new houses on the fringe of the city, and it was this demand which the new development was intended to satisfy. The land was advertised on forty-year leases in 1820, and the houses went up between 1822 and 1833 (see p. 188) under the overall direction of a local surveyor, Henry Dixon. There were two new streets, Beaumont Street and St John Street, each of them designed to focus on a landmark: Worcester College at the western end of the gently curving Beaumont Street, and the Radcliffe Infirmary to the north of St John Street (now largely hidden from view). The brick-built houses are faced in Bath stone;

The north side of Beaumont Street, looking east

The University Galleries (Ashmolean Museum) and Taylor Institution from the southern end of St Giles

their plain classical façades are enlivened by carved door-cases and, in Beaumont Street, by cast-iron balconies like those of contemporary Cheltenham.

The building of Beaumont Street was followed in 1841–5 by the erection of Oxford's finest building of the first half of the 19th century, housing the University Galleries (now the **Ashmolean Museum**) and the **Taylor Institution** for modern languages. Here, for the first time for over fifty years, Oxford acquired a new building of national, even international, distinction. The galleries were intended to display the University's art collection, which had grown through the gift of the Pomfret (Arundel) Marbles in 1755. The only purpose-built gallery for the display of works of art in Oxford was on the top floor of the Schools Quadrangle (the present Upper Reading Room of the Bodleian Library), and this was coveted by the Bodleian as a space for storing books; the marbles meanwhile were housed temporarily in the former School of Natural Philosophy in the Schools Quadrangle. Those who took the visual arts seriously argued that a suitable new building was essential if new gifts were to be attracted and the study of art fostered in the University, and in this they were proved right, for the construction of the building was swiftly followed by the gift of Sir Thomas Lawrence's collection of Old Master drawings—one of the finest in England—acquired by Lord Eldon after the death of the artist in 1830 and by other donations which have made the Ashmolean one

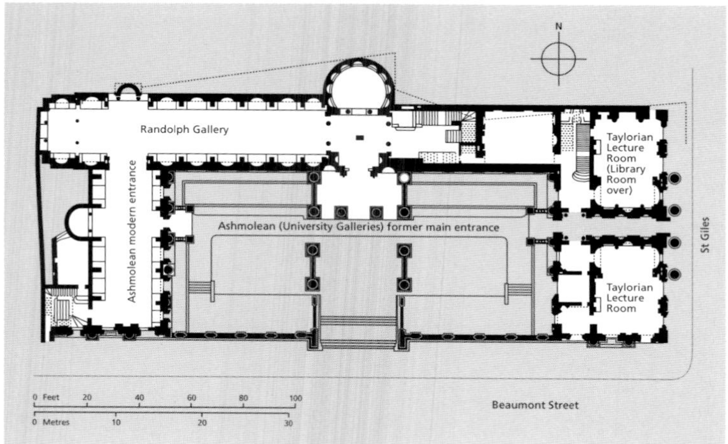

The Ashmolean Museum and Taylor Institution: plan as first built

of the finest galleries of its size in England. Equally important was the legacy of the architect Sir Robert Taylor (d.1788) to the University 'for establishing a foundation for the teaching and improving the European languages'. Taylor's will was contested by his son, but when he died in 1834 the money accrued to the University, and the Registrar, Philip Bliss, conceived the idea of housing the new Institution in a building shared with the University Galleries. Its construction could be financed in part by the profits of the University Press, and in part by a gift in 1797 from the Revd Francis Randolph, Principal of St Alban Hall, intended for the building of new galleries.

The site chosen was a rectangular one at the St Giles end of Beaumont Street, with the short side of the rectangle facing St Giles. On the grounds of both stylistic consistency and appropriateness to the function of the building, Bliss insisted that the new building should be 'Grecian' in character, and a competition was held in 1839. The winner was England's most scholarly and creative classical architect, Charles Robert Cockerell. Cockerell was no stranger to university architecture. He had already produced several designs for the remodelling of the central area of Cambridge University, but they had for the most part remained unexecuted. His Oxford building stands well above street level on a massive rock-like plinth, with a long and seemingly windowless north range facing Beaumont Street, flanked by higher wings projecting forward, lit by very large windows. This rather unconventional arrangement was mainly determined by practical considerations: the need to give equal prominence to the two institutions sharing the building, and the need to allow the best kind of natural lighting for the galleries in the north and west ranges and the Taylorian library and lecture-rooms in the east wing.

Cockerell believed that modern architects should not so much imitate Grecian architecture as 'appropriate [it], engraft it on our wants, and recast it for our necessities'. In his handling of the façades he moved away from the flat and often monotonous neoclassicism of much early 19th-century public architecture to something much more sculptural and expressive, even Baroque. This involved synthesizing elements taken from across the whole range of the European classical tradition: Grecian, Roman, and Renaissance. The unusual version of the Ionic order which knits the structure together was taken from the *cella* at the Temple of Apollo at Bassae in the Peloponnese which Cockerell had himself visited in 1811; later he published a description of it. The order is used in the portico facing Beaumont Street, and it also appears on the inner sides of the east and west wings, and at the centre of the St Giles front, where the four free-standing columns, surmounted by statues representing the main European languages, allude to the idea of a Roman triumphal arch. The plaited decoration of the frieze which runs all the way around the building can be taken back to Hellenistic temples in Asia Minor, and the placing of arches over columns in the wings—one of Cockerell's favourite devices—was derived from a vanished Roman temple at

The Randolph Gallery of the Ashmolean Museum, looking east *c*.1895. One of the candelabra from Hadrian's Villa, presented to the University by Sir Roger Newdigate in the 18th century, stands in the foreground

Bordeaux illustrated by Perrault in his edition of Vitruvius (1674). Finally, the low-pitched roofs of the east and west ranges with their bracketed cornices allude to the *palazzi* of the Italian Renaissance, notably Vignola's Palazzo Farnese at Caprarola. The complex effect is heightened by contrasts of colour, the free-standing columns of white Portland stone—hitherto unknown in Oxford—contrasting with the yellow Bath stone of the walls; the basement, now faced in Portland stone, was originally covered in a brown stone from Whitby.

Part of the appeal of the building lies in Cockerell's exploitation of architectural surprises. There are two approaches, from St Giles and from Beaumont Street, reflecting the separate identities of the Taylorian Institution and the Ashmolean Museum. The first, for the Taylorian, leads from the street through a passageway flanked by Doric columns and covered by a segmental vault; from here there is an enticing vista up a flight of steps to the portico of the Ashmolean, while a side doorway gives access to the beautifully proportioned lecture-rooms and the spacious, galleried, and richly decorated library, one of the finest 19th-century classical interiors in Oxford. The approach to the Museum from Beaumont Street is dominated by the portico at the centre of the north range. On entering through it the visitor was originally confronted by an apse or exedra containing classical statuary in niches, approached through a screen of Doric columns (this was later removed to make way for more galleries). The main gallery, originally used to display the University's collection of casts after the antique (but now housing the Arundel Marbles), is to the left of the portico, screened off at either end by arches supported on Doric columns; it is lit by rectangular windows high on the south wall, following the latest German ideas on the display and lighting of works of art. To the right of the portico is the staircase, cantilevered out from the walls, with a cast of the frieze from the Temple at Bassae (the original is in the British Museum) at cornice level; it leads to the much-remodelled top-lit picture galleries above the sculpture gallery and to other galleries in the west wing.

Cockerell's building was the last major example of classical architecture in Oxford. Elsewhere in the University Gothic architecture reigned supreme, largely because of the questionable but widely held belief that it alone was appropriate to the *genius loci*. This belief was strengthened by a growing scholarly interest in medieval buildings, expressed in the formation of the Oxford Architectural Society in 1839. This influential group of enthusiasts contributed to the gradual adoption of a more robust and archaeologically correct form of Gothic in place of the generally unimaginative manner of the 1820s and 1830s, a late example of which was Edward Blore's

The Hall of Pembroke College from the east.

unfortunate remodelling of the interior of the Chapel of St John's College in in 1843–4. Some architects adopted a late or Tudor form of Gothic, like Charles Barry, architect of the Houses of Parliament, in his discreet but unmemorable block of rooms for University College (1840–2) which took the place of the Three Tuns inn in the High Street. A similar style was used by J. C. and C. A. Buckler in their Magdalen College School of 1849–51 (now the College Library), built to the west of Magdalen College on the site of the former Greyhound inn at the corner of Longwall Street and replacing the old school facing the College, part of which was allowed to survive as the 'Grammar Hall' (it now houses the Home Bursary); the new schoolroom, with its high open timber roof, was lit by large square-headed traceried windows.

Somewhat similar in character is the new Hall at **Pembroke College**, built in 1847–8 to the designs of one of Charles Barry's pupils, the Exeter-based architect John Hayward. One of the smallest and least well-endowed of the colleges, Pembroke had largely missed out on the great rebuilding of the 18th century, but it underwent an intellectual renaissance under the mastership of Francis Jeune, a vigorous University reformer, and in 1845–6 Hayward designed a large and dull block of rooms on the northern side of the garden, containing one of the first purpose-built lecture-rooms in any Oxford college. The Hall, which stands close by at the western end of the garden, is built of rubble stone from Bladon, near Woodstock—a material much employed in Oxford in the late 19th century—and is raised up to first-floor level, like the Hall at Christ Church, with the kitchens placed underneath and a flight of stairs leading to a porch and a screens passage. Externally the various elements of the building are composed into a picturesque and convincingly medieval-looking composition, and inside there is a hammer-beam roof, the first to be constructed in Oxford since that in the Hall at Oriel College two centuries before.

A more prominent emblem of the new approach to Gothic architecture is the **Martyrs' Memorial**, built in 1841–2 to commemorate Cranmer, Latimer, and Ridley, the Anglican bishops who had been burnt at the stake in Broad Street during the reign of Mary Tudor. It stands next to the church of St Mary Magdalen, terminating the southward view from St Giles, and confronting the exactly contemporary Taylor Institution only a few yards away: a vivid reminder of the stylistic rift within early Victorian architecture. The architect, chosen after a competition, was the young George Gilbert Scott, son of a Buckinghamshire clergyman of Evangelical views, whose early career was taken up largely with the design of workhouses. Following the competition instructions, he based his design on the late 13th-century Eleanor Cross at Waltham (Essex), a well-known, if somewhat battered, example of the Decorated style, deemed by contemporary pundits of ecclesiology to be the most perfect of the styles of English medieval architecture; Scott also employed the Decorated style in his rebuilding of the north aisle of St Mary Magdalen's church, carried out at the same time, and in his spiky, profusely pinnacled, and crocketed Memorial he asserted the widespread contemporary belief that architectural imitation is the sincerest form of flattery.

The Martyrs' Memorial is a reminder of the strength of religious feeling in mid-19th-century Oxford, and it was religious animosity which prevented the rebuilding of a complete College—Balliol—by the most inspiring and most influential of all early 19th-century Gothic architects, A. W. N. Pugin. Pugin's ideas about the moral as well as the practical superiority of Gothic over all other forms of architecture found a ready hearing in the Oxford of the 1840s, and in 1843 he was approached by the senior Fellow of Balliol, Frederick Oakeley—soon to follow Newman along the well-trodden path to Rome—to prepare a series of designs for a remodelling of the College

An aerial view of the central University area, looking north. St Mary's church and All Souls College are in the foreground, with Radcliffe Square and the Radcliffe Camera beyond and Brasenose College to their left. In the distance are (left to right) Exeter College, the Sheldonian Theatre and Bodleian Library, and the Clarendon Building. Trinity College and the New Bodleian Library are at the top of the picture

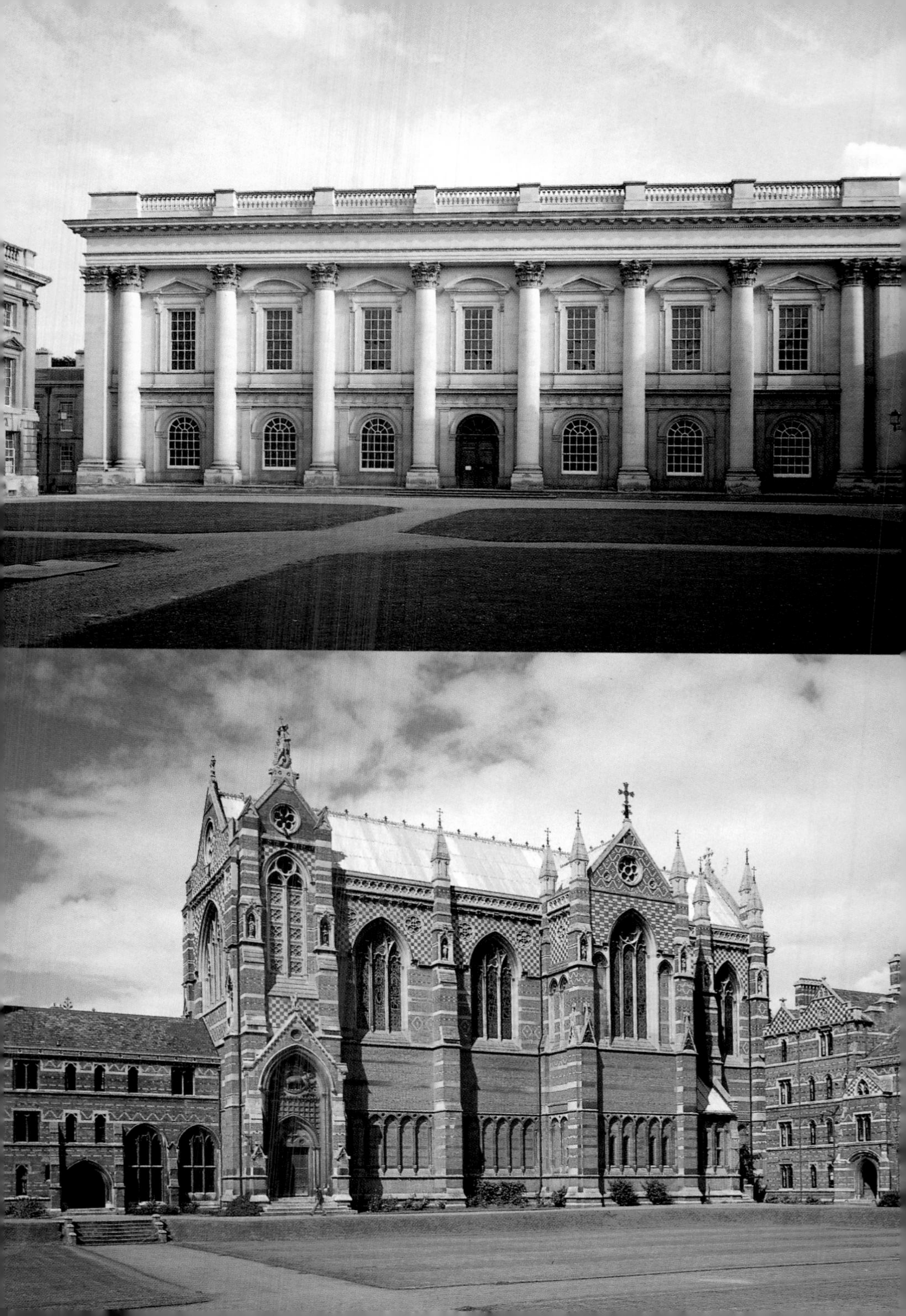

The southern end of St Giles in 1850, showing the Martyrs' Memorial and the remodelled north aisle of St Mary Magdalen's church. On the left is the Basevi Building at Balliol College

along uncompromisingly medieval lines, following the rejection of an earlier and duller scheme by Basevi. Pugin proposed an almost total rebuilding of the Broad Street front and the construction of a new Chapel in the Decorated style; his meticulous drawings, still preserved in the College, also show an octagonal timber-roofed kitchen and an undergraduate's room complete with appropriate furniture designed by Pugin himself. But the scheme was quashed by the Master, Richard Jenkyns, who refused to contribute to the building fund or to let his house—an integral part of the design—be designed by a Roman Catholic, and in the end the only building Pugin was allowed to design in Oxford was a new outer gateway at Magdalen, erected in 1844 through the good offices of J. R. Bloxam, a prominent Tractarian and Fellow of the College. Even this lasted for only forty years, falling victim finally to the present St Swithin's Quadrangle (see p. 247), a building of which Pugin would probably have approved, had he lived to see it. It was not until the 1850s that the intensity inherent in Victorian Gothic architecture was unleashed on Oxford with its full force.

(top) The north façade of Christ Church Library from Peckwater Quadrangle

(bottom) The Chapel of Keble College from the south

6 Victorian Gothic

Oxford in 1850 was a city which had not expanded much beyond its medieval boundaries. Despite the recent growth of the working-class districts of Jericho and St Ebbe's, open country still extended almost to Magdalen Bridge in the east, to Folly Bridge in the south, Osney in the west, and St Giles church in the north. Peter de Wint's view of the western approach to the city for the *Oxford Almanack* of 1852 shows the city's towers and spires rising directly out of the surrounding water-meadows, and in *The Scholar Gipsy*, published in 1853, Matthew Arnold movingly evoked a world in which town gave way to country without any intervening zone of suburbs. This world had already changed irrevocably by the time of Arnold's death in 1888, and out of this change grew the modern city of Oxford.

Already by the 1850s the tranquillity of the city was being threatened by the coming of the railway. The Great Western Railway opened a branch line from Didcot in 1844, terminating south of the river, and in 1850 it was extended northwards, following the line of the Oxford Canal. A new station of the most utilitarian kind followed in 1852, alongside the road to Botley and points west; it survived in a state of increasing decrepitude until 1970. Meanwhile in 1851 the London and North Western Railway opened its own line to Oxford from Bletchley (Bucks), and brought in the engineering firm of Fox and Henderson, contractors for the celebrated Great Exhibition building (the Crystal Palace) in London, to build the iron and glass train shed for their station, which stood next to the GWR building. Fox and Henderson used identical iron castings to those employed in the Crystal Palace, and a similar ridge-and-furrow roof structure, giving the modest building—especially modest since its closure and partial demolition—a minor place in the architectural history of the period; it is now (1997) threatened with removal altogether as part of a proposed redevelopment of the former station yard. Plans to establish the repair works of the GWR in Oxford were formulated in the 1860s, but they came to nothing and large-scale industrialization was postponed until after the First World War.

The interior of the University Museum in the late 19th century

A late 19th-century photograph of the former LNWR station

Without any new industries to attract newcomers, Oxford's population grew only modestly in the second half of the 19th century, dropping from thirty-third in the league table of England's largest towns at the beginning of the century to sixty-eighth by the end, though the population in 1900 was five times what it had been a century earlier. The increase in numbers led inevitably to physical expansion, but the timing and character of that expansion were profoundly influenced by changes within the University and in the social habits of Oxford's middle classes. Despite recent reforms, the University in 1850 was still a network of wealthy and exclusive corporate societies whose main social functions were to train Anglican clergymen and to provide a higher education for those of the social élite who cared to avail themselves of it. Most college fellowships were still sinecures, occupied by clerics waiting for lucrative livings, for whom neither scholarship nor teaching was a priority. Internal reforms, starting with a Royal Commission in 1852, and the removal of religious restrictions made the University increasingly attractive to ambitious middle-class parents, eager to launch their sons on careers in the professions and in the burgeoning home and imperial civil service. Numbers of students began to rise, and by 1900 twice as many undergraduates were being matriculated each year as in the 1820s. Meanwhile, encouraged by the growing desire of the colleges for student housing, the merchants and professionals of the city began to abandon their city-centre houses, where they had often lived cheek by jowl with artisans and the poor, in favour of new suburban residences.

Already in the 1850s detached and semi-detached villas were being built along the Woodstock and Banbury Roads, on the well-drained gravel to the north of the city. The transformation of this area into the fashionable suburb of North Oxford was heralded in 1853–5 by the building of **Park Town** on a long, narrow piece of ground to the east of the Banbury Road, about a mile north of the city centre, originally bought by the Oxford Board of Poor Law Guardians as the location for a new workhouse. Under the supervision of the City Surveyor, Samuel Lipscomb Seckham, a planned development of houses sprang up here for families with comfortable though not vast incomes of £500 to £1000 a year, local estate agents having already bewailed the fact that 'Oxford should be excluded from the advantages possessed by Cheltenham, Leamington, and many other places, where provision was made for parties of limited income'. Some of the houses were detached and semi-detached villas of an Italianate character, each of them capable of housing a normal Victorian middle-class family, complete with servants; at the centre of the development there is an oval-shaped space densely planted with trees and shrubs, overlooked by two crescents of terraced houses faced in Bath stone, with a similar crescent at the far end. They look back to the formality of Beaumont Street, Oxford's most impressive planned housing development of the early 19th century, but the villas with their larger gardens clearly satisfied the growing middle-class yearning for space, privacy, and the

Park Town from the west

Headington Hill Hall from the south

illusion of *rus in urbe*. This was to be the dominant theme in the later development of North Oxford.

Another potentially attractive area for middle-class housing development lay at the top of Headington Hill, to the east of Magdalen Bridge. But here the land belonged to the brewer James Morrell, owner of a sizeable country estate of more than 3000 acres, and in 1856–8 he built a magnificent new house, **Headington Hill Hall**, overlooking the city in which his family fortune had been made. Designed by John Thomas, the architect of some of the estate buildings in Windsor Great Park, this is a full-scale Victorian country house in an enriched Italianate style, with an ample complement of reception rooms grouped around a central staircase and an extensive service wing fashioned out of the existing villa on the site. The house stands on the crest of the hillside, commanding a view of terraces and pleasure grounds—now a public park—dotted with specimens of exotic trees, with a stretch of open meadow land (now South Park) acting as a *cordon sanitaire* between the gardens and the working-class district which was growing up on the former common fields of Cowley. Having been for many years the secretive home of the notorious publisher Robert Maxwell, Headington Hill Hall has recently assumed a public role as the administrative offices of Oxford Brookes University.

In the three decades starting in the 1850s Oxford acquired a collection of new University and collegiate buildings unmatched in quantity and originality since the era of 'Hawksmooring and Townesending' in the early 18th century. This outburst of new building was partly a response to the continuing religious fervour unleashed by the Oxford Movement, but it also reflected the process of reform whose long-term effect was to establish a modern, mainly secular University in which religion was increasingly marginalized. The reform of the University began tentatively with the Royal Commission of 1852, followed two years later by an Act of Parliament which enabled the colleges to reform their statutes so as to open up their fellowships to competition. Clerical control effectively ended in 1871, when non-Anglicans were allowed to become members of the University, and an increasing number of college fellowships were opened up to married men after a second Royal Commission and a second Act of Parliament in 1877. By 1900 most fellowships were, as they have remained, the preserve of lay, professional teachers and scholars. These changes were accompanied by improvements in the system of teaching and by an expansion of the curriculum. A more rigorous tutorial system was gradually adopted, in order to prepare undergraduates for the all-important final examinations, and new honours schools, headed by University professors, extended the range of subjects taught to include the natural sciences, modern history, jurisprudence, and eventually many others. Thus the principle of academic pluralism was enshrined, and has flourished ever since.

The advent of a new era was vividly highlighted by the construction of a new scientific **University Museum** on land acquired from Merton College to the north of the city. The chief promoter of this singular building was Henry Acland, Reader in Anatomy and subsequently Regius Professor of Medicine. A leading light in the establishment of an honour school of natural science in 1850, he recognized the need for a new building in which the sciences could be taught, especially to medical students, and exhibits of 'all the materials explanatory of the structure of the earth, and of the organic beings placed upon it' displayed. There was £30,000 in hand from the profits of the University Press, and a competition was held in 1854, which resulted in the shortlisting of two designs: a classical one by Charles Barry's son, Edward Middleton Barry, and one in the Gothic style by the young and little-known Benjamin Woodward, junior partner in the Irish firm of Deane and Woodward. Woodward had recently designed a new museum for Trinity College, Dublin, in a style based on that of medieval Venice, and, largely through the influence of Acland, his design was chosen, work starting in 1855.

The University Museum from the south-west in 1860. The chemistry laboratory is to the right of the main building, and behind it is the Keeper's house (since demolished), also designed by Benjamin Woodward

Coming only a decade after the resolutely classical Ashmolean Museum, the University Museum proclaimed the newly rediscovered glories of Continental Gothic. Henry Acland was a friend of the Oxford-educated John Ruskin, author of *The Seven Lamps of Architecture* (1849) and *The Stones of Venice* (1851–3), and Woodward, like many other young architects of the 1850s, was deeply influenced by Ruskin's often confused, though passionately argued and persuasive prose. For him, as for Acland, Gothic was more 'natural' than classicism, allowing for the creation of a spontaneous system of architectural ornament freed from the rigid rules of the orders. It could thus be used to convey messages about the building's main function: to display and expound the wonders of the natural world. George Edmund Street, architect to the diocese of Oxford, argued in his *Plea for the Revival of True Principles of Architecture in the Public Buildings of Oxford* (1853) that 'where nature is to be enshrined, there especially ought every carved stone and every ornamental device bear her marks and set forth her loveliness.' And in a pamphlet about the Museum, published in 1859, Ruskin and Acland reiterated that 'all art employed in decoration should be informative, conveying truthful statements about actual facts.' Previously in Oxford, the Gothic style had been chosen for its religious or historical associations. Now it was to be a bearer of ideas about the very meaning of creation: ideas which were hotly disputed in the famous confrontation over the theory of evolution between Thomas Huxley and Samuel Wilberforce, Bishop of Oxford, which took place within the Museum in 1860.

The Museum's bold, almost symmetrical façade, with its pointed central tower, has no ecclesiastical or monastic overtones, and is completely free of any aura of 'collegiate Gothic'. The main inspiration comes from the medieval secular architecture of northern Europe, especially the Low Countries, though the almost free-standing chemistry laboratory to the south was based on the 14th-century kitchen at Glastonbury Abbey. Bath stone was used for the walls, but colour and variety are imparted by the choice of Bristol sandstone and north Oxfordshire ironstone for the dressings.

The carved detail of the main building was delegated to two of the he craftsmen who had worked for Woodward on the museum at Trinity College, Dublin—James and John O'Shea from Ballyhooly. Thus Ruskin's belief that 'all architectural ornamentation should be executed by the men who design it' was put into practice: something almost unheard-of at the time (Ruskin also made a design for a window himself). The O'Shea brothers' carvings, with animals crawling over the pointed arches and the jambs of the windows, and peeping out of the foliage of the capitals, are certainly more inventive than anything of their kind seen in Oxford since the Middle Ages; James O'Shea told Acland in 1859 that he 'would not desire better sport than putting monkeys, cats, dogs, rabbits and hares . . . in different attitudes on those jambs'. Unfortunately the building proved to be much more expensive than originally envisaged and, even though the brothers offered to continue the work without payment, they were dismissed, having in the meantime offended some of the stuffier dons by boasting of having carved caricatures of them between the carvings of parrots and owls inside the porch (the caricature heads were obliterated, but the parrots and owls can still be seen). Although the building was structurally complete by 1860, its external decoration has never been completed, and there is little likelihood that it ever will be.

James O'Shea carving one of the window jambs on the west front of the University Museum

The interior of the Museum is even more remarkable than the exterior. The competition specifications insisted that the exhibits should be placed in a courtyard covered by a glass roof and enclosed by three ranges of buildings containing lecture-rooms, laboratories, and a library; the east side was left empty for future expansion. Woodward chose to surround the courtyard with a corridor on the ground floor and a gallery on the first, giving access to the rooms and enclosed by Gothic colonnades, as in the courtyard of a medieval Italian *palazzo*. Several of the capitals were carved from specimens in the Botanic Garden by the O'Sheas, who were recalled in the 1860s, but others date from 1905–10. The first-floor columns are each formed from a different kind of stone from the British Isles, with the name of each neatly carved at the base, thus integrating the building with the exhibits in the closest possible way. Elsewhere Woodward remained content with bare brick walls, jagged brick arches, and tough-looking wooden furniture characteristic of the vigorous style espoused by many of the younger Gothic Revivalists in the 1850s.

The most spectacular feature of the interior is the glass roof, made by Francis Skidmore of Coventry, and resting on cast-iron columns supporting pointed Gothic arches, with copious decoration in wrought iron. Glass and iron roofs were common in mid-19th-century shopping arcades, greenhouses, and railway stations, and a glass roof had been used in James Pennethorne's long-demolished Geological Museum in Piccadilly in London (1846–51). But the University Museum was the first major English building in which the technology of glass and iron was harnessed to the architectural language of the Gothic. Though on purely practical grounds the roof was not a great success, largely because the steep pitch was vulnerable to wind pressure, aesthetically it was a triumph, with the sinewy curved forms of the Gothic structure strangely complementing the natural forms of the beasts and monsters on display. No Oxford building is stranger, more unexpected, or in its peculiar way more uplifting.

Woodward's other major Oxford commission came in 1856–7, a year after the beginning of the Museum. It was for a debating room for the **Oxford Union Society**, a club for members of the University which had recently moved to new premises in St Michael's Street. Here too Woodward reinterpreted the Gothic style in a highly original manner. The exterior is of polychromatic brick—stone being too expensive—and the interior consisted at first of one large room, three-sided at one end, with an open timber roof, and a heavy wooden gallery around the sides from which spectators could watch the debates. The sturdy, almost uncouth architecture suggested the halls of medieval romance to the impressionable minds of the young William Morris and Edward Burne-Jones, recently graduated from Exeter College and freshly fired by an enthusiasm for the Middle Ages as a mental refuge from the utilitarian modern world; together with their Pre-Raphaelite mentor Dante Gabriel Rossetti and others, they set about painting the upper parts of the walls with Arthurian scenes in the summer of 1857. These amateurish efforts all but vanished because of inadequate preparation of the surface, but Morris later returned to paint the roof, which has survived in much better condition; the room was turned into a library when the present debating hall was built by Alfred Waterhouse in 1878.

In contrast to the excitements offered by Woodward, much of the

The library (formerly the debating chamber) of the Oxford Union

collegiate building of the 1850s was carried out in the unadventurous and undemanding Tudor-Gothic style. Anthony Salvin's northern extension to the Garden Quadrangle at Balliol (1853) is a good example of the genre, with its gate tower satisfyingly closing the vista east from Beaumont Street. 'Collegiate Gothic' was also employed by J. C. Buckler in his new Turl Street frontage to Jesus College (1854–6); following not long after the refacing of Lincoln and Exeter Colleges, its construction completed a process whereby the façades of the colleges in Turl Street acquired a somewhat lifeless homogeneity which they had never possessed in the past (see p. 196). But by the end of the 1850s men like Buckler were being supplanted by younger architects who took a more detached, even iconoclastic, view of the University's architectural inheritance. Like Woodward, they believed passionately in the possibility of creating a distinctive form of Gothic architecture appropriate to the age, and as a result of their efforts Oxford leapt once more to the forefront of English architecture.

Most of the new generation of architects had acquired their reputations though the building of churches, and their initial impact was made through the remodelling and rebuilding of college chapels: something demanded by a new generation of dons fired with the enthusiasm of the Oxford Movement. The new taste made its first appearance in Oxford in the Chapel of Merton College (see p. 30), restored in 1849–56 by William Butterfield, one of the fiercest

The Chapel of Balliol College from the north

members of the younger generation. He removed the 17th-century woodwork, introduced new stalls, and laid a colourful tiled floor; the roof was painted by John Hungerford Pollen, a young Fellow of the College sympathetic to the Pre-Raphaelites. Butterfield's sturdy furnishings still complement their 13th-century surroundings in a most effective way, but his stone and marble screen—dubbed the 'garden wall' by a later generation—was removed in 1960 and his Grove Building of 1860–3, to the south of Mob Quad, was given a bland Tudor-Gothic face-lift in the 1920s, when his reputation was at its lowest. Butterfield was also chosen instead of Salvin as architect of the new Chapel at **Balliol** (1856–7). Ever since the building of his All Saints, Margaret Street, in London, the 'model church' of the Ecclesiological Society, 'constructional polychromy' had been an important element in his style, and the contrasting bands of red Worcestershire and white Somerset stone on the outside of the new Chapel struck a bold and strident new note in the architecture of Oxford. The oddly shaped bell turret on the north side was equally unexpected, and the building subsequently attracted much criticism, like everything Butterfield built in Oxford, narrowly escaping total demolition in 1912; even so, the interior was extensively remodelled in the 1930s, resulting in the unfortunate destruction of Butterfield's woodwork, his colourful wall decoration, and the iron screen.

The most prolific mid-Victorian architect in Oxford was George Gilbert Scott. He first made his mark on the city with his Martyrs' Memorial, but by the 1850s he had abandoned the delicacy of the English Decorated style in favour of a tougher and more vigorous manner which owed much to the early Gothic of France. His finest Oxford building in this style is the Chapel at **Exeter College**, built in 1856–9. Exeter had become the second most populous College in the University by the 1850s, and Scott was first employed in 1854–6 to build a new block of rooms and a gate tower overlooking Broad Street, and an attractive new Library in the Fellows' Garden, lit by lancet windows of unimpeachably 'early' character. But these buildings pale into insignificance beside the new Chapel, which replaced the existing 17th-century Chapel on the north side of the main quadrangle; each of the Fellows donated a year's salary towards the building costs. The tall, generous proportions of the new building were unparalleled in any Oxford college chapels since those of All Souls and Magdalen in the 15th century. As in the infinitely more delicate Sainte-Chapelle in Paris, to which it has often been compared, there is a single vaulted space, lit by tall traceried windows, with boldly projecting buttresses, an apsidal east end, and a spire or *flèche* surmounting the west gable, best seen from Ship Street where it

Exeter College Chapel, looking east

closes the eastward view. The dark interior, glowing with excellent stained glass by Clayton and Bell, captures something of the solemn, numinous atmosphere of the medieval French churches so much admired by Scott and his contemporaries. The effect is enhanced by carved work in stone, wood (by G. F. Bodley), and iron. Nowhere in Oxford has the spirit of romantic medievalism been more compellingly conveyed.

Scott was the most prolific church architect of his day, and from Exeter he went on to restore the Chapels of University College, **Christ Church** (the **Cathedral**), All Souls, and New College. The results, like so much of Scott's work, vary in quality. At University College, where he was employed from 1859 to 1862, his heavy timber roof succeeded in destroying much of the delicate character of the 17th-century Chapel, though the old panelling and glass were fortunately allowed to remain; he also designed a new Library like that of Exeter. In **Christ Church Cathedral** he took over as restorer from John Billing of Westminster, who had carried out alterations in 1853–6, and from Benjamin Woodward, who replaced the east window of the 14th-century Latin Chapel in 1858, filling it with stained glass of Pre-Raphaelite intensity by the young Edward Burne-Jones. Scott was first consulted in 1870, and it is to him that we owe the introduction of the present woodwork and ironwork, the splendid marble floor, the remodelling of the southern end of the south transept, and the rebuilding of the east wall of the sanctuary (see p. 70); the latter involved replacing the existing 14th-century east window with two round-arched windows surmounted by a circular one, thus re-creating what Scott, with some justification, believed to be the original 12th-century appearance. The habit of replacing genuine medieval work in the interests of 'authenticity' was vehemently attacked by Ruskin and Morris, but from a purely aesthetic point of view Scott's restoration of the Cathedral must be counted a success; the effect was enhanced by the quality of the fittings, especially the stained glass by Clayton and Bell in the east windows of the chancel and, later, by Burne-Jones's willowy figures in the east windows of the Lady Chapel and choir aisles. Here Oxford showed itself once again to be one of the main nurseries of Pre-Raphaelite art in England.

The present appearance of the Chapels at All Souls and New College is also to a large extent the result of restorations by Scott. At All Souls (1873–6) he uncovered the long-obscured 15th-century stone reredos and installed new seating, though Sir James Thornhill's screen was allowed to survive. And at **New College**, recently awakened from its 18th-century torpor after the adoption of new statutes in 1857 to become one of the largest and most successful colleges in the

University, he succeeded in 1877–80 in obliterating the work of James Wyatt (see p. 188), still less than a century old. Scott had already restored the Hall (1862–5), removing the 18th-century plaster ceiling and replacing it by an open timber roof of a late medieval type, but his pleas for a similar low-pitched tie-beam roof in the Chapel were ignored by the Fellows, who insisted on an inappropriate hammer-beam roof to replace Wyatt's plaster vault. The proportions of the building suffered accordingly, and the new stalls, in stained oak, and the vapid figures of saints and prophets in the reredos (carried out in 1884–92 under the supervision of J. L. Pearson after Scott's death) did little to improve matters. By the time this extensive and unnecessarily destructive 'restoration' had finished, Oxford had entered a more secular era, and the remaining college chapels were allowed to stay undisturbed for the enjoyment of later generations.

The finest of Oxford's Chapel restorations took place at **Worcester College** in 1863–4. Here too Wyatt was the victim, but Scott was passed over in favour of William Burges, one of the most original architects of his time. The result is one of the finest 19th-century interiors in Oxford. Burges was brought in by a group of Fellows of advanced aesthetic tastes, notably the Chaplain, W. E. Daniel. Like most of his contemporaries, Burges had no time for Wyatt's delicate neoclassical style of interior decoration, which he called 'the vilest Renaissance of George III's time', and in his hands a much more ornate and richly coloured scheme was imposed on Wyatt's framework, drawing on early Renaissance sources and introducing representations of birds and animals to illustrate 'man and nature combining in the worship of God'. Wall and ceiling paintings by Henry Holiday explore the themes of the Temptation and the Fall, the Te Deum and the Benedicite, while the stained-glass windows introduce the idea of 'Christ as the Light of the World', with paintings of the four Evangelists standing guard at the corners. New woodwork was also introduced, a mosaic floor installed (using authentic Roman techniques learnt by Burges), and a splendid marble lectern carved by Thomas Nicholl. Burges went on in 1873 to prepare designs for a similarly extravagant programme of redecoration in the Hall, but this proved too expensive, and a tamer set of proposals was adopted in its place and carried out in 1876. Even these were too much for a later, more timid generation of dons, and in 1966 Wyatt's original scheme was re-created; the chimneypiece and sideboard were fortunately rescued, and can now be seen at Knightshayes Court (Devon), a house designed by Burges. An equally colourful Renaissance-style redecoration of an 18th-century Chapel took place at **Pembroke College** in 1884. This was a modest stone box constructed by William

Townesend, but in the hands of the decorator and stained-glass designer C. E. Kempe—another follower of the Pre-Raphaelites and an old member of the College —its dimly lit interior took on a new sense of mysterious richness characteristic of the era.

In several colleges the rebuilding or restoration of a chapel was accompanied by the construction of new accommodation for the growing number of undergraduates. At Christ Church this task fell to Thomas Deane, partner of Benjamin Woodward, who had died in 1861; his firm was also responsible for several new scientific buildings which clustered around the new University Museum, including the Clarendon (physics) Laboratory of 1867–9 (since rebuilt beyond recognition) and the Pitt-Rivers Museum (1885–6), a galleried iron-roofed shed which shelters an extraordinary collection of objects of anthropological interest. Deane's massive four-storeyed Meadow Building (1863–6) recalls the University Museum, albeit in a coarser vein; standing on the site of a 17th-century block facing Christ Church Meadow, it contained fifty-seven sets of rooms, each with a sitting-room, bedroom, and study. Gilbert Scott's block of rooms for New College of 1872–7 makes an equally ponderous intrusion into the delicate streetscape of Holywell, to the north of the city wall on the site of the Townesends' masonry yard. But the most thorough mid-Victorian expansion of an older college took place at **Balliol**. Here a

Balliol College from the south in 1932. On the right is the frontage to Broad Street designed by Alfred Waterhouse, with Butterfield's Chapel and the medieval Library behind it. Next to the left on the street front is the Master's Lodgings, also by Waterhouse, and at the bottom left corner is Henry Keene's Fisher Building, refaced in 1870. The Hall is at the far end of the Garden Quadrangle

The Hall of Balliol College from the south. The Senior Common Room, to the right, was built by the Oxford Architects' Partnership in 1965–8

gift from a putative descendant of John de Balliol caused the Fellows to revive plans first mooted in the 1840s (see p. 210) for rebuilding the south and east sides of their 15th-century quadrangle and building a new Master's Lodging. The architect was Alfred Waterhouse, best known for large public buildings in his native north of England, like the awe-inspiring Town Hall at Manchester, from which city the donor's fortune was derived. According to the future Master, Benjamin Jowett, the college wanted 'to avoid eccentricity and un-English styles and fancies'—a clear reference to Butterfield—and Waterhouse's design, with its central gate tower, showed a considerable debt to Pugin's abandoned plans. His detailing, though, is less delicate than Pugin's, and his use of Bath stone cut into small blocks and pointed with dark mortar ensured that his buildings, which went up in 1867–8, have a hard, even forbidding quality common to much of his architecture. Carefully varied in height, they dominate the western end of Broad Street and cast a severe eye over the inside of the quadrangle, dwarfing the remaining 15th-century structures (the Hall and Library) and making even Butterfield's Chapel appear smaller than it is in fact; in the possibly apocryphal words of Oscar Wilde: 'C'est magnifique, mais ce n'est pas la gare.' But Waterhouse's buildings clearly satisfied the College, for in 1873–7 he was called back to design a new Hall—one of the largest in Oxford—on the northern side of the Garden Quadrangle. What this impressive structure lacks in decorative finesse it makes up for in brooding power, and with its completion the College achieved its definitive form, which later changes in taste have not succeeded in removing.

Though William Butterfield was passed over for the rebuilding of Balliol, he was selected as the architect of the first complete new college in Oxford since Wadham in 1612. This was **Keble College**, built in 1868–82 on an empty site opposite the University Museum, and named after John Keble, the saintly Anglican divine whose Assize Sermon of 1833 had launched the Oxford Movement. Keble College was not designed to attract young aristocrats or ambitious middle-class careerists; its members were to be 'diligent students living simply', many of whom, it was hoped, would enter the Anglican priesthood. This was a conscious revival of the medieval ideal of a college of poor scholars, an idea close to the heart of the founders of the Oxford Movement. The choice of Butterfield as architect stemmed from his reputation as a staunch High Churchman and builder of Anglican churches and educational establishments over a period of thirty years. As his Chapel at Balliol had showed, he was no tame copyist, and at Keble he showed a disregard for convention and the *genius loci* which has never been forgiven by those who equate good architecture with 'good taste'. The result is one of the most startling, yet also one of the most impressive, buildings of the Gothic Revival.

The most radical deviation from hallowed Oxford tradition came with Butterfield's decision to use brick in place of stone as the main building material, and for this decision he believed that no apology was needed:

> I set small store by popularity, and intend, as long as I continue to work, to take the responsibility of thinking for myself and to use the materials which this locality and this age supply, without caring to ascertain first whether any course is to find immediate favour or not . . . The older Oxford colleges were of bad local stone, and there was not brick to be had. Oxford has nowadays brick, but not stone.

The brickwork at Keble was handled in a dazzling display of polychromy, with patterns of blue and white brick enlivening the red walls, and chequered decoration of brick and stone adorning some of the gables: something for which there was ample medieval precedent not only in Germany and northern Italy, but also in England. Only by drawing on such disparate sources, Butterfield believed, could the Gothic style be properly adapted to the needs of the modern world.

The dominant building is the Chapel (see colour plate facing p. 211),

The chancel of Keble College Chapel

with its bold buttresses, thrusting pinnacles, and jagged spiky skyline It was built in 1873–6 out of funds contributed by the Anglo-Catholic Gibbs family, merchant bankers from Bristol whose fortune had been based on the import of guano from South America for use as fertilizer; their generosity ensured that no expense was spared either in the embellishment of the exterior or in the decoration of the interior. Like the Chapel at Exeter College, it is a tall vaulted building without internal partitions, but in its design Butterfield drew inspiration from Italy rather than France. The windows, filled with stained glass by one of his favourite craftsmen, Alexander Gibbs, are placed high on the walls, as in the upper church of S. Francesco at Assisi, allowing for the introduction of a band of mosaic panels (also by Gibbs) depicting, in a somewhat crude and naïve fashion, scenes from the Old Testament prefiguring the Christian revelation. Colour is omnipresent, as it was in the great medieval churches in their heyday: in the windows, the patterning of the walls, the mosaics, the alabaster reredos, the floor tiles, and in the tiles behind the blind Gothic arcade below the mosaics. And to emphasize the central importance of the Eucharist, so important in Anglo-Catholic worship, the altar is raised up on steps, and the not very comfortable seating—designed, like all the fittings, by Butterfield—is arranged in rows facing forward, as in a normal church, thus breaking deliberately with the communal cosiness of the traditional college chapel.

Butterfield also radically rethought the overall layout and internal design of the College. The entrance lodge is placed opposite the eastern end of the Hall and Library block which separates the main quadrangle from the smaller Liddon Quadrangle to the south, and for the first time in Oxford, the undergraduates' rooms were placed not around staircases but along corridors: an economical arrangement thought appropriate for the simple life envisaged by the founders. They take up the east and west sides of the main quadrangle, with ranks of chimneystacks and low towers for the staircases to add a note of picturesque variety. The south range, facing the Chapel, is horizontal in emphasis, with a long, unbroken, pitched roof covering the Hall and Library; they are placed at first-floor level, with common-rooms underneath and an internal staircase lit by a huge oriel window in the centre, imparting an almost Baroque sense of drama to the approach. In 1877, when the building was nearing completion, the Balliol-educated Gerard Manley Hopkins wrote to Butterfield, hoping that 'you will long continue to work out your beautiful and original style. I do not think this generation will ever much admire it. They do not understand how to look at a Pointed building as a whole, having a single form governing it throughout . . . They like it to be a sort of

The landing at the top of the Hall and Library staircase at Keble College

farmyard, a medley of ricks and roofs and dovecots.' The architects of the next generation were to prove the truth of this observation.

The architecture of Keble College and the University Museum is echoed, albeit in less insistent tones, in the suburban housing of North Oxford. In 1854 the University bought from Merton College a large tract of land north of the University Museum, long used as a 'public walk'. In the 1860s it was laid out as the University Parks, with paths, flower-beds, and carefully planted trees to the designs of James Bateman, graduate of Magdalen College and creator of the extraordinary garden at Biddulph Grange, Staffordshire. In many Victorian towns the creation of a public park was accompanied by the development of the surrounding land for middle-class housing, and this proved to be the case with the University Parks. The land to the north belonged to St John's College, and in 1855 an Act of Parliament was passed, allowing the College to develop its estate on building leases. This gave the signal for the creation of one of the most successful middle-class housing developments in Victorian England.

As in most planned suburbs, the building of the first houses was accompanied by the construction of a church. The architect, George Edmund Street, was architect to the diocese of Oxford, in which capacity he had already designed the former St Barnabas school (1855–6) in Great Clarendon Street, Jericho (see p. 202), and the former school in Paradise Square, St Ebbe's (1858). He occupied an office in Beaumont Street in the 1850s, into which he had taken the young Philip Webb and William Morris as pupils, and, like others of his generation, he admired the bold, powerful, sculptural effects of early French Gothic architecture. The church of **St Philip and St James**, Woodstock Road (1860–5), makes full use of the expressive

St Philip and St James church, Woodstock Road, from the west

The Norham Manor estate as conceived by William Wilkinson *c.*1860. The University Parks are in the foreground, with Banbury Road to the left

potential of this style. It is built of rugged-looking rubble stone, with plate-traceried windows seemingly punched out of the surfaces, and there is a superb tower and broach spire over the crossing. Inside, the effect is dark, rich, and spacious (most of the original fittings were removed when the building became the Oxford Centre for Mission Studies in 1983). The increasingly ritualistic worship of the period demanded a chancel clearly demarcated from the rest of the church, but equally clearly visible from it, so the nave is unusually wide, lit by clerestory windows of different shapes, and is separated from the narrow aisles by low, stumpy, marble columns with carved capitals supporting very wide pointed arches; at the east end the walls are canted inwards to focus attention on the raised apsidal chancel, which is vaulted and lit by large bar-traceried windows. This magnificent building, like the Chapels of Exeter and Keble Colleges, can vie with any of Oxford's medieval churches.

By the time St Philip and St James was finished the first houses on the **North Oxford** estate were already occupied. The land was divided into two portions: Walton Manor, west of Woodstock Road, for which a plan was prepared in 1860 by Samuel Lipscomb Seckham, the builder of Park Town; and Norham Manor estate, to the north of the University Parks, where the layout was entrusted to William Wilkinson, the son of a builder from Witney, who came in Oxford in

1856 and succeeded J. C. Buckler as architect to the local Police Committee. Wilkinson was an enthusiast for Gothic architecture, and a bird's-eye view of the Norham Manor estate prepared in about 1860 shows irregular Gothic and Italianate villas dotted around an extensively planted landscape crossed by winding roads. Though development was slow—only thirty-seven houses had been built by 1866—it was eventually built up along the lines envisaged by Wilkinson, and by the mid-1860s he had replaced Seckham as architect for Walton Manor too. As supervising architect to St John's College, his influence can thus be seen over the whole of the southern part of the North Oxford estate.

The first occupants of the new houses were drawn mainly from the richer tradespeople of the city, with a sprinkling of clergymen, University professors—who had always been allowed to marry—and women living on private incomes. By 1890, following the relaxation of celibacy rules for college Fellows, there were sixty or so dons living on the estate, but there were also many newcomers from outside Oxford, attracted by the social cachet of the burgeoning suburb and the increasing presence of good schools. In 1897 John Meade Falkner in his *History of Oxfordshire* wrote: 'Instead of being a University pure and simple, with just so much of town attached as was sufficient to minister to University wants, [Oxford] has become to some extent a residential resort to which a great many are attached who have no ostensible connection with the University at all.' The residents shared a way of life which presupposed the presence of three or four living-in servants in each house, with two and sometimes three large reception rooms, four or five bedrooms for family and guests, and a large garden. And middle-class incomes were high enough, and prices low enough, to ensure that houses built according to these generous standards remained in demand down to the First World War.

The largest houses were purpose-built for clients who selected their own architects. These were not the well-known London names who were currently monopolizing work in the University and colleges. Several of the earliest houses were designed by Wilkinson himself, and he illustrated some of them in his *English Country Houses* (1870). The remainder were by locally based architects like E. G. Bruton, Surveyor to the Dean and Chapter of Christ Church and later to Oxford City Council, and Charles Buckeridge, a pupil of Gilbert Scott who settled in Oxford in 1856 and built up a large practice specializing in churches and schools. Two of the largest and most eccentric houses, 56 and 58 Banbury Road (1865–6), were designed by John Gibbs, the architect of Banbury Cross; their first occupants were a chemist and a draper. Everywhere yellow or red brick was used in place of the Bath stone and stucco facings of Park Town, with stonework limited to carved detail, and great store was set by originality and individuality. Gables, porches, turrets, and bay windows proliferate, as in Benjamin Woodward's spiky, Germanic-looking house for the curator of the University Museum (now demolished), and there is much inventive 'Ruskinian' Gothic detailing, like the carvings of animals, allegedly by John Hungerford Pollen, around the doorway of 62 Banbury Road—now the University's Department of Earth Sciences—built to Bruton's designs in 1864–5 for the vicar of St Mary Magdalen's church.

Carving over the doorway of number 62 Banbury Road

Most of the houses were built speculatively by developers, St John's College carefully controlling their construction and ensuring that noxious trades were excluded and poorer inhabitants kept at bay. Several are semi-detached, with the kitchens and services placed in a basement underneath the main reception rooms and the Gothic detailing pared down to a minimum. Many of these houses were designed by Wilkinson's pupil Frederick Codd, who eventually succeeded Seckham as City Surveyor; he was the designer of, *inter alia*, number 2 Bradmore Road, home of the arch-aesthete Walter Pater, a Fellow of Brasenose College. The houses became progressively smaller on the western fringe of the estate, and in

Holy Trinity Convent, Woodstock Road (now St Antony's College). The church of St Philip and St James is to the left

1870–5 some attractive rows of artisan terraced houses were built in Kingston Road, the northern continuation of Walton Street, by Wilkinson's nephew C. C. Rolfe; they have Gothic doorways, and the upper windows are set within gables enlivened by mock half-timbering.

Numbers 13 and 14 Bradmore Road, by Frederick Codd, built in 1872 and 1874

An important part of the character of North Oxford derives from its religious and educational buildings. The Oxford Movement opened the way to the establishment of Anglican religious communities in the city, and in 1864 Marian Hughes, the first woman to take religious vows in the Church of England since the Reformation, founded the Convent of the Holy Trinity on a site to the south of St Philip and St James's church in the Woodstock Road. The architect was Charles Buckeridge, and his first scheme was a highly original attempt to express the doctrine of the Holy Trinity in architectural form: triangular in plan, with three curved ranges encircling a centrally planned chapel joined by corridors to circular rooms at the corners. This plan was abandoned in favour of a more conventional one with two ranges of residential buildings extending back from the entrance range to enfold the chapel, and the buildings went up in 1866–8. The south range was devoted to the nuns, but the northern part of the building was largely given over to educational purposes, with a schoolroom for children of the 'industrial classes'; two other schoolrooms, carefully graded according to social rank, along with an orphanage, were built in the grounds. Buckeridge's architecture is a tough and uncompromising, almost brutal, expression of the early Gothic style, chosen to complement Street's adjacent church. The gabled walls of rubble stone from Kirtlington, a few miles north of the city, are punctuated by lancet windows arranged in groups of twos and threes, and there is scarcely any decorative carving. The spacious, beautifully proportioned chapel was built in 1891, after Buckeridge's death, under the supervision of John Loughborough Pearson, one of the greatest architects of the Gothic Revival; with its plain lancet windows and quadripartite stone vault, it remains true to the spirit of early French Gothic architecture, and now serves as the Library of St Antony's College, which took over the convent's buildings in 1950 (see p. 321).

The largest school in North Oxford is St Edward's School for boys, built in 1873–81 on the edge of the hamlet of Summertown, to the north of the St John's College estate. The architect was William Wilkinson, and the original buildings, all in a somewhat coarse version of the early Gothic style, are grouped around a large windswept quadrangle; they include a hall and an appropriately 'muscular' chapel, with a tall tower. St Edward's was a brainchild of the Revd Thomas Chamberlain, the Anglo-Catholic vicar of St Thomas's church, and he also founded St Anne's school for girls, which moved in 1872 to Rewley House (now the University's Department for Continuing Education and Kellogg College), a dour set of brick buildings in Wellington Square, to the west of St Giles. The architect was E. G. Bruton, who had recently, in his capacity as City Architect, laid out the square itself—Oxford's largest surviving residential square—on the site of the city's 18th-century workhouse; earlier plans for building a Roman Catholic oratory here were dashed by the papacy's unwillingness to encourage Catholics to attend the University. Meanwhile, a new and larger workhouse (since demolished) was built to the north of Cowley Road.

With the commercial and professional middle classes—at the most a fifth of the city's population—ensconced in North Oxford, and to a lesser extent in and around the Iffley Road, the low-lying areas to the west, north-west, south, and east of the city centre were gradually colonized by those on smaller incomes. Until the middle of the 19th century the workers of Oxford had lived close to their work, many of them in the parishes of St Ebbe's and St Thomas's, where workers and tradesmen had resided ever since the Middle Ages. But by 1850 the population of the central districts (including St Ebbe's and St Thomas's) had virtually reached its peak, and by 1881 it had been overtaken by that of the outlying parishes. With overcrowding and lack of sanitation rife, the first attempts were made to improve housing in the close-packed districts to the south and west of the city centre, and in 1866 a three-storeyed brick block of thirty tenements known as Christ Church Model Dwellings (now Christ Church Old Buildings) went up in the Hamel, near Morrell's Brewery, to the

Christ Church Old Buildings, the Hamel

designs of the ubiquitous E. G. Bruton: Oxford's only surviving example of this type of housing. Outside the central areas, new working-class housing took the form of two-storeyed brick terraces of the 'two up and two down' variety, their monotony often redeemed by the attractive chequerboard patterning of the brickwork. Many houses of this kind were built in the 1850s and 1860s at Osney, to the west of the site of the long-vanished Oseney Abbey; beyond St Clement's, between the Cowley and Iffley Roads, following the enclosure of the parish of Cowley in 1853; and in Jericho, to the north of the University Press. The initiative was taken by small speculators, often local tradesmen or college servants who then lived on the letting income. It was no doubt this kind of building which Gerard Manley Hopkins had in mind when he referred (in his poem 'Duns Scotus's Oxford') to Oxford's 'base and brickish skirt', which 'sours / That neighbour-nature thy grey beauty is grounded / Best in'.

While Oxford expanded, the spiritual needs of the poor were not neglected. St Ebbe's church was enlarged by G. E. Street in 1862, and in the same year the picturesque though much altered medieval church of St Aldate, opposite Christ Church, was totally rebuilt in the Decorated style by J. T. Christopher, a cousin of the rector. These churches were (and are) strongly Evangelical in character, but it was Anglo-Catholicism which became most strongly established in the new working-class suburbs: in the church of St Frideswide, Botley Road (1872), an uncharacteristically sober (and unfinished) work by the normally eccentric S. S. Teulon; and in the large and impressive St Mary and St John, Cowley Road, built in 1883 to the French Gothic designs of A. Mardon Mowbray, a pupil of Charles Buckeridge who later went on to build the equally spacious, but never finished, church of St Michael, Summertown (1909).

St Barnabas church and Cardigan Street, Jericho, looking east

But the most impressive monument to the Anglo-Catholic mission to Oxford's working class is the church of **St Barnabas**, whose Italianate tower still dominates Jericho. It was built in 1869–72 at the expense of Thomas Combe, Printer to the University, a zealous High Churchman and a notable collector of Pre-Raphaelite pictures, including Holman Hunt's *Light of the World*, now in Keble College Chapel (others are on display in the Ashmolean Museum). The architect, Arthur Blomfield, had already in 1864 designed the conventionally Gothic Radcliffe Infirmary chapel, but at St Barnabas, with Combe's active support, he adopted a style which can best be called Early Christian, combining, in his own words, 'the greatest economy with the greatest strength and durability, and in total disregard of all conventional notions as to fitness and external appearance'. The Early Christian style was cheaper than Gothic, since it did not require the expensive carved ornament without which Gothic architecture becomes dull and lifeless; it also emphasized the continuity of the Church of England with the primitive Church, something which lay at the core of Anglo-Catholic doctrine. The church is built not of brick or stone but of 'rubble-work of local stone set in a mortar composed of blue lias lime and very coarse sand, forming a sort of fine concrete', coated externally in Portland cement. It follows the basilican plan, with an aisled and clerestoried nave and a shallow apse containing the high altar, and another apse at the west end for the baptistery; the choir, surrounded by low walls, is brought forward into the nave, allowing the congregation close visual contact with the services. Though the interior decoration was not begun until 1893, and was never completed in full, it still conveys something of the passionate intensity of belief which sustained the pioneers of the Oxford Movement. And from the outside the church, on its marshy site next to the Oxford Canal, succeeds in evoking the melancholy glories of Torcello and Ravenna.

Spurred perhaps by the spate of Anglican church building, the Roman Catholics made their first significant architectural statement in Oxford since the Reformation with the church of **St Aloysius**, built

St Aloysius church, Woodstock Road, looking east

in 1873–5 on a site given by a notable recent convert, the Marquess of Bute, to the south of the Radcliffe Infirmary. The architect, Joseph Hansom, was the designer of many Roman Catholic churches, including the splendid French Gothic St Philip Neri (now the Roman Catholic Cathedral) at Arundel (Sussex). St Aloysius also draws on France for its inspiration, with its tall, aisled nave, apsidal chancel, lancet windows in the clerestory, and rose window in the east wall facing the Woodstock Road; the chief point of interest internally is the elaborately carved reredos made up of two layers of niches enclosing effigies of saints. But funds were limited, a dull yellow brick was chosen for the walls, and the internal effect is somewhat lacking in warmth, especially since the removal of much of the painted decoration during the 1960s.

As Oxford's population grew, the centre of the city was gradually transformed. With the middle-class residents decamping to the suburbs, the way lay open for large-scale commercial and academic redevelopment: something which has gone on intermittently ever

The Chapel of Worcester College looking east

O YE PRIESTS OF THE LORD BLESS YE THE LORD

The Randolph Hotel with the Martyrs' Memorial to the left

since the 1860s. The process began with the construction of William Wilkinson's mammoth **Randolph Hotel** (1863–6) at the eastern end of Beaumont Street, facing the Ashmolean Museum. This was a new type of hotel for Oxford, large and luxurious, with rooms for 68 guests: an assertively uncompromising symbol of the transition from the coaching age to the age of the railway. Four storeys high plus attics, it is built of yellow brick, with Gothic detailing—especially stiff-leaf capitals of the kind found all over North Oxford—and a high-pitched roof which has unfortunately lost its spiky iron cresting. Its ponderous bulk and lumpish form expose Wilkinson's limitations as an architect, but the interior, with its vaulted vestibule, vertiginous staircase, and spacious, high-ceilinged dining-room and drawing-rooms, is brashly impressive. Wilkinson went on in 1864 to build new premises in Cornmarket Street for the grocers Grimbly Hughes (since demolished), in a version of North Italian Gothic, and Gothic was also used for the London and County (now National Westminster) Bank (F. and H. Francis, 1866) in the High Street and the Post Office (by the Office of Works architect E. G. Rivers, 1880) in St Aldate's. Soon afterwards a long process of remodelling, extending, and re-roofing the 18th-century **Covered Market** was completed with the construction of the present wooden roofs by E. G. Bruton between 1886 and 1897, giving Oxford what is still its most attractive commercial interior.

The Garden Quadrangle at St John's College, showing the residential accommodation on the first-floor deck, with the dining-room next to the ground-floor courtyard below

The interior of the Covered Market

The building of the Randolph Hotel marked the end of the reign of stucco in the streets of central Oxford. When a new street, King Edward Street, was cut through land owned by Oriel College to the south of the High Street in 1871–5 the elevations, by Frederick Codd, a member of Wilkinson's North Oxford team, were in a dull though 'honest' yellow brick; the building of the street, one of Oxford's dreariest, involved the demolition of numerous old buildings, some of them dating back to the Middle Ages. Codd also inaugurated the rebuilding of Queen Street—now one of the main shopping streets—in 1875–8 with the construction of Hyde's clothing factory (numbers 31–32), a tall brick structure whose façade is enlivened by rows of round-arched windows. The extension of New Inn Hall Street north to George Street in 1872 also led to a major change of scale. Here the most important building was the **Wesley Memorial Church** of 1877–8.

Designed by Charles Bell and built of a rugged grey ragstone, it retains the galleried arrangement typical of earlier Nonconformist chapels (like the modest Wesleyan chapel it replaced), but the architecture is Decorated Gothic, with a tall broach spire (see p. 200) happily closing the westward vista from St Michael's Street.

In the 1870s and 1880s a new generation of Oxford architects turned away from the highly-charged Gothic of Butterfield and his generation. A persistent undercurrent in the criticism of buildings like Keble College was that they were 'un-English', both in their style and in their materials, the implication being that new architecture should merge effortlessly into its surroundings. So Victorian Gothic fell into a sharp critical decline, reaching its nadir perhaps in the 1920s when, as Kenneth Clark recalled in *The Gothic Revival*, 'it was universally believed that Ruskin had built Keble, and that it was the ugliest building in the world. Undergraduates and young dons used to break off on their afternoon walks to have a good laugh at the quadrangle.' A sense of continuity and respect for tradition and context became the new touchstones, proclaimed by most of Oxford's new buildings down to the 1950s, when another radically alien style came to the fore.

The north side of Queen Street. The three most prominent buildings are (left to right) the former Hyde's clothing factory, the former Wilberforce Temperance Hotel (F. W. Albury, 1888) and, nearest the camera, numbers 36–37 (Herbert Quinton, 1912), which served until 1932 as a showroom for Morris Garages Ltd. In the distance is the Westgate Centre

The Wesley Memorial Methodist church, looking west

The new mood of respect for Oxford's past caused a return to the careful, restrained English Gothic which had been elbowed out by the Continental style of the 1850s and 1860s. This is seen above all in the work of G. F. Bodley, who claimed kinship with the founder of the Bodleian Library and later took up residence in a Jacobean manor house at Water Eaton, just to the north of Oxford. Like Pugin, Bodley extolled the virtues of English medieval architecture, and, like his contemporary William Morris, he had great respect for the traditional architecture of the city and the University. His towers over the Hall staircase at **Christ Church** (see p. 77)and at the north-eastern corner of Tom Quad (1876–9) are so discreet and so seemingly inevitable that they can easily be mistaken for work of Cardinal Wolsey's time, and

The High Street front of St Swithin's Quadrangle at Magdalen College

with their completion the 350-year-long story of the building of Tom Quad was finally brought to an end. Together with his partner, Thomas Garner, who supervised the domestic parts of the practice, Bodley went on in 1879 to win a competition for a set of new rooms for **Magdalen College**, a project which involved the destruction of Pugin's gateway of 1844. They stand on the long-vacant site of Magdalen Hall, and in describing their designs the architects wrote that they had 'endeavoured to obtain a sufficiently dignified character to harmonize with the College, but avoiding much elaborate ornament . . . Nor is it a place for the display of much originality of design, or for the imitation of any foreign treatment of architecture. The Gothic should be not only that of Oxford, but that of Magdalen.' The buildings, which became known as St Swithin's Quadrangle (1881–5), consisted of two ranges of Burford stone entered through a gate tower echoing, though not imitating, the 15th-century Muniment Tower and Founder's Tower to the east. The masonry and the detailing were carried out with complete confidence, and an equally assured approach was adopted in the President's Lodgings of 1888, facing the new entrance to the College from the High Street. Here discretion and conformity to the *genius loci* were elevated to supreme virtues; as H. S. Goodhart-Rendel remarked in the 1930s: 'Looking at Garner's buildings, one might fancy the Gothic style had never died, and to Garner I do not think that it ever had.'

The Examination Schools: first-floor plan showing the original uses of the rooms

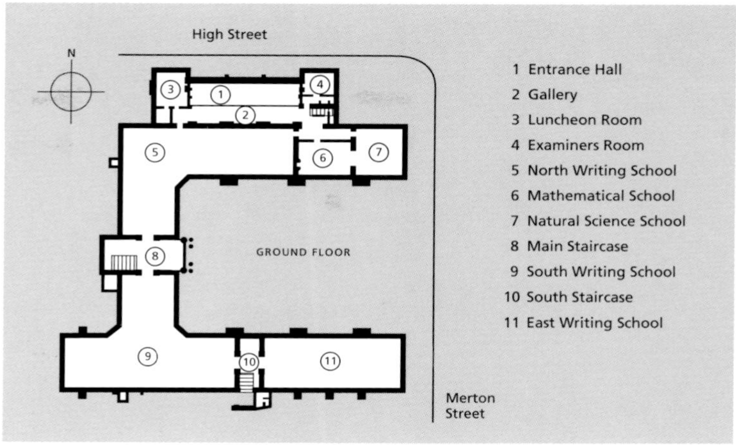

The key figure in the architecture of late 19th- and early 20th-century Oxford was Thomas Graham Jackson. He was a pupil of Gilbert Scott, but, like his contemporary Norman Shaw and many other architects of his generation, he reacted against the 'modern Gothic' of the 1850s and 1860s. His rise to prominence owed much to the fact that he was elected to a prize fellowship of his old college, Wadham, in 1864. This fellowship, like most under the old unreformed system, did not involve any teaching responsibilities, but it enabled him to build up an extensive practice within the University, starting in 1872 when he remodelled the Warden's Lodgings at Wadham. Then in 1875 he won a competition for the new **Examination Schools**, to be built on the site of the Angel Inn at the eastern end of the High Street. This large and striking building, erected between 1876 and 1882, launched him on a career which made him one of the most prolific and influential of all Oxford's architects.

The Examination Schools are a monument to the 19th-century reform of the University. The publication of new Examination Statutes in 1849–50 came as the culmination of a trend in which written examinations replaced the long discredited and largely meaningless oral examinations which had originated in the Middle Ages. Space was needed both for the examinations and for the increasing numbers of lectures given by the new generation of University professors, and for these purposes the Old Schools next to the Bodleian Library soon became inadequate. The building was in any case coveted by the Bodleian officials, who were clamouring for more space for the ever-growing number of books in their care, and in 1859 it was handed over to the Library, the University's art collection having already been removed from the gallery (now the Upper Reading Room) on the top floor of the building. In his design for the

The Examination Schools from the High Street

new Schools Jackson rejected the Gothic favoured by the other competitors and, taking his cue from what he called in his memoirs 'the haunting vision of Elizabethan and Jacobean work, and especially of those long mullioned and transomed windows at Kirby Hall in Northamptonshire [1570]', he opted for an eclectic style made up of elements from English, Italian, and Flemish architecture. This, he believed, was

> eminently suitable to modern usage, more elastic than Gothic or free classic . . . It seemed to me that it is possible to refine English Renaissance by avoiding its eccentricities, retaining that Gothic feeling which gave it life and instead of imitating the gross ornamentation to which it was prone, looking rather to the lovely decorative work of the early or Bramantesque Renaissance in Italy.

Jackson made this style—later dubbed 'Anglo-Jackson'—his own, and it reappeared in many of his later Oxford buildings.

Jackson claimed that the Examination Schools possessed a 'collegiate character which would harmonize with the traditions of Oxford', but this is true only in a general sense. The building is closer in appearance to a large Elizabethan or Jacobean country house, albeit one of a rather idiosyncratic kind, with its open courtyard plan and large, square-headed, mullioned and transomed windows. The courtyard faces east onto the narrow Merton Street, thus ensuring peace and quiet for the examinees, with a 'tower of the orders' at the centre of the west range, purely picturesque and emblematic like Hawksmoor's towers in the North Quadrangle at All Souls. The Schools are in fact entered from the High Street, through a porch with an arch in the form of a *Serliana* or Venetian window, which leads into a large and echoing open-roofed hall, encircled by a gallery and lit by vast windows of the type which Jackson had admired at Kirby Hall. This serves as a grandiose vestibule, and from it corridors lead by devious routes to the rest of the building: rooms for lectures and *viva voce* examinations on the ground floor and three large 'writing schools' above, cunningly shaped so as to allow maximum ease of invigilation. Jackson's amateurish planning would have appalled anyone educated at a Continental architecture school (such places scarcely existed in England), but criticism is largely stilled by the sumptuous quality of the decoration, no expense being spared, especially in the the main staircase, to recapture the rich effects of the Renaissance buildings which had entranced Jackson during his extensive travels in northern Italy. This lavish decoration of an essentially utilitarian structure can partly be explained by the dictates of official entertaining, but it also reflects an academic system which ritualizes examinations as the ultimate goal of a student's career; even

The entrance hall of the Examination Schools, looking east

in 1997, both students and dons still have to appear for examinations in full academic costume. For this, the University found itself saddled with a bill three times larger than the original estimate, largely recouped out of the profits of the University Press, and especially from the sale of the Revised Version of the Bible.

Jackson was as innovative in his choice of building materials as he was in the choice of style. Abandoning both the Bath stone used by Waterhouse at Balliol and the brick of Keble and North Oxford, he turned to the yellowish limestone of Clipsham (Rutland) for the main elevations, with rubble stone from Bladon, a few miles north of Oxford, for the rear of the building. These materials were not only attractive in themselves; both also proved resistant to ever-increasing pollution, and they were used in most of Oxford's new University buildings of the late 19th and early 20th centuries. When Jackson was asked in 1878–84 to replace the decayed Headington ashlar on the upper floor of the Old Schools he again used Clipsham stone (see p. 94), setting a precedent which has been followed over and over again down to recent times.

While the Examination Schools were still going up, Jackson was employed to design the pretty cricket pavilion in the University Parks (1880–1), introducing, for the first time in Oxford, the timbered gables and neo-vernacular detailing made popular by Norman Shaw

The Cricket Pavilion in the University Parks

and other architects of his generation. These features also appear in J. O. Scott's Oxford University Boat Club (1881), another reminder of the growing cult of organized sport and outdoor pursuits in the Oxford of Max Beerbohm's *Zuleika Dobson*. The University also employed Jackson to build two smaller buildings on the remaining parts of the Angel Inn site. The first, dating from 1886–8 and now the Ruskin School of Drawing, was built as a non-residential headquarters for students who could not afford the fees charged by the colleges: an indication of a growing concern to establish a wider and more meritocratic pool of entrants. It stands immediately to the east of the Examination Schools, and in order to stress its separate identity Jackson used Bladon rubble for the main elevations, which were designed in an elaborate version of the Tudor-Gothic style, with several characteristically playful touches, like the pretty lantern lighting the staircase on the Merton Street side. The second building, originally occupied by the Oxford Local Examinations Delegacy (1895–7), occupies a narrow tongue of land betwen the Schools and Merton Street, where it announces its identity with a bold curved gable of Jacobean character.

Jackson also worked extensively for the colleges. Though they were suffering from falling rents through the agricultural depression which devasted landed incomes in Britain from the 1880s onwards, there was still a desperate demand for new accommodation to house the ever-growing numbers of undergraduates. Some of Jackson's college buildings were squeezed onto confined spaces, like his block of rooms behind the Hall at Lincoln (1880–3) and his block on the northern side of Merton Street for Corpus Christi (1884–5), though here he rose to the opportunity of designing an elaborate gabled street

The Library of Mansfield College

selected as architect after earlier French Renaissance-style schemes by Alfred Waterhouse—an architect with a considerable reputation in Nonconformist circles—were set aside. His Tudor-Gothic buildings gave the new establishment a comforting air of permanence, but at the same time he introduced some innovations in planning and layout. Since all the students lived out of the College at first, no residential quarters were needed, and buildings were disposed around a spacious open-ended courtyard, with the Hall, some lecture-rooms, and a functionally useless but picturesque gate tower on the long north side, the Perpendicular Gothic Chapel—intended as a place of worship for all Nonconformist students in Oxford—facing the street to the east, and the Library to the west. In his internal detailing Champneys revealed his Arts and Crafts sympathies, especially in the aisled Library, apparently inspired by the famous late medieval tithe barn at Harmondsworth (Middlesex), with its steeply pitched roof adorned with stylized floral paintings. Here, as in many of Oxford's buildings of the 1870s and 1880s, there is a palpable feeling of relaxation after the rigours of High Victorian Gothic, and the air of undemanding charm which Champneys so effectively captured at Mansfield College was to pervade much of the architecture of Oxford down to the 1960s.

LLOYDS BANK LIMITED
LLOYDS BANK LIMITED

7 Into the Twentieth Century

The architectural history of Oxford over the past 300 years has been punctuated by periods of intense activity and creativity, followed by longer periods of relative stagnation. No one could write a comprehensive history of English architecture in the first forty years of the 18th century or the mid-19th century—or, for that matter, the 1960s—without referring to Oxford, but after each of these periods Oxford slipped out of the limelight. The reasons are partly economic and partly cultural; in each case, the tastes of those who commissioned new buildings ceased to be in touch with whatever was most vital in English and European architecture. So at the end of the 19th century, following the excitement of High Victorian Gothic, Oxford settled into a less adventurous frame of mind, first announced in the work of G. F. Bodley and T. G. Jackson in the 1870s. In this Oxford was, for all its peculiarities and idiosyncrasies, in many ways a microcosm of England as a whole. And, as in England, a sense of cultural individuality encouraged some architects to design buildings of real distinction.

Ever since the 13th century the architectural initiative in Oxford had been taken by the University. But in 1893–7 the city marked its growing sense of self-confidence by building a new **Town Hall**. The city of Oxford has a corporate history longer than that of the University, and by the end of the 19th century the elected council had been largely freed from the University interference under which it had chafed ever since the Middle Ages. In 1889 Oxford obtained county borough status, putting it on a par with the largest cities in the country, and at the same time the civic boundaries were redrawn to incorporate outlying areas like Summertown and Headington. Two years later, prompted by the arguments of Robert Buckell, a Liberal alderman, some of the council members embarked on a tour of town halls in the north of England before announcing a competition for new municipal buildings on the site of the 18th-century Town Hall on the eastern side of St Aldate's. The competition was won by H. T. Hare, a young architect who went on to design several public and

Lloyds Bank, Carfax

The Town Hall from the south-west, soon after completion. The doorway on the right led into the Public Library (now the Museum of Oxford)

municipal buildings of great distinction all over England, and with the construction of the new building the inhabitants of Oxford at last acquired an appropriate architectural expression of their civic pride.

Town halls served many purposes in late Victorian and Edwardian England. Not only were they expected to house the council chambers, police courts, and official accommodation for the mayor, which they had contained from time immemorial; now there was also a growing municipal bureaucracy whose task was to put into effect the legislation concerning public health, sanitation, and education, which transformed urban life in the late 19th century. Oxford's new Town Hall, like many others, also contained a public library and a large hall for concerts and public meetings. The building therefore covers a much larger area than its predecessor, and its construction entailed the demolition of several old buildings, including the picturesque mid-17th-century Nixon's School and the Corn Exchange by S. L. Seckham, built as recently as 1861–2.

The main façade, to St Aldate's, is a virtuoso rendition of the neo-Jacobean theme employed by T. G. Jackson in his University buildings of the previous twenty years, and, like Jackson, Hare made the wise

Town Hall: plan of first floor

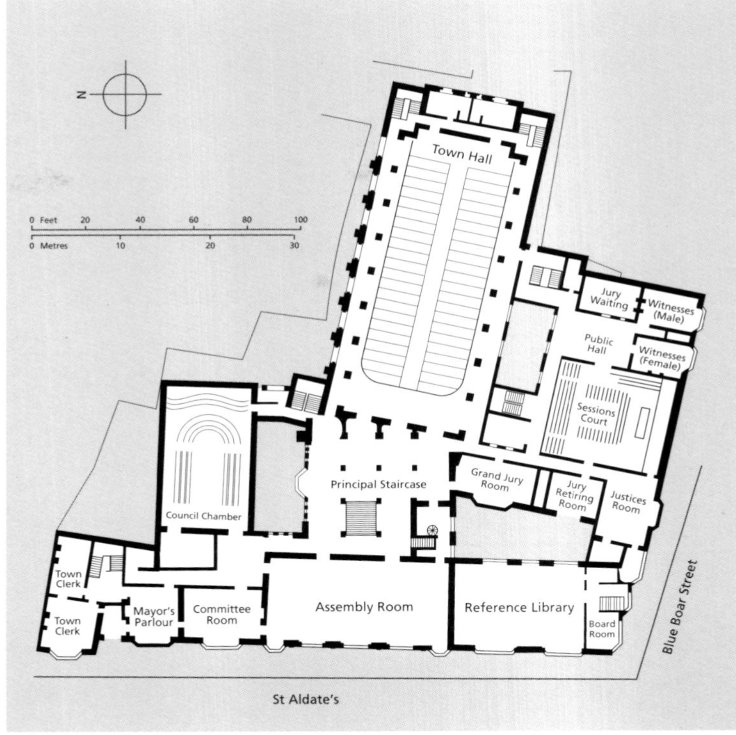

decision to use Clipsham stone for the walls. Large mullioned and transomed windows light the main rooms on the first floor overlooking the street front, some of them treated as projecting oriels, and there is a display of richly embellished gables on the roof-line, carved with great panache by William Aumonier, along with a cupola, seen to especially good effect from Carfax; the subsidiary frontage to Blue Boar Street is handled more freely, and here too there is some excellent detailing, down even to the ironwork guarding the entrance to the public lavatories, almost worthy of Charles Rennie Mackintosh. But there is an underlying discipline behind the exuberant ornamentation. Unlike Jackson, Hare had received a rigorous classical architectural training in Paris and, despite the irregularly shaped site, he was able to balance clarity of planning with dramatic effect, paying due attention to practicality and convenient means of access. The approach to the main rooms on the first floor is handled superbly, with a staircase of Baroque magnificence leading up to the barrel-vaulted Hall, and to the timber-roofed Assembly Room on the street front. The internal decoration is as inventive as that on the outside of the building, from the writhing Michelangelesque figures in the spandrels of the arches supporting the Hall vault to the dark neo-Jacobean woodwork in the Mayor's Parlour, Council Chamber, and Magistrates' Court. With the completion of this lavish and expensive building (the cost was £91,500, £40,000 more than the estimate), the city of Oxford, for the first and only time, showed itself to be more than a match for the University as a patron of architecture.

The building of the new Town Hall was followed by the improvement of **Carfax**, a project which had intermittently occupied the minds of architects and city fathers for the past two centuries. Work began in 1896 with the demolition of the Regency Gothic church of St Martin, leaving only the 14th-century tower standing and an open space in front. Hare prepared plans for heightening and embellishing the tower as a civic monument to rival the towers and spires of the University. But antiquarian prejudice intervened, and in the end the tower was restored and refaced much more discreetly by T. G. Jackson in 1897. But Hare was employed in 1896–7 to design the adjacent Tower House in Queen Street and the Midland Bank at the southern end of Cornmarket Street, both of them pretty turreted exercises in the 'free style'. Not to be outdone, Lloyds Bank decided in 1901 to rebuild its premises at the corner of Cornmarket Street and High Street. Their architect was Stephen Salter, whose office was in

The main hall of the Town Hall *c.*1900

Carfax, looking west *c.*1900 after the demolition of the body of St Martin's church. H. T. Hare's Tower House is to the left of the 14th-century church tower and his Midland Bank to the right

Oxford, and his curvaceous, exuberant, neo-Jacobean façade with its extravagent display of 'Ipswich' windows is the most original of Oxford's commercial buildings of its time, memorably closing the vista north from St Aldate's (the south-west and south-east corners of Carfax were rebuilt in a plainer and duller style between the two World Wars).

The growth of retailing in Edwardian Oxford led to extensive building in the main shopping streets. By 1914 many of the old stuccoed buildings which had lined Queen Street, Cornmarket Street, and George Street had gone (see pp. 144, 178); more disappeared in the 1930s, and still more in the 1950s and 1960s. Most of the architects of the new buildings were locally based, and several were involved in the design of houses on St John's College's North Oxford estate. They included William Wilkinson's nephew H. W. Moore, architect in 1894–6 of the rather fussily detailed red-brick Corn Exchange and Fire Station (now the Old Fire Station Arts Centre) in George Street; Herbert Quinton, who was responsible for the attractive white stone façade of number 30 Cornmarket Street; and N. W. and G. W. Harrison, whose prominent premises for Messrs Baker (1914; now Dillon's bookshop) at the corner of Cornmarket Street and Broad Street introduced a note of classicism with its large plate-glass windows separated by Ionic columns of stone to conceal

The northern end of Cornmarket Street at the junction with Broad Street and George Street. On the left is the former William Baker House, and to the right is St George's Mansions (Homer and Lucas, 1910). In the foreground is St Mary Magdalen's churchyard

the steel-framed structure. By 1914 the crossroads at the northern end of Cornmarket Street—one of Oxford's main shopping areas—had achieved its present unmistakably Edwardian appearance.

The eastern end of the High Street also underwent extensive rebuilding. The main architect here was E. P. Warren, brother of the President of Magdalen College, which owned much of the property. It is to him that we owe the carefully detailed Eastgate Hotel of 1899–1900, echoing the vernacular architecture of late 17th-century Oxford, and the impressive neo-Tudor block of shops and undergraduate rooms at 49–52 High Street on the opposite side of the road (now part of St Edmund Hall), complementing but not competing with the nearby Examination Schools. Warren also designed the pretty fountain and clock which stand to the west of the traffic roundabout at the Plain on the far side of Magdalen Bridge (1899), and went on to do some work for St John's and Balliol Colleges, but his largest Oxford commission came in 1911–13 when he added a large neo-Georgian extension to the south of the Radcliffe Infirmary in the Woodstock Road, the first of several additions which in due course swamped the original 18th-century structure.

Among the most inventive turn-of-the-century buildings in central Oxford are a pair of schools designed by Leonard Stokes, an architect best known for his telephone exchanges and Roman Catholic churches and convents (he also made extensive additions to Emmanuel College, Cambridge). The passing of the Education Act of 1870 led to the establishment of a School Board in Oxford, but nothing of architectural note was done until the Board took over three of the schools formerly funded by the Nonconformists: the Central Schools for boys and girls, and the East Oxford British School. The Board employed Stokes to design new premises for all three schools: the Central Schools for boys (at Gloucester Green) and girls (in New Inn Hall Street), both built in 1901, and the East Oxford School (in Cross Street, St Clements: since remodelled). The girls' school (now part of St Peter's College) is a particularly impressive piece of architecture, with its long mullioned and transomed windows lighting the main schoolrooms on the ground floor, and wings on either side, each with its own entrance leading upstairs to the separate training rooms for male and female pupil teachers. Stokes's Arts and Crafts sympathies showed themselves in the careful choice of materials—rubble stone for the walls, Yorkshire slate for the roof—and the carvings around the door-cases to the schoolrooms introduced a note of symbolism characteristic of the period, with a pomegranate tree representing Life over one door and a myrtle with seven doves for the gifts of the Holy Spirit representing Knowledge over the other. The boys' school (now the City Information Centre) is more domestic in character and more conventional in its detailing, the Board having expressed the wish that it should be 'of a picturesque character' in deference to the old buildings which it replaced. But here too Stokes's handling of the materials—stone for

The former Central School for Girls, New Inn Hall Street

the façade and stone slates for the roof—is most effective, and the planning, with the classrooms grouped round a circular top-lit hall, highly ingenious.

Oxford at the beginning of the 20th century was still a country town, with a large proportion of the population involved in the service economy which had grown up alongside the University, but a certain amount of industrial building nevertheless went on in the western fringe of the city centre. The gabled, vaguely Flemish, red-brick façade of the former Lucas's clothing factory (H. G. Drinkwater, 1892) is still a prominent feature at the western end of George Street, and in the ensuing years a series of depressing red-brick warehouses sprang up in Park End Street, the western continuation of New Road leading from the city centre to the railway stations. More inventiveness was shown by Herbert Quinton in Cooper's marmalade factory (1903) at the western end of Park End Street, with its free-style façade of red brick with stone embellishments facing the LNWR railway station; it and its rather less distinguished red-brick neighbours are the first buildings seen by those visitors to Oxford who arrive by train.

Frank Cooper's marmalade factory, Park End Street

Brickwork of a more Ruskinian variety was used in the façade of the former Electric Lighting Station, built in 1892 to the designs of P. Brevit beside the River Thames at Osney. But the building with the most significance for Oxford's industrial future was opened in 1910 by a young manufacturer of bicycles and motor-cars, William Morris, on the other side of the city centre, at the corner of Longwall Street and Holywell Street. This was a garage and workshop, and behind the rather prim red-brick neo-Georgian façade by the firm of H. J. Tollit & Lee (now part of New College) the first bull-nose Morris was assembled in 1912. With the beginning of mass production of the popular new cars at Cowley in the following year, a new phase in the history of Oxford began.

Oxford's suburban expansion gathered pace during the 1890s, when there was a nationwide building boom fuelled by rising real wages. Terraces of lower middle-class and artisan housing sprang up on the lower ground to the east of Magdalen Bridge, to the south of Folly Bridge, and to the west along Botley Road. Rather more substantial houses went up to the south of Iffley Road and north of Cowley Road, on the slopes of Headington Hill, some of it on land acquired by the Oxford Industrial and Provident Land and Building Society; some of the owners supplemented their income, as they have done ever since, by letting out rooms as lodgings for students who, from 1868 onwards, were allowed to live out of college. There was also extensive building in 'New Headington', some two miles north-east of the city, and in Summertown, hitherto an isolated hamlet of brickworks and market gardens beyond the North Oxford estate, and in each case the rows of red-brick houses were served by parades of shops which still flourish. Thus Oxford began to acquire its distinctive pattern of a central commercial and academic area from which fingers of suburban development stretch out, separated from each other by the low-lying meadows of the Thames and Cherwell flood plains.

The most favoured residential area remained North Oxford, and here building proceeded apace until the 1920s, by which time the St John's estate had been almost entirely built over. The dominant North Oxford architect in the late 19th century was H. W. Moore, who went into partnership with his uncle William Wilkinson in 1881 and, like him, was employed widely throughout the city. Like Wilkinson too, Moore was more successful on a small than a large scale, and his St Clements Mission Hall (1886–9) and St Giles Parish Room, Woodstock Road (1887–91) are particularly good examples of his eclectic style, made up of elements taken from Flemish architecture, from English home counties vernacular and 'Queen Anne', and from

Number 10 Northmoor Road, by H. W. Moore (1904)

the late Gothic. Moore's houses are usually built of red brick, and in the larger ones, in St Margaret's Road and Banbury Road, there is abundant detailing in terracotta. The last parts of the estate, north of Park Town, were not completed until the first three decades of the 20th century, and here neo-vernacular and, eventually, neo-Georgian detailing reigned supreme. Most of the houses here were designed by locally based architects deeply influenced by the Arts and Crafts movement, including Herbert Quinton (in Rawlinson Road), George Gardiner (in Linton Road), Frank Mountain (in Northmoor and Chadlington Roads), Stephen Salter (in Charlbury Road), and N. W. Harrison (in Chadlington and Charlbury Roads); Harrison replaced Moore as surveyor to the estate in 1903. But by the 1920s, when the development was completed, neo-Georgian had become all the rage, and there are some excellent houses in this style by the London architect Christopher Wright in Northmoor and Belbroughton Roads. There are more houses in a similar vein in the prosperous northern fringe of North Oxford beyond Summertown; placed among them is the Arts and Crafts-influenced Roman Catholic church of St Gregory and St Augustine, Woodstock Road, built in 1911 to the designs of Ernest Newton, one of the leading domestic architects of the Edwardian era, who also carried out alterations to the neighbouring Apsley Paddox.

The acres of red-brick housing in Oxford's late 19th- and early 20th-century suburbs are interruped periodically by strategically placed churches and public houses. The 1890s saw an explosion of pub building, in Oxford as in the rest of urban England. The largest brewery, Morrell's, rebuilt its premises in St Thomas Street in 1892–6, and the firm's inappropriately named architect H. G. Drinkwater went on to rebuild several of the tied houses, of which he former Cape of Good Hope at the Plain (1892), in a broadly neo-vernacular style, with red-brick walls and timbered gables, is a typical example. Drinkwater also showed himself to be an able exponent of Gothic architecture in his church of St Margaret in North Oxford (1893). The finest of Oxford's many pubs of this period were designed by H. T. Hare, and sprang from his involvement in the Town Hall and the remodelling of Carfax. The former White House (1897–8) in the Abingdon Road, south of Folly Bridge, is a pleasing example of an 'improved' pub of the Arts and Crafts variety, with its white-painted rendered first floor and tiled roof evoking an idyllic, though increasingly threatened, rural world. But the more striking of the two is the Elm Tree in Cowley Road (1899), adjoining Oxford's oldest surviving cinema, of 1910–11 (now called the Ultimate Picture Palace) and facing the Cowley Road Methodist Church (1903–4), itself a highly original reinterpretation of English late Gothic architecture by the most eccentric of Oxford's turn-of-the-century architects, Stephen Salter. Here too Hare employed neo-vernacular detailing and materials, but in this case he adapted the butterfly-shaped plan of the

The Elm Tree, Cowley Road

kind used in some of the more innovative houses of the period to the needs of the drinker, and in doing so he enlivened an otherwise drab part of the city.

A different kind of nostalgia pervades the best of Oxford's late Victorian and Edwardian churches. Here the finest results were achieved by the Anglican religious communities which developed in the wake of the Oxford Movement: especially in its more ritualistic manifestations, still a potent force in turn-of-the-century Oxford, though increasingly marginalized in the University. England's first Anglican community for men, the Society of **St John the Evangelist** or Cowley Fathers, had been established in 1868 by the Anglo-Catholic Richard Meux Benson, vicar of Cowley, in Marston Street, south of the Cowley Road, and for thirty years his 'congregation of mission priests' occupied a plain red-brick Mission House with a top-floor chapel. But in 1894–1902 G. F. Bodley expanded the buildings, linking them by a cloister to a large new church facing the Iffley Road. The church is one of the finest buildings of its date in Oxford, light and spacious, with a high arched roof of wood, a short aisled nave, and a much longer monastic-style chancel, entered through a carved wooden rood screen; externally the main feature is the tower, plain and somewhat gaunt in character, rising up from the west bay of the nave. Throughout the building Bodley remained true to his favoured English late Gothic style, but the detailing is of an almost Cistercian simplicity, contributing to the calm, contemplative effect; as in all of his work, great attention was paid to the smooth, highly finished quality of the masonry and to the internal decoration, notably the painting of the roof and the design of the screen, the organ-case, and the pulpit. Since 1980 the buildings have been occupied by St Stephen's House, an Anglican theological college.

Benson also founded St John's Home for old people in Leopold Street, a little to the east of the Cowley Fathers' community. The rather dull neo-Tudor buildings went up in 1873–5 to the designs of Charles Buckeridge, though under the supervision of J. L. Pearson, who took over his practice, and they were extended by Pearson in 1882–3. By this time the home had come under the care of the All Saints Sisters of the Poor, a community of nuns, and they commissioned Ninian Comper, a pupil of Bodley, to build a chapel in 1905–7. Comper had already in 1900 designed the light and spacious—though never finished—church of St John, New Hinksey, in the straggling suburb south of Folly Bridge, and he was also the architect, with his partner Bucknall, of the red-brick St Mary and St John's infant school in Hertford Street (1903). His chapel for St John's Home is a tall, narrow, aisleless building, Perpendicular Gothic in character but smaller and

The interior of St John the Evangelist, Iffley Road

more lavish in its detailing than Bodley's church for the Cowley Fathers. The short nave is separated from the chancel by a richly carved stone screen with flattened Gothic arches, beyond which there are beautifully carved wooden stalls; the roof is of wood, with tiny pendants within the panels, and the east window is filled with stained glass designed by Comper himself. Like Bodley, Comper believed passionately in the continuing relevance of Gothic architecture within—or perhaps as a refuge from—the modern world, and in this little-known building he expressed that feeling in a way which can suspend the most troubling disbelief.

The last great monument to Oxford Anglo-Catholicism is **Pusey House**, established in 1884 after the death of Edward Bouverie Pusey, Canon of Christ Church and one of the spiritual leaders of the movement. It was intended as a 'house of sacred learning', manned by resident clergy, with Pusey's library of theological books at its core:

a modern version of the medieval college of secular priests. Like Keble College, it was seen as a spiritual citadel, keeping modernization and secularization at bay. The priests first took up residence in a row of houses on the western side of St Giles, but a large bequest from a Leeds solicitor, John William Cudworth, enabled work to start in 1911 on the construction of new and permanent buildings on the same site. The architect was Temple Moore, a pupil of the younger George Gilbert Scott, who had designed a well-detailed range of Tudor-Gothic rooms for St John's College on the opposite side of St Giles in 1880 (completed by E. P. Warren in 1900). Moore's chaste, beautifully proportioned churches, mainly in the north of England, had already shown him to be one of the most successful exponents of the Gothic style in late Victorian and Edwardian England, and his buildings at Pusey House exploit that style with great sensitivity. They are of coursed rubble stone and take their cue from monastic architecture, with the Chapel (of 1911–14) taking up the whole of the north side of the quadrangular courtyard; a cloister, dining-room, and sacristies occupy the two-storeyed east range, facing onto St Giles, the domestic offices (built in 1924–6, and now used by St Cross College) were on the south side of the courtyard, and the Library and lecture-rooms stand on the western side. Everywhere the detailing is well thought out, the overall effect calm and restrained, above all in the aisleless Chapel; divided into two, like most monastic churches, by a stone screen or *pulpitum*, it is vaulted throughout in concrete (though it looks like stone), with the buttresses making a bold effect on the north side, facing the narrow Pusey Street. The decoration is restrained, except for the gilded Renaissance-style *baldacchino* by Comper over the high altar (1937), and the proportions impeccable. Here, as much as in any post-medieval Gothic building in Oxford, the 'last enchantments of the Middle Ages' are evoked in a totally convincing and moving way.

The Chapel of Pusey House, looking east

The non-Anglican churches, with less money at their disposal, achieved less satisfying architectural results. The dour **Manchester College**, a non-denominational establishment with strong Unitarian connections, built in Mansfield Road in 1891–3 to the designs of the Manchester architect Thomas Worthington, is a rather heavy-handed reinterpretation of the Tudor-Gothic idiom, redeemed mainly by a superb set of stained-glass windows by Burne-Jones in the Chapel; its construction, following soon after that of Mansfield College to the north, hastened the development of the area between Holywell Street and the University Parks, a process which was carried forward by the erection of several attractive detached houses for dons, including T. G. Jackson's characteristically inventive King's Mound of 1892–3,

designed as a home for Balliol College's married tutors. The opposite end of the ecclesiastical spectrum to Manchester College is represented by the forbidding flint-built Roman Catholic church of St Edmund and St Frideswide in the Iffley Road, designed by Benedict Williamson in 1911; it stands next to a 'house of studies', built in a similar style in 1921 for Franciscans studying at the University, something allowed after the papacy relaxed its earlier veto on Catholics studying in Oxford in 1895. The Dominicans also returned to Oxford in the wake of this ruling, but they showed a greater understanding of the *genius loci* in their new priory, built immediately to the south of Pusey House in 1921–9 to the sensitive designs of E. Doran Webb, architect of the Oratory in Birmingham; in his chapel Webb succeeded in recapturing something of the atmosphere of the lost medieval churches of the preaching orders.

The architecture of the University before the First World War was still to a large extent dominated by T. G. Jackson and Basil Champneys. Jackson's last and most extensive work for an Oxford college was at **Hertford**, refounded in 1874 following a large gift of money by the banker Charles Baring. Here he faced the task of giving some coherence and sense of identity to a very disparate collection of earlier buildings on a confined site: the plain and much remodelled 16th-century remnants of Hart Hall; the former chapel of the abortive Hertford College of 1740; and the residential blocks erected after Magdalen Hall had taken over the site in 1820 (see p. 194). Rebuilding and expansion proceeded in fits and starts, beginning with the construction of a new Hall and porter's lodge on the Catte Street front

The western side of St Giles, with the façades of Blackfriars and Pusey House

The Hall of Hertford College from the quadrangle

in 1887–8; this was accompanied by the remodelling of the north side of the old quadrangle, incorporating the old Hall of Hart Hall. A new Chapel on the south side of the quadrangle followed in 1906–8, and in 1901–7 residential blocks went up on the site of a group of old houses on the north side of New College Lane, acquired from the city corporation; they were joined to the older parts of the College in 1913–14 by what has inevitably come to be known as the Bridge of Sighs (it is in fact much more like the Rialto). Finally, after the end of the First World War, the new North Quadrangle was extended north to Holywell Street and a new entrance opened into Catte Street (1923–6), incorporating the remains of the octagonal early 16th-century Chapel of Our Lady which stood beside one of the long-vanished postern gates in the city wall.

Jackson's boldest stroke at Hertford was to place his new Hall over the entrance lodge, between the two existing classical blocks of 1820–2. It is lit on each side by large Venetian windows placed side by side and is reached from within the quadrangle by a staircase very loosely based on that of the French Renaissance château at Blois; the effect is unforgettable, though strangely disorientating. The Chapel also draws on a wide range of sources: essentially Gothic in its construction and proportions, but with detailing, including some excellent carved woodwork, taken almost entirely from the early Renaissance. The north range, on the site of the former kitchens, is in a relatively restrained neo-Palladian style, but the frontage of the North Quadrangle to Catte Street and New College Lane is neo-Jacobean, save for the remnants of the Chapel of Our Lady. deftly remodelled for the maximum picturesque effect (it is now the Junior Common Room). Even more picturesque is the 'Bridge of Sighs', a characteristic reinterpretation, on a miniature scale, of the Renaissance idea of a covered bridge. By drawing so widely, and seemingly so indiscriminately, on the varied legacy of the European Renaissance, Jackson's work at Hertford was bound to offend the purists, and the shameless mixture of motifs anticipates some of the excesses of recent post-modernism. Yet the ensemble is redeemed by the superb quality of the craftsmanship, and it would be a harsh critic indeed who would deny that it adds to the visual pleasures of Oxford: an aim which Jackson always kept in the forefront of his mind.

The north quadrangle of Hertford College, with T. G. Jackson's covered bridge spanning New College Lane

Detail of the gate tower of Oriel College's Rhodes Building, facing the High Street. Cecil Rhodes occupies the topmost niche

While Hertford College was being transformed, important extensions were made to **Merton** (1904–10) and **Oriel** (1908–11). Here Basil Champneys was the architect, and in both cases the space was made available by swallowing up neighbouring academic halls. St Alban Hall, which stood to the east of Merton, was all but demolished, and in its place Champneys designed a sensitively detailed set of undergraduate rooms arranged around an open courtyard looking south over Christ Church Meadow; he also designed the former Warden's Lodgings (1908) on the opposite side of Merton Street in a rather overbearing version of the neo-Jacobean style. A similar process of assimilation—this time of the former St Mary Hall—made it possible for Oriel College to build a new block of undergraduate rooms facing north onto the High Street, financed out of money left by Cecil Rhodes, who had attended Oriel in the intervals of making his fortune as a young man in the diamond mines of South Africa. This is another beefy neo-Jacobean building, with a central gate tower, a gabled roof-line, and statues of worthies both ancient and modern, including a besuited Rhodes and two armoured kings. But a different, more sympathetic Champneys emerges in the earlier Shelley memorial, erected in 1892–3 to the west of the front quadrangle of University College, from which the poet had been sent down after publishing an atheistic pamphlet in 1811. The domed, top-lit space houses Onslow Ford's androgynous figure of Shelley, originally commissioned for the Protestant Cemetery in Rome, but now placed

The Shelley memorial at University College

behind a grille and approached down steps, as if under the sea: an appropriate conceit. The whole ensemble exudes a languid sensibility entirely characteristic of the 1890s, just as the Rhodes Building expresses the bombastic self-confidence of the Edwardian era.

The most interesting new developments in collegiate architecture in the years before the First World War took place in the women's colleges. Women's higher education in Oxford began modestly in 1879 with the opening of a 'small hall or hostel in connection with the Church of England' in a house at the furthest end of Norham Gardens in North Oxford, leased from St John's College and accommodating nine students. It became Lady Margaret Hall, and in the same year a second college, Somerville, a non-denominational foundation, was established for eleven students in Walton House, an early 19th-century villa to the west of the Woodstock Road, near the Radcliffe Infirmary. The Colleges prospered, even though the students were not allowed to take degrees, and both expanded in the last two decades of the 19th century, acquiring the freehold of their houses and grounds in the process. Neither College felt the need to make bold architectural statements or to make the new buildings conform in style, planning, or materials to traditional ideas of what a college should look like; instead the emphasis was upon supplying a protective, domestic environment of the kind then deemed essential for well-bred young ladies. The time-honoured staircase plan still used in the male colleges (except Keble) was abandoned in favour of the more convenient corridor arrangement, Basil Champneys

Lady Margaret Hall from the south-east. The Wordsworth Building is to the left, the Talbot Building in the centre, and the Toynbee Building to the right

The west façade of the Talbot Building at Lady Margaret Hall. It now forms part of the front quadrangle, completed in 1966

remarking somewhat patronizingly in 1912 that 'You cannot turn girls out into the air when they pass from room to room.' And the idea of a monumental agglomeration of large buildings placed around a quadrangle was dropped in favour of a looser arrangement of houses, believed to provide a less intimidating environment for the students, and thus one more conducive to academic endeavour.

The first extension to **Lady Margaret Hall** came in 1880–4, when Champneys designed a new block next to the existing house with red-brick walls, white-painted oriel windows, and pretty Dutch gables: features which had all appeared in his designs for Newnham College, Cambridge, another women's foundation (the gables have been obscured by later additions). Further expansion became possible after a large stretch of land stretching down to the River Cherwell was acquired in 1893, much of it laid out as a strikingly beautiful garden. Champneys was now replaced as architect by Reginald Blomfield, a graduate of Exeter College and son of the architect of St Barnabas, Jericho, and it is to him that we owe the prevailing character of the College as it developed and expanded in the early 20th century. He was first employed in 1896 to build the Wordsworth Building, designed for twenty-four students and two tutors, and containing single bed-sitting rooms—at the time an innovation largely confined to the women's colleges—arranged on either side of an axial corridor, with common-rooms at either end. Elizabeth Wordsworth, the first Principal of the College, wanted the new building to have 'somewhat of a homelike character', and, with its red-brick walls, white woodwork, hipped roof, and classical proportions, it reflects the growing taste for English domestic architecture of the late 17th and early 18th centuries, already anticipated in Jackson's rather less refined High School for Girls (see p. 255). Two more additions—the Talbot and Toynbee Buildings—were made in 1909–15, and here Blomfield introduced a more monumental note, with elements derived from the architecture of the later French Renaissance (about which he had written a book) and the English Baroque; the Talbot Building, which for many years closed the eastward view from Norham Gardens. contained a panelled dining Hall with a Library above it, divided into bays by columns supporting transverse barrel vaults. But the use of brick, and the pervasive sense of a single architect's mind in control, impart a visual unity which help make Lady Margaret Hall the most architecturally satisfying of the women's colleges.

A more piecemeal process of expansion took place at Somerville, where new residential blocks by T. G. Jackson and H. W. Moore were erected in 1881–5 and 1894, followed in 1902–3 by a long, low, red-brick Library block by Basil Champneys, and finally in 1913 by a neo-Georgian Hall designed by Edmund Fisher, brother of the historian H. A. L. Fisher, a Fellow of New College and President of the council of Somerville; they form part of a large, grassy, and architecturally diverse quadrangle into which several later buildings have been inserted. Meanwhile, two more women's colleges were founded: St Hugh's (1886), which at first occupied houses in Norham Gardens, and St Hilda's, founded in 1893 in the 18th-century Cowley House on the east bank of the River Cherwell. St Hilda's stayed on its attractive riverside site, and was extended southwards in 1897. St Hugh's, by contrast, acquired in 1913 a new site in the grounds of The Mount, a mid-19th-century villa between the Banbury and Woodstock Roads in North Oxford, using money donated by Clara Morden, a keen suffragette who had inherited a fortune from her father, a manufacturer of propelling pencils. Here over the next three years the Birmingham architects H. T. Buckland and W. Hayward erected an inoffensive but unremarkable red-brick neo-Georgian block with wings, typical of many educational buldings of the period. It was enlarged between the wars, when a large and beautiful garden was created by one of the fellows, Annie Rogers, a devoted follower of

Map 4
North Oxford and the Science Area

1 University Museum
2 Pitt Rivers Museum
3 Clarendon Laboratory
4 Electrical Laboratory
5 Radcliffe Science Library
6 Physiology Department
7 Biochemistry Department
8 Organic Chemistry (Dyson Perrins) Laboratory
9 Physical Chemistry Laboratory
10 Inorganic Chemistry Laboratory
11 Plant Sciences (Forestry and Botany) Department
12 Sir William Dunn School of Pathology

Wolfson College
Boat House
RIVER CHERWELL
N
St Hugh's College
Maison Française
Lady Margaret Hall
Church of S S Philip & James
Nissan Institute of Japanese Studies
St Antony's College
Surveyingand Geodesy
Pitt Rivers Musuem Annexe
Biological Anthropology
Appointments
Wycliffe Hall
Department of Education
UNIVERSITY PARKS
University Cricket Pavillion
KEBLE ROAD TRIANGLE
Green College
St Anne's College
Acland Hospital
Radcliffe Observatory
Dept. of Materials
Computing Services
Radcliffe Infirmary
Departments of Engineering Science, Materials
UNIVERSITY SCIENCE AREA
Nuclear Physics
Keble College
Linacre College
Zoology and Psychology
Somerville College
St Aloysius' Church
St Giles' Church
Mathematical Institute
Dartington House
Queen Elizabeth House
Halifax House
University Offices
St Benet's Hall
Department of Pharmacology
Institute of Virology
Social & Administrative Studies
Kellogg College
Rhodes House
Mansfield College
Regent's Park College
St John's College
LINTON ROAD
BARDWELL ROAD
PARK TOWN
NORHAM ROAD
CANTERBURY ROAD
CRICK ROAD
NORHAM GARDENS
BEVINGTON ROAD
KEBLE ROAD
PARKS ROAD
SOUTH PARKS ROAD
MANSFIELD ROAD
ST CROSS ROAD
MUSEUM ROAD
BLACKHALL ROAD
LITTLE CLARENDON STREET
BANBURY ROAD
WOODSTOCK ROAD
ST GILES'
NORTHMOOR ROAD
CHARLBURY ROAD
BRADMORE ROAD
FYFIELD ROAD
1
2
3
4
5
6
7
8
9
10
11
12

William Morris and the Arts and Crafts, who, in Mavis Batey's words, 'always wore stout boots, an old macintosh and a kind of trilby hat when working in the garden'.

The building of the women's colleges was part of a process in which the architectural centre of gravity of Oxford University began to move northwards. Another important factor was the growth of scientific teaching and research. In 1887 only 5 per cent of Oxford's undergraduates were reading for scientific degrees, and men like R. B. Clifton, for many years Professor of Experimental Philosophy, could claim that 'the wish to do research betrays a certain restlessness of mind.' But scientific teaching and research began to expand in Oxford after the turn of the century, and with it came a growing demand for new and larger buildings. At first the commissions fell into the lap of T. G. Jackson, largely through the influence of Henry Boyd, Principal of Hertford College and a former Master of the Drapers' Company of London, which funded new scientific projects in both Oxford and Cambridge. With scientific books bursting out of the library in the University Museum, Jackson was commissioned in 1897–1901 to design the adjacent Radcliffe Science Library in a characteristically mongrel style, part Gothic and part Renaissance, with tall round-arched windows lighting the reading rooms and projecting buttresses to counteract the outward thrust of the walls. It was Jackson too who designed the red-brick neo-Georgian Electrical Laboratory, to the north of the Museum, in 1909–10. The Dyson Perrins Organic Chemistry Laboratory, funded partly out of money contributed by Lea and Perrins, the manufacturers of Worcestershire Sauce, followed in 1913–16 on a site facing South Parks Road to the east of the Radcliffe Science Library, but here the architect was not Jackson but Paul Waterhouse, son of the architect of Balliol College (where he was educated himself). Though neo-Georgian in its general character, with red-brick walls and detailing inspired by the English Baroque, Waterhouse made no attempt to conceal the building's function, and much of the wall surface is taken up by large windows lighting the laboratories. Here, to a much greater extent than in the collegiate buildings of the early 20th century, changes in architectural form were brought about by changing needs rather than changing fashion. Further genteel inroads into the areas on the edge of the University Parks were made with the red-brick Engineering Laboratory (W. C. Marshall, 1914), at the apex of what later became known as the Keble Road Triangle, and the Biochemistry Laboratory to the east of the University Museum (H. Redfern, 1924–7). Most impressive of all was the Dunn School of Pathology (1925–7), designed by E. P. Warren on a prominent site at the eastern end of

The Sir William Dunn School of Pathology, South Parks Road

South Parks Road; here in its leafy setting the red-brick neo-Georgian elevations evoke the 18th-century country houses which to many educated Englishmen of the inter-war era were the acme of architectural excellence.

By 1914, after the spate of rebuilding at the turn of the century, the central streets of Oxford's academic quarter, with one or two exceptions—and allowing for the post-Second World War refacing of decayed and blackened stonework—looked much as they do now. The 1920s were a time of economic depression, and the older colleges built relatively little of note, save for a new Library at Trinity (J. Osborn Smith, 1925–7) and a new house for the Rector of Lincoln at the southern end of Turl Street, designed in 1929–30 by Herbert Read, architect of the College's attractive pre-war Library (1906); both are well-proportioned stone buildings in the neo-Georgian manner. The one new college was **St Peter's**, founded in 1929 as a 'private hall' in New Inn Hall Street, on the unfashionable western side of the city centre, by the Evangelical Bishop F. J. Chavasse of Liverpool and his son, later Bishop of Rochester, as a low-church equivalent of Keble College. There was already a heterogeneous collection of earlier buildings on the site, including the church of St Peter-le-Bailey, which became the college Chapel, the former Wyaston House, recycled as the porter's lodge, and Hannington Hall, built in 1832 in connection with an abortive revival of the ancient New Inn Hall but remodelled at the end of the 19th century; the top floor of this rather ungainly building became the Hall of St Peter's College. To these the locally based architect Fielding Dodd added a block of red-brick neo-Georgian residential buildings (see p. 200), with spacious, well-proportioned rooms, on the opposite side of a rudimentary quadrangle. Lack of funds ensured that the plans were only partially carried out (in 1930), but subsequent building down to the 1950s remained true to the original undemandingly attractive model. Dodd later went on, in 1933–4, to make an unobtrusive extension to the one surviving independent academic hall, St Edmund Hall, following its recent elevation to the status of a college. Meanwhile at the largely 16th-century **Holywell Manor**, next to the medieval church of St Cross, Balliol College set a precedent by establishing a graduate hostel in 1930 well away from the main site, employing Gilbert Spencer—brother of the more famous Stanley—to paint frescoes in one of the rooms; the picturesque rubble-stone building was extended in 1938 and again in the 1990s.

In preparing the designs for St Peter's, Fielding Dodd was helped by Herbert Baker, who was the sole architect of one of Oxford's most successful inter-war buildings, **Rhodes House** (1926–9). Like the Radcliffe Camera, Rhodes House was designed both to commemorate its founder and to benefit the University, and the Rhodes trustees, who funded it out of the diamond magnate's immense fortune, ensured that it was built on a suitably lavish scale. The site chosen was

The Library of Rhodes House

Lady Margaret Hall: the Chapel and Deneke Building

have appealed to a Willliam Butterfield or a James Stirling, but it did at least ensure that Oxford's inter-war buildings are pleasant both to live and to work in: something that cannot always be said of their successors.

Some of the largest building schemes of the 1930s were carried out by the women's colleges, which expanded after 1920, when women were allowed to read for Oxford degrees as well simply attending lectures. The Front Quadrangle at Somerville, with its attractive arched entrance from the Woodstock Road, was built in 1932–3 to the designs of the Arts-and-Crafts-trained Percy Morley Horder, brought in at the suggestion of the art critic Roger Fry, the brother of the College's Principal. And at Lady Margaret Hall a major expansion to the north of the original buildings was placed in the hands of Giles Gilbert Scott, a pupil of Temple Moore and architect of Liverpool Anglican Cathedral, perhaps the finest Gothic building of the 20th century anywhere. Scott's first Oxford commission, carried out in 1928–30, was for a discreet extension to Bodley and Garner's St Swithin's Quadrangle at Magdalen College, but at Lady Margaret Hall, where work began in 1931, he was asked to virtually double the size of the College by erecting a large new block of undergraduate rooms (the Deneke Building), including a new Hall, lit by clerestory windows, with a Chapel attached to the main block by a corridor. For the bulk of the building he adopted a simplified version of the neo-Georgian manner used earlier, though with greater sensitivity, by Reginald Blomfield. But in the Chapel he adopted what for him must

The Radcliffe Science Library extension from Parks Road

have been a much more sympathetic style, part Byzantine and part Romanesque. Built of a light-coloured brick, like the rest of his buildings for the college, it has a concrete dome and a light, spacious interior admirably suited (apart from acoustical problems) to corporate worship. Together with Lutyens's Chapel at Campion Hall, it is Oxford's finest ecclesiastical building of the inter-war years. And it was presumably Scott's success at Lady Margaret Hall which caused him to be employed in 1937–8 by the Society for Home Students, a long-established organization for the education of women at Oxford, to design their new library and common-rooms (the latter not built until after the Second World War) at the southern end of the Woodstock Road, opposite the Radcliffe Infirmary. This rather amorphous set of buildings, faced with the inevitable Bladon rubble, became in due course the nucleus of St Anne's College (see p. 321).

The most prolific architect in the Oxford of the 1930s was Sir Hubert Worthington. He was the son of Thomas Worthington, architect of Manchester College, and he spent a short time in Lutyens's office before the First World War, before becoming Professor of Architecture at the Royal College of Art and Slade Lecturer in Oxford. Worthington's first Oxford building was an extension of 1933–4 to Jackson's **Radcliffe Science Library**, and it epitomizes his immediately recognizable style. Flat-roofed and faced with punch-faced Bladon rubble, and the windows arranged in long vertical strips, there are few of the vernacular details employed by Baker or Lutyens. Instead, the mannered and slightly fussy detailing, like that of many 1930s buildings in England, is influenced by contemporary Dutch and Scandinavian models. But the internal planning is spacious, the craftsmanship excellent, and there is at least one notable work of decorative art in the form of a pair of wooden doors carved by Eric Gill, depicting scientists who had worked in Oxford. Worthington went on in 1936 to design new premises for St Catherine's Society—formerly the Delagacy for Non-Collegiate Students—replacing a group of picturesque but run-down houses in St Aldate's, to the south of the Christ Church Memorial Gardens, created ten years earlier, and now the Faculty of Music; this was followed by a new Library for New College (1939), a block of undergraduate rooms for Merton College in Rose Lane, facing the Botanic Garden (1939–40), and a group of mainly scientific buildings for the University, erected after the Second World War (see p. 303).

The largest architectural commission of the inter-war years was the **New Bodleian Library**, built to the designs of Giles Gilbert Scott. The rapid growth of printed material in the 20th century imposed a severe strain on old library buildings everywhere, and at Cambridge Scott had already designed a completely new University Library on a site well away from the historic centre of the city. In Oxford the decision was taken, perhaps unwisely, to remain on the existing site and to build a large extension—effectively a huge warehouse for five million books—with new reading-rooms and offices on the site of some older

The New Bodleian Library from the south

Map 5 'Greater Oxford'

houses on the opposite side of Broad Street, linked to the older building by an underground tunnel with a conveyor belt to move the books to the reading-rooms in the Old Library. Funding came in large measure from the Rockefeller Foundation—one of the first instances of large-scale overseas funding of a kind which was to become more common after the Second World War—and the building went up in 1937–40.

In its layout and construction the New Bodleian broke completely with earlier Oxford traditions of library building. The central core is a steel-framed book stack—an idea borrowed from American libraries visited by the Bodleian staff—which the local building regulations insisted should not be more than 50 feet high. The stack—not designed by Scott—has eleven decks, three of them underground, and is surrounded by corridors, offices, and quiet, spacious reading-rooms. What is visible from the outside is an agglomeration of rubble masonry wrapped around the stack, broken up by openings for windows and doors, some of which—like the never-used ceremonial entrance to Broad Street—do not lead anywhere very obvious. Despite Scott's efforts to impart a 'friendly texture' and a 'characteristically English' synthesis of functionalism and classical decorum, the detailing—an odd mixture of classical and Art Deco motifs—does little to relieve the inert, shapeless mass of the wall surfaces, and the decision to use small blocks of rubble stone for so massive a building was visually unfortunate. Matters were not improved by the creation of an area of 'dead space' on the Broad Street front, necessitated by the fact that the square book stack does not align with the street. The New Bodleian exposes the limitations of the belief that large buildings of modern materials can be easily humanized by dressing them up in period details, and its widely perceived inadequacies prepared the ground for a more radical approach to modern architecture which took hold in Oxford in the 1950s.

By the outbreak of the Second World War Oxford had become, for the first time in its modern history, a major manufacturing town. As early as 1925 William Morris (later Lord Nuffield) had become Britain's biggest car manufacturer, producing 41 per cent of all British cars and ensuring employment not only for the local population but also for a growing number of immigrants from the 'depressed areas' of South Wales and the north of England. By 1931 the city's population had risen to over 80,000, and in the 1930s it increased by another third to over 100,000: a rate of growth unmatched by almost any other town in England. While many of the older manufacturing towns of Britain suffered through the loss of their staple industries, Oxford enjoyed unprecedented prosperity. By 1939 Morris Motors and

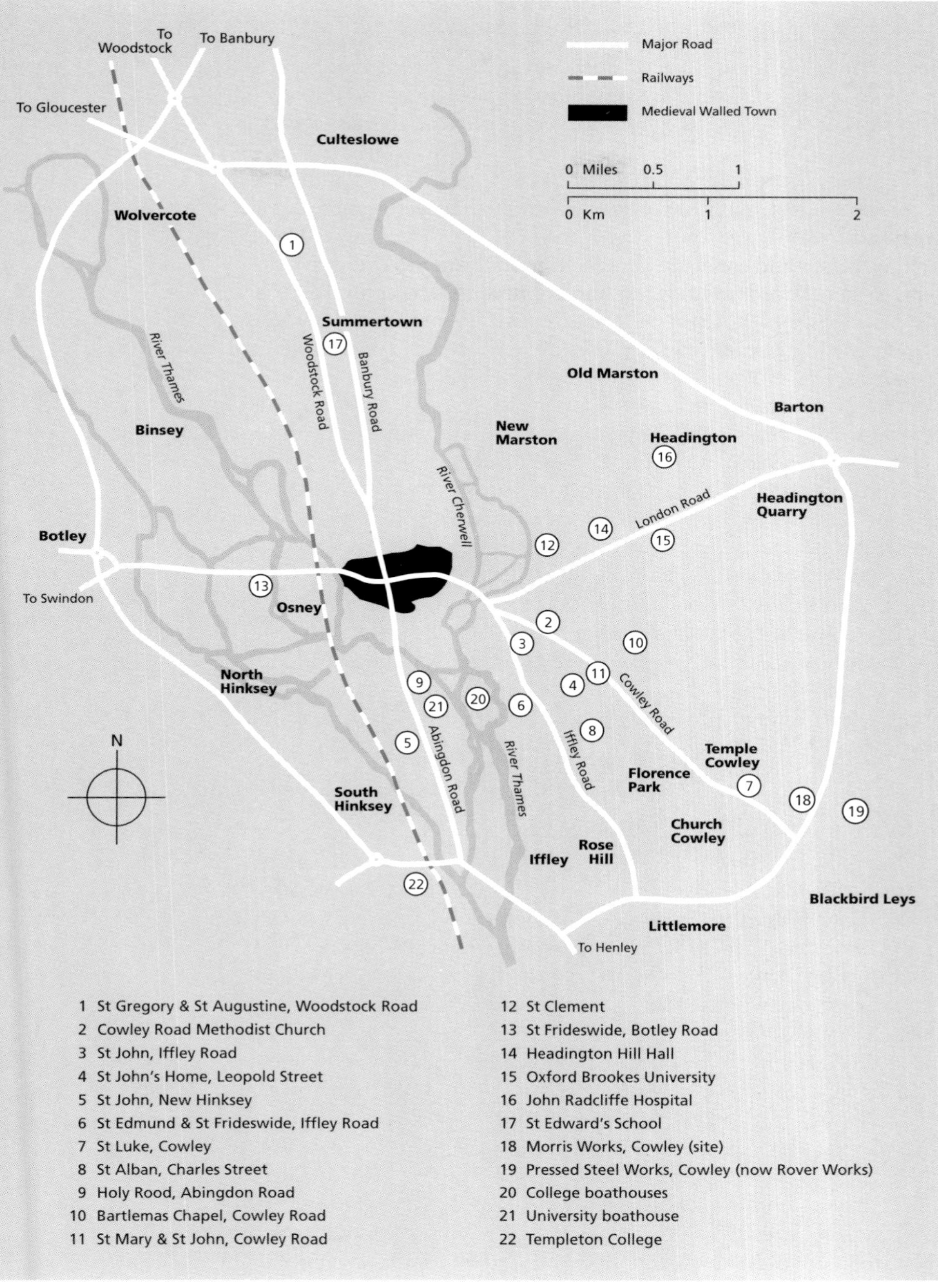

1 St Gregory & St Augustine, Woodstock Road
2 Cowley Road Methodist Church
3 St John, Iffley Road
4 St John's Home, Leopold Street
5 St John, New Hinksey
6 St Edmund & St Frideswide, Iffley Road
7 St Luke, Cowley
8 St Alban, Charles Street
9 Holy Rood, Abingdon Road
10 Bartlemas Chapel, Cowley Road
11 St Mary & St John, Cowley Road
12 St Clement
13 St Frideswide, Botley Road
14 Headington Hill Hall
15 Oxford Brookes University
16 John Radcliffe Hospital
17 St Edward's School
18 Morris Works, Cowley (site)
19 Pressed Steel Works, Cowley (now Rover Works)
20 College boathouses
21 University boathouse
22 Templeton College

Pressed Steel—the car-body manufacturing firm founded by Morris in 1926—were employing more than 10,000 people, most of them earning what were, by the standards of the period, high industrial wages.

Oxford was one of the boom towns of inter-war Britain, but the architectural results for the city were meagre in the extreme. Morris's operations were based at first in a former Military Training College by T. G. Jackson, close to the rural hamlet of Temple Cowley; as the business expanded in the 1920s, development took place on open ground to the east, and by 1939 a vast area had been covered by the utilitarian sheds necessary for modern assembly-line production. Meanwhile the city expanded fast in an easterly direction, finally taking in most of the parishes of Church Cowley, Headington, Marston, and Iffley. Rural villages of thatched, stone-built farmhouses and cottages clustered around their modest medieval churches now became part of an amorphous built-up area made up predominantly of low-density terraced and semi-detached houses for a mainly working-class and lower middle-class clientele.

During the 1920s the city council took the lead in providing new houses, building 1556 houses for rental: three times the number built by private builders. Local authorities were now, for the first time, given generous help from central government in building new

Inter-war council houses at the foot of Morrell Avenue, visible from the London road at the foot of Headington Hill and carefully detailed in the neo-Georgian manner

houses for the working classes, allowing some at least of the poor to move out of the slums which still disfigured parts of the city centre, to the dismay of social investigators like C. V. Butler, whose *Social Conditions in Oxford* (1912) was one of the first of many learned books anatomizing the lives of Oxford's working class. The first small estates of council houses, at the far ends of the Iffley and Cowley Roads, were built in 1921–2, to designs by a group of local architects; with their steeply gabled roofs and careful Arts and Crafts detailing, they show a strong debt to the work of Parker and Unwin at Letchworth Garden City and Hampstead Garden Suburb. But much more was done after 1928, when the city's boundaries expanded to twice their former area. The corporation had obtained powers to borrow money in order to buy land for housing four years before, and, with government grants still in operation, the houses built at the end of the decade were notable for their generous scale and careful detailing, often neo-Georgian in character. The architect was Kellett Ablett, who came to work for the City Engineer's department in 1925; good examples of his work can be seen in the gently curving Morrell Avenue (1929–31), alongside the Morrell family's estate on Headington Hill, and in the Gipsy Lane estate at the top of Headington Hill. Judged from both an architectural and an environmental point of view, these houses were as good as any of this kind built in England at the time.

The council houses of the 1920s were deliberately let at high rents in order to attract the 'better sort' of working man and his family, thus in theory enabling the poor to move out of the city centre slums into the houses vacated by the new council tenants. But with slum conditions persisting, and with the Depression of 1929–31 exacerbating unemployment throughout much of England, the Labour government passed an Act of Parliament in 1930, directing local authorities to concentrate their efforts on providing low-rental housing for occupation by the slum-dwellers, whose noxious dwellings were to be eradicated. So the council houses of the 1930s were planned on a less generous scale than those of the 1920s, and less attention was paid to architectural effect; the results can be seen in the huge estates built on the city boundaries at Cutteslowe, Rose Hill, and elsewhere. Meanwhile, the newcomers attracted by the car works were largely housed by private builders, responsible for about four-fifths of the estimated 5280 new houses constructed in Oxford during the 1930s. Some of the builders operated on a very large scale, like F. E. Moss, who developed the huge Florence Park estate at Church Cowley in 1933–7 for letting to car workers who could not afford to buy their own houses; elsewhere he built houses for sale, charging between £600 and £700 in the late 1920s. His houses were small and externally extremely plain, with roughcast elevations and slate roofs, but at Florence Park he made an attempt to create a sense of identity through the provision of a park, opened in 1936, with a wide approach road lined with shops. Elsewhere on the eastern fringes of the city there is little to break the monotony. And when Lord Nuffield embarked on a traditional gesture of patronage by paying for a new church, St Luke, Oxford Road, a well-proportioned Gothic building by a talented local architect, H. S. Rogers, in 1938, he was criticized by some malcontents for wasting money which could have been used to increase the wages of the workers; the church is now redundant. The only other inter-war parish church of any note is St Alban, Charles Street (T. L. Dale, 1928–33), hidden among the turn-of-the-century artisan housing to the north of the Iffley Road. But it is a mere fragment of what was originally intended and the interest lies more in the fittings, including a set of stations of the cross by Eric Gill and his son (1938–45), than in the architecture, pleasing though this is.

The showrooms for Morris Garages Ltd (now the Oxford Crown Court) at the southern end of St Aldate's

Oxford's inter-war prosperity led to a certain amount of commercial building in the city centre, but even the greatest enthusiast for the architecture of the 1930s would find it difficult to single out more than one or two buildings from the general mediocrity. The Royal Oxford Hotel near the railway station (E. T. Leed, 1935) is fairly typical in its neo-Georgian elevations, though the effect is marred by the use of a bilious-looking yellow stone from Temple Guiting in Gloucestershire. Large-scale alterations took place on the northern side of George Street with the building of the depressing brick-clad New Theatre (W. and F. R. Milburn, 1933–4) and the equally insensitive ABC Cinema on the site of a 19th-century church to the south of Gloucester Green. But the most far-reaching changes took place to the south of the city centre, between Christ Church and Folly Bridge, where a congeries of courts and alleys had grown up over the centuries outside the long-vanished south gate of the city. On the site of these overcrowded and insanitary dwellings there sprang up the pompous ashlar-faced Morris car showroom (Henry Smith, 1932; now the Oxford Crown Court) and the bland though well-proportioned Police Station (H. T. Hurcombe, 1936), both of them neo-Georgian in character, as well as Hubert Worthington's new premises for St Catherine's Society. Thus the transformation of the southern approach to the city began, and a precedent was set for the more extensive clearances carried out to the south-west of the city centre in the 1960s.

8 From Modernism to Post-Modernism

The Second World War left the physical fabric of Oxford almost unscathed, but it led indirectly to fundamental changes in the character of the University. The first and most obvious change was an increase in the number of students, attracted by the principle of universal grants enshrined in the Education Act of 1944 and by the determination of successive governments down to the 1980s to encourage the ancient universities as nurseries of a meritocratic managerial élite. Largely through this influx of State-funded students—among the most fortunate beneficiaries of the Welfare State—student numbers, including those of graduate students, doubled to about 12,000 between 1939 and 1985.

An equally important result of the war was the great increase in research activity, especially in the sciences and social sciences. Oxford had built up a reputation for pioneering work in certain of the sciences, especially chemistry, between the wars, and during the Second World War and afterwards it became one of the world's leading scientific universities. The main paymaster in the post-war years was the University Grants Committee, funded by both Labour and Conservative administrations in the belief, unchallenged until the 1980s, that publicly funded research was an essential component of economic growth. The growing importance of research increased the power of the University, both as the co-ordinator of the increasingly complex academic life of Oxford and as a conduit for government grants. But private benefactors also stepped in to fund new colleges, housing ever more post-graduate students, whose numbers increased by 40 per cent during the 1960s. There are now (1997) thirty-nine colleges, eleven of them post-war foundations, of which three—St Catherine's, Mansfield, and Manchester (recently renamed Harris Manchester)—existed before the war as societies or halls. All but three of the post-war colleges cater for post-graduate students.

The Florey Building, Queen's College

The most important architectural project of the immediate post-war years was the building of a new college for graduates engaged in research into the social sciences. It bears the name of William Morris, Lord **Nuffield**, the founder of Morris Motors and the man who, more than anyone else, was responsible for Oxford's growth as an industrial city. In 1937 Nuffield offered a million pounds to the University in order to establish what would in effect have been a post-graduate business school specializing in 'engineering and accountancy'. This proposal did not meet with the approval of the left-wing Vice-Chancellor, A. D. Lindsay, Master of Balliol, and he persuaded the reluctant benefactor to shift the academic focus to 'the study by co-operation between academic and non-academic persons of social (including economic and political) problems'. The site was one which Nuffield had himself purchased, in New Road to the north of the castle mound, an area hithero occupied by the largely defunct Oxford Canal basin. Thus the shabby western approach to the city centre would be improved and beautified by the man whose car factories had done so much to transform (though not to beautify) the area to the east of Magdalen Bridge. Meanwhile the University would establish a significant outpost in the western part of the city centre.

Designs were procured from a number of architects, and in 1938 the University opted, somewhat perversely, for a scheme prepared by Austen Harrison, the expatriate designer of several British government buildings in the Middle East. This represented a highly original, though somewhat forbidding, reworking of the traditional quadrangular layout, with a research institute placed on the western side of Worcester Street, and the residential part of the college disposed around two courtyards to the east. The courtyards were to be separated by a flight of steps, with the upper one dominated by a stark lantern tower concealing the vestibule and staircase to the aisled Hall, raised up to first-floor level and divided by rows of round arches resting on massive columns of Greek Doric profile. But Nuffield told the University in 1939 that the design was 'un-English and out of keeping with the best tradition of Oxford architecture; as well as contrary to my expressed wishes that it should be in conformity with that tradition'. He threatened to withdraw his support, and Harrison was forced to produce a new design 'on the lines of Cotswold domestic architecture'. It was this design which, after many modifications and savings, formed the basis of the College whose construction finally began in 1949.

The building of Nuffield College took place against a background of post-war economic stringency which dictated a slow pace of construction and the omission of several of the key features in Harrison's original plan. The research institute to the west of Worcester Street was never built, and the site is now ignominiously

Nuffield College, looking east

occupied by a car park. The Chapel and the Library were resited in a redesigned tower to the north of the New Road entrance. This ungainly structure—a parody of the steeples of medieval Oxford—is essentially a masonry-clad steel-framed book stack, lit by a monotonous array of windows punched out of the wall surface, and capped by a copper-covered spike. The rest of the college is less gauche in appearance, though the architecture lacks the power of Harrison's original design. Gables, mullions, smooth ashlar walls of Cotswold stone, and stone slate roofs all work their familiar charm, albeit in the context of a classically inspired plan derived from the original scheme. A rectangular strip of water runs through the lower quadrangle and a flight of steps leads up to the Hall, lit by large mullioned and transomed windows, with an open timber roof supported on pointed arches of concrete: an effective reinterpretation of the traditional collegiate pattern.

Meanwhile, building resumed in the older colleges. In the mid-1950s less than half of the male undergraduates were housed in college rooms, the remainder renting rooms from landladies in the town. But in the last forty years the proportion of students residing 'in college' has steadily increased, and several colleges now accommodate students on site or in satellite hostels for the whole of

Queen's College: the Provost's Lodgings from Queens Lane

their undergraduate career. Funding came from the colleges' own endowments, from private benefactors and, increasingly, from appeals to old members and well-wishers, supplemented by loans from the University and, in a few cases, by funds from the University Grants Committee. The accent at first was on an understated and undemanding continuity with pre-war traditions. At Mansfield College Thomas Rayson, the last of Oxford's Arts and Crafts-inspired architects, designed a new block of undergraduate rooms as late as 1960–2, which are all but indistinguishable from the 'collegiate Gothic' work of Basil Champneys, built when Queen Victoria still had several years to live. Elsewhere the neo-Georgian idiom held sway: in the Dolphin Quadrangle at St John's (1948), designed by an old member of the college, Edward Maufe, architect of the equally unassuming façade of the Oxford Playhouse in Beaumont Street (1938), and later of Guildford Cathedral; in [Sir Albert] Richardson and Houfe's Principal's Lodgings and Wolfson Building at St Hilda's (1954–61); and above all in Raymond Erith's Provost's Lodgings at Queen's (1958–9), the most consistently classical of all the Oxford colleges. This is a robust ashlar-faced building, square in plan, with a simple two-storeyed elevation towards the College and a highly original frontage to the high-walled Queen's Lane. Heavily rusticated on the ground floor, with three tiny windows to break up the bare expanse of ashlar walling above, it has a vitality and intellectual integrity absent from most of the other rather effete neo-Georgian buildings of the time.

Erith also worked on a larger scale at **Lady Margaret Hall**. His first building here was a new Library (1959–61), which makes up the east range of the front quadrangle, facing Reginald Blomfield's Lodge Building of 1926. Like Blomfield's buildings, it is of red brick, and the first-floor reading-room is lit by windows placed between the study carrels, with semicircular lunette windows—a favourite English Palladian motif—above; there is a squashed-looking stone colonnade below, possibly echoing Lord Burlington's rather more elegant early 18th-century dormitory at Westminster School. Erith claimed that 'the elevations are simply the outcome of the internal arrangements, the design is functional even though the style is not.' And, despite the awkward external proportions, the spacious, well-lit interior vindicates his statement. Erith was also responible for the barrack-like range of 1963–6 which served as a new entrance to the College, facing Blomfield's Talbot Building. This was financed by the Wolfson Foundation, which contributed generously to building projects at several of the women's colleges in the 1960s, and Erith hoped that the street front would 'do something to rest the eyes and nerves of North Oxford'. With its bare red-brick walls and massive pedimented archway, it certainly presents a forbidding face to the outside world: a contrast of mood, if not the rest for overstrung academic sensibilities that the architect intended.

Continuity with the past was strongly emphasized in the first post-war buildings to go up in the **Science Area** south of the University Parks. A new phase of development began here in 1939–40 with the building of a utilitarian-looking Physical Chemistry laboratory, funded by Lord Nuffield and designed by the firm of Lanchester and Lodge, who later went on to design buildings for the Departments of Physiology (1949–53) and Inorganic Chemistry (1954–60), the latter coated more attractively in a rubble-stone façade echoing that of Hubert Worthington's Radcliffe Science Library extension of the 1930s. Worthington himself designed similar buildings for the Forestry and Botany departments on nearby sites in 1947–50, notable mainly for their spacious, well-finished interiors; the interior of the Forestry building is adorned with wood from the different countries of the Commonwealth supplied by, among others, the Rajah of Sarawak. Worthington was also the architect of the rubble-faced, flat-roofed History Faculty Library (now the Philosophy Sub-Faculty), built in Merton Street to a discreet pre-war design in 1954–6.

It was against this placid background that the Modern Movement made its first impact on post-war Oxford. In 1952 the influential critic

J. M. Richards launched a broadside in the *Architectural Review* against the recent architecture of both the ancient universities, calling Nuffield 'a missed opportunity of a really tragic kind', and bemoaning the lack of 'any awareness of what is happening in the arts in the contemporary world, or any marked sense of what are the contemporary issues'. He singled out for special criticism the fashion of 'outsentimentalizing the sentimentalist by peppering the dignified ashlar stone city with buildings of rubble masonry entirely foreign to its character—more appropriate to a Cotswold village', as in Worthington's recent buildings in the Science Area, or the otherwise modernistic new buildings for Wadham designed in 1948–53 by H. G. Goddard, an old member of the College. These views were echoed by a handful of architecturally minded dons, including David Henderson, an economist and a Fellow of Lincoln College, who criticized the 'completely unreflective conservatism in matters of building' which prevailed throughout the University and became a leading member of a University committee for 'elevations and the choice of architects'. The stage was thus set for an architectural upheaval comparable to those which had transformed the design of Oxford buildings in the 1660s and the 1850s. University committees and college governing bodies were gradually persuaded to commission buildings from a younger generation of architects trained under the new ideas which had recently swept through the schools of architecture. Taking their inspiration from the Continental architects of the inter-war period—Gropius, Mies van der Rohe, Le Corbusier, and their followers—these younger architects saw a virtue in bold experimentation and took a positive delight in the use of forms and materials which they believed would express the spirit of the age.

The modernist idiom first made its impact on Oxford in the late 1950s, starting with the construction of four new college boat-houses immediately to the east of Christ Church Meadow in 1957–9, to the designs of Bridgewater and Shepheard, and Henry Goddard; with their nautical flavour, characteristic of much inter-war modernism, these are still among the most attractive monuments of the Modern Movement in the city. The progress of the new style can also be clearly charted in the Science Area. Here the key building also went up in 1957–9 as a home for the Dyson Perrins Organic Chemistry laboratories and lecture-room; the architect, Basil Ward, first made his reputation in the 1930s as a member of the partnership of Connell, Ward, and Lucas. Now a member of the firm of Ramsey, Murray, White, and Ward. he was chosen on the urging of David Henderson in preference to Lanchester and Lodge, and his stark

The Dyson Perrins laboratories and lecture-room

concrete and glass structure was later described by the Oxford Design Society as an 'exciting display of structural virtuosity . . . it crouches ill at ease among its stuffy neighbours, lightly draped with glass, but taut and poised as if to spring away': something not immediately apparent to the casual observer. The same firm went on in 1960–3 to design a nine-storey concrete and glass tower block for the Department of Engineering on a site to the north of Keble College, in an area of Victorian houses (the 'Keble Road Triangle') set aside for University buildings by Oxford's post-war town planners. This characterless structure was of unprecedented height, and in 1962, with plans for another tower for the Zoology Department in the offing, the City Council imposed height guidelines for future buildings, enabling the city's skyline—one of its greatest aesthetic assets—to be preserved. A more humane example of the modernist idiom is the **Maison Française** (Jacques Laurent, with Brian Ring, Howard and Partners, 1962–3), hidden away among the Victorian villas of Norham Road in North Oxford; its simple geometric shapes and lack of ornament exemplify the principles of clarity and puritanical restraint which inspired the founding fathers of the Modern Movement in architecture.

The first uncompromisingly modernist college building was the 'Beehive' block in the North Quadrangle at **St John's**, built in 1958–60 to the designs of Michael Powers of the Architects' Co-Partnership.

The 'Beehive' building at St John's College. The Senior Common Room of 1673–6 is to the right

The firm, which had designed an extension to the President's Lodgings at Corpus Christi in the previous year, was recommended by the architectural historian John Summerson, a member of the avant-garde MARS (Modern Architecture Research) group in the 1930s, and through the efforts of some of the younger Fellows the College was persuaded to drop earlier Tudor-Gothic plans by Edward Maufe, the architect of the northern side of the quadrangle. Though relatively small, the new building represented a radical departure from the norms of Oxford collegiate architecture. The pairs of rooms which had been thought appropriate for the 'young gentlemen' of the 19th and early 20th centuries now gave way to single study-bedrooms with under-floor heating. They are hexagonal in shape, possibly reflecting what Philip Opher has called 'an interest in organic form current among architects at the time', and are arranged on either side of hexagonal staircases lit from above through lanterns surmounted by pyramid roofs. The hexagonal shape of the rooms determines the unconventional serrated elevation of the building, and the architects were equally bold in their choice of materials. The carved mouldings which had been a feature of Oxford buildings, both Gothic and classic, from time immemorial, were now abandoned, to be replaced by unbroken expanses of Portland ashlar stone—hitherto little used in Oxford—with dark metal panels underneath the broad sliding plate-glass windows. Here, as much as in the choice of style, the Beehive signified an important new initiative.

The triumph of modernism in Oxford was secured by the erection of a completely new college designed according to the purest and most uncompromising precepts of the International Style. **St Catherine's College** grew out of St Catherine's Society for Non-Collegiate Students, which had for the last twenty-five years occupied premises in St Aldate's designed by Hubert Worthington (see p. 291), but with the growth of undergraduate numbers in the 1950s, especially among students reading for science degrees, it soon became obvious that new buildings would be needed. Plans for a road across Christ Church Meadow (see p. 329) precluded expansion on the existing site, so in 1957 Merton College offered to sell an empty site to the north-east of the city centre among the water meadows by the River Cherwell, close to Holywell Manor and St Cross church; the buildings in St Aldate's were earmarked for the newly founded graduate-only Linacre College. The Master of St Catherine's, Alan (later Lord) Bullock, now embarked on an energetic programme of fund-raising, mainly from commerce and industry, but, declaring himself 'somewhat perplexed' by recent British architecture, he decided to search Europe for an architect: an unprecedented decision which was much criticized at the time. Accompanied by the University Surveyor and other Oxford luminaries, including the ebulliant Maurice Bowra, Warden of Wadham College, he therefore embarked on a tour of recent Continental buildings before settling on the Danish architect Arne Jacobsen, whose work, embodying the much-admired welfarist social ethic of the Scandinavian countries, was brought to his attention by David Henderson. Bullock later wrote: 'From the moment I walked into Munkegaards School [near Copenhagen], I felt convinced that after nearly two years of looking we had found the architect we wanted.' It was therefore to Jacobsen's designs that the buildings were erected between 1960 and 1964.

In both its layout and its architectural character, St Catherine's represents as sharp a break from Oxford tradition as Keble College a century earlier. In contrast to Nuffield College, where the patron had intervened to force the architect to give his designs a more traditionalist flavour, Alan Bullock and his colleagues were happy to give Jacobsen free rein in transplanting his minimalist, puritanical style to Oxford. He was told to use the quadrangular layout, with staircase entry to the rooms, but his strictly geometrical plan and rigidly unified pseudo-functionalist aesthetic bear very little relationship to collegiate architecture as hithero understood. Everywhere the much-admired virtues of the picturesque and the pragmatic give way to the remorseless working out of a single idea. Two long parallel blocks of rooms are placed on either side of an often

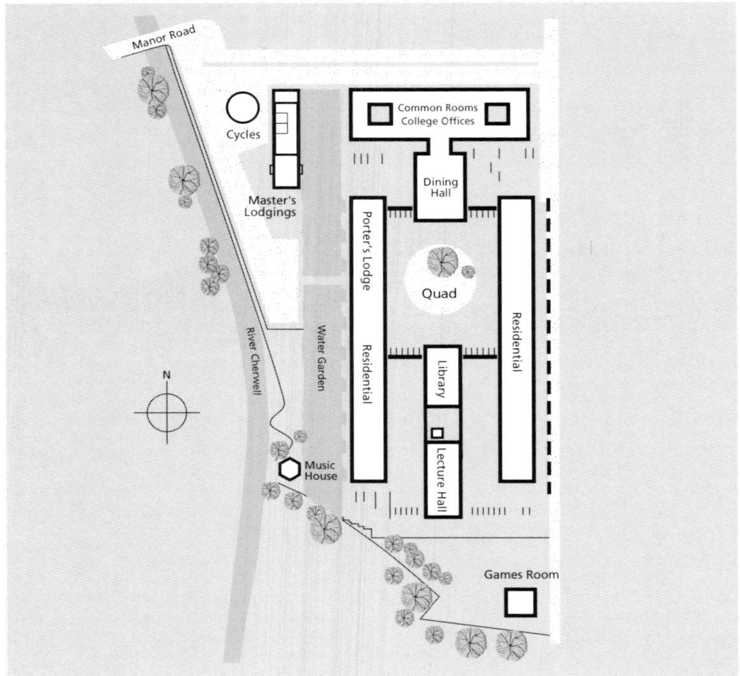

St Catherine's College: ground plan

windswept open space, in which are set detached buildings housing the Hall, Library, and lecture-rooms (in another departure from precedent no chapel was provided); a low common-room and administrative range joins the two residential blocks at the northern end. Verticality is banished, apart from a perfunctory bell tower, and ornament non-existent. Writing in the *Architectural Review*, the critic Reyner Banham mischievously described the college in 1964 as 'the best motel in Oxford'.

St Catherine's does not announce itself to the outside world, and visitors sidle in past the circular bicycle sheds before seeing the westernmost residential block across an expanse of lawn, with a rectangular strip of water and a sculpture by Barbara Hepworth in front. The College was among the first in Oxford to abandon traditional load-bearing walls in favour of frame construction, and the upper floors of the residential blocks are cantilevered out, their plate-glass curtain walls—reflecting the work of Mies van der Rohe—interrupted only by massively protruding concrete beams which form the constructional leitmotif throughout the College, even in the low, one-storeyed common-rooms. The other materials are plate-glass, copper—for the facing of the Library block—and buff-coloured bricks, made to special dimensions determined by the architect, and

The west range of St Catherine's College, with a sculpture by Barbara Hepworth in the foreground

as alien to Oxford's traditions as the red brick of Keble (and arguably less attractive). Visual relief comes mainly from the sensitive planting, making use of numerous low brick walls which form part of Jacobsen's plan, and the pervasive feeling—rare in the older colleges—of unenclosed space. The undergraduate rooms, built within cost limits laid down by the University Grants Committee, are noticeably lacking in privacy. But a real sense of nobility was achieved in the Hall, a vast room capable of seating all the members of the College at one time: an important factor in establishing the sense of corporate identity and loyalty which Bullock and the founding Fellows wished to promote. The shadowy, uninterrupted space is defined by the rectilinear trabeated structure of polished concrete beams resting on massive uprights, and lit by windows placed high in the bare walls of exposed brick. Expense was not a prime consideration here, though the floor was laid in Westmorland slate instead of the marble which Jacobsen had wanted. Like the other communal rooms of the College, the Hall was designed as a 'total work of art', with the tables, chairs, benches, and even the cutlery designed, Bauhaus-fashion, by Jacobsen himself; the curvaceous swivelling chairs at the high table prompted one unsympathetic observer (H. Plommer) to complain that 'they seem so carefully

The interior of the Hall at St Catherine's College

designed for bodies of one particular shape, that one fears for any diner not built on the generous lines of a thegn or a jarl.' Throughout the College it is impossible to escape the presence of a ruthlessly logical, almost obsessive mind at work. Nowhere in Oxford is there a stronger sense of a modern university as a secular, essentially utilitarian institution, and nowhere in England is there a purer statement of the architectural ideals of the Modern Movement as understood in its heroic earlier years.

A different, though equally uncompromising approach was adopted in the nearby **St Cross Building** (1961–4). This massive pile houses the English and Law Faculties and the Institute of Economics and Statistics, each with its own library and offices: an indication of the new emphasis on the University as a research institution. Funding came in part from the Rockefeller Foundation and the University Grants Committee, and the design was placed in the hands of the uncompromising modernist Leslie Martin, Professor of Architecture at Cambridge University, and his partner Colin St John Wilson. In their recent and much-publicized Harvey Court for Gonville and Caius College, Cambridge, Martin and Wilson had drawn upon the work of the influential Finnish architect Alvar Aalto, especially in their expressive use of brick. The St Cross Building is more complex in plan than Harvey Court, but it employs a similar architectural language. Martin subscribed to Le Corbusier's belief that 'the plan is the generator [of form]', and the form of the building is determined by the internal arrangement of differently sized boxes—offices, top-lit L-shaped libraries, and windowless lecture-rooms—placed at different levels and ingeniously interlocking with one another. The resulting agglomeration of massive cubic blocks is clad in buff brick—chosen, though this is not very apparent to the observer, to harmonize with the stone of the adjacent Holywell Manor and St Cross church—and broken up by long strips of plate-glass windows with metal frames: a favourite Corbusian mannerism. The most striking feature, though, is the monumental external staircase, leading from St Cross Road to the English and Law Libraries on the top floor, and conjuring up subliminal images of the Odessa steps in Eisenstein's *Battleship Potemkin*—a film much admired in the 1960s. The effect is impressive, but lacks humanity: a criticism which can be applied to much of Martin's work.

Martin went on in 1963 to prepare grandiose schemes for a series of scientific buildings on the south side of South Parks Road, an area of Victorian houses overlooking college playing fields. The orignal intention was to build a tower block for the Department of Zoology,

The St Cross Building (English and Law Faculties, and the Institute of Economics and Statistics) from the south-west

plans for which were commissioned from the firm of Chamberlin, Powell, and Bon, but they provoked an outcry and were rejected. Martin's scheme, matured through a series of theoretical studies, set out to provide equivalent amounts of space in much lower buildings, not only for zoology and but also for other sciences. By the time work started on the block housing the **Zoology and Psychology Departments** (1966–71), Harold Wilson's Labour government had come to power, with its emphasis on the need for Britain to invest in the 'white heat of the technological revolution', and Martin's design embodies the prevalent mood of scientific triumphalism. The forbidding concrete megastructure consists of two sets of laboratories arranged like giant flights of steps on either side of a central spine, which contains artificially lit libraries and lecture-rooms, along with the inevitable corridors and lifts. The walls are of pre-cast concrete, deliberately left rough to show the marks of the wooden shuttering: a favourite mannerism of the 1960s derived ultimately from the later works of Le Corbusier. With its gargantuan scale and shabby, greying exterior, the building shows no regard for the existing urban fabric, and precious little for the sensibilities of those who have to use it: a criticism which can be levelled with even more force at the same architect's University Offices, built for a growing University administration on the southern side of Little Clarendon Street and completed in 1974.

The Zoology and Psychology Departments from the south-west

Powell and Moya's new buildings at Brasenose College, looking south

The 1960s and early 1970s saw a 'great rebuilding' in the Oxford colleges, comparable in scale and scope to any of its earlier counterparts. This was a time of economic growth—though the academic pundits continually bemoaned the fact that it was not as fast as in other countries—and few societies escaped the virus of competitive building, often funded by appeals to old members or benefactions from rich donors. Meanwhile the architects, many of them from well-known London firms, vied with one another to provide original solutions to the age-old—and, in principle, not very complex—problem of housing the transitory student population. Of the many architects involved, the most prolific were Philip Powell and J. H. Moya. They had first made their mark in the post-war Churchill Gardens housing estate at Pimlico in London, and had subsequently built up a reputation in the school and hospital building programmes demanded by the Welfare State. Their Oxford début came in 1959 when they were commissioned by **Brasenose College**, whose Bursar was an enthusiast for modernist architecture, to construct a new set of rectangular study-bedrooms on a very confined site behind T. G. Jackson's New Quadrangle. As Powell later said, '[the] College's requirements, typical and rational for such a site, were simple—fit in, squeeze in, as many rooms as you can without being anti-social about it.' Like Michael Powers at St John's, they employed Portland stone

A top-floor room in the Blue Boar Quadrangle at Christ Church, looking towards Tom Quad

from the mollusc-rich Roach beds, together with large metal-framed plate-glass windows and extensive lead cladding. But their plan is more complex, with a series of low one-storeyed 'pavilions' placed in the cramped space next to the Jackson building, and two four-storeyed blocks at the southern end of the site, overlooking the churchyard of All Saints church. From there the effect is highly sculptural and, by carefully relating the scale of the new buildings to those of their neighbours, Powell and Moya showed that it was possible to use the architectural language of the Modern Movement in a creative and original way in Oxford, without detracting from the historic appeal of the surroundings: something which eluded several of their contemporaries.

Powell and Moya went on to design a larger L-shaped set of study-bedrooms at Blue Boar Quad in **Christ Church** (1964–7), deftly fitted into the College's former car park between Tom Quad and Blue Boar Street. Here too they used Portland stone, notably in the heavy masonry buttresses which counteract the dominance of the blank window surfaces. Further variety and contrast came from the retention of a 17th-century brewhouse and the old gently curving rubble-stone wall along Blue Boar Street; this serves as the ground-floor wall on the northern side of the north range, the upper floors of which peep over it to enliven the view along the street. An equal respect for the *genius loci* was shown in their Christ Church Picture Gallery of 1967–8, designed to house the College's splendid art collection, which had hitherto been housed in the Lower Library,

The glazed eastern wall of the Christ Church Picture Gallery, with the back of James Wyatt's Canterbury Quadrangle in the background

now required for readers. The new building was sunk below the Dean's garden and is externally totally invisible to the visitors, who approach through a discreet entrance in the Canterbury Quad. Inside, however, there is a series of well-lit, minimally detailed galleries which rank among the most successful modernist interiors in Oxford.

In their new building for **Corpus Christi** in Magpie Lane (finished in 1969), Powell and Moya abandoned Portland stone in favour of local limestone rubble, redolent of Baker and Worthington, though used now in conjunction with an exposed concrete frame and characteristically large windows. Great efforts were made to fit the new building into its surroundings: an exuberantly detailed block by T. G. Jackson immediately to the south, the boundary wall of Oriel College to the west, and the tower of Merton closing the southward view down the narrow street. As in all the firm's best Oxford work, the visual appeal lies in the highly textured surfaces and carefully contrived outlines, tempering the ideals of modernism with the pragmatic, picturesque virtues of much 19th- and early 20th-century English architecture.

Powell and Moya were also responsible for the building of **Wolfson College**, one of two new foundations established by the University in the mid-1960s to cater for the growing number of academics and post-graduate students without collegiate affiliations (the other was St Cross College, which took up residence in 1981 in part of Pusey House). Founded as Iffley College in 1964, the new society changed its name after a generous grant from the Wolfson Foundation, and the

An aerial view of Wolfson College from the east, with the River Cherwell in the foreground and the villas of North Oxford behind. The pyramid roof covers the Hall, and the married students' flats are on the extreme right

buildings were erected in 1969–74 on a site close to the River Cherwell in deepest North Oxford, well away from the city centre. As at St Catherine's, the choice of an architect was preceded by an extensive tour of recent university buildings, in Holland and Finland as well as Britain, and advice was also sought from two of the gurus of English modernism, J. M. Richards and Nikolaus Pevsner. But here a home-bred partnership was preferred, and Powell and Moya's solution to the problem of designing a new college was revealingly different from Arne Jacobsen's at St Catherine's. The layout is more intimate, the planning less rigidly rationalistic. The college aimed to instil a 'decent and reasonable egalitarianism' and the buildings were intended, in the words of one of the founding Fellows, to be 'on a scale suited to their surroundings and suited also to their human occupants': a modern reinterpretation of the late Victorian ideals of 'sweetness and light'. So there are two closed quadrangles, smaller than anything at St Catherine's, one of which is masked by a colonnade from blocks of married students' flats—the first to be provided on this scale in Oxford. A residential block stretches out from the Hall and Library quadrangle towards the willow-fringed river, where the architects created an artificial island and 'punt harbour'. The architecture is somewhat monotonous, with its repetitive use of exposed reinforced concrete frames, large plate-glass windows, and flat roofs, and the entrance from Linton Road is unnecessarily grim. But the changes of level are carefully managed and the buildings are beautifully integrated with the landscape of the Cherwell valley, showing once again the architects' sympathy for the English picturesque tradition.

Apart from Powell and Moya, the most widely employed architectural firm in Oxford in the 1960s and early 1970s was Arup Associates. Their guiding spirit was Philip Dowson, a graduate of the avant-garde Architectural Association school in London, who had entered the office of the engineer Ove Arup, one of the pioneer English modernists, in the 1950s, and had established a 'building group' within the organiszation so as to integrate all the varied aspects of building within a single design team: an idea which can be taken back to Gropius and the Bauhaus in the 1920s. Dowson's first Oxford commission came about as a result of a recommendation by the Nobel Prize-winning scientist Dorothy Hodgkin to Janet Vaughan, Principal of **Somerville College**. Like all the heads of the women's colleges, she was under pressure from central government to increase the number of women in Oxford, and in 1962–6 two blocks of study-

The south range of Wolfson College

The north side of Little Clarendon Street, with the Fry Building for Somerville College perching above the shops

bedrooms were built to Dowson's designs to the south of the College's main quadrangle, with a façade to Little Clarendon Street, until then an unpretentious thoroughfare linking Woodstock Road and Walton Street. The Vaughan and Fry Buildings, as they became known, perch like packing-cases on a brick-faced plinth containing shops, approached from the street through a row of segment-headed concrete arches—influenced by Le Corbusier's much-admired Maisons Jaoul in Paris—and the rooms are inserted within an exposed frame of pre-cast concrete, reflecting the frequently reiterated rationalist belief that the structure of a building should be comprehensible to the viewer; Dowson also believed that the arrangement would allow privacy and shade to the plate-glass-windowed rooms, although, like other architects of the time, he does not seem to have bothered greatly about noise, which was described as 'intolerable' by some of the occupants. A more jagged and 'brutalist' version of the same system was adopted in the Fry and Wolfson Buildings, on the western side of the quadrangle, facing Walton Street (1964–7), but here the box-like plate-glass windows were brought forward to project beyond the jagged concrete frame.

Dowson employed the 'structural grid' again after his firm won a limited competition for the Sir Thomas White Building at **St John's**

(1970–5). This is a large L-shaped development of study-bedrooms and common-rooms for 145 students, built on the college's northern boundary adjoining Museum Road and funded out of the abundant income which fell into the College's lap after the sale of houses on the North Oxford estate. The frame, of 'bush-hammered' concrete, is the dominant feature in the design, leaping over an old rubble-stone wall in Museum Road and establishing an insistently rectangular pattern on all the elevations. But its repetitive form is broken up by the intrusion of concrete turrets, clad in French limestone and housing the staircases, and by the lead-covered pavilions on the roof-line. With the completion of the building, St John's was now able to offer all its undergraduates three years of living in College: an important factor in the competition to attract the best students, and one which was imitated by other colleges when they could afford to do so.

The Arup firm was also heavily involved in the development of the 'Keble Road Triangle'. Dowson had already experimented with the application of industrialized techniques to scientific research buildings in the Mining and Metallurgy building at Birmingham University, and, following the completion of Basil Ward's tower block for the Engineering Department, he was brought in to design a

A recent bird's-eye view of St John's College, showing the Front Quadrangle, Canterbury Quadrangle, and Dolphin Quadrangle in the foreground, with the North Quadrangle, and the Sir Thomas White Building to the left. The Garden Quadrangle is at the far side of the garden in the distance

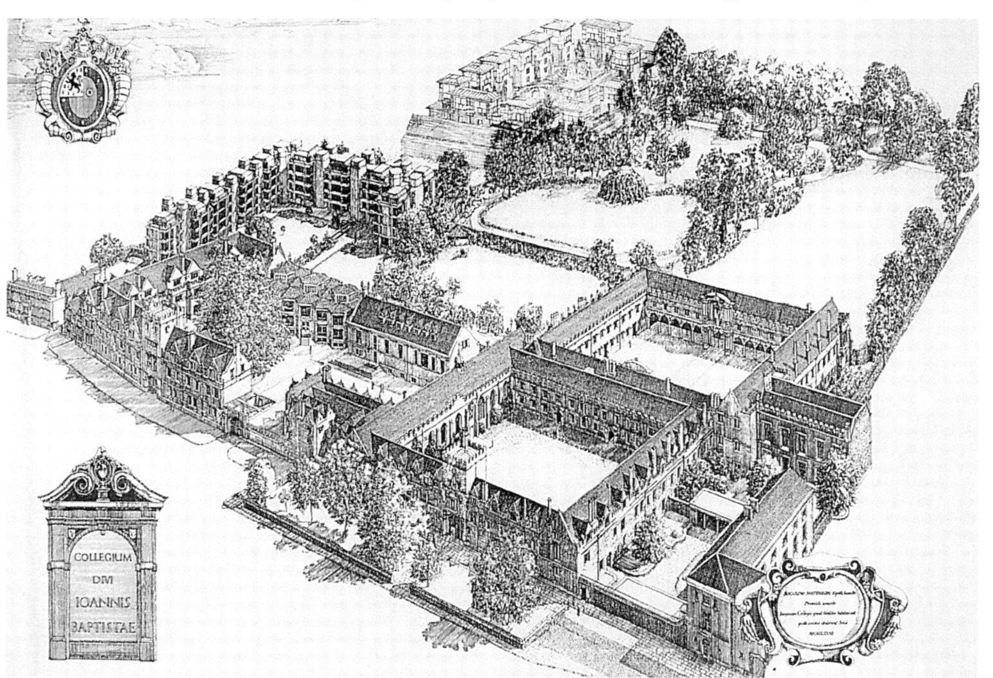

Nuclear Physics laboratory at the southern end of the site. Vying with Leslie Martin's Zoology and Psychology complex for the dubious title of the most brutalist building in Oxford, this ungainly pile, completed in 1970, is notable mainly for the extraordinary fan-shaped concrete superstructure to the Vandergraf generator (a kind of linear accelerator) which greets the visitor approaching the centre of Oxford along the Banbury Road. A new block for the Departments of Engineering and Metallurgy followed in 1971–6, its concrete frame and insistent horizontal lines of the cantilevered floors conveying an air of intimidating power. And, in accordance with much-touted Corbusier-influenced theories of the time, a first-floor 'deck access' was instituted, ensuring that the massive complex bears no relationship to the streets around it.

The brutalist idiom can also be experienced in an unadulterated form in the Oxford buildings designed by the firm of Howell, Killick,

The Nuclear Physics Laboratory from Banbury Road

Partridge, and Amis. Graduating from the Architectural Association, they had all worked in the 1950s for the London County Council, one of the main nurseries of avant-garde architecture at the time, where they had been involved in the design of the influential Alton West housing scheme at Roehampton, made up of concrete blocks set in a verdant landscape of lawns and trees. In 1960 they supplied an imaginative scheme for new buildings at **St Anne's College**, which by now had expanded beyond its uninspiring pre-war block by Giles Gilbert Scott to incorporate several Victorian houses with their gardens. A Hall had already been built, in 1958–60, to designs by Gerald Banks, with the kitchens placed alongside the Woodstock Road and a large lantern projecting above the roof-line to light the spacious interior; HKPA's proposals were for a tower block and a set of six four-storeyed residential buildings of oval shape and restless, almost expressionist character, clad in pre-cast concrete with projecting balconies and arranged like links on a S-shaped chain weaving elegantly through the gardens overlooking a lake. In the event only two of the blocks were ever built (in 1966–9), together with a new gate tower on the Woodstock Road, echoing the residential blocks in both its shape and its mannered detailing. The lake was never made, and the whole ensemble, which has weathered to a dismal grey, now looks distinctly sad and dated.

Fresh from St Anne's, the same firm was employed to extend **St Antony's College**, just to the north on the Woodstock Road. This was a new graduate college, founded out of a gift of a million pounds from a Frenchman, Antonin Besse, some of which went to fund new buildings at the poorer undergraduate colleges, including Pembroke and St Edmund Hall. Besse had made his fortune in the then British colony of Aden and left it to Oxford in order to further 'ideas that are dear to me'. They included the study of international relations, deemed essential to the maintenance of stability in a troubled and dangerous post-war world, and in 1950 the new college was established in the former nunnery of Holy Trinity. Like Nuffield, it also served as a research institute, attracting scholars and *savants* from many countries and many walks of life. The new buildings, first conceived in 1960, were designed to provide much-needed housing and to encourage the Fellows, students, and visitors to enjoy the communal meal-centred life which has been a characteristic of Oxford ever since the Middle Ages. The first design was more disquietingly expressionist than the first St Anne's project, and something of the same character survived in the revised and much smaller-scale scheme which was carried out in 1968–70. It consists of a single rectangular building to the north of the former convent

The Hall and common-room block at St Antony's College

building, with a first-floor Hall and common-rooms, and kitchens and a 'buttery' or informal dining-room on the ground floor. Even without the weird flights of fancy which had characterized the 1960 design, the box-like concrete-framed building is as novel a reinterpetation of the age-old idea of a communal collegiate building as can be found in Oxford. The upper floors, clad with pre-cast concrete panels, rest on concrete stilts, recalling Corbusier's famous *pilotis*, and the Hall and common-rooms, with their 'diagrid' roofs of criss-crossing diagonal concrete beams, are lit by windows with peculiar hooded surrounds which oddly anticipate the shape of computer screens: a case of life imitating art. Intended, like the *brise-soleils* of Corbusier's later buildings, to reduce glare, they help give this strange but oddly compelling building something of the sinister aura of a high-security institution. Had economic recession not intervened in the 1970s, the College might also have acquired a building by the Brazilian modernist architect Oscar Niemeyer, who offered to design it free of charge, but in the event nothing happened until the 1990s, by which time the architectural climate had changed radically.

The characteristically 1960s obsession with novelty was nowhere more strikingly expressed than in James Stirling's **Florey Building** for Queen's College (1968–71; see p. 298). This extraordinary block of study-bedrooms was built well away from the rest of the College buildings on the eastern side of Magdalen Bridge overlooking the

River Cherwell, and is approached from the street through a public car park, with which it has often been confused. Stirling had already achieved almost legendary status among the architectural avant-garde with his Engineering Building at Leicester University and his History Faculty Building at Cambridge. The Florey Building, as original in its way as either of these much-publicized oddities, represents a radical reinterpretation of the idea of the grandstand or amphitheatre, with its four levels of rooms arranged around a semicircle raised up from the ground on concrete stilts to command a pastoral view over the river to the arcadian grounds of Magdalen College. The inside of the semicircle is glazed all over, reflecting the obsession with glass which had been a characteristic of the Modern Movement since its earliest days. But the rear walls are almost windowless and are clad throughout in bright red tiles: a material also found in Stirling's buildings at Leicester and Cambridge, and as much at variance with Oxford's building traditions as the concrete used by Howell, Killick, Partridge, and Amis. On practical grounds, both of maintenance—the building now looks distinctly the worse for wear—and of the comfort of the students, who are obliged to contemplate each other in their box-like split-level rooms like goldfish in a bowl, roasting in the summer and freezing in the winter, the building must be counted a failure. But it looks impressive in pictures, and it continues to be admired by those who count originality as a primary aesthetic virtue.

The Florey Building represents the culmination of Oxford's flirtation with experimental modernism. Most of the other major projects of the late 1960s and early 1970s, like Powell and Moya's Wolfson College and Philip Dowson's Sir Thomas White Building at St John's, are more sober in their approach. The same is surprisingly true of the Garden Building at **St Hilda's College** (1968–70), the one Oxford building by those *enfants terribles* of the Architectural Association in the 1950s, Alison and Peter Smithson. St Hilda's differs from other Oxford colleges in being linear and additive in plan, with buildings of disparate dates and styles strung out along the bank of the Cherwell to the south of Magdalen Bridge. The Smithsons' elegant glass-walled structure, consisting of fifty-one study-bedrooms grouped around a concrete and brick service core, exploits the scenic potential of the site, and at the same time points a sharp contrast to the adjacent red-brick Cowley Grange, designed by William Wilkinson in 1877–8 and bought by the college in 1921; the most unusual feature of the Garden Building is the external framework of timber, structurally independent of the rest of the building, and designed both to give privacy to the students and to serve as a support for climbing plants.

The southern portion of St Hilda's College, with William Wilkinson's Cowley Grange to the left and the Smithsons' Garden Building to the right

Glass also figured largely in the Oxford work of Ahrends, Burton, and Koralek, a younger partnership whose members had come under the influence of the Smithsons while at the Architectural Association in the 1950s. Richard Burton had worked under Powell and Moya at Brasenose, and in 1968–9 the firm was employed to design the Oxford Centre for Management Studies—now Templeton College—on an open site at Kennington, just outside the city boundary. Over the next twenty years a series of extensions resulted in the creation of an impressive set of buildings arranged around courtyards, with sloping glazed walls to the study-bedrooms, zinc-clad external walls, and a top-lit Library or 'information centre' at the core. The same firm was responsible in 1970–1 for a sensitive addition to the Catholic Chaplaincy in the Old Palace in St Aldate's (see p. 119), containing a bare and cunningly-lit Chapel appropriate to the reformed liturgy which took hold after the Second Vatican Council. And in 1973–7 they designed the Hayward and De Breyne Buildings at **Keble College**, the first major addition since Butterfield's time. The task here was to fit a hundred bedrooms and a common-room onto a narrow site formerly occupied by a group of Victorian houses in Blackhall Road, on the western boundary of the site, and the solution was both elegant and effective. The building is only one room deep and follows the line of the street, coiling 'organically' round at its southern end to enclose a small courtyard. The plain and almost windowless external walls are of yellow brick, punctuated by turrets containing the staircases, which summon up an image of medieval fortifications. But inside there is a sinuous, unbroken curtain wall of brown tinted glass with aluminium mullions, sloping diagonally outwards and reflecting the vivid

The top-lit Library at Templeton College

patterning of Butterfield's buildings opposite. Butterfield had spoken eloquently about the need to use the materials of his own age, but where his buildings are hard, spiky, and richly patterned, those of Ahrends, Burton, and Koralek are sleek, shiny, and curvaceous. His architecture proclaims faith in God, theirs in technology. Nowhere in Oxford is the language of modernism used with more subtlety.

It would be wrong to imply that the colleges were all as adventurous and enlightened in their patronage of modern architecture as Keble, or even—for all the bizarre impracticality of James Stirling's building—Queen's. Some colleges commissioned buildings of numbing banality, like Exeter's at the corner of Broad Street and Turl Street, finished in 1964 and now containing Blackwell's Art and Poster shop; the architect, Lionel Esher, claimed that Oxford 'gave

The Hayward and De Breyne Building at Keble College, looking north to Butterfield's Hall and Library range

him stage-fright'. Others were disastrously inappropriate, like the red-brick and concrete Waynflete Building for Magdalen College (Booth, Ledeboer, and Pinckheard, 1960–1), which sadly fails to live up to the potential of its superb site at the eastern end of Magdalen Bridge, or David Roberts's crude, insistently horizontal Sacher Building for New College graduates, irredeemably blighting the western side of Longwall Street (1961–2). Roberts, who also worked extensively at Cambridge, also designed the jagged, red-brick Wolfson and Kenyon Buildings at St Hugh's (1964–6), equally assertive—a quality much admired in the 1960s—but less damaging to the surrounding environment.

Some colleges employed local firms like that of Kenneth Stevens and Partners, inheritors of Fielding Dodd's practice. They were responsible in 1965–9 for carrying out a large programme of new building on a highly constricted site to the east of the existing quadrangle at St Edmund Hall, including a new Hall, common-rooms, and seventy-seven study-bedrooms, some of which are

Keble College: the Hayward and De Breyne Building from Blackhall Road

placed above the Hall in a gable-roofed tower. Though rather crudely detailed, they are cleverly slotted into their constricted site with relatively little adverse effect on the surroundings. At Balliol the Oxford Architects' Partnership, whose members were trained in the Oxford Polytechnic School of Architecture, were employed in 1965–8 to add a new block of bedrooms and a Senior Common Room on either side of Waterhouse's Hall (see p. 228). Brutalist in character, they provide an interesting context for Waterhouse's dour Gothic. A less successful addition to an older college is the gauche concrete pyramid-roofed block built in 1964–8 next to the Library at Trinity College to the designs of Maguire and Murray, head of the School of Architecture at Oxford Polytechnic and City Architect respectively; the huge underground Norrington Room in Blackwell's bookshop was part of the same project.

It is a paradox that the heyday of modernism in Oxford should coincide with a massive programme of restoration of the older buildings of the University. In his influential *Oxford Stone* (1947) the geologist W. A. Arkell advocated the 'systematic refacing' of those buildings whose façades had, by the indiscriminate use of Headington ashlar, fallen victim to the depredations of time and atmospheric pollution: a problem worsened by a rise in car emissions. Arkell's advice was accepted by the University and most of the colleges, bringing to an end a long period in which repairs had all too often been carried out in a partial and haphazard manner, leaving the buildings with a patched and pock-marked appearance; an exception was Peckwater Quadrangle at Christ Church, successfully refaced in Clipsham stone in 1924–30. So, encouraged by influential figures like W. F. Oakeshott, Rector of Lincoln College, the Oxford Historic Buildings Fund was established in 1957 and, aided by contributions from the Ford Foundation and elsewhere, the last decaying traces of the older stone were gradually removed from the crumbling, blackened façades of Oxford's older buildings, like the Bodleian Library and the Sheldonian Theatre.

As a result of this ambitious programme, which lasted until 1974, walls threw off generations of grime, and re-carved details, like the herms or 'emperors' heads' around the Sheldonian precinct, became visible for the first time for many years. Clipsham limestone remained the most popular material, sometimes, as at Wadham (refaced in 1957–66), taken from beds with a blue vein in order 'to relieve the uniformity of the surface', as Oakeshott put it. And where necessary, as at Christ Church Library (refaced in 1960–2), Clipsham was used together with other kinds of stone to provide the necessary contrast in colour and texture. As Clipsham stone began to run out,

Left:
Part of the ground floor of the Sheldonian Theatre in the 1950s, showing the decayed Headington stone

Right:
The Sheldonian Theatre after refacing in 1958–61; the grievously decayed herms or 'emperors' heads' around the precinct wall were replaced in 1970–2

stone from French quarries began to be used in its place, as at Magdalen College, which carried out an independent £6.2m repair programme lasting from 1974 to 1989; here the tower was beautifully refaced in Clipsham stone, but in the rest of the buildings, including the High Street front, a greyish French stone was employed with less success.

No one looking at pictures of buildings like the Sheldonian and Christ Church Library before and after restoration could reasonably deny that refacing was unavoidable, and that on balance it improved the appearance of Oxford. But something was also lost: not only the sentimental appeal of crumbling stonework, but also a tangible link with the past. This was less true of the re-use of older buildings, another striking feature of the last thirty years. The most successful instances of architectural conservation in the University were the conversion of two city centre churches, St Peter-in-the-East and All Saints, into libraries for St Edmund Hall and Lincoln College respectively. Both colleges had unusually cramped sites, and both succeeded in ensuring new leases of life for little-used buildings which had played an important part in the architectural history of the city. At St Edmund Hall, the conversion was skilfully carried out in 1969–70 by the college architect, Kenneth Stevens and Partners (see p. 330). It did not involve any major structural alterations to the interior, but at Lincoln the floor was raised in order to allow the construction of a basement reading-room. This ambitious project was carried out in 1975 by Robert Potter, the architect for the equally effective restoration of the Bodleian Library (1959–68), causing little adverse effect to the appearance of the building and imparting great benefit to the users.

The rebuilding of Oxford's academic quarter in the 1960s and 1970s was matched by an even more extensive rebuilding of parts of the city centre. Here the motives were different: the insistent demands for more space on the part of commerce and local administration; the need to clear what were perceived as slums to the west and south-west of the city centre; and the growing problem of traffic in the city centre. These problems, it was widely believed, could be solved by planning, seen in the post-war years as a panacea for many of society's ills, and planning often involved extensive rebuilding. Thomas Sharp's influential planning survey of 1948, commissioned by the City Council and published as *Oxford Replanned*, not only endorsed earlier proposals for the building of a relief road for the High Street through Christ Church Meadow; it also argued for an almost total clearance of the western and south-western parts of the city centre, which would become a nexus for commercial and administrative activity, leaving the academic quarter largely untouched.

The Meadow road was never built, due partly to a well-orchestrated campaign from within the University in general and Christ Church in particular, and Sharpe's proposals for the complete rebuilding of the city centre (which would have involved the demolition of theTown Hall and the Covered Market) were mercifully never put into effect. But there was much commercial redevelopment. The rebuilding of the main shopping streets began in 1955, when, contrary to Sharp's proposals, and in the teeth of opposition from the City Council, the Clarendon Hotel in Cornmarket Street (formerly the Star Inn) was demolished to make way for Woolworth's, designed by Lord Holford and since meretriciously revamped as the Clarendon Centre.
The Council had meanwhile decided on the 'comprehensive redevelopment' of the St Ebbe's area in 1953, against the expressed wishes of two-thirds of the inhabitants, but with the support of the commercial interests which were strongly represented among the Council members. The clearance was not carried out until after 1966, when the population was moved out to a new estate at Blackbird Leys, to the south-east of Cowley, begun in 1957, one of several new council estates built around the fringe of the city in the post-war years. Much of the cleared area in St Ebbe's was given over to a new inner ring road (intended to link up to the abortive Meadow road) and its associated car parks. Meanwhile the areas closest to the city centre were devoted to offices and shopping, notably a covered shopping mall, the Westgate Centre, planned and financed by the City Council and built in 1970–2.

The church of St Peter-in-the-East, looking east, after its conversion into the Library of St Edmund Hall

The architectural results of this extensive programme of rebuilding, which reached its climax in the late 1960s and early 1970s, varied from the mediocre to the disastrous. Driven by the crudest notions of cost effectiveness, and lacking either the financial resources or the aesthetic concerns which allowed the colleges to employ the best architects, public authorities and commercial enterprises—mainly the former—filled large areas to the south-west and west of Carfax with large, insensitively detailed buildings rising up from car-strewn open spaces. Even the most doctrinaire modernist would find it difficult to find a good word to say for the new telephone exchange and magistrates' courts in Speedwell Street (1957, 1966–9); for the appallingly insensitive Westgate Centre at the western end of Queen Street, designed by the City Architect's Department; for the brutal multi-storey car park which takes up one side of the former Paradise Square, St Ebbe's—a strong contender for the title of Oxford's ugliest building; or for the shapeless County Council offices of 1974 which face the Westgate Centre across the realigned and blighted Castle Street. The concrete and glass Beaver House in Hythe Bridge Street, built in 1971–2 as the headquarters of the Blackwell bookselling empire, is little better, though mercifully some distance away from the city centre. So too is the distressingly banal complex of curtain-walled buildings housing Oxford Polytechnic, now Oxford Brookes University (City Architect's Department, 1953–63) at the top of Headington Hill, ironically incorporating Oxford's only School of Architecture, and the vast and featureless John Radcliffe Hospital, also at Headington, begun in 1968 to the designs of Yorke, Rosenberg, and Mardall. With the exception of the top-lit centrally planned Roman Catholic church of the Holy Rood in the Abingdon Road (Gilbert Flavell, 1959–61), it is hard to think of a single public building of any distinction in Oxford, outside the University, dating from the first three post-war decades: an indictment all the worse for the fact that these decades saw a level of prosperity unmatched in any earlier period in English history. Fortunately, economic recession and public revulsion against the worst architectural excesses intervened before more damage could be done.

The economic and financial crises which crippled Britain in the mid-1970s led to a virtual cessation of large-scale building activity in Oxford. Along with these difficulties and the mood of national introspection they engendered, a widespread revulsion against the cultural legacy of modernism took root, especially once some of the buildings of the 1960s had begun to be dogged by irritating maintenance problems. Out of this climate there emerged a new concern with environmentalism and architectural conservation. Though too late to save the St Ebbe's district, public pressure helped mitigate the proposed redevelopment of Jericho, where once-doomed Victorian terraced houses began to be eagerly bought up by young academics and professionals in the 1970s. It also led to the establishment of Conservation Areas, not only in the city centre but also in North Oxford, whose Victorian character was being eroded by demolitions (often for flats) after the expiry of the original 99-year leases. When the economy recovered in the 1980s the skills of conservation architects, and of the City Council's energetic conservation officer, succeeded in saving and improving some of the relatively small number of surviving pre-19th-century buildings in the central shopping streets. The way had already been led by the architect Thomas Rayson, who had sensitively restored the former Plough Inn (now the Austin Reed shop) in Cornmarket Street as early as 1925, and the northern part of the late 14th-century New Inn opposite (see p. 47), long turned into shops. In 1985–7, long after Rayson's death, the adjoining part of the Inn's street front (now the Laura Ashley shop) was restored, with rather more concern for archaeological accuracy, using the expertise of F. W. B. Charles, an authority on medieval timber-framed buildings. An equally intelligent approach was adopted at the Golden Cross in 1986–7, involving not only the restoration of the dilapidated exterior of the former inn, but also the conservation of the extensive 16th-century wall paintings (see p. 83) and the creation of a passageway from the old inn yard to the Covered Market.

The collapse of faith in modernism also led to far-reaching changes in the character and appearance of Oxford's new buildings, changes which are still in the process of working themselves out as the 20th century nears its close. This was first detectable in the design of housing schemes, both for students and for the inhabitants of the city. Economic recession, combined with a revulsion against the work of architectural prima donnas like James Stirling, led in many cases to the employment of locally based firms like the Oxford Architects' Partnership, who were employed at Alan Bullock Close (completed in 1976), a development of forty-seven flats for graduate students on a site by the River Cherwell in St Clements. Here they moved from brutalism towards a more humane and less experimental style. Though the minimal detailing lends a certain bleakness to the brick elevations, the small domestic scale shows a welcome respect for the setting and for the sensibilities of the occupants, qualities also in evidence in the new quadrangle for Hertford College in Holywell Street, completed in the same year to the designs of Shepheard, Epstein, and Hunter. A similar transition to domesticity can be seen in the work of another local firm, the Architects' Design Partnership, where the brutalism of their Old Members' Building at Jesus College (1971) gradually gave way to a more human scale. In the devastated area between the new inner ring road and the River Thames to the south-east of the city centre, a mixture of private and council housing was slowly constructed by several firms, including the Oxford Architects' Partnership, starting in 1978. Here the architecture is more traditionalist in character, with great emphasis laid on the visual appeal of steep-pitched roofs and red brick walls, and of the luxuriant vegetation which surrounds several of the houses: a welcome contrast to the tarmac and concrete wastes of the car parks near the Westgate Centre.

Economic recession, followed in 1979 by the election of a Conservative administration unsympathetic to massive government subsidies to universities, created great disaffection among the dons,

Houses by the Oxford Architects' Partnership to the south of Thames Street, St Ebbes

but it had the welcome effect of killing off the University's more megalomaniac building schemes. The space-age detailing of the Lankester Reading Room for the Radcliffe Science Library, built to the designs of the University Surveyor and opened in 1976, makes no impact whatsoever on the environment, since it is cunningly hidden beneath the front lawn of the University Museum. And where the University's recent buildings have ventured above ground they have in general been both tactful and discreet in character. The Virology, Microbiology, and Pharmacology laboratories (Architects' Design Partnership, 1985 and 1990) occupy a site once intended to house a westward extension of Leslie Martin's Zoology and Psychology building, but their restrained brick elevations and pitched slate roofs are more humanely scaled and make less of an assault on the eyes.

As public funding declined in the late 1970s and 1980s, the architectural initiative shifted decisively from the University to the colleges. The first new college to be founded since the 1960s was Green College, established on a site which included the Radcliffe Observatory. Here on the Woodstock Road frontage a collection of almost excessively well-mannered neo-Georgian residential buildings was erected in 1978–81 by the office of the University Surveyor, Jack Lankester: something which it is almost impossible to imagine having occurred ten years before. A more significant new commission was the Sainsbury Building at **Worcester College**, built after a limited competition to the designs of Richard MacCormac of the firm of MacCormac, Jamieson, and Pritchard, out of funds contributed by the grocery magnate Lord Sainsbury, and completed in 1983. This cleverly planned structure marks a decisive shift in architectural taste. It stands on the north-eastern boundary of the College's extensive grounds, at the far end of the lake created in the early 19th century, and is designed not so much to dominate the landscape as to form a part of it. It is constructed of brick on a base of rubble stone, there are sloping slate roofs, and wood is used extensively, both internally and externally. The plan is complex, allowing for the creation of numerous intimate, private spaces, with the L-shaped rooms—themselves a significant departure from the ubiquitous rectangular boxes of the 1960s—grouped around kitchens, each room being, in MacCormac's own words, 'a unique destination, special and slightly secret'. Stylistically, there is an obvious debt to the English vernacular tradition, but there are also hints of Frank Lloyd Wright and Japan: a mixture of motifs and historical influences entirely typical of what was already being called post-modern architecture.

After the architectural and planning disasters of the 1960s and 1970s, Oxford's City Council made a welcome return as a patron of significant new architecture in 1984 with the building of an **Ice Rink** on marshy ground at Oxpens, to the south-west of the city centre. The architect, Nicholas Grimshaw, is a devotee of the 'high-tech' school of neo-modernist architecture, otherwise unrepresented in Oxford, and the building consists of a lightweight shed with a glazed front wall supported by a long horizontal beam hanging between two tall steel masts of a somewhat nautical character. But the most ambitious architectural project undertaken by the City Council in recent years

The Sainsbury Building at Worcester College

The Oxford Ice Rink

has been the redevelopment of **Gloucester Green**. This bleak open space between George Street and Beaumont Street, to the north-west of the city centre, formerly housed the city gaol and was used for many years as a cattle market before being turned into a bus station. In 1983, after much public consultation, the Council chose to adopt the 'Romantic Option' for the site, which was to be used for shops, offices, and flats, with an underground car park and two open spaces, one of which could be used for a weekly open-air market and the other as a new bus station. In their design the architects, Kendrick Associates, rejected the architectural language of modernism in favour of an exuberant post-modern eclecticism, recalling the wilder excesses of the turn-of-the-century 'free style', and it was this design which was carried out between 1987 and 1990. The buildings are clad in red brick, interspersed with patterning in different coloured brick, and stone dressings, and no effort was spared to exploit the picturesque possibilities of the site, notably in its south-western corner, where three Disney-like domed turrets close the vista eastwards from Hythe Bridge Street and the elegant new railway station completed in 1990. The Gloucester Green development can easily be criticized for the the kitsch quality of some of the detailing. But it brings a festive, carnivalesque note to what had been a drab part of the city, and has provided a much-needed public open space for the benefit of residents and visitors alike.

As the economy revived in the boom years of the later 1980s, the colleges began building on a large scale again. An important motive

The south-western corner of the Gloucester Green development from Hythe Bridge Street

was the growing need to house as many as possible of the students in college-owned accommodation: something resulting partly from a decline in privately rented property, partly from City Council policy favouring the use of local housing for local residents, and partly from a change in the funding of student grants wrought by Margaret Thatcher's government. Another significant factor was a growing desire to benefit from the lucrative conference trade in the summer months. In this new surge of collegiate building the firm of MacCormac, Jamieson, and Pritchard has played a role equivalent to that of Powell and Moya in the 1960s, and, as in the 1960s, there has been a supporting cast of very varied abilities.

In the Bowra Building at **Wadham College** (1990–2), MacCormac followed in the uncompromisingly modernist footsteps of the Glasgow firm of Gillespie, Kidd, and Coia, architects of Robinson College, one of the most impressive buildings of the 1970s in Cambridge. Their first work for Wadham was the conversion of a row of old houses on the north side of Holywell Street into extra student rooms, deftly fitting in a new Blackwell's Music Shop in the process; this was carried out in 1970–2, and a few years later in 1977, with the help of funds contributed by the Imperial Organization for Social Services of Iran, they built a new Library to the east of the college, its yellowish concrete exterior proclaiming their continuing indebtedness to the brutalist idiom. The intention was to extend the building southwards at some future date, but when that time arrived architectural taste had changed, and that change is reflected in MacCormac's design. The new building consists of four blocks of eighty-five bedrooms, of yellow brick with pre-cast concrete detailing, standing on a first-floor deck or terrace—an idea first developed in an abortive project for extra buildings at Worcester College in 1986—with the ground floor given over to common-rooms and a dining-room for conferences. The blocks are grouped on either side of a narrow 'internal street' focusing at the southern end on the tower of New College, and they are broken up by an array of towers—also a feature of the abandoned Worcester design—with overhanging eaves and large windows on the upper floors, necessary in view of the close spacing of the buildings on the confined site. MacCormac has called his work 'vertebrate architecture . . . like cabinet work', but there is also an impressive range of historical references, from the work of Alvar Aalto, Frank Lloyd Wright, and other heroes of the Modern Movement back through the traditional architecture of Japan to the works of the Elizabethan country-house architect Robert Smythson and the Mannerist architecture of Renaissance Italy. Here there is sufficient wealth of meaning to satisfy the most demanding post-modern taste.

Fresh from his success at Wadham, MacCormac went on to design a larger and even more monumental set of buildings overlooking the north side of the garden at **St John's** (see p. 319 and colour plate facing p. 243), finished in 1994. The arrangement of 'public' rooms (including a small concert hall) at ground level, with residential accommodation punctuated by towers on a first-floor deck, is essentially the same as at Wadham, but here the effect is more dramatic and the classical allusions more insistent. The rooms are arranged around the edges of the deck, in the centre of which there is a huge circular opening allowing light into the shadowy ground floor. Here massive segmental arches of pre-cast concrete, Piranesian in character and textured to look like stone, support the deck and give access to the main 'public' rooms—a dining-room and a small concert hall—each of them roofed with a shallow pendentive dome, recalling the architecture of Sir John Soane, one of the key influences on the more historically minded English architects of the late 20th century. The effect is noble enough and inventive enough to evoke the palmy days of Oxford classicism in the early 18th century. Upstairs there is

The Bowra Building at Wadham College, with the tower of New College in the distance framed by the two sides of the 'internal street'

almost an excess of visual incident, with low walls enclosing beds of plants, circular lanterns projecting upwards from the downstairs rooms, and isolated pavilions reminiscent of Japanese temple architecture on the garden side. But the dominant impression, as at Wadham, derives from the towers, knitting together the composition like those of Robert Smythson's Hardwick Hall (Derbyshire). In its lucid plan, its concern for surface texture and skyline, and its generous scale the Garden Quadrangle demonstrates that, given a sympathetic patron and a generous budget, the architects of late 20th-century Oxford are capable of designing buildings of a quality matching those of their earlier predecessors.

The most striking characteristic of Oxford's most recent architecture is its extreme stylistic variety, greater even than in the heyday of the late 19th- and early 20th-century 'free style'. In the architecture of *fin-de-siècle* Oxford, as in that of *fin-de-siècle* Britain, anything goes, inevitably perhaps in view of the prevailing climate of aesthetic and moral relativism. At one extreme of the stylistic spectrum is a handful of uncompromisingly modernist buildings, including a block of rooms at St Peter's College by Chamberlin, Powell, and Bon (1989), notable mainly for its glass-clad external staircase, and a well-massed and well-detailed extension to St Catherine's by the Manchester-based Hodder Associates (completed in 1995), reinterpreting and humanizing the style of Arne Jacobsen. The brick-clad Jacqueline du Pré Concert Hall at St Hilda's (van Heynigen and Haward, also completed in 1995), one of the few Oxford buildings in which a female architect has played a leading role, is an impressive reminder of the continuing vitality of modernist architecture as the 20th century nears its close; the recent extension to the premises of the Oxford University Press (IDC Ltd/Amec Group, 1991) also contains some striking internal spaces. Meanwhile the radical claims of low-energy architecture have been advanced in the externally unprepossessing brick-clad Arco Building (Rick Mather, completed in 1995), sunk into the ground on the north side of the garden at Keble College, and in an extension by the ECD Partnership to Linacre College, housed since 1977 in Cherwell Edge, a red-brick 'Queen Anne' house of 1886–7 at the south-eastern corner of the University Parks; internally highly innovative in its concern for energy-saving, from the outside it is stylistically indistinguishable from its neighbour.

Most architects have opted for various forms of post-modern eclecticism, appealing to the prevailing public demands for meaning, memory, and respect for context in architecture. They include the long-established partnership of Maguire and Murray in their riverside

The interior of the Jacqueline du Pré Concert Hall at St Hilda's College

Geoffrey Arthur Building for Pembroke College (completed in 1989), the first college building to go up on the south side of the Thames; built of concrete blocks, its steep-pitched roofs and stark detailing conjure up, whether intentionally or not, images of a medieval Germanic fortress, hence the nickname of 'Colditz' conferred by local residents. Maguire and Murray were also responsible for the stuccoed Linbury Building at Worcester College, finished in 1991 and notable mainly for its array of pyramid-roofed turrets peeping like watch-towers over an old rubble-stone wall along Hythe Bridge Street. Here their appointment came after earlier designs by MacCormac, Jamieson, and Pritchard had been rejected on the grounds of cost, but this firm has continued to attract commissions in Oxford, most recently from Balliol College, for which they have recently designed a block of rooms on the south side of the College's sports grounds in Jowett Walk, to the north of Holywell Street; completed in 1996, they are a smaller-scale and starker variation on the theme explored earlier in MacCormac's buildings for Wadham and St John's. A more domestic approach was adopted by the Alec French Partnership in the brick-clad, pitched-roofed Clare Palley Building on the south side of the quadrangle at St Anne's (1993), and by the Architects Design Partnership in their well-proportioned and carefully detailed Nissan Centre for Japanese Studies at St Antony's (1993), clearly influenced both by Japan and by Frank Lloyd Wright. Elsewhere, as in the recent buildings put up by Merton College on the south side of Jowett Walk, or by Christ Church and Corpus Christi in the Iffley Road, the desire not to offend has led to the creation of façades as deeply unmemorable as—and far less well-crafted than—the dullest architecture of the immediate post-war period, when Hubert Worthington still reigned supreme.

Freedom of stylistic choice has led in some cases to a complete rejection of the architectural legacy of the 20th century, seen at its most trite in a set of ham-fisted extensions to Manchester College by Peter Yiangou Associates, where crudely detailed red-brick façades of neo-Georgian character mask the structural steel frame. An even more decisive step forward into the past has been taken at Magdalen—architecturally always among the most conservative of Oxford colleges—where the Grove Buildings on the western edge of the College's deer park (first stage completed in 1995), have not only been designed in a rather loose version of the Tudor-Gothic style, but have been built with masonry construction throughout; the architect is Demitri Porphyrios, a man much favoured by that scourge of the Modern Movement, the Prince of Wales. Other colleges have created new accommodation and teaching space out of older buildings, usually former houses whose retention has been decreed by the city planners, as eager to conserve the vernacular buildings of the city in the 1990s as they were to destroy them in the 1960s. In the Dorothy Hodgkin Building at Somerville (Oxford Architects Partnership, 1988–91) a set of study-bedrooms and a conference room have been fitted in behind a row of stuccoed houses and shops in the Woodstock Road. More ambitious schemes of a similar kind, all but invisible to the outside world, have been carried out by Lincoln and Oriel Colleges in their extensive holdings to the south of the High Street, the latter

Pembroke College's Geoffrey Arthur Building from the west

including a clever conversion of a former indoor tennis court into a set of lecture and seminar rooms. Here, as in much recent Oxford architecture, discretion appears to be the better part of architectural valour.

Collegiate building slowed down in the mid-1990s, partly because the demand for student rooms has been satisfied in many colleges, partly because of the difficulty of finding space on which to build, especially in view of the tough planning constraints imposed by the City Council. Several privately funded new projects are currently (1997) under active consideration by University departments, among them a Humanities or Classics Centre at the back of the Ashmolean Museum, designed by the classical architect Robert Adam, and an Institute for American Studies close to Mansfield College, to be designed in the modernist idiom by the firm of Kohn, Pedersen, and Fox. But a scheme by Jeremy Dixon for a new Business School on a playing field in Mansfield Road was set aside in the autumn of 1996, partly on the grounds of its adverse impact on the surrounding environment: something which will inevitably surface again as pressures grow to build on the open spaces of Oxford. A new proposal (June 1997) places the Business School on derelict land next to the railway station, but another plan for a Centre for Islamic Studies, complete with mosque and minaret, seems certain to cause further controversy.

Anthony Wood once wrote: 'If you except the Colleges and Halls, the City of Oxford, in relation to building, is a very inconsiderable place, and no better than an ordinary Market Town.' With the recent scaling down of the former Morris (latterly British Leyland, now Rover) car works in Cowley, Oxford has cast off much of the industrial character implanted between the wars, and has reverted to its commercial roots, diversified by a smattering of high-tech industry—and even an embryonic Science Park—around the fringes, and a large public sector, especially in the medical services. No one contemplating the 'tide of human existence' at Carfax on a Saturday afternoon can doubt that for most of its inhabitants Oxford is first and foremost a trading and service centre, as it has been since the days of the Anglo-Saxons. Yet Oxford's architectural future will surely be determined primarily by the University which was planted, cuckoo-like, in the midst of its uncomprehending citizens 800 years ago. Oxford's buildings have always reflected the idiosyncrasies of the University: its extreme degree of decentralization, its marked tendency in certain eras to swim against the political and social tide, its taste for ceremony and nostalgia, its habit of sinking into long periods of torpor followed by

Robert Adam's scheme for a new Cast Gallery on the northern side of the Ashmolean Museum, part of a proposed Classics Centre

shorter periods of intense activity. And as the University changes, Oxford's architecture will no doubt change too.

Gerard Manley Hopkins grasped the essential visual character of Oxford when he hailed it as a 'Towery city and branchy between towers'. That character emerged in the later Middle Ages, and over the last 500 years it has proved remarkably resilient, due in large part to the extraordinary continuity of the academic institutions comprising the University. Within its Gothic framework, Oxford has been diversified and enriched by buildings in two very different architectural styles: the classicism of the later 17th and 18th centuries and the modernism of the later 20th century. It is the juxtaposition of beautiful and distinctive buildings of different styles, functions, and materials within a relatively small area which goes a long way to explain the continuing fascination of Oxford for both the historian and the casual visitor. At the close of the 20th century, Oxford's architecture stands at a crossroads. The historic fabric of the city, threatened though it is by the pressure of traffic—modern Oxford's greatest curse—is cared for as never before, but architects and patrons have lost any common sense of purpose. This confusion of aims reflects a broader confusion and fragmentation within modern English culture and society, yet the pluralism which is so characteristic of our age could provide a creative opportunity for the architects of the 21st century. Out of a deeper understanding of Oxford's eclectic, idiosyncratic, architectural past there might well grow the as yet unimagined architecture of Oxford's future.

Walks around Oxford

The following four maps show a selection of the most important buildings in central Oxford and are organized by major architectural periods.

1 **Medieval Oxford: 1000–1530**
2 **Early Modern Oxford: 1530–1750**
3 **Late Georgian and Victorian Oxford: 1750–1900**
4 **Twentieth-Century Oxford**

Using the maps, visitors to Oxford can devise their own walks around the city, based on personal interests and the time available. The buildings listed in bold are those which should be visited if time is limited.

Please note that not all buildings and sites shown on the maps will be accessible at all times; colleges have specific opening times for visitors, and special arrangements may be needed to visit private locations.

The quadrangle of St Catherine's College, showing the Library and bell tower

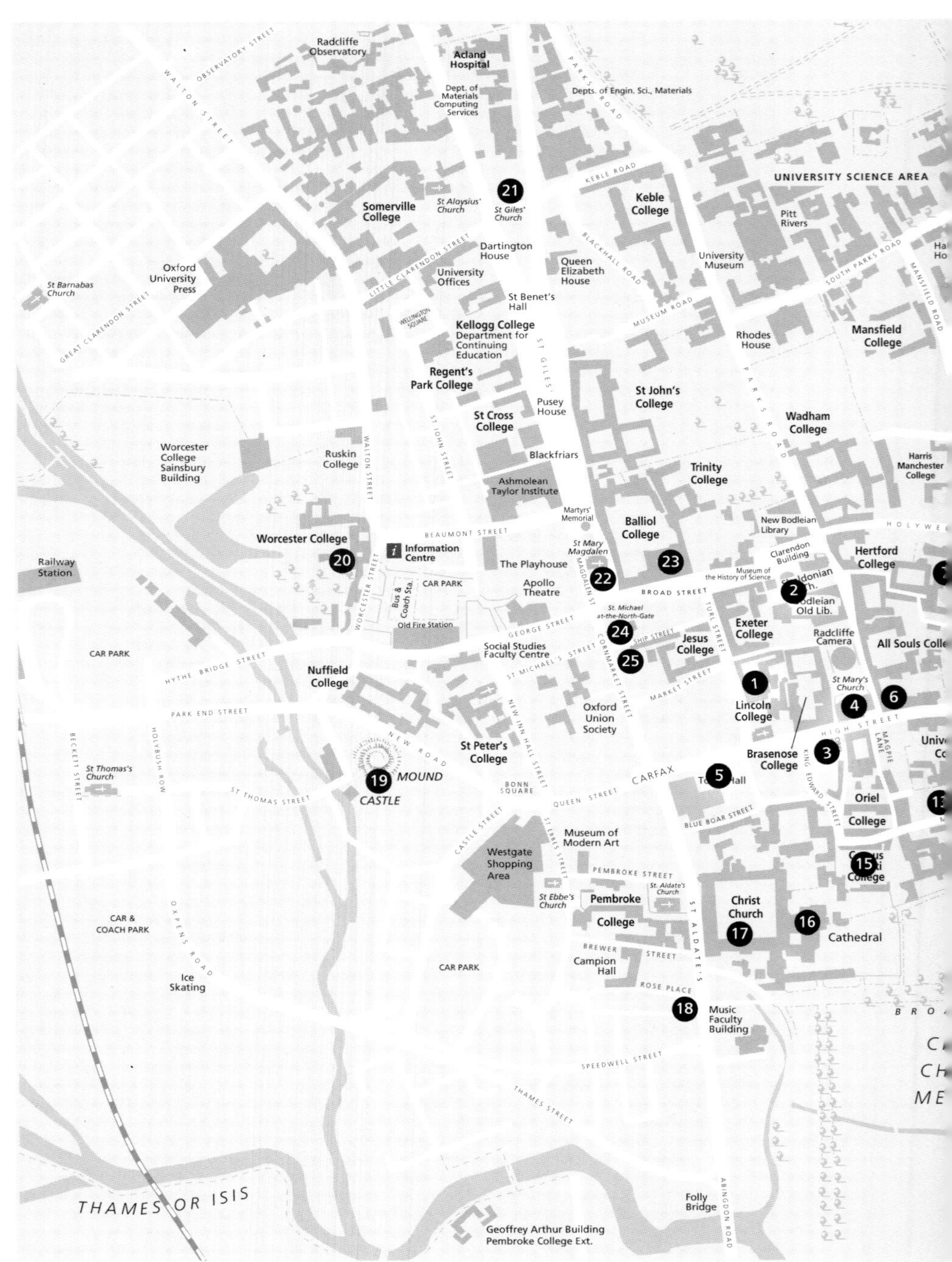
Radcliffe Observatory
Acland Hospital
Dept. of Materials Computing Services
Depts. of Engin. Sci., Materials
UNIVERSITY SCIENCE AREA
Somerville College
St Aloysius' Church
St Giles' Church
Keble College
Pitt Rivers
Dartington House
Queen Elizabeth House
University Museum
Oxford University Press
University Offices
St Benet's Hall
St Barnabas Church
Kellogg College Department for Continuing Education
Rhodes House
Mansfield College
Regent's Park College
St John's College
St Cross College
Pusey House
Wadham College
Worcester College Sainsbury Building
Ruskin College
Blackfriars
Trinity College
Harris Manchester College
Ashmolean Taylor Institute
Martyrs' Memorial
Balliol College
New Bodleian Library
Worcester College
Information Centre
St Mary Magdalen
Clarendon Building
Hertford College
Railway Station
The Playhouse
Museum of the History of Science
Apollo Theatre
CAR PARK
Bus & Coach Sta.
Old Fire Station
St. Michael at-the-North-Gate
Exeter College
Radcliffe Camera
All Souls College
Jesus College
Social Studies Faculty Centre
Nuffield College
Lincoln College
St Mary's Church
Oxford Union Society
St Peter's College
Brasenose College
St Thomas's Church
MOUND
CASTLE
Oriel College
Museum of Modern Art
Westgate Shopping Area
St. Aldate's Church
St Ebbe's Church
Pembroke College
Christ Church
Cathedral
CAR & COACH PARK
Campion Hall
Ice Skating
Music Faculty Building
THAMES OR ISIS
Folly Bridge
Geoffrey Arthur Building Pembroke College Ext.
WALTON STREET
OBSERVATORY STREET
PARKS ROAD
KEBLE ROAD
BLACKHALL ROAD
SOUTH PARKS ROAD
MANSFIELD ROAD
LITTLE CLARENDON STREET
GREAT CLARENDON STREET
WELLINGTON SQUARE
MUSEUM ROAD
ST GILES'
ST JOHN STREET
BEAUMONT STREET
WORCESTER STREET
MAGDALEN ST
BROAD STREET
HOLYWELL
GEORGE STREET
SHIP STREET
TURL STREET
HYTHE BRIDGE STREET
ST MICHAEL'S STREET
CORNMARKET STREET
MARKET STREET
PARK END STREET
NEW INN HALL STREET
NEW ROAD
HIGH STREET
MAGPIE LANE
BECKETT STREET
HOLYBUSH ROW
ST THOMAS STREET
BONN SQUARE
QUEEN STREET
CARFAX
KING EDWARD STREET
BLUE BOAR STREET
CASTLE STREET
ST EBBES STREET
PEMBROKE STREET
ST ALDATE'S
OXPENS ROAD
BREWER STREET
ROSE PLACE
SPEEDWELL STREET
THAMES STREET
ABINGDON ROAD
1
2
3
4
5
6
15
16
17
18
19
20
21
22
23
24
25

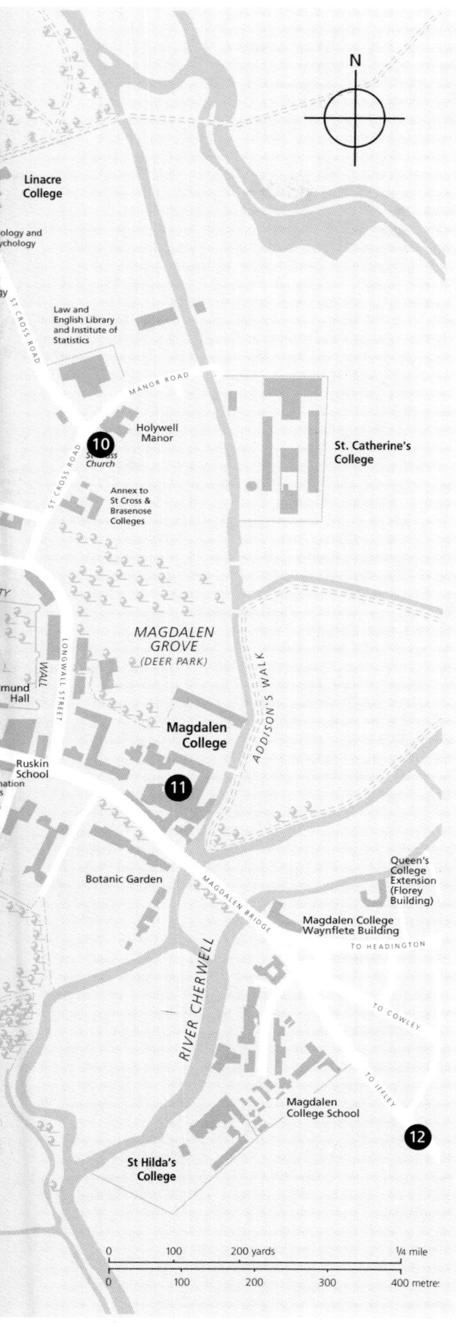

Medieval Oxford
1000–1530

1 **Lincoln College** (p. 49)
2 **Divinity School** (p. 65)
3 107 High Street, formerly Tackley's Inn (p. 25)
4 **St Mary's (University) church** (p. 34)
5 126 High Street (p. 48)
6 **All Souls College** (p. 57)
7 **New College** (p. 39)
8 **St Peter-in-the-East** (St Edmund Hall Library) (p. 11)
9 **City walls: in the garden of New College** (p. 22)
10 St Cross church (p. 69)
11 **Magdalen College** (p. 60)
12 Iffley church—2 miles to the south-east (p. 12)
13 Beam Hall: Merton Street (p. 49)
14 **Merton College: Front Quad, Mob Quad, and Chapel** (pp. 28, 31, 29)
15 **Corpus Christi College** (p. 72)
16 **Christ Church Cathedral** (p. 15)
17 **Christ Church: Tom Quad and Hall** (p. 73)
18 Littlemore Hall: St Aldate's (p. 49)
19 **Castle tower and mound** (p. 5)
20 **Worcester College: the former *camerae*** (p. 55)
21 St Giles church (p. 30)
22 St Mary Magdalen church (p. 35)
23 Balliol College: Front Quad (p. 51)
24 **St Michael's church** (p. 3)
25 Laura Ashley shop: Cornmarket, formerly New Inn (p. 47)

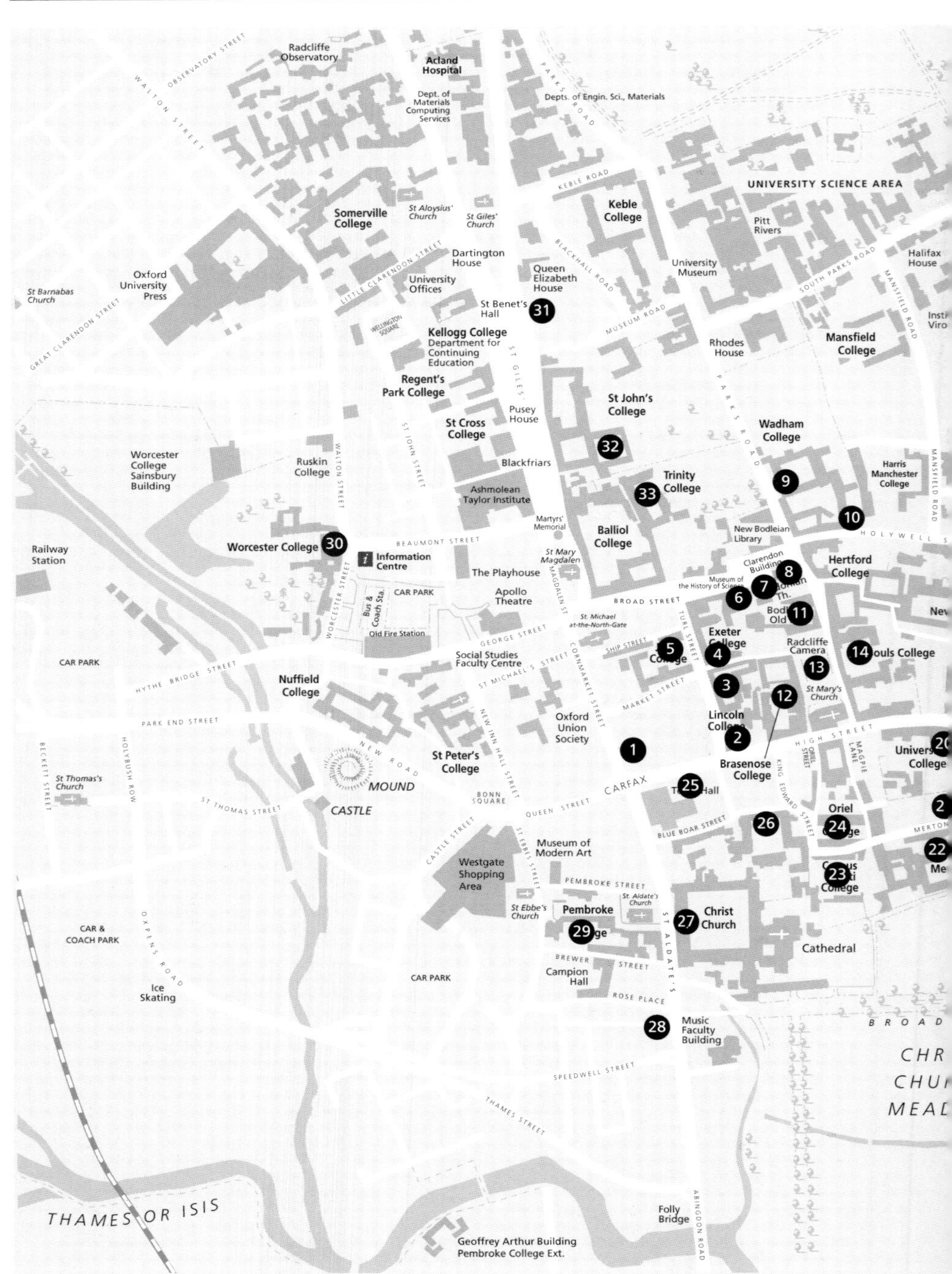

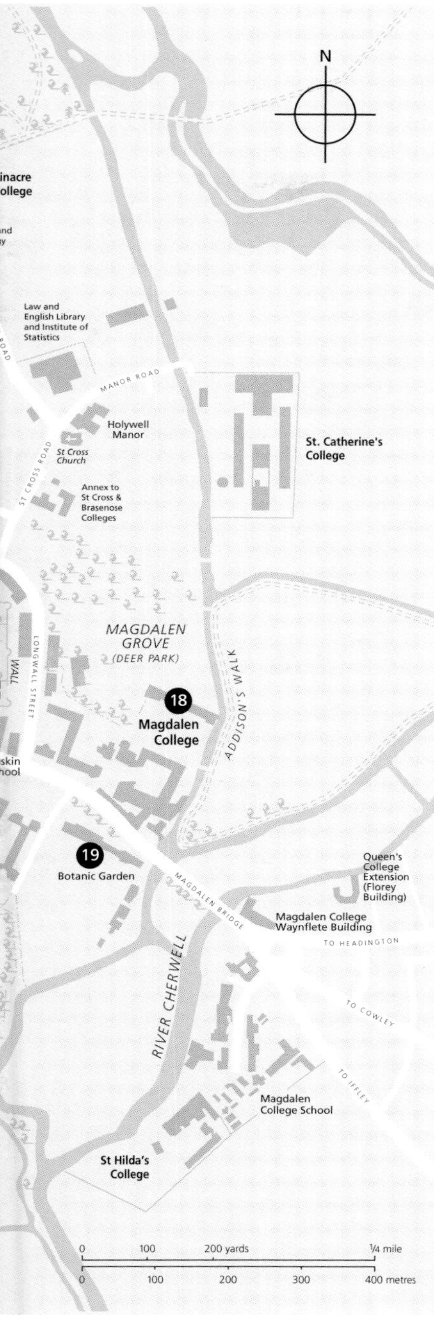

Early Modern Oxford 1530–1750

1 Golden Cross, Cornmarket Street (p. 118)
2 **All Saints church** (Lincoln College Library) (p. 145)
3 **Lincoln College: Chapel** (p. 105)
4 **Exeter College: Hall** (p. 103)
5 Jesus College (p. 105)
6 **Old Ashmolean** (p. 127)
7 **Sheldonian Theatre** (p. 123)
8 **Clarendon Building** (p. 150)
9 **Wadham College** (p. 98)
10 Holywell Street (p. 116)
11 **Bodleian Library and Schools Quad** (p. 92)
12 **Brasenose College, Chapel and Library** (p. 114)
13 **Radcliffe Camera** (p. 167)
14 **All Souls College: Hall, North Quad, and Codrington Library** (p. 159)
15 New College: Garden Quad (p. 132)
16 **Queen's College** (p. 152)
17 **St Edmund Hall, Chapel and Old Library** (p. 133)
18 **Magdalen College: New Building** (p. 164)
19 **Botanic Garden** (p. 107)
20 **University College** (p. 102)
21 Merton Street: Postmasters' Hall and tennis court (p. 120)
22 **Merton College: Library, Fellows' Quad** (p. 86)
23 Corpus Christi College: Chapel cloister, and Fellow's Building (p. 149)
24 **Oriel College** (p. 101)
25 Kemp Hall, off High Street (p. 120)
26 **Christ Church: Peckwater Quad** (p. 142)
27 **Christ Church: Tom Tower, Hall staircase** (p. 112)
28 Old Palace (Catholic Chaplaincy), St Aldate's (p. 119)
29 Pembroke College (p. 106)
30 **Worcester College** (p. 157)
31 St Giles House (p. 145)
32 **St John's College: Canterbury Quad** (p. 108)
33 **Trinity College** (p. 135)

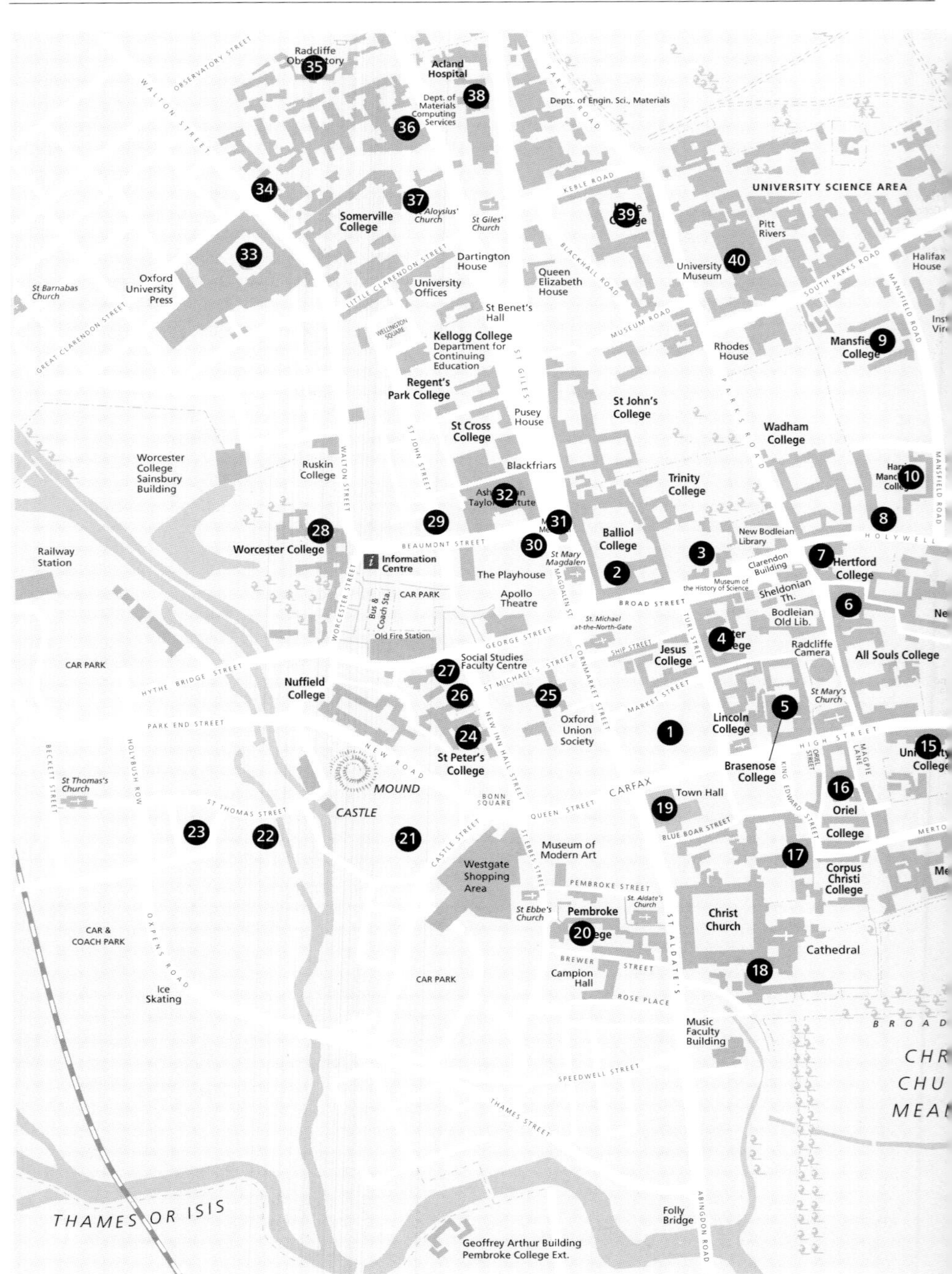

Radcliffe
35
Acland Hospital
Dept. of Materials Computing Services
38
36
Depts. of Engin. Sci., Materials
OBSERVATORY STREET
WALTON STREET
PARKS ROAD
KEBLE ROAD
UNIVERSITY SCIENCE AREA
34
37
Somerville College
St Aloysius' Church
St Giles' Church
39
Pitt Rivers
33
Dartington House
Queen Elizabeth House
University Museum
40
Halifax House
St Barnabas Church
Oxford University Press
LITTLE CLARENDON STREET
University Offices
BLACKHALL ROAD
SOUTH PARKS ROAD
MANSFIELD ROAD
St Benet's Hall
GREAT CLARENDON STREET
WELLINGTON SQUARE
MUSEUM ROAD
Kellogg College
Department for Continuing Education
Rhodes House
9
Regent's Park College
ST GILES'
St John's College
Pusey House
Wadham College
St Cross College
Worcester College Sainsbury Building
Ruskin College
ST JOHN STREET
WALTON STREET
Blackfriars
Trinity College
10
32
29
31
28
8
Railway Station
Worcester College
BEAUMONT STREET
30
Balliol College
3
New Bodleian Library
HOLYWELL
St Mary Magdalen
7
Hertford College
Information Centre
2
Clarendon Building
The Playhouse
Museum of the History of Science
CAR PARK
Apollo Theatre
Sheldonian Th.
6
BROAD STREET
Bus & Coach Sta.
WORCESTER STREET
Bodleian Old Lib.
St. Michael at-the-North-Gate
Old Fire Station
GEORGE STREET
4
Radcliffe Camera
SHIP STREET
Jesus College
All Souls College
CAR PARK
Social Studies Faculty Centre
TURL STREET
27
HYTHE BRIDGE STREET
Nuffield College
ST MICHAEL'S STREET
CORNMARKET STREET
St Mary's Church
26
25
MARKET STREET
5
PARK END STREET
Oxford Union Society
Lincoln College
1
24
HIGH STREET
15
NEW INN HALL STREET
St Peter's College
Brasenose College
BECKETT STREET
St Thomas's Church
HOLYBUSH ROW
NEW ROAD
MOUND
KING EDWARD STREET
ORIEL STREET
MAGPIE LANE
16
BONN SQUARE
Town Hall
CARFAX
ST THOMAS STREET
CASTLE
QUEEN STREET
19
Oriel College
23
22
21
CASTLE STREET
ST EBBES STREET
BLUE BOAR STREET
Museum of Modern Art
17
Westgate Shopping Area
PEMBROKE STREET
Corpus Christi College
St Ebbe's Church
Pembroke
St. Aldate's Church
Christ Church
CAR & COACH PARK
20
ST ALDATE'S
Cathedral
OXPENS ROAD
BREWER STREET
18
Campion Hall
CAR PARK
Ice Skating
ROSE PLACE
Music Faculty Building
BROAD
SPEEDWELL STREET
THAMES STREET
THAMES OR ISIS
Folly Bridge
ABINGDON ROAD
Geoffrey Arthur Building Pembroke College Ext.

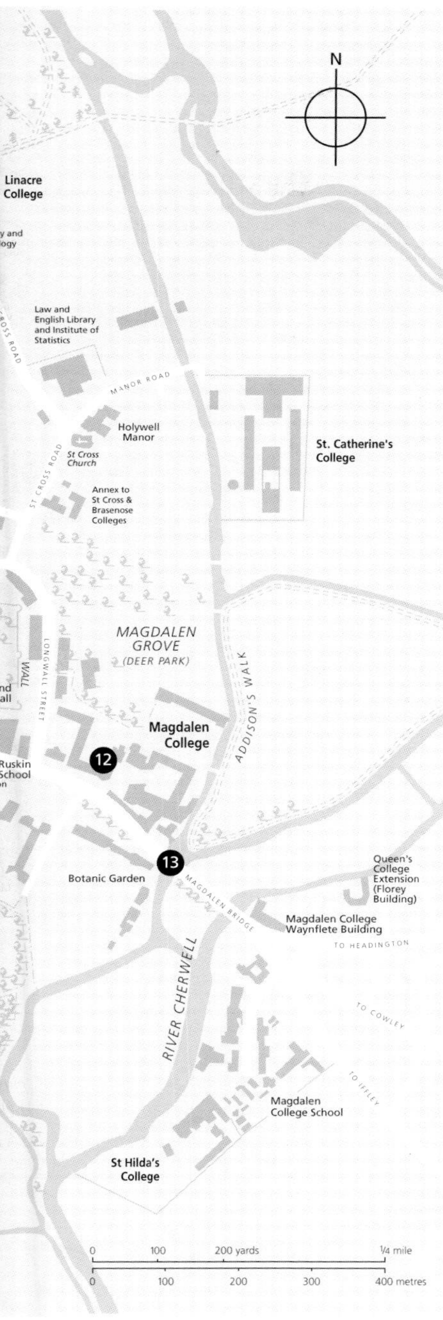

Late Georgian and Victorian Oxford 1750–1900

1 Covered Market (p. 242)
2 Balliol College (p. 227)
3 Trinity College: Front Quad (p. 253)
4 Exeter College: Chapel, etc. (p. 223)
5 Brasenose College: New Quad (p. 253)
6 Hertford College (p. 274)
7 Indian Institute, now History Faculty Library (p. 256)
8 Holywell Music Room (p. 187)
9 Mansfield College (p. 256)
10 Manchester College (p. 272)
11 New College: Holywell Building (p. 227)
12 Magdalen College: St Swithin's Quad (p. 247)
13 Magdalen Bridge (p. 264)
14 Examination Schools (p. 248)
15 University College, Shelley Memorial (p. 277)
16 Oriel College: Library and former St Mary Hall (p. 186)
17 Christ Church: Canterbury Quad (p. 185)
18 Christ Church: bell tower, and Meadow Building (p. 227)
19 Town Hall (p. 259)
20 Pembroke College: Hall (p. 209)
21 County Court and Prison (p. 202)
22 Morrell's Brewery and former brewer's house and almhouses (p. 269)
23 Christ Church Model Dwellings (p. 238)
24 St Peter's College: entrance block (p. 200)
25 Oxford Union (p. 220)
26 Wesley Memorial church (p. 244)
27 Oxford School for Boys; Social Studies Centre (p. 254)
28 Worcester College: Hall and Chapel (p. 188)
29 Beaumont Street and St John Street (p. 203)
30 Randolph Hotel (p. 243)
31 Martyrs' Memorial (p. 210)
32 Ashmolean Museum and Taylor Institute (p. 205)
33 Oxford University Press (p. 193)
34 St Paul, Walton Street (p. 201)
35 Radcliffe Observatory: Green College (p. 183)
36 Radcliffe Infirmary (p. 264)
37 St Aloysius church (p. 240)
38 Oxford School for Girls; Department of Materials (p. 255)
39 Keble College (p. 229)
40 University Museum (p. 217)

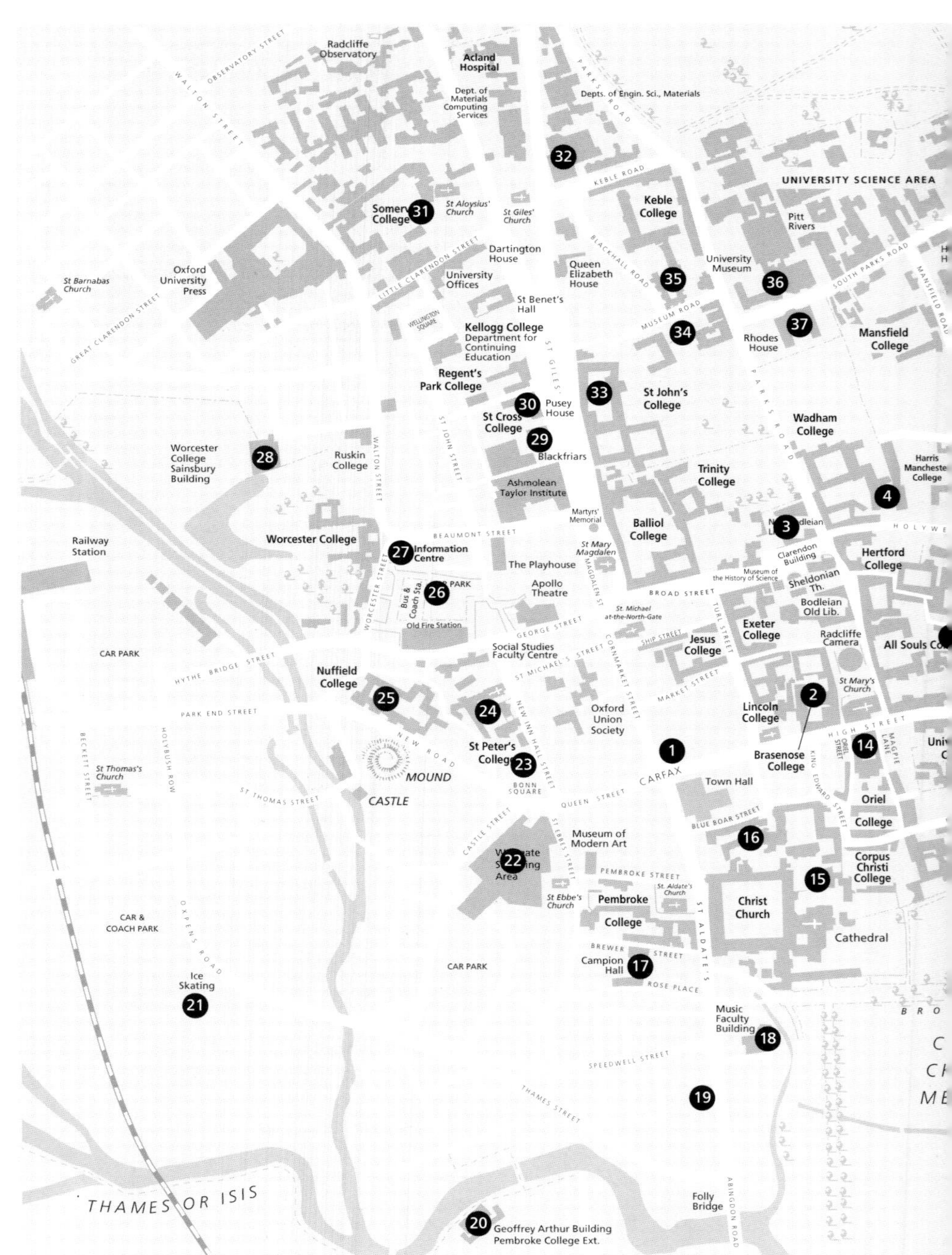
Radcliffe Observatory
Acland Hospital
Dept. of Materials Computing Services
Depts. of Engin. Sci., Materials
UNIVERSITY SCIENCE AREA
Somerville College
St Aloysius' Church
St Giles' Church
Keble College
Pitt Rivers
Dartington House
Oxford University Press
St Barnabas Church
University Offices
Queen Elizabeth House
University Museum
St Benet's Hall
Kellogg College Department for Continuing Education
Rhodes House
Mansfield College
Regent's Park College
Pusey House
St John's College
St Cross College
Wadham College
Blackfriars
Worcester College Sainsbury Building
Ruskin College
Trinity College
Ashmolean Taylor Institute
Harris Manchester College
Martyrs' Memorial
Balliol College
Railway Station
Worcester College
Information Centre
St Mary Magdalen
Clarendon Building
Hertford College
The Playhouse
Museum of the History of Science
Sheldonian Th.
Apollo Theatre
Bodleian Old Lib.
Bus & Coach Sta.
Old Fire Station
St. Michael at-the-North-Gate
Exeter College
Radcliffe Camera
Jesus College
All Souls
CAR PARK
Social Studies Faculty Centre
Nuffield College
St Mary's Church
Lincoln College
Oxford Union Society
St Peter's College
Brasenose College
St Thomas's Church
MOUND
CASTLE
Town Hall
Oriel College
Museum of Modern Art
Westgate Shopping Area
Corpus Christi College
St Ebbe's Church
St. Aldate's Church
Pembroke College
Christ Church
Cathedral
CAR & COACH PARK
Campion Hall
CAR PARK
Ice Skating
Music Faculty Building
THAMES OR ISIS
Folly Bridge
Geoffrey Arthur Building Pembroke College Ext.
WALTON STREET
OBSERVATORY STREET
PARKS ROAD
KEBLE ROAD
BLACKHALL ROAD
SOUTH PARKS ROAD
MANSFIELD ROAD
LITTLE CLARENDON STREET
GREAT CLARENDON STREET
WELLINGTON SQUARE
MUSEUM ROAD
ST GILES'
ST JOHN STREET
BEAUMONT STREET
HOLYWELL
BROAD STREET
TURL STREET
GEORGE STREET
SHIP STREET
MAGDALEN ST
CORNMARKET STREET
WORCESTER STREET
HYTHE BRIDGE STREET
ST MICHAEL'S STREET
MARKET STREET
PARK END STREET
NEW ROAD
NEW INN HALL STREET
HIGH STREET
ORIEL STREET
MAGPIE LANE
BECKETT STREET
HOLYBUSH ROW
CARFAX
BONN SQUARE
KING EDWARD STREET
ST THOMAS STREET
QUEEN STREET
CASTLE STREET
ST EBBES STREET
BLUE BOAR STREET
PEMBROKE STREET
ST ALDATE'S
BREWER STREET
ROSE PLACE
OXPENS ROAD
SPEEDWELL STREET
THAMES STREET
ABINGDON ROAD
1
2
3
4
14
15
16
17
18
19
20
21
22
23
24
25
26
27
28
29
30
31
32
33
34
35
36
37

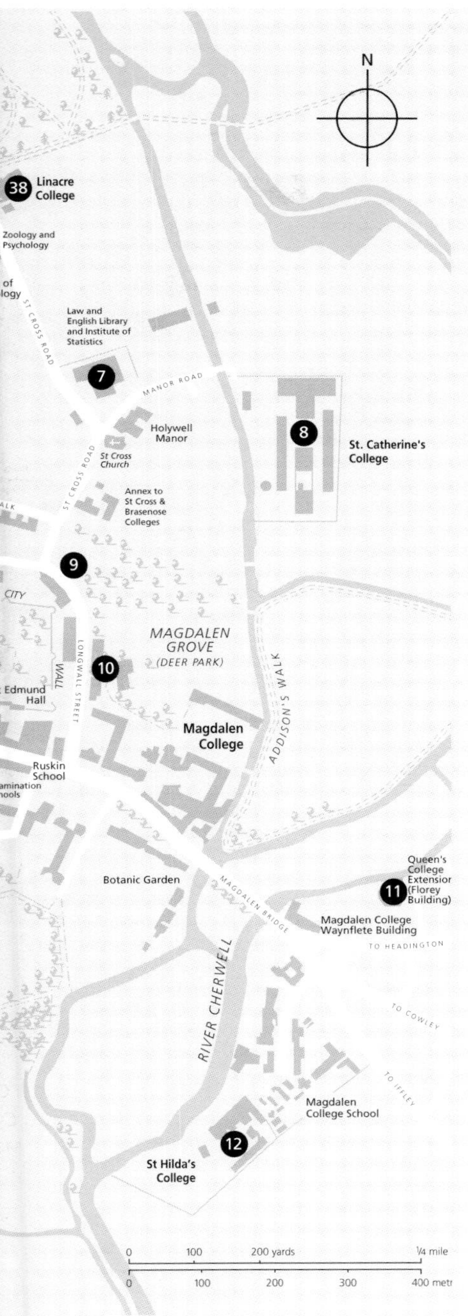

Twentieth-Century Oxford

1 Carfax rebuilding (p. 262)
2 Brasenose College: new buildings (p. 313)
3 New Bodleian Library (p. 291)
4 Wadham College: Bowra Building (p. 336)
5 Queen's College, Provost's Lodgings (p. 302)
6 Balliol College: new building in Jowett Walk (p. 340)
7 St Cross Building (p. 310)
8 St Catherine's College (p. 307)
9 Former Morris garage, Longwall Street (p. 267)
10 Magdalen College: Grove Building (p. 341)
11 Queen's College: Florey Building (p. 322)
12 St Hilda's College (p. 280)
13 Merton College: Warden's Lodgings and St Alban's Quad (p. 277)
14 Oriel College: Rhodes Building (p. 277)
15 Christ Church: Picture Gallery (p. 314)
16 Christ Church: Blue Boar Quad (p. 314)
17 Campion Hall (p. 286)
18 Music Faculty (p. 291)
19 Former Morris showroom, St Aldate's (p. 297)
20 Pembroke College: Geoffrey Arthur Building (p. 339)
21 Oxford Ice Rink (p. 335)
22 Westgate Centre (p. 329)
23 Former girls' school, New Inn Hall Street (p. 265)
24 St Peter's College (p. 283)
25 Nuffield College (p. 300)
26 Gloucester Green (p. 335)
27 City Information Centre; former school (p. 265)
28 Worcester College: Sainsbury Building (p. 333)
29 Blackfriars (p. 274)
30 Pusey House (p. 271)
31 Somerville College (p. 278)
32 Engineering & Nuclear Physics Laboratories (p. 282)
33 St John's College: North Quad, Sir Thomas White Building (p. 305)
34 St John's College: Garden Quad (p. 337)
35 Keble College: Hayward and De Breyne Buildings (p. 324)
36 Radcliffe Science Library (p. 282)
37 Rhodes House (p. 284)
38 Linacre College (p. 307)

Acknowledgements

The publishers wish to thank the following for their permission to reproduce the illustrations in this book: Robert Adam Architects: 343; Ahrends Burton and Koralek: 325, 326 (photos John Donat, London); Warden and Fellows of All Souls College, Oxford: 57 (Hovenden Maps no. 1); Architects Design Partnership: 48; *Architectural Review*: 314 (photo Richard Einzig), 317 (photo Bill Toomey); Ashmolean Museum, Oxford: pen and wash drawings by Frederick Mackenzie, 36, 198, 205, 211; 5 (*Almanack*, 1874), 8 (*Almanack*, 1873), 11 (watercolour, 1806, by H. O'Neill), 35 (*Almanack*, 1754), 73 (watercolour, 1794, by Edward Dayes), 120 (*Almanack*, 1868), 167, 178, 184 (wash drawing by John Dixon), 209 (*Almanack*, 1858). Bodleian Library, Oxford: 25 (MS Gough Oxon. a.50, f.18), 27 (Loggan), 52 (MS Bodley 13, f.12v); 66 (reconstruction by Robert Potter), 84 (MS Don. a.2, f.26), 100 (Ackermann), 116 (MS Don a.3, f.96), 119 (MS Don. a.2, f.10), 121 (MS Don. a.2, f.19), 124 (Loggan), 131 (W. Williams, *Oxonia Depicta*, 1733), 136 (Ackermann), 148 (Minn. 6/39), 174 (Minn. 15/30), 181 (Ackermann), 185 (Ackermann), 190 (Ackermann), 234 (MS Top. Oxon. d.501, f.89); British Library, London: 144 (Add. MS 36376, f.79); British Motor Industry Heritage Trust/Rover Group: 296; photos Barry Capper: 23(b), 172, 179, 233, 239, 255, 264, 268, 269, 294, 333. Country Life Picture Library/IPC Magazines Ltd: 72, 286, 287; Chris Donaghue Photography (The Oxford Photo Library): 252, plate facing p. 210; photo Kerry Downes, York: 163. Dunthorne Parker Architects/photo Geoff Dann: 84(b). Fotomas Index, West Wickham: 10; Francis Frith Collection, Shaftesbury: 152. Nicholas Grimshaw & Partners Ltd/photo Jo Reid and John Peck, Newport: 335; © Sonia Halliday/Laura Lushington, Weston Turville: plate facing p. 114. Kendrick Associates/photo Dennis Gilbert: 336; photos A. F. Kersting, London: xiii, 12, 37, 47, 51, 53, 56, 59, 68, 76, 78, 86, 87, 92, 94, 110, 117, 127, 128, 137, 138, 139, 142, 150, 151, 153, 154, 155, 160, 162, 165, 170, 175, 177, 180, 184(b), 186, 187, 192, 195, 197, 200, 204, 221, 222, 228, 232, 236(b), 256, 273, 274, 275, 276, 277(a), 285, 289, 301, 306, 324, 330, plates facing pp. 82, 83, 211. MacCormac Jamieson Prichard: 319 (President and Fellows of St John's College, Oxford), 334 (© Richard Bryant/Arcaid), 338 (photo Peter Durant, London), plate facing p. 242 (photo Peter Durant, London); Maguire & Co. /photo Nicholas Meyjers: 341. National Monuments Record/RCHME © crown copyright: 17, 19, 21, 60, 277. Oxfordshire County Council Department of Leisure and Arts (Oxfordshire Photographic Archive): 7 (photo Henry Taunt), 23(a) (Taunt), 118, 146, 188, 193 (Taunt), 202, 203(a), 207, 213 (Taunt), 214 (Taunt), 215, 242, 244, 251 (Taunt), 253, 260, 262, 263, 266, 271; Oxford University Museum: 219. Powell Moya Partnership : 315 (photo Paul Proudman, Oxford), 316 (© Shepherd Building Group Ltd). Rhodes House Library/photo R. Judges: 284; Royal Institute of British Architects (British Architectural Library): 237 (*The Builder*, 5 Feb 1870), 243 (*The Builder*, 23 April 1864), 265 (*The Builder*, 18 May 1901); Royal Photographic Society, Bath: vii. St Catherine's College, Oxford: 310; St Hilda's College, Oxford/photo Charlotte Wood, Wallingford: 340. Photo Thomas Photos, Oxford: ii, xiv, 4, 13, 14, 18, 30, 32, 38, 42, 43, 45 (by permission of the Warden and Fellows of New College), 46 (*Almanack*, 1844), 55, 61 (Loggan), 64, 67, 70, 77, 85, 89, 91, 97, 98, 99, 103, 104, 105, 107, 109, 111, 113, 115, 122, 130, 133, 134, 140, 141 (Loggan), 143, 145, 147, 156, 158, 166, 170, 183, 196, 203(b), 216, 218 (*Almanack*, 1860), 224, 227 (E. H. New, *A New Loggan View of the Oxford Colleges*, 1932), 230, 241, 245, 246, 247, 248, 254, 257, 258, 278, 279, 283, 290, 291, 298, 302, 305, 309, 311, 312, 313, 318, 320, 322, 327, 328, 344, plates facing pp. 115, 211. From David Loggan, *Oxonia Illustrata* (1675): 27, 33, 50, 54, 61, 124, 141, 168. From Rudolph Ackermann, *History of the University of Oxford* (1814): 100, 136, 181, 185, 190.

Bibliographical References

All historians of Oxford are indebted, directly or indirectly, to the 17th-century antiquary Anthony Wood, whose voluminous collections on the history of the city and the University were edited by J. Peshall under the title of *The Ancient and Present State of the City of Oxford* (1773) and by J. Gutch as *The History and Antiquities of the University of Oxford* in 1786–96. Much additional material is included in Wood's *Survey of the Antiquities of the City of Oxford*, ed. A. Clark (Oxford Historical Society, 1889, etc.) and in A. Clark (ed.), *The Life and Times of Anthony Wood* (Oxford Historical Society, 1891, etc.). Thomas Hearne's collections were edited by the Oxford Historical Society in 11 volumes, starting in 1885. Among the plethora of later histories and guidebooks, J. Ayliffe, *The Ancient and Present State of the University of Oxford* (1723), T. Salmon, *The Present State of the Universities* (1744), and J. Ingram, *Memorials of Oxford* (1837) can be singled out. John Bereblock's frequently reproduced drawings of the colleges of 1566 (Bodleian Library, MS Bodley 13), David Loggan's bird's-eye views in *Oxonia Illustrata* (1675), and those of W. Williams, *Oxonia Depicta* (1733) are invaluable in picturing the University before the great rebuilding of the 19th century. For other early visual sources, see H. M. Petter, *The Oxford Almanacks* (1974), J. R. Green's mid-18th-century drawings of vanished buildings in the Bodleian Library (MS Gough Oxon 50), J. B. Malchair's late 18th-century drawings in the Ashmolean Museum and elsewhere, the mostly unpublished early 19th-century drawings of J. C. Buckler in the Bodleian Library (MS Don A 2–3), R. Ackermann's *History of the University of Oxford* (1814), J. B. Skelton, *Oxonia Antiqua Restaurata* (2nd edn, 1843), and the photographs of Henry Taunt and others in the Centre for Oxfordshire Studies at the Central Library, Westgate, Oxford.

The buildings of both city and University before 1714 are described, many of them in exhaustive detail, in the report of the Royal Commission on Historic Monuments, *An Inventory of the Historical Monuments of the City of Oxford* (1939). H. S. Goodhard-Rendel, 'Oxford buildings criticized', *Oxoniensia*, 17–18 (1952–3), pp. 200–15, provides a stimulating corrective to the tone of uncritical admiration adopted by most writers on Oxford's buildings; his often caustic comments can also be read in a series of articles in *Architect and Building News*, 13 Dec 1935, pp. 324–32, etc. The most recent comprehensive account of the history of the city can be found in A. Crossley (ed.), *The Victoria History of the County of Oxfordshire* (*VCH*), vol. 4 (1979); the University and each of the individual colleges is covered, often with invaluable architectural detail, in vol. 3 (1954). For the history of the University, C. E. Mallett, *A History of the University of Oxford* (1924–7), is still useful, though the multi-volume *History of the University of Oxford*, the final volume of which will appear in 1999 (vol. 7), brings together the most recent scholarship on the subject; the relevant architectural sections are cited below. See also L. Stone, 'The size and composition of the Oxford student body', in L. Stone (ed.), *The University in Society* (1974). College histories are legion, and of variable value for the history of architecture; the most useful ones are mentioned below. Nikolaus Pevsner's introduction to Oxford, and his accounts of individual buildings, in J. Sherwood and N. Pevsner, *The Buildings of England: Oxfordshire* (1974), is invariably acute, and H. M. Colvin, *Unbuilt Oxford* (1983), is the best book on the architectural history of the University to have appeared in recent years. Among less specialized recent books, C. Brooke and R. Highfield, *Oxford and Cambridge* (1988), offers an approachable and scholarly recent summary of the history of the University, as does J. Prest (ed.), *The Illustrated History of Oxford University* (1993). A. F. Kersting and J. Ashdown, *The Buildings of Oxford* (1980), is concise and beautifully illustrated. C. Hibbert (ed.), *The Encyclopedia of Oxford* (1988), is an excellent and reliable source of information on individual buildings, and there is much useful information, especially about 19th- and 20th-century buildings, in M. Graham's booklets, *On Foot in Oxford* (Oxfordshire County Libraries, various dates). Among books and articles dealing with different aspects of Oxford's architectural history, W. J. Arkell, *Oxford Stone* (1947), J. Sherwood, *A Guide to the Churches of Oxfordshire* (1989), M. Archer *et al.*, *English Heritage in Stained Glass: Oxford* (1988), A. Crossley *et al.*, *Shopping in Oxford: A Brief History* (Oxford Preservation Trust, 1983), M. Batey, *Oxford Gardens* (1982), J. Newman, 'Oxford libraries before 1800', *Archaeological Journal*, 135 (1978), pp. 248–57, and G. Barber, *Arks for Learning* (Oxford Bibliographical Society, 1995), deserve special mention. For Oxford's architects, H. M. Colvin, *A Biographical Dictionary of British Architects 1600–1840* (3rd edn, 1995), is invaluable.

Chapter 1: Origins: 900–1350

Recent archaeological research on Oxford's origins is briefly summarized in T. G. Hassall, *Oxford: The Buried City* (1987) and at greater length in J. Blair, *Anglo-Saxon Oxfordshire* (1994). For the early history of St Michael's at the North Gate, see B. Durham *et al.*, 'Oxford's northern defences', *Oxoniensia*, 48 (1983), pp. 13–40 and V. H. H. Green, *The Tower and Church of St Michael at the North Gate* (1987). For the Castle, see T. G. Hassall, *Oxford Castle* (1971) and T. W. Squires, *In West Oxford* (1928), which also discusses Oseney Abbey. The best comprehensive history of St Frideswide's Priory (Christ Church Cathedral) is still S. A. Warner, *Oxford Cathedral* (1924), but the conclusions, especially on the early history of the building, are modified by the papers brought together in *Oxoniensia*, 53 (1988), published separately as J. Blair (ed.), *St Frideswide's Monastery at Oxford* (1990). B. Durham *et al.*, 'The Infirmary and Hall of the medieval hospital of St John the Baptist at Oxford', *Oxoniensia*, 56 (1991), pp. 17–75, and J. Blair, 'Frewin Hall, Oxford', *Oxoniensia*, 43 (1978), pp. 49–55, discuss two early buildings which survive in a much altered form. The origins of the University are authoritatively discussed in J. Catto (ed.), *The Early Oxford Schools* (*History of the University of Oxford*, vol. 1, 1984). For the history and buildings of the academic halls, see W. A. Pantin, 'The Halls and Schools of mediaeval Oxford: an attempt at reconstruction', in *Oxford Studies presented to Daniel Callus* (Oxford Historical Society, new series 16, 1964), W. A. Pantin, 'Tackley's Inn, Oxford', *Oxoniensia*, 7 (1942), pp. 80–92, and J. Munby, 'J. C. Buckler, Tackley's Inn and three medieval houses in Oxford', *Oxoniensia*, 43 (1978), pp. 123–69. The origins of the collegiate plan are discussed in W. A. Pantin, 'Chantry priests' houses and other medieval lodgings', *Medieval Archaeology*, 3 (1959), pp. 244–6. For the early buildings of Merton College, see J. R. L. Highfield, *The Early Rolls of Merton College* (Oxford Historical Society, new series, 18 (1964)) and A. Bott, *Merton College: A Short History of the Buildings* (1993), and for the University Church, T. G. Jackson, *The Church of St Mary the Virgin* (1897).

Chapter 2: The Later Middle Ages

The architectural history of the University in the later Middle Ages is covered in J. Harvey's chapter on 'Architecture in Oxford 1350–1500' in J. Catto and R. Evans (eds), *Late Medieval Oxford* (*History of the University of Oxford*, vol. 2, 1992). See also R. H. C. Davies, 'The chronology of Perpendicular architecture in Oxford', *Oxoniensia*, 11–12 (1946–7), pp. 75–89, E. A. Gee, 'Oxford masons 1370–1530', *Archaeological Journal*, 109 (1952), pp. 63–8, and E. A. Gee, 'Oxford carpenters 1370–1530', *Oxoniensia*, 17–18 (1952–3), pp. 112–84. All previous accounts of the architecture of New College have been superseded by G. Jackson-Stops's chapters in J. Buxton and P. Williams (eds), *New College, Oxford* (1979). For other colleges, see V. H. H. Green, *The Commonwealth of Lincoln College 1427–1977* (1979), J. Jones, *Balliol College* (2nd edn, 1997), H. M. Colvin and J. Simmons, *All Souls College: An Oxford College and its Buildings* (1989), E. W. Allfrey in *Brasenose Quatercentenary Monographs* (Oxford Historical Society, 1909), and J. G. Milne and J. Harvey, 'The building of Cardinal College, Oxford', *Oxoniensia*, 8–9 (1943–4), pp. 137–53. See also A. Bott and J. R. L. Highfield, 'The sculpture over the Gatehouse at Merton College, Oxford', *Oxoniensia*, 58 (1993), pp. 233–40. For the monastic colleges, see R. B. Dobson, 'The Religious Orders 1370–1540' in *History of the University of Oxford*, vol. 2, pp. 541–56 and J. Blair, 'Monastic Colleges in Oxford', *Archaeological Journal*, 135 (1978), pp. 263–5; individual monastic colleges are discussed in H. M. Colvin, 'The building of St Bernard's College', *Oxoniensia*, 24 (1959), pp. 37–44, R. Gameson and A. Coates, *The Old Library at Trinity College* (1988), pp. 15–34, and J. Blair, 'Frewin Hall, Oxford: a Norman mansion and a monastic college', *Oxoniensia*, 43 (1978), pp. 48–99 (for St Mary's College). For late medieval buildings in the city, see J. Munby *et al.*, 'Zacarias's: a 14th century Oxford New Inn', *Oxoniensia*, 57 (1992), pp. 245–309 and J. Munby *et al.*, '126 High Street: the archaeology and history of an Oxford house', *Oxoniensia*, 40 (1975), pp. 254–91. The most recent accounts of the architectural history of the Divinity School and Duke Humfrey's Library can be found in J. N. L. Myres, 'Recent discoveries in the

Bodleian Library', *Archaeologia*, 101 (1967), pp. 151–68 and S. Gillam, *The Divinity School and Duke Humfrey's Library at Oxford* (1988).

Chapter 3: From Reformation to Restoration

The architectural history of the University in the 16th century is recounted in J. Newman, 'The physical setting: new building and adaptation', in J. McConica (ed.), *The Collegiate University* (*History of the University of Oxford*, vol. 3, 1986) and for the 17th century see *History of the University of Oxford*, vol. 4 (1997). For collegiate and University buildings, see the relevant parts of *VCH*, vol. 3, and also W. H. Stevenson and H. E. Salter, *The Early History of St John's College* (Oxford Historical Society, new series 1, 1939), D. Sturdy, E. Clive Rouse, and C. Cole, 'The painted roof of the Old Library, Christ Church', *Oxoniensia*, 26–7 (1961–2), pp. 215–43, T. G. Jackson, *Wadham College* (1893), N. Briggs, 'The foundation of Wadham College, Oxford', *Oxoniensia*, 21 (1956), pp. 61–81, C. S. L. Davies and J. Garnett (eds), *Wadham College* (1994), and H. M. Colvin, *The Canterbury Quadrangle* (1988). For the architecture of the early 17th century, see T. W. Hanson, 'Halifax craftsmen in Oxford', *Transactions of the Halifax Antiquarian Society* (1927–8), pp. 253–317, and also I. G. Philip, 'The building of the Schools Quadrangle', *Oxoniensia*, 12 (1948), pp. 39–48, G. W. Wheeler (ed.), *Letters of Thomas Bodley to Thomas James* (1926), C. Cole, 'The building of the Tower of the Five Orders', *Oxoniensia*, 38 (1968), pp. 92–107, I. G. Philip, *The Bodleian Library in the 17th and 18th Centuries* (1983), and M. R. A. Bullard, 'Talking heads: the Bodleian Frieze, its inspiration, sources, designer and significance', *Bodleian Library Record*, 14 (1994), pp. 461–500. See also W. L. Spiers (ed.), *The Note-Books and Account Books of Nicholas Stone* (Walpole Society, vol. 7, 1918–19). For buildings in the city, see W. A. Pantin, 'The development of domestic architecture in Oxford', *Antiquaries Journal*, 26 (1947), pp. 120–50, D. Sturdy *et al.*, 'Eleven small Oxford houses', *Oxoniensia*, 26–7 (1961–2), pp. 323–32, C. Cole, 'Carfax Conduit', *Oxoniensia*, 29–30 (1964–5), pp. 142–66, W. A. Pantin, 'The Golden Cross, Oxford', *Oxoniensia*, 20 (1955), pp. 46–89, E. Clive Rouse, 'Some 16th and 17th century domestic wall paintings in Oxford', *Oxoniensia*, 48 (1983), pp. 119–30, and J. Potter, *Tennis in Oxford* (1994).

Chapter 4: The Age of Classicism

The architecture of the late 17th-century University is discussed in *History of the University of Oxford*, vol. 4 (1997). An essential starting-point for the buildings of the early 18th-century University is H. M. Colvin, 'Architecture', in L. S. Sutherland and L. G. Mitchell (eds), *The Eighteenth Century* (*History of the University of Oxford*, vol. 5, 1986), and many of the important projects of this period are discussed in Colvin, *A Catalogue of 18th and 19th century Architectural Drawings in Worcester College Library* (1964). For the Sheldonian Theatre, see *Wren Society*, vol. 19, pp. 91–9 and C. Saumarez Smith, 'Wren and Sheldon', *Oxford Art Journal*, 6 (1983), pp. 45–50. J. R. L. Highfield, 'Alexander Fisher, Sir Christopher Wren, and Merton College Chapel', *Oxoniensia*, 24 (1959), pp. 70–82 deals with one of Wren's minor commissions. For Wren's work at Trinity College and for Tom Tower, see *Wren Society*, vol. 5, pp. 14–21, and for his buildings in Oxford generally K. Downes, *The Architecture of Wren* (1982). Celia Fiennes's comments can be found in C. Morris (ed.), *The Journeys of Celia Fiennes* (1947). For architects and craftsmen involved in Oxford buildings, see J. C. Cole, 'William Byrd, stonecutter and mason', *Oxoniensia*, 14 (1949), pp. 63–74, M. J. H. Liversidge, 'Prelude to the Baroque: Isaac Fuller at Oxford', *Oxoniensia*, 57 (1992), pp. 311–29, W. G. Hiscock, *Henry Aldrich* (1960), and K. Downes, *Hawksmoor* (1969). William Townesend's work is discussed in Hiscock, *Christ Church Miscellany* (1946), pp. 40–59. The history of the Old Ashmolean is recounted in R. F. Ovenell, *The Ashmolean Museum 1688–1894* (1986). For Trinity College, see T. Warton, *The Life of Ralph Bathurst* (1761); for St Edmund Hall, A. B. Emden, *An Account of the Chapel and Library Building, St Edmund Hall* (1932); for Queen's College, J. R. Magrath, *The Queen's College* (1921), and R. H. Hodgkin, *Six Centuries of an Oxford College* (1949); for Christ Church, Hiscock, *Christ Church Miscellany* and *The Building Accounts of Christ Church Library 1716–1779*,

lunette A window or opening in a Renaissance building in the form of a half-circle or half-moon.

mullion A vertical post within a window.

nave The western arm of a church, furthest from the main altar.

ogee A double S-shaped curve, often used in English late medieval architectural decoration.

oriel A projecting bay window in a medieval building, often, but not invariably, upstairs.

pediment The gable-end of a classical temple, often used in diminutive form as an embellishment (e.g. over a window) in Renaissance architecture.

piano nobile In Italian Renaissance architecture, the main upper floor of an important domestic building.

pilaster A flattened, two-dimensional, classical column used as decoration on a building.

pinnacle A small spire on the roof-line of a building, usually at the top of a buttress (q.v.).

portico A porch or entrance to a building designed in the manner of a classical temple front.

reredos A carved screen behind the altar of a church.

rotunda A circular, usually classical, building or part of a building, often covered by a dome.

rustication In Renaissance architecture, the practice of either leaving masonry deliberately rough in order to convey an impression of strength or of carving deep indentations between blocks of masonry for the same purpose.

tie-beam A horizontal timber beam spanning the width of a building.

tracery The intersecting embellishment of the upper part of a Gothic window. Bar tracery is made up of bars of carved stone, plate tracery (found only in early Gothic) is pierced through the wall surface at the top of the window, and blind tracery signifies traceried forms applied as decoration to the wall-surface of a building.

transept One of the two cross-arms of a cruciform (q.v.) church, between the nave (q.v.) and chancel (q.v.).

transom A horizontal bar within a window.

triforium An arcaded wall-passage inside a medieval church, between the main arcade and the clerestory (q.v.).

undercroft A vaulted space underneath the main room in a building; in a church, often called a crypt.

vault An arched masonry ceiling of a building, usually a church. A groin vault is made up of tunnel- or barrel-vaults intersecting at right angles in each bay or subdivision of the building. In a rib vault - one of the main component features of Gothic architecture - the intersections are emphasized by mouldings or ribs of stone. A lierne vault has mouldings linking the main ribs across the webs of the vault so as to form ornamental, sometimes star-shaped, patterns on the surface. A fan vault is made up of concave-sided half-cones embellished with the fan-like decoration.

Venetian window A window with three openings, the central one of which is arched, with those to the side demarcated by classical columns; sometimes called a *Serliana*.

voussoir A wedge-shaped stone forming part of an arch.

Index

Italic figures indicate a colour plate, photograph, map, or illustration
Bold figures indicate where a main reference to the topic can be found